No Adult Left Behind

For decades, Americans have debated why our students consistently score lower than their peers in other developed countries. While most debates have focused on school spending, curriculum, teacher quality, and teachers' unions, *No Adult Left Behind* argues that local democratic control is the root of the problem. Elected school boards govern local school districts, but only adults vote in local elections – and most of voters don't have school-aged children or care about academics. This leads to educational debates that are centered around issues that most arouse adult passions, such as partisanship, identity politics, property values, and employment concerns, while the needs of students get left behind. In identifying the misalignment between the interests of school children and the political and policy agendas of the adults who control education, *No Adult Left Behind* stands to become a landmark study on modern education politics.

Vladimir Kogan is Professor in the Department of Political Science at the Ohio State University and one of America's leading scholars of education politics. Kogan previously covered education at the Voice of San Diego, a pioneering nonprofit news organization specializing in investigative journalism.

CAMBRIDGE STUDIES IN THE COMPARATIVE POLITICS
OF EDUCATION

No Adult Left Behind: How Politics Hijacks Education Policy and Hurts Kids

Editor

Terry M. Moe, Stanford University

Education and its reform are matters of great political salience throughout the world. Yet as Gift and Wibbels observed, "It is hard to identify a community of political scientists who are dedicated to the comparative study of education." This series is an effort to change that. The goal is to encourage a vigorous line of scholarship that focuses squarely on the politics of education across nations, advances theoretical thinking, includes a broad swath of educational terrain – from elementary and secondary education to vocational education to higher education – and explores the impacts of education on key aspects of society. The series welcomes books of very different types. Some may be grounded in sophisticated quantitative analysis, but qualitative work is welcome as well, as are big-think extended essays that develop agenda-setting ideas. Work is encouraged that takes on big, important, inherently messy topics, however difficult they may be to study. Work is also encouraged that shows how the politics of education is shaped by power, special interests, parties, bureaucracies, and other fundamentals of the political system. And finally, this series is not just about the developed nations, but encourages new work on developing nations and the special challenges that education faces in those contexts.

Books in the series

The Comparative Politics of Education: Teachers Unions and Education Systems around the World
Edited by Terry M. Moe and Susanne Wiborg

A Loud but Noisy Signal? Public Opinion and Education Reform in Western Europe
Marius R. Busemeyer, Julian L. Garritzmann and Erik Neimanns

The Politics of Comprehensive School Reforms: Cleavages and Coalitions
Katharina Sass

Making Bureaucracy Work: Norms, Education and Public Service Delivery in Rural India
Akshay Mangla

Education for All? Literature, Culture and Education Development in Britain and Denmark
Cathie Jo Martin

A Liberal Education: The Social and Political Impact of the Modern University
Brendan Apfeld, Emanuel Coman, John Gerring, and Stephen Jessee

Mobilizing Teachers: Education Politics and the New Labor Movement in Latin America
Christopher Chambers-Ju

No Adult Left Behind

How Politics Hijacks Education Policy and Hurts Kids

VLADIMIR KOGAN
Ohio State University

Shaftesbury Road, Cambridge CB2 8EA, United Kingdom

One Liberty Plaza, 20th Floor, New York, NY 10006, USA

477 Williamstown Road, Port Melbourne, VIC 3207, Australia

314–321, 3rd Floor, Plot 3, Splendor Forum, Jasola District Centre, New Delhi – 110025, India

103 Penang Road, #05-06/07, Visioncrest Commercial, Singapore 238467

Cambridge University Press is part of Cambridge University Press & Assessment, a department of the University of Cambridge.

We share the University's mission to contribute to society through the pursuit of education, learning and research at the highest international levels of excellence.

www.cambridge.org
Information on this title: www.cambridge.org/9781009606318
DOI: 10.1017/9781009606349

© Vladimir Kogan 2025

This publication is in copyright. Subject to statutory exception and to the provisions of relevant collective licensing agreements, no reproduction of any part may take place without the written permission of Cambridge University Press & Assessment.

When citing this work, please include a reference to the
DOI 10.1017/9781009606349

First published 2025

A catalogue record for this publication is available from the British Library

Library of Congress Cataloging-in-Publication Data
NAMES: Kogan, Vladimir author
TITLE: No adult left behind : how politics hijacks education policy and hurts kids / Vladimir Kogan, Ohio State University.
DESCRIPTION: New York, NY : Cambridge University Press, 2025. | Series: Cambridge Studies in the Comparative Politics of Education | Includes bibliographical references and index.
IDENTIFIERS: LCCN 2024059585 | ISBN 9781009606325 hardback | ISBN 9781009606318 paperback | ISBN 9781009606349 ebook
SUBJECTS: LCSH: Education – Political aspects – United States | Curriculum planning – Political aspects – United States | Education and state – United States | Social justice and education – United States
CLASSIFICATION: LCC LC71 .K63 2025 | DDC 379–dc23/eng/20250428
LC record available at https://lccn.loc.gov/2024059585

ISBN 978-1-009-60632-5 Hardback
ISBN 978-1-009-60631-8 Paperback

Cambridge University Press & Assessment has no responsibility for the persistence or accuracy of URLs for external or third-party internet websites referred to in this publication and does not guarantee that any content on such websites is, or will remain, accurate or appropriate.

In memory of Dr. Taylor Lyen,
who proved that educators can change lives

Contents

List of Figures		*page* ix
List of Tables		xi
Acknowledgments		xiii
1	What Are Schools For?	1
	Well-Intentioned Adults, Dysfunctional Schools	4
	Student Outcomes as Our North Star	9
	Chief Justice Earl Warren Was Wrong	12
	Looking beyond Money and Unions	13
	Politics, Markets – and Hacks	16
	Prebunking the Critics	19
	A Note on Organization and Style	28
	The Cancellation of James Ragland	29
2	Skin in the Game	34
	Measuring the Quality of Democracy	38
	Assessing Processes and Outcomes	42
	Illustrative Example: San Francisco	43
	National Data	48
	Lesson 1: Voters ≠ Parents	50
	Lesson 2: Voters Don't Care Much about Student Learning	52
	Lesson 3: School Board Elections Don't Provide Voters Much Choice	58
	Why Broken Elections Matter	59
	Democratic Myths versus Realities	64
3	Adults Follow Partisan Leaders on Education Policy	65
	The Trump Effect	67
	Obama Derangement Syndrome?	72

	A Top-Down Model of Mass Preferences	74
	A Tale of Two Ballot Measures	77
	A New Era of Polarized Education Politics?	94
4	All Curriculum Politics Is National	97
	Honest History or Political Indoctrination?	100
	Reading World War III	106
	Curriculum in the State House	120
	Lessons Learned?	124
5	Adult Culture Wars and Student Achievement	131
	Measuring Culture Wars	136
	Empirical Strategy	138
	Conflicts and Test Scores	141
	Getting More in the Technical Weeds	146
	It Should Be about the Students, Stupid	148
6	The Color of School Employment	154
	Race and Government Employment	159
	Untold Story of Southern Desegregation	163
	Hurricane and Reform in New Orleans	175
	An Impossible Trinity?	186
7	Bootleggers, Baptists, and Building Closures	190
	Competing Narratives	196
	Coalition Merchants and Narrative Construction	207
	What We Know	211
	Causes and Consequences of Closure: New Evidence	213
	Myths and (Political) Realities	225
8	Housing Markets Create Educational NIMBYs	229
	Policing the Boundaries of Educational Opportunity	234
	Political Power of Homeowners	240
	What Affects Home Prices – and What Doesn't	242
	Residential Sorting versus Gerrymandering	249
	How Housing Markets Undo Education Reforms	251
	Can Homeowners Do Well by Doing Good?	256
9	A Framework for Education Reform	259
	Reform 1: Hold School Board Elections in November of Even Years	263
	Reform 2: Make *Good* Performance Information More Salient	265
	Reform 3: Promote Smart School Choice Options	268
	10% Less Democracy?	273
	From Satan to Other Deluders	275
References		279
Index		303

Figures

3.1	Relationship between city-level voter partisanship and support for two California education ballot initiatives	page 93
4.1	Legislative roll call votes on Critical Race Theory bans and "science of reading" legislation	121
5.1	Coachella Valley High School "Arab" Mascot	132
5.2	Event study plot for the effect of local controversy on student achievement	143
5.3	Student achievement impact by the topic of controversy	145
5.4	Alternative event study estimates for the effect of local controversy on student achievement	147
6.1	Trends in Black teacher employment over time	171
7.1	Student demographic composition and school closures in selected cities	215
7.2	Predicting school closures	217
7.3	Effect of school closure on student achievement (in standard deviation units)	221
7.4	Effect of school closure on district enrollment and staffing	222
7.5	Effect of school closure on teacher salaries and local revenues	224
8.1	"Homevoter" political power and student achievement	247

Tables

2.1	Comparing participation in three San Francisco elections	*page* 46
2.2	Representation of parents in local school board elections	50
2.3	How school board elections compare to other legislative contests	58
5.1	Summary statistics, measured in 2010	139
5.2	Effect of local culture war controversy on student achievement	141

Acknowledgments

This project is the culmination of nearly a decade of research on school governance – examining how the decisions voters make on Election Day ultimately impact student learning in the classroom. My interest in education began even earlier, reflecting some of the personal experiences I recount in these chapters as a student, parent, journalist, and all-around gadfly.

In addition to my own firsthand knowledge and the extensive academic literature on the topics I cover, many of the ideas of this book came out of the approximately forty interviews I conducted in the process of doing research. Some of those materials evolved into the chapters of this book. However, there were also many other insightful observers who generously shared their time with me and who I don't quote by name but whose ideas are woven into the narrative. In incorporating the interview materials, I have done my best to avoid cherry-picking quotes that are most convenient for my arguments. Instead, I have tried to fully convey the nuance and complexity of the perspectives that I heard and, in particular, highlight counterarguments that challenge some of the ideas I put forward.

I owe a particular debt of gratitude to Terry Moe, whose coauthored book *Politics, Markets, and America's School* was truly transformational for both the field and for how I came to understand public education. He proved that political scientists had important theoretical and empirical contributions to make to the study of education, and it is hard to imagine that today's vibrant Education Politics and Policy Section of the American Political Science Association would exist without his foundational work. In addition, Terry graciously read my original book proposal and a draft of this book cover to cover, providing invaluable and constructive comments that have made the final product much better.

This book also would not have been possible without my long-time collaborators and dearest friends Stéphane Lavertu and Zac Peskowitz. Many of the ideas I discuss build on our coauthored work. In addition to Terry and Stéphane, Michael Hartney (who came up with the title of the book) and Laura Kogan provided comments on early drafts, and Parker Baxter, Craig Burnett, A. J. Crabill, Leslie Finger, Doug Harris, Jeff Henig, David Houston, Tom Loveless, Mimi Lyon, Robert McGrath, Ajat Mehta, Bob Moranto, James Strickland, and Adam Tyner offered great feedback on individual chapters. I have also benefited greatly from my conversations with Paul Hill.

The research discussed in Chapter 2 and the data collected for those analyses (as well as the figure presented in Chapter 8) were made possible by the generous financial support of the Spencer Foundation (2015 Lyle Spencer Research Grant, "The Education Governance and Accountability Project"). The school board election and Catalist voter records we collected were hand-coded by a team of outstanding research assistants that included Kezia Atta, Cory Barnes, Victoria Bartos, T. J. Beavers, Emily Cooner, Annie Curie, Kayleigh Feldkircher, Hannah Flaten, Adam Friend, Natalie Fritz, Ray Gans, Tessa Gilcher, Thomas Graham, Brennan Hall, Tommy Kaczkowski, George Kutrolli, Kristie Lam, Kyle Larson, William McCracken, Hayley McKinley, Jared Michael, Eleni Packis, Evan Posner, Namrata Pujara, Jordan Schultz, Katy Scruppi, Sarah Souders, Chaekwang You, and Megan Young. Many of these students were supervised by Carolyn Abott, who designed the collection protocols and cleaned much of the final data. The state legislative roll calls analyzed in Chapter 4 were collected and coded by Casey Thompson and Cordelia Van der Veer.

I

What Are Schools For?

Anything for the children.
—Former Columbus school board member Stephanie Groce

June 7, 2023, was the day a group of homophobic Armenians from Glendale, California, almost got me canceled. I will explain what happened shortly – and how the controversy perfectly encapsulates the thesis I put forward in this book. But first, it is important to set the scene.

That June was a big month for education policy. The federal government released the latest installment of the National Assessment of Educational Progress (NAEP) – an exam given to a nationally representative set of thirteen-year-olds for decades that allows academic achievement to be tracked over time. The NAEP is often called the "nation's report card" because of its ability to take stock the state of American education and put current performance in historical context. It was the first update of this series since the start of the COVID-19 pandemic, and it painted a terrifying picture of the toll the historic disruption had produced.

"In reading, average scores have declined to levels last seen in the 1970s, erasing decades of progress won through political blood, sweat, tears – and billions in public investments," I wrote in a piece published by *The 74*, an online education news platform associated with education reformers. "But the scores among the most disadvantaged students are even more shocking. Those in the bottom quarter of achievement are less proficient in reading than similar-aged peers were in 1971, posting the lowest scores ever recorded. In math, the bottom 10 percent students are back to their all-time low. Although racial breakdowns are not available for earlier years, the gap between Black and white students has grown markedly over the past decade. Not only has average achievement posted a record decline, but the effects have been concentrated among the most at-risk students" (Kogan, 2023).

The NAEP numbers should've been big news – a wake-up call and urgent reminder about the need to double down on postpandemic academic recovery. Although national outlets did write about the results, the announcement seemed to attract little attention among the broader population. To the extent that Americans were thinking about education during the summer break, they were focused on the culture wars that were roiling schools across the country over the preceding three years. The first round focused on Critical Race Theory (discussed in Chapter 4), the next on pandemic masking requirements, and the most recent on allegedly sexually explicit books that conservative critics charged were being made available to young children in school libraries. By June 2023, the arguments had found a new target – the rainbow flag that had become the symbol of LGBT acceptance and pride.

June is celebrated as Gay Pride Month, and many communities mark the occasion by displaying the rainbow flag and by issuing symbolic proclamations. The Glendale Unified School District had been planning to mark Pride Month by adopting such a resolution, just as it had every year since 2019. In 2023, however, the move attracted considerable attention and newfound opposition. Both supporters and opponents packed the room to speak at the school board meeting, and many others remained outside to protest. Members of the Los Angeles Armenian community led the resistance to the resolution, citing their religious convictions and criticizing broader LGBT-friendly policies in the district (McGahan, 2023). Eventually, the protests outside of the board meeting devolved into punches and pepper spray – and videos of the brawl appeared on newscasts across the country.

According to Google Trends, a tool that tracks queries on the search engine, more people googled "Glendale pride" than "NAEP" that month. It was a reflection of how much academic considerations had receded on the list of priorities of Americans and the extent to which adult political conflict had come to dominate education policy.

Which brings me to my tweet on June 7: Perhaps, I suggested sarcastically, school districts should put up flags with line charts tracking the achievement trajectories of their students? Maybe then people would start to actually care about the dismal state of education, and angry adults might show up at school board meetings and fight with each other about how to improve academic performance?

The blow back from other scholars of education policy began almost immediately. "This is SUCH dangerous rhetoric," tweeted Rachel White, a professor at the University of Texas, Austin, and a former collaborator of mine on an abandoned research project. "Pitting (a) showing care for/supporting LGBTQIA+ community against (b) increasing student performance on a single state assessment & condoning violent attacks not only on schls supporting LGBTQIA+ students, but also schls w low test scores?!"

Jack Schneider, an education historian at University of Massachusetts, Amherst, and longtime critic of standardized testing (e.g., Schneider, 2017), piled on. "Wow. This seems like a real 'delete your account' moment," he responded to White. "Perhaps he didn't *mean* to suggest that he's a fan of the anti-LGBTQ+ assault that is in the news? And perhaps he didn't *mean* to suggest that he'd like to see such attacks on schools with low standardized test scores?"

White and Schneider's reaction was hardly surprising. A year earlier, I had penned an article for *Education Next*, a journal published by Harvard University. The thesis of the article was summarized aptly by the headline: "Locally Elected School Boards Are Failing" (Kogan, 2022). The pandemic had stress-tested public education, I wrote, and revealed the extent to which adult politics had come to distort education policy, often at the expense of student learning.

Schneider and White (along with several coauthors) wrote a response, challenging the premise of my argument. "But are locally elected school boards actually *failing*?" they asked. "Answering this question isn't merely a matter of determining whether they ensure the academic outcomes Kogan prizes. It also requires us to examine the democratic purpose and practices of school boards. Taking into account the mission, stakeholders, and procedures of public schools and their governing boards – the what, who, and how of their activity – we believe that publicly elected school boards continue to play a vital role in serving children, communities, and democracy" (White et al., 2023).

In the months since our exchange, I have grown more confident that I was right and they were wrong. This book is an effort to articulate my argument, which has two parts. First, the Achilles' heel of public education is the system of local democratic control we have opted to use to govern it. At the root of almost every barrier standing in the way of efforts to improve student learning are perverse political and electoral incentives that this governance system creates. Second, by design, local democratic control serves the interests of adults (who get to vote in local elections), not the kids that public schools actually educate. Sometimes the interests of the two happen to be aligned, but when they conflict, democracy stacks the deck in favor of adults.

To borrow from science journalist Gary Taubes (2016), if this were a criminal case against local democratic control of public education, *No Adult Left Behind* would be the argument for the prosecution.

WELL-INTENTIONED ADULTS, DYSFUNCTIONAL SCHOOLS

Many readers, I suspect, will instinctively push back on my premise that the political interests of adults and the well-being of students are often in conflict. Perhaps not in the abstract, but when applied to specific education policy debates playing out today. That was certainly the reaction of economist Doug Harris when he read Chapter 5 of this book for a recent academic conference. The chapter examines the impact of adult culture wars on student academic outcomes and shows how conflicts about school mascots, free speech, racism, and evolution ultimately disrupt local schools and hurt student learning.

In his discussant comments, Harris rejected the idea that these were "adult" conflicts. Although the data used in the chapter ends a few years ago, before the rise of recent arguments about the appropriate care for transgender youth, Harris noted the relevance to that issue. Schools are not typically involved in health care – including decisions about whether to prescribe puberty blockers – but many have become embroiled in the controversy by enacting policies allowing students to socially transition in school and prohibiting teachers from notifying parents that their child changed their preferred pronouns. This was, according to Harris, not just an adult political issue. Trans-identifying youth have historically experienced high rates of depression and anxiety and elevated risk of suicide and self-harm – although the direction of causality in these correlations remains disputed. School policies designed to protect trans students are not about adults at all, they are a sincere attempt to save lives. There is, in short, no conflict between adult and student interests. Only raging transphobes who deny the efficacy of gender-affirming care would suggest otherwise.

This is definitely a powerful and appealing argument – but ultimately an unsatisfying one, for two reasons. The first is that it assumes the policies that adults – the kind of sincere and well-meaning adults who are mobilized and show up at local school board meetings and who vote in local school board elections – believe are good for students actually help them. There is, for example, no high-quality evidence showing that school policies prohibiting teachers from notifying parents about their child's social transition improve mental health outcomes for trans-identifying students. There is also no research showing that flying a rainbow flag in June on school district buildings increases the sense of inclusion for LGBT youth. It's possible that these policies work as intended – and I certainly hope they do! – but it's also possible that they backfire by increasing bullying of LGBT students, for example.

The second problem is that this argument ignores the collateral consequences and disruption to learning that can result from making school boards one of the primary forums for debating and ultimately resolving our society's most contentious and divisive political debates.

It's helpful to illustrate both of these points by looking back 100 years, to reexamine two of the most charged political controversies of the 1920s – over evolution and the prohibition of alcohol. Both became entangled in education policy and, looking back with the benefit of hindsight, we can appreciate why this development probably didn't serve public education well.

Readers familiar with the controversy over the teaching of evolution will almost certainly think of the famous "Scopes Monkey Trial" in Dayton, Tennessee. The 1925 case involved the prosecution of a teacher named John T. Scopes, who was criminally charged with teaching evolution to his students in violation of state law. The popular memory of the case is greatly influenced by the 1960 film "Inherit the Wind," which dramatized the trial. Many people today believe the effort to outlaw evolution was being driven by poorly educated rubes intent on writing their fundamentalist religious beliefs into school curriculum.

As historian Edward Larson (2003) has shown, however, almost everything we think we know about the case is wrong. The entire fiasco was a slick public relations stunt cooked up by the local business community to attract national media attention for Dayton. It's unclear whether Scopes had even taught evolution. In fact, he had already made plans to leave Tennessee when the trial began and volunteered to be prosecuted in exchange for modest compensation paid by the American Civil Liberties Union and local business leaders. And although religion certainly motivated many opponents of evolution, this is a simplistic and incomplete account. For example, William Jennings Bryan, the populist Democrat and President Woodrow Wilson's secretary of state who became the public face of the anti-evolution movement, was indeed a devout Christian, but his faith was only one of several motivations behind his activism. Bryan was a Presbyterian, not a Fundamentalist.

For Bryan, the main problems with teaching evolution in schools was not the biology but the social norms and mores these Darwinian ideas encouraged. We must remember that the 1920s were a decade when scientific racism, eugenics, and social Darwinism were all in vogue. These ideas had shockingly high levels of support from some of the nation's most highly visible scholars and public intellectuals, who argued they were the logical conclusion of Darwin's theory.[1] Such ideas remained popular until they were discredited after becoming embraced by and forever linked to Nazism in Germany a decade later.

To his credit, Bryan was appalled by the eugenicists from the start – long before the Holocaust – and believed social Darwinism was immoral. By teaching students the theory of evolution, he believed schools were inculcating support for these vile ideas among the next generation. Worse, he worried they were making war more likely. According to his biographer, Bryan's opposition to evolution stemmed in large part from his belief that a "survival of the fittest" mentality had contributed to German militarism in the run up to the first world war (Levine, 1965, pp. 259–264). Darwin, Bryan believed, had laid "foundations for the bloodiest war in history" (Larson, 2003).

Prohibiting schools from teaching evolution for Bryan was not about adults imposing their religious beliefs on school children – it was about stopping the spread of horrible ideas like eugenics that threatened the most vulnerable members of society and potentially even world peace. I suspect many modern progressive activists would be sympathetic with these goals, although they would almost certainly reject the premise that eugenics is a necessary logical conclusion of biological evolution, as many believed during this period.

While Bryan's intentions were no doubt noble, the fight against the teaching of evolution had unintended consequences he never imagined. (He died unexpectedly just days after the 1925 trial.) It would trigger political battles in states and school districts around the country for nearly a century, pitting neighbor against neighbor. And it

---

[1] Indeed, the evolution textbook at issue in the Scopes trial, George W. Hunter's *A Civic Biology*, included a rank-ordering of "five races," starting with "the Ethiopian or negro type" and proceeding through several others before describing "the highest type of all, the Caucasians" (Moran, 2003).

spawned massively expensive lawsuits that drained resources that otherwise could've been spent in the classroom. Chapter 5 details one recent case.

The second historical example about the potentially pernicious role of adult interests in education is related to efforts to outlaw the consumption of alcohol. Almost all Americans are familiar with Prohibition – a thirteen-year experiment during which the Eighteenth Amendment prohibited the manufacture, sale, and transportation of booze. Most also know that Prohibition was a failed policy, one that gave rise to underground bootlegging controlled by organized crime and considerable violence (e.g., Owens, 2014). Fewer may remember what motivated the Women's Christian Temperance Union (WCTU), the activist group that led the successful advocacy campaign for Prohibition. The WCTU believed alcohol was a major cause of vice, contributed to domestic violence against women, led to premature deaths, and created poverty – all claims for which we have considerable empirical support today!

Even fewer know the role that public education played in the story. Beginning in the 1880s, the WCTU turned its focus to school curriculum. The group developed pro-temperance lesson plans, providing children "scientific" information about the harms of alcohol. Persuading state politicians to teach about the evils of alcohol was also an easier political lift than convincing them to outlaw alcohol outright: "Even politicians in favor of temperance were not sure they wanted to alienate voters by proscribing drinking. Children, however, were another matter. They did not vote, and they might safely be taught to shun what their parents cared little to abandon" (Tyack and James, 1985, pp. 515–516). By the mid 1890s, forty-five states had passed laws mandating temperance instruction, and more than twenty-five required teachers to pass a test on the subject in order to receive their certification.

Although WCTU leaders were no doubt sincere in their belief that encouraging children to abstain from alcohol would be good for them in the long run, they also had other motivations. Here was an opportunity to shape the political opinions and behaviors of the future electorate during their formative school years. It should not be surprising that many voters who initially supported Prohibition in the early 1920s came of age during a period when temperance instruction was mandated in the schools. Would Prohibition have been enacted at all if school curriculum had not been used as a tool of political indoctrination to push what many reputable scientists at the time viewed as anti-alcohol propaganda (Mezvinsky, 1961)? Do the pure and entirely praiseworthy intentions of WCTU activists let them off the hook for the many problems failed Prohibition-era policies ultimately created?

These are hardly unique examples. As noted education historian David Tyack has written, public schools have attracted the attention of almost every well-organized adult interest at some point in American history. School attendance is mandatory, creating a captive audience of children. Influencing school curriculum is an opportunity to shape the political outlook of the next generation of voters. If you believe in the righteousness of your political cause, the temptation is just too great. Individually, many of these efforts and ideas may have considerable merit. But collectively, they strip the school curriculum of coherence and divert precious, finite classroom time away from teaching essential skills in core academic subjects:

> Throughout the twentieth century, dozens of interest groups have stood ready to cure civic ills or help business by adding another course to the curriculum (usually on a subject remote from the traditional academic disciplines). The National Association of Manufacturers supported vocational education. The Women's Christian Temperance Union lobbied states and the federal government until they legislated an antialcohol message in every school in the nation. Driver education was cheerfully advocated by car dealers and insurance companies. ... State legislators enacted laws requiring compulsory physical education after huge numbers of draftees failed their physical exams. When public health officials battled an epidemic of venereal disease around 1900, they proposed classes in sex education. The American Legion and the Daughters of the American Revolution lobbied tirelessly to Americanize America. A major challenge to educational leaders was to create some coherence in the many programs added to the curriculum. (Tyack, 2001)

Another education historian, Lawrence Cremin, has argued that there is an "inextricable relationship between social reform, reform *through* education, and reform *of* education ... Humanitarians of every stripe [see] education at the heart of their effort toward social alleviation" (1961, p. 85). As Cremin's mentee, the famous Diane Ravitch noted in one of her early books, "Defined as they so often were as instruments of national purpose, educational institutions became focal points for large areas of consensus (there is much, after all, on which Americans agree), but they also served as magnets for dissention, attracting all those who wanted to change the social order, preserve threatened traditions, challenge historic wrongs, or make sure the next generation was not tainted by the errors of their predecessors" (Ravitch, 1983, p. xii). This often proved unproductive, she recognized. "Throughout history, Americans have expected much of their educational institutions; sometimes schools have been expected to take on responsibilities for which they were entirely unsuited. When they have failed, it was usually because their leaders and their public alike had forgotten their real limitations as well as their real strengths."

That social and political reformers truly believe what they're doing is right and will benefit student well-being makes their efforts no less of an adult political project. The jugular question, I argue in this book, is how such advocacy efforts impact the quality of the education that students ultimately receive.

STUDENT OUTCOMES AS OUR NORTH STAR

This book is a scholarly endeavor to engage in careful empirical research. It seeks to describe the world as it is, not as I wish it to be. In the interest of transparency, however, I should lay my normative cards on the table.

Implicit in the discussion in the remainder of this book is my view about what public education is all about. Just as fire stations exist to save property and people by putting out fires, police departments exist to protect residents from crime, and municipal water agencies exist to deliver clean and safe water, I believe public schools exist to teach children academic skills. We evaluate the quality of fire services by tracking response times to 911 calls, measure police performance by looking at changes in crime and case clearance rates, and assess water quality by testing it for the presence of toxins such as lead and arsenic. None of these metrics are perfect or capture every relevant dimension of service quality we ultimately care about (see, e.g., Mosher, Miethe and Philips, 2002), but they provide invaluable insights and allow us to identify problems and course-correct when necessary. Similarly, we can evaluate whether schools are doing their jobs by examining student achievement, as measured using standardized test scores.

My perspective is well summarized in a pithy memo written by a governance coach[2] brought in by the San Francisco school board in the aftermath of a recall that removed three of their colleagues (the recall is discussed in Chapter 2):

First, school systems exist to improve student outcomes. That is the only reason school systems exist. School systems do not exist to have great buildings, happy parents, balanced budgets, satisfied teachers, student lunches, employment, or

---

[2] The governance coach is former Kansas City School Board Chair AJ Crabill, who I interview in detail in Chapter 7 and who provides the opening epigraph for Chapter 2.

anything else. Those are all means – and incredibly important and valuable means at that – but none of them are the ends; none of those are why we have school systems. They are all inputs, not outcomes. None of those are measures of what students know or can do. School systems exist for one reason and one reason only: to improve student outcomes.

W. E. B. Du Bois put it well in his 1935 address to the Georgia State Teachers Convention. "The school has but one way to cure the ills of society and that is by making men intelligent. To make men intelligent, the school has again but one way, and that is, first and last, to teach them to read, write and count," he argued. "And if the school fails to do that, and tries beyond that to do something for which a school is not adapted, it not only fails in its own function, but it fails in all other attempted functions. Because no school as such can organize industry, or settle the matter of wage and income, can found homes or furnish parents, can establish justice or make a civilized world" (quoted in King, 1971, p. 257).

To assert that schools exist to improve student outcomes says nothing about *how* they should do so. Perhaps serving nutritious meals and making them available free of charge to all students improves learning (Frisvold, 2015; Schwartz and Rothbart, 2020). Perhaps replacing exclusionary disciplinary policies with restorative justice practices improves student behavior and attendance (Adukia, Feigenberg and Momeni, 2023). Perhaps reducing class sizes is the best policy lever for improving achievement (but see Chingos, 2013). The important thing is to set clear goals tied to student outcomes and measure how well schools are meeting them, not to impose prescriptive mandates about how the goals should be achieved. We've tried prescriptive mandates before, and it didn't work out well (see Manna, 2011).

Equally importantly, my formulation does not take a firm position about *why* schools should focus on improving academic achievement. As historian David Labaree has argued, lack of agreement on the why question has long provided the raison d'être for education politics. "[T]he problem is not that we do not know how to make schools better but that we are fighting among ourselves about what goals schools should pursue," he famously wrote. "Goal setting is a political, not a technical, problem. It is resolved through a process of making choices and not through a process of scientific investigation. The answer lies in values (what kind of schools we want) and interests (who supports which educational values) rather than apolitical logic" (Labaree, 1997, p. 40). In his accounts, public education has lurched from one reform to the next for decades in part because different reformers were interested in different goals. Some believed schools were there to produce "democratic equality" by preparing students for citizenship, others that schools were responsible for training the future workforce ("social efficiency"), and yet others focused on using education to promote the "social mobility" of individuals.

This book does not take a position on this debate. I believe all three are important and reasonable people can disagree about how to make trade-offs between these goals. Critically, however, ensuring that students are skilled in core academic subjects – that they are numerate and literate – is required for accomplishing all three goals. That is another reason for making student academic achievement – "what students know or can do" – the North Star to guide education policy decisions.

To be sure, my framing sidesteps hugely important and deeply political questions. If educational resources are finite, how do we fairly allocate them among different schools and students? Is it better to group students by ability, providing an opportunity for advanced students to accelerate further but concentrating low-achieving students in classrooms with other disadvantaged peers? When teaching history, should we emphasize the lasting legacies of slavery or encourage students to celebrate the country's founding ideals, even if we have not always lived up to them? These are truly complex questions, and this book offers no simple or satisfying answers to any of them.

But it turns out that there is a great deal that Americans agree about. Everyone thinks kids should be able to read. All believe children should be able to do basic math – the kind of math required to balance one's checkbook as an adult. And there is almost certainly consensus about the need to develop students' critical thinking and reasoning skills – habits of thought they'll need to successfully navigate personal relationships, excel in their careers, and contribute to our democracy as responsible citizens. Indeed, as I discuss in Chapter 4, there is also a surprising degree of agreement about what we should teach school children about American history, even if today's polarized political debates suggest otherwise.

This book seeks to explain why so many public schools fail to accomplish even the limited academic objectives around which there is no disagreement. Why so many students enter middle school unable to read, why they graduate from high school unable to do algebra, and why so many American adults do not know even the basic facts about the structure of American government. Our public education system fails too many students – disproportionately the students who come from the most disadvantaged families and who need good schools to compensate for all of the other challenges they face in their homes and neighborhoods and to give them a decent shot to live healthy, happy, and meaningful lives. My argument is that dysfunctional governance is ultimately responsible for these disparities and that failure is hardwired into the political processes and institutions through which our society has chosen to govern our schools.

CHIEF JUSTICE EARL WARREN WAS WRONG

For many years after his retirement from the Supreme Court, Earl Warren was frequently asked what he thought was the most important decision during his tenure as chief justice. It was a difficult question, because the Warren court had issued so many landmark rulings affecting almost every aspect of American government and life. Despite the embarrassment of riches – so many important cases to choose from – most people expected Warren to say *Brown v. Board of Education*, the 1954 unanimous decision striking down the system of legally segregated schooling in the South. But that was not the case Warren ultimately singled out.

Writing in his memoirs, Warren said "this accolade should go to the case *Baker v. Carr* (1962), which was the progenitor of the 'one man, one vote' rule" (quoted in Charles and Fuentes-Rohwer 2016). The 1962 ruling found for the first time that malapportionment – the drawing of legislative districts with unequal population to dilute the political power of some groups and amplify the influence of others – was unconstitutional. At the time, malapportionment was intentionally used to limit the influence of large urban centers, where most African-Americans lived, and to reduce their representation in state legislatures throughout the country. Segregated and unequal schools, the retired chief justice argued, were a symptom of an electoral system stacked against Black voters. "If we had already had universal voting," Warren said in one interview, and if every vote counted equally, "then we wouldn't have had many of the problems *Brown* attempted to correct."

My contention is that Warren is wrong, on two counts. The first has to do with the *Brown* case itself. As I show in Chapter 6, a great deal of the opposition to school integration came from *within* the African-American community. Some were attached to high-profile, beloved all-Black schools (Buck, 2011). And many were worried – with good reason, as it would turn out – that integration would mean the elimination of well-paying public sector jobs that Black educators had found in the segregated system. One uncomfortable possibility I consider in Chapter 6 is that integration happened precisely *because* the Jim Crow South had found ways to keep African-Americans from exercising their voting rights and political power.

But Warren's broader thesis was also incorrect. Equality at the voting booth does not guarantee an equitable, high-quality public education system if the population that uses the school system – children – are not eligible to vote. In fact, it could make good schools less likely.

The potential disconnect between the interests of voters and other non-voting constituents was itself baked uncomfortably in to the Supreme Court's one-man, one-vote decisions. "Legislators represent people, not trees or acres," the court ruled in another famous malapportionment case, *Reynolds v. Sims* (1964) "Legislators are elected by voters, not farms or cities or economic interests." But what to do if the "people" legislators are supposed to represent are different, and need different things, than the "voters" who elect them? The court never answered that question.

The same dilemma plagues public education. Schools exist to serve students, not trees or acres. School board members are elected by adult voters, not farms or cities or economic interests. This book documents the many ways in which the interests of these two groups can and often do diverge. When such divergence happens, our governance system is effectively gerrymandered to amplify the interests of adults at the expense of educational needs of public school students.

LOOKING BEYOND MONEY AND UNIONS

Much of the academic debate on how to improve public education is split between two camps – those who argue that the main problem is lack of financial resources and those who blame teachers' unions. Both of these accounts are valuable, but both are also incomplete.

It is true that, for much of American history, public education was financed in a way that was deeply inequitable, leaving disadvantaged communities and schools serving students of color with far fewer dollars to spend than schools educating their wealthier, whiter counterparts. The culprit was heavy reliance on local property taxes to raise the operating revenues for public schools, which linked school quality to the size of each community's tax base and the willingness of its residents to pay taxes. The hugely unfair system that resulted was described in *Savage Inequalities*, a devastating account by Jonathan Kozol (1991).

But we must also recognize that this is not the system we have today, thanks to two waves of legal interventions and a number of important state court decisions (see Koski and Hahnel, 2015 for overview). Since the early 1970s, a number of state Supreme Courts have struck down their states' school finance models for violating equal protection guarantees written into state constitutions. Starting in 1989, another series of lawsuits challenged systems too heavily reliant on local revenues as violating constitutional requirements guaranteeing some minimal level of educational quality or "adequacy." In each case, the courts ordered state governments to pony up money to supplement local sources, channeling additional resources to communities that needed them the most. The evidence shows that these interventions were effective, narrowing resource gaps and improving the achievement and attainment of students from disadvantaged areas (Jackson, Johnson and Persico, 2016; Lafortune, Rothstein and Schanzenbach, 2018).

These state finance reforms have fundamentally changed the reality of school funding in this country. "Average spending per pupil, measured at the school district level, is approximately the same for nonpoor students and for free-lunch students. Average class sizes are also approximately the same across high and low-poverty schools," economists Lisa Barrow and Diane Whitmore Schanzenbach (2012) concluded after reviewing the data a decade ago. "The big differences across high- and low-poverty schools are in teacher characteristics, facilities, and school crime rates. Low-poverty schools have more experienced teachers, less teacher turnover, fewer crimes, and more specialized facilities." The incentives and distortions created by local democracy contribute to many of these remaining differences.

The evidence clearly shows that educational spending has a causal effect on student performance (Jackson and Mackevicius, 2024). But to acknowledge that more money is, on average, better does not imply that lack of resources is the primary cause of unacceptably low achievement in many schools and districts. It is not. In most places, spending is now high enough to have reached the point of diminishing marginal returns (Abott et al., 2020; Lee, Shores and Williams, 2022). Local political processes dictate how money is allocated within schools – and explain why it's often spent so unproductively and why school districts fail to maximize the academic returns on these investments (Handel and Hanushek, 2023). The problem in most districts is not a lack of money but how it's spent.

More importantly, the effects of additional spending are just far too small to address our existing achievement gaps any time soon. The widely cited meta-analytic estimates from Jackson and Mackevicius (2024) show that $1,000 in sustained additional spending per year over four years improves test scores in math and reading by about 0.03 standard deviations. By contrast, the difference in the achievement of students who qualify for free and reduced-lunch price and those who don't is on the order of 0.7 standard deviations (Hanushek et al., 2019). Closing this gap through money alone would mean boosting spending by $90,000 for every low-income student over their time in school (assuming, optimistically, no diminishing returns), or nearly $7,000 per year. That represents a roughly 50 percent increase over current levels. The Black–white achievement gap is even larger, which means the amount of additional spending needed to close it is even greater. No realistic observer of American politics believes that this kind of increase is in the cards.

Teachers' unions also play a central role in education, particularly in school board elections. I highly recommend two excellent book-length scholarly accounts of union influence local politics by political scientists Terry Moe (2011) and Michael Hartney (2022a). In addition to their ability to swing school board elections, unions intervene to directly shape policies that impact learning.

The evidence that teachers' unions generally – and collective bargaining in particular – negatively affects school quality is overwhelming. It is clear that teachers' unions are motivated to look out primarily for their own members and have no problem selling out students when their interests conflict (Cook, Lavertu and Miller, 2021). The various job rules and protections that unions win on behalf of teachers often have a net negative impact on students (Lovenheim and Willén, 2019; Moe, 2009).

One of the most persuasive studies on this issue focuses on Boston and was written by a team of MIT economists (Abdulkadiroğlu et al., 2011). Previously, these authors published a series of careful analyses on Boston charter schools – publicly funded schools that operate independently of the city's school district and have considerable flexibility in how they are run. The earlier studies consistently found that the charter schools were doing a great job, far outperforming traditional public schools serving similar students.

As more families left the Boston schools for the high-performing charters, the district decided to create its own system of "pilot" schools trying to replicate the success of charters. Just like charters, the pilot schools received "more flexibility and decision-making powers over school budgets, academic programs, and educational policies" (Abdulkadiroğlu et al., 2011, p. 700). Unlike charters, however, the pilot schools were still unionized and covered by the district's collective bargaining agreement with the teachers' union.

Both charter schools and pilot schools in Boston proved to be popular – so popular, they had wait lists to get in. To ration the limited spots, the law required each type of school to run random admissions lotteries. This also provided the economists a perfect way to evaluate the impact of attending these schools – comparing the academic outcomes of students who won each lottery to those who lost and thus had to attend their neighborhood public schools instead. Students who got into the charter schools consistently did better. Surprisingly, those who got into the pilot schools did *worse* – they would've been better served attending their neighborhood public school instead. Since the only difference between the two was whether the school was covered by the teachers' union contract, the study provided compelling evidence about the negative impacts of such contracts on student learning.

I discuss teachers' unions (and school employees more broadly) throughout this book, and they play a particularly prominent role in Chapter 6, which examines the politics of school closures. However, my argument is that teachers' unions are just one of many relevant adult interests who exercise political power in education, often in ways that negatively impacts students. Unions are especially engaged on issues most likely to impact the employment interests of their members – policies related to teacher compensation, evaluation, assignment, and dismissal. These are hugely consequential in light of the reality that teacher quality is the single most important in-school factor that can make the difference in a student's academic trajectory. But there are many other policy debates in education that are more peripheral to teachers' unions core concerns and in which they play a much smaller role. Much of my book focuses on these topics because they have been largely overlooked in the scholarly research on education governance.

POLITICS, MARKETS – AND HACKS

This volume builds on arguments first laid out by political scientists John Chubb and Terry Moe more than thirty years ago, in their pathbreaking book *Politics, Markets, and America's Schools* (1990b). Education reformers, Chubb and Moe argued, were focusing their energies on all of the wrong things and ignoring the biggest problem – the institutions through which public schools are governed. "It is our view that the most fundamental causes [of low academic performance] are far less obvious, given the way schools are commonly understood, and far less susceptible to change," they wrote. "They are, in fact, the very institutions that are supposed to be solving the problem: the institutions of direct democratic control" (p. 2).

In their study, the authors analyzed data from the High School and Beyond Survey, constructing measures of school quality based on growth in student test scores in a variety of academic subjects between sophomore and senior year. They found that differences in the amount of homework, graduation requirements, administrative routines in classroom, and disciplinary policies didn't seem to affect how much students learned in high school. One of the things that did matter, however, was having an effective school organization – characterized by strong leadership provided by building principals with the authority to hire and manage their teaching staff. School organization predicted achievement gains as much as initial student test scores and parents' socioeconomic status.

The problem with the public education system, Chubb and Moe argued, was that democratic control was inherently incompatible with effective school organization. Elected officials pushed for more and more bureaucratization, both to impose their political values on principals and teachers who might not share their goals and to lock in their preferred policies and insulate them from change in case the political tide turned in the future. Vested interests with selfish motives for keeping schools operating just as they were – in particular, teachers' unions – also used their political power to block institutional reforms necessary to improve academic achievement.

The result was a system in which the public schools functioned largely as adult employment agencies, overseen by principals who mostly acted as compliance officers rather than instructional leaders and lacked the autonomy needed to maximize student learning, including by hiring the good teachers and dismissing the bad ones. Parents and their kids were the ones who lost out – by design. "The fundamental point to be made about parents and students is not that they are politically weak, but that, even in a perfectly functioning democratic system, the public schools are not meant to be theirs to control and are literally not supposed to provide them with the kind of education they might want," the authors concluded. "The schools are agencies of society as a whole, and everyone has a right to participate in their governance. Parents and students have a right to participate too. But they have no right to win. In the end, they have to take what society gives them" (p. 32).

As will become clear in the remainder of this book, I wholeheartedly agree with Chubb and Moe's diagnosis of the problem and their big-picture argument. When it comes to low academic achievement of America's students, to quote former Brookings Institution President Bruce McLaury (who wrote the foreword to the Chubb and Moe book), "government has not solved the education problem because government is the problem." I do quibble with some of the details, however.

In particular, I believe Chubb and Moe underestimate the importance of real estate markets and the extent to which the capitalization of perceived school quality into home prices influences local politics and what school districts do, a topic I take up in Chapter 8. In addition, I offer a somewhat different diagnosis for why urban school districts suffer from the greatest governance dysfunctions. "The nation's largest cities are teeming with diverse, conflicting interests of political salience – class, race, ethnicity, language, religion – and their schools are plagued by problems so severe, wide-ranging, and deeply rooted in the urban socioeconomic structure that the situation appears out of control and perhaps even beyond hope," Chubb and Moe concluded. All of these things are true, but as I argue in Chapter 2, another reason for the poor performance in these communities is the especially large disconnect between who votes in local school board elections and the students that these schools actually serve.

The final area of mild disagreement is that I believe the problems created by local democratic control are actually even more extensive and severe than Chubb and Moe suggest. They focus on bureaucratization and vested interests, which are both major impediments to creating and sustaining effective schools. But the range of adult interests in local politics is vast, and the number of things adults care about – including partisanship and identity politics – is large. As a result, school board members face strong incentives to engage in symbolic and performative politics – activities that David Mayhew described as "advertising," "position-taking," and "credit-claiming" (1974) – that are at best orthogonal to providing a good education to students and often come at the expense of doing so. The barriers to running school well is not just the bureaucracy and vested interests hardwired into democracy but also the political hacks elections tend to reward and put into office.

What Are Schools For?

PREBUNKING THE CRITICS

The arguments made and empirical findings reported in the remainder of this book will no doubt be controversial. Before proceeding, therefore, I want to take a moment to anticipate the most likely criticisms and preemptively address them.

Schools Aren't Failing

Passionate defenders of American public education will almost certainly push back on my starting proposition – that public schools are failing many American children. They might point to Gallup polling data showing that three-fourths of parents are satisfied with their kids' schools, although probably not to other figures from the same poll showing that the vast majority give low marks to the education system as a whole (Barnum, 2023).

That is exactly what happened in 1983, in response to the release of "A Nation at Risk" by the National Commission on Excellence in Education. The report was a call-to-arms for education reformers, and it used incredibly evocative language to describe the perilous state of American public education. "Our Nation is at risk. Our once unchallenged preeminence in commerce, industry, science, and technological innovation is being overtaken by competitors throughout the world," the report began. "If an unfriendly foreign power had attempted to impose on America the mediocre educational performance that exists today, we might well have viewed it as an act of war. As it stands, we have allowed this to happen to ourselves. ... We have, in effect, been committing an act of unthinking, unilateral educational disarmament."

The report had a tremendous impact on American policy, but many critics continue to charge that it misrepresented the data to attack public schools. When comparing SAT scores over time, for example, the report did not account for the changing demographic mix of students taking the college admission test. When comparing the performance of American students on international exams to kids in other countries, it also did not account for differences in who participated in the testing samples.

These are entirely fair critiques, and it is important not to overstate the magnitude of the problems. Public schools work just fine for a great many families and children. The issue, however, is that they don't work for precisely the students who need them to work the most.

As economist Helen Ladd – hardly a right-wing public school hater – noted more than a decade ago, America's middling performance on international exams is driven in large part by the scores of our most economically disadvantaged students. It is these students who most lag behind similar peers in other countries. "U.S. students in families with [socioeconomic status (SES)] below the median perform particularly badly relative to their low-[SES] peers in other countries, while U.S. students from more advantaged backgrounds perform reasonably well by international standards," she pointed out. "That is, the largest shortfalls in performance among U.S. students are concentrated among those with relatively low [SES]. These shortfalls suggest there is room for the United States to do better by its disadvantaged students" (Ladd, 2012, p. 210).

Some of the blame might lay with the threadbare nature of the American welfare state and other social policies. But these cannot explain why our education system exacerbates existing inequalities. Poor students are consistently assigned less experienced teachers, suffer from higher rates of teacher absenteeism, and are far less likely to receive a substitute teacher when theirs is out (Barrow and Schanzenbach, 2012; Liu, Loeb and Shi, 2022). There are policy choices that drive these disparities, and these choices reflect the pressures and incentives created by the local political process that governs public schools.

Test Scores Miss Too Much

Some readers might take issue with my reliance on standardized test scores to assess whether schools are serving students well and to quantify the observable variation of school quality across communities. There are a range of possible arguments in this vein often heard from skeptics of standardized testing, and some are more reasonable than others.

One version is that test scores simply don't matter, and that differences in test scores we see between schools just reflect how well a school is teaching to the test. This is just plain wrong. In a fascinating series of papers linking standardized test scores measured during childhood to the same individuals' future tax returns several decades later, economist Raj Chetty and his coauthors found clear evidence that scores predicted important long-run outcomes, including college attendance, homeownership, and retirement savings rates. More importantly, the researchers showed that teachers who most improved their students' test scores also improved their labor market outcomes in adulthood while reducing teenage pregnancy (Chetty et al., 2011; Chetty, Friedman and Rockoff, 2014).

A different, more sophisticated argument acknowledges that test scores matter. But it raises worries about the unintended consequences of attaching high-powered incentives to these scores and about the potential harms from accountability pressures, like those in place under the No Child Left Behind Act (NCLB). Not only do these encourage the narrowing of curriculum – cutting instruction in subjects such as art and theater to focus on the tested content – but also give rise to all sorts of problematic gaming incentives, such as reclassifying students as needing special education to remove them from the testing sample (Deming et al., 2016) or even suspending low-achieving students on test days so they are not there to participate in the exams (Figlio, 2006). Such gaming behaviors give the impression of higher performance without actually improving learning.

These are legitimate concerns. Indeed, one of the major problems with the NCLB accountability regime is that it focused only on increasing the number of students gaining proficiency in math and reading (and later science). The unintended but entirely predictable consequence of doing so was that it caused school districts and teachers to prioritize the kids on the "bubble" – just below or barely above the proficiency threshold – while ignoring the needs of advanced learners and those far behind academically (Neal and Schanzenbach, 2010).

In my discussion throughout the book, I am very attentive to these issues. Throughout, I emphasize the importance of using the *right* performance metrics. My preferred measure of school quality – student achievement growth over time – has a number of desirable properties. It isolates the schools' contributions to student learning and removes factors such as poverty and parental involvement, over which educators have no control. In addition, the mathematically complex nature of this measure also makes it very difficult to game.

The final, and most serious, critique of emphasizing test scores is that it might cause us to overlook other dimensions of school quality that are even more important for students' long-term success. This argument is mostly closely associated with the work of economist Bo Jackson (2018), who constructed different measures of teacher quality based on their ability to increase test scores, improve school attendance, and reduce disciplinary infractions (see also Kraft, 2019). Jackson showed that teacher effects on these "noncognitive" outcomes were most important for predicting student success over the long run, including for outcomes such as educational attainment.³ Worryingly, the teachers that seem most effective at improving noncognitive outcomes tend to be different from the teachers who produce the largest growth in short-run test scores.

This was important work that had a profound impact on my thinking and which has clear policy implications. Particularly when it comes to teacher evaluations, it is important to examine multiple outcomes. When looking at impacts on test performance, it is also important to focus on learning gains that persist over longer periods of times, discounting short-term increases in achievement.⁴

But it is also important to emphasize that these findings are about individual teachers. In this book, my focus is on schools and school districts. Most of the variation in teacher quality is actually within schools and when we aggregate up to the school (or district) level, a lot of the idiosyncratic teacher effects cancel out. Even though impact on test scores and behaviors may have low correlations when we compare teachers, their relationship is likely to be much stronger at higher levels of aggregation.

This should not be surprising: Personal attributes that make individual teachers particularly skilled are likely quite different than practices and policies that produce building-wide academic gains. And if the whole school is struggling to grow students academically, whatever problems are responsible almost certainly impact the student experience in other domains as well. In the real world, I doubt we can find many schools that struggle to improve student achievement but hit it out of the ballpark in terms of attendance, discipline, and school climate.

Recent work by Jackson and coauthors confirmed that this is indeed the case. Using data from high schools in Chicago, they built several different measures of school quality – based on test score growth, student responses surveys measuring students' social emotional skills, and behavioral metrics that included attendance and school discipline. These different dimensions of school quality turned out to be positively correlated with each other, in many cases quite strongly (see bottom panel of Table 2 in Jackson et al., 2022). Most worryingly, the authors found that across each measure, access to good schools was not equitable within the district – students in need of the best schools received the least access

---

³ This may also explain why early childhood education intervention, which seem to produce only short-run test score effects that fade out quickly, are found to improve outcomes decades later in domains such as labor market participation and criminal involvement.
⁴ As it turns out, effects on long-term test score growth is much more strongly correlated with teacher effects in "noncognitive" domains (Gilraine and Pope, 2021).

to them. "Our estimates suggest that the least-advantaged students gain the most from attending effective schools," they concluded. "However, in our data, the least-effective schools are disproportionately attended by the least-advantaged students."

To summarize, school quality is multidimensional, and test scores don't capture everything. But they can differentiate the best schools from the worst, help us understand how access to each is stratified among students, and allow us to examine the political processes that contribute to this variation.

Schools Are "Community Institutions"

For those who follow education policy debates closely, it is common to hear the refrain that schools are "community institutions." And it is hard to disagree – until you actually think through what this statement implies. Usually, the "community institutions" argument is trotted out to defend policy choices that serve the interests of various adults. Yes, the argument often goes, the policy we've adopted may negatively impact student learning, but that's OK because schools are community institutions. They don't just exist to serve kids.

Such arguments come up a lot in the context of school closures (see Chapter 7). Shuttering an existing school is one of the most divisive and contentious decisions a school district could make. Proposing to do so brings out all sorts of angry and mobilized adults – proud alumni with fond memories of their time there, diehard supporters of the football team, nearby homeowners who worry that an empty building will hurt their property values, and school employees who stand to lose their jobs. It doesn't matter if the school is half-empty and if keeping it open diverts precious financial sources from other high-value educational programming. It doesn't matter if it has atrocious academic outcomes and has failed students for years. It is a "community institution" and must stay open.

In their response to my *Education Next* essay, Schneider, White and their coauthors wholeheartedly embraced this view. "Kogan's argument suggests that schools should primarily serve the interests of students and that we can tell whether they are doing their jobs by examining performance-based accountability scores," they wrote. "But public schools in the U.S. have a wide range of stakeholders, including a diversity of students and families, as well as the economic, civic, and social sectors in those families' surrounding communities. ... Students aren't the only ones who benefit from public education. Local and regional communities have a serious stake in their schools and gauge their success far more broadly than can be captured by standardized test scores. Public schools are valued for many reasons, among which is their function as community hubs, providing a means to discover shared educational interests that are locally and regionally distinct."

To understand why this argument, although highly seductive, is ultimately flawed, it is useful to think by analogy. How persuasive would it be when applied to other types of public services? After all, we could argue that *all* government organizations are "community institutions" and agencies that operate physical buildings even more so. Yet rarely do we use this logic to justify or excuse bad performance in other policy domains.

Consider firefighting. In many cities, the fire houses are beautiful, ornate buildings with striking architecture. In our neighborhood, the fire house really is a community institution – the property parcel on which it sits also hosts a community garden that is used by many neighbors and as a location for public events. But no one would dispute that the ultimate responsibility of the fire department is to put out fires, and we should hold it accountable for doing so.

Imagine that a city has multiple fire stations but is facing financial pressures. It notices that some of its fire stations are used much more often than others – perhaps because most fires break out on the urban–wildlife interface. The station in that part of town is always responding to calls. Firefighters there are overworked and the response time horrible. The station across town is rarely dispatched, on the other hand. The firefighters there spend most of their time pumping iron and grilling out.

In reviewing this data and facing financial exigencies, the city might decide to shutter the second fire station and then transfer some of its firefighters to the first location. This will save money, helping balance the budget, and also improve service quality – ultimately saving more homes from being burned to the ground.

It is difficult to imagine that many people would show up at the city council meeting opposing the consolidation on the grounds that the underused fire station is a "community institution." It's even less plausible that policymakers would take such arguments seriously – that they would accept suboptimal response time to 911 calls and ineffective fire protection just to keep a building open.

To be sure, the closure of fire station is often highly contested and controversial. Firefighters' unions fight them, often effectively. But they usually do so by making arguments about service quality – about how the closure of the fire station will affect response times and ability to fight fires. They don't claim that fire houses should remain open because they are "community institutions."

Similar thought experiments can be done in other service areas. Would local voters overlook poorly run public hospitals with dismal excess mortality rates as a result of incompetent doctors and unsanitary surgery rooms because these hospitals' policies on elective abortions match local community sentiment, whether pro-choice or pro-life? Would residents be OK with drinking contaminated water, laced with dysentery and typhoid, in order to protect the jobs of those who work for public water agencies?

When it comes to things adults ultimately care about, these types of arguments don't fly when writing off poor performance. Yet we take them at face value all the time in education, when it is kids who are negatively impacted. Again, politics explains why these arguments gain so much traction in the context of public education (but not other policy domains) and why elected officials willingly make decisions that are bad for students to keep politically powerful adults happy.

What about Racism, Poverty, and Other "Root Causes"?

A few years ago, I started seeing the same older woman at the Columbus school board meetings. One day, we started chatting and it turned out she was getting ready to run for the school board. She had begun her career as a corporate attorney, then switched tracks, and became a high school teacher serving high-need students with disabilities. Her passion for students and learning was infectious and her sincerity obvious. We quickly became friends and my wife and I even hosted a fundraiser at our house for her campaign. (She ended up winning).

But we could not disagree more about our theories of change. "If we want to improve academic outcomes," she would say, "we have to help the families. We have to increase parental involvement. And we have to fix poverty." It was the standard "root causes" argument. Many proponents of this view support the establishment of "community schools," a model in which various community partners build a presence at school buildings and deliver social services to students.

And it's not a crazy idea. We know that most of the variation in student achievement is not explained by school or teacher quality (Chingos, Whitehurst and Gallaher, 2015). Things happening outside of the classroom – and outside of the school day – matter much more. So it would stand to reason that our efforts to improve student outcomes should focus on out-of-school factors as well. It is an intellectually compelling argument, but ultimately a bad one.

Start with the practicalities. Teaching young children to read seems to me a much more tractable goal than eliminating poverty or rooting out racism. If political dysfunction stands in the way of good academic outcomes in a school, it's hard to imagine that the same school is well positioned to effectively tackle much more complex social challenges.

There are other reasons to be skeptical. In the aftermath of the violent urban riots in the 1960s, President Lyndon Johnson appointed a National Advisory Commission on Civil Disorders to figure out what went wrong and to make recommendations about how to prevent it from happening again. The group, which became known as the Kerner Commission after its chairman, took a hard look at education. It found deep inequities in funding and racial segregation. Poor education created cycles of poverty and exacerbated racial disparities. America, the commission's final report warned, is "moving toward two societies, one Black, one white – separate and unequal." To fix the problems, it advocated school funding reform, school desegregation, early childhood education, and investment in social services. (The report also called for greater school choice and vouchers, although many overlook that recommendation.) It was, in other words, an embrace of the "root cause" approach.

These recommendations were given life in President Johnson's "War on Poverty," which created most of the programs that make up today's welfare state. Six decades have passed since the commission's report was issued. Yet here we are, with many folks still arguing that the way to improve public education is to eliminate poverty and fight racism. It's a good bet people will be making the same arguments in sixty years, too. The school children trapped in underperforming schools today just can't wait that long.

As with the "community institutions" argument, it is useful to reason by analogy and look at other types of government services. The Kerner Commission wasn't just interested in education – it had a lot to say about crime as well. And, just like education, it argued that the way to reduce crime was to address the "root causes." That argument has been clearly debunked.

During the 1990s and early 2000s, we saw a dramatic decrease in violent crime in America's largest cities, and disadvantaged populations benefited the most. Sociologist Patrick Sharkey has estimated that the crime decline increased life expectancy of African-American men by nearly an entire year on average – a "public health breakthrough" on par in magnitude with the hypothetical effect of wiping out obesity (Sharkey and Friedson, 2019). Although criminologists continue to debate what most contributed to this success, it is clear that we didn't fix all of the "root causes." Better policing – more police officers patrolling mostly in crime hot spots and targeting high-risk, repeat offenders – were a big part of the story (Abt, 2019; Kennedy, 2011).

In his 2019 book on urban gun violence, former Obama administration Department of Justice official Thomas Abt argued: "[A]ddressing root causes cannot and will not stop the bleeding. Ending poverty, inequality, and even racism are all important long-term goals, but they are not concrete plans for anti-violence action. Meaningful progress on fundamental socioeconomic conditions will take generations to achieve. People living with the reality of urban violence need relief right now" (Abt, 2019). Replace "urban violence" with "failing schools," and the same argument applies to education.

And too often, the "root causes" argument becomes an excuse to tolerate failing schools and a way to pass the buck. A great example is provided in the opening page of journalist Richard Whitmire's book *The Bee Eater* about reformer Michelle Rhee's efforts to fix the Washington, DC, school district. At one of the city's most chronically underperforming elementary schools, the author found a sign: "There is nothing a teacher can do to overcome what a parent and a student will not do."

"It was posted low on the wall, precisely at eye level for the elementary school children moving through the hallways. For those children, the sign was a daily reminder," Whitmire wrote. "For those children, the sign was a daily admonition that the teachers [at the school] were not responsible for students' failings. We're not the reason the test scores at this school are awful. We're not why D.C. schools rank at the bottom of all the nation's schools. Look at yourself, look to your parent. *You* are to blame" (Whitmire, 2011, p. v).

In this book, I advocate for a version of the Serenity Prayer as applied to education – "God, grant me the serenity to accept the things I cannot change, the courage to change the things I can, and the wisdom to know the difference." As I frequently told my school board member friend, public schools have students for seven hours a day, 180 days a year. Yes, we need to be realistic about what we can accomplish during this period. But we must also be laser-focused on maximizing this limited time and ensuring that every child has access to the very best teachers. Public schools cannot fix poverty, and they cannot dismantle racism. Maybe, just maybe, they could move the needle on student learning. But local politics often prevents them from doing so.

A NOTE ON ORGANIZATION AND STYLE

Although this book is a scholarly project, it is written with a much broader audience in mind. The issues I discuss are simply too important to our society to be debated only within the cloistered ivory towers of academia. As a result, it intentionally ignores many of the norms usually expected of academic writing. I want to briefly highlight and discuss them here.

First, as this chapter makes clear, the book makes liberal use of first-person references. This is an intentional choice, in part because the evolution of my thinking around these issues was deeply informed by my own experiences (some of which I discuss at the beginning of Chapter 8). I first started attending school board meetings in 2002, when I became the editor of my high school newspaper. After college, I worked as an education reporter covering the San Diego Unified School district for the pioneering online nonprofit Voice of San Diego, which specialized in investigative reporting. And over the past six years, I have watched or attended every school board meeting here in Columbus – sometimes speaking at public comment with very large signs. For me, following school board meetings has become a hobby in the same way that many other people enjoy watching professional sports, and some of the observations and anecdotes in this book come from those experiences.

Second, I have sought to make this book readable and accessible to a broad range of readers, including those not steeped in the academic literature on education politics and policy. It intentionally avoids – to the maximum extent possible – indecipherable and arcane jargon often favored by scholars in this field. Of course, specialized vocabulary has its uses when communicating with other experts and specialists. But for everyone else, it can come across as "sociological gobbledygook," to quote Chief Justice John Roberts from a recent partisan gerrymandering case.

Third, this book does not begin with a detailed "literature review," summarizing the state of the scholarly knowledge and articulating how my findings contribute to various academic debates in the field. Instead, I address the relevant literatures in each respective chapter – in a subtle and hopefully unobtrusive way that does not detract from the reading experience of non-academics. And I discuss the new insights and contributions from my analysis in the short concluding section of each chapter.

Fourth, every chapter in this volume is organized around original quantitative analyses that use cutting-edge statistical methods. Most are designed to estimate causal effects. In presenting the results of these analyses, however, I have tried to keep the discussion intentionally non-technical and accessible. (Chapter 5 does include some equations, but these can be safely skipped by readers who want to avoid them without any major loss of comprehension.) Every chapter opens with at least one memorable case study or example that illustrates the findings or mechanisms implied by the large-N regression analyses that follow.

Finally, although the book is intended to be read in chronological order, each chapter can stand on its own. They can be read (or assigned in classes) separately without depriving the reader of essential background knowledge covered earlier. The first half of this book, Chapters 2 through 4, focus on examining adult interests in public education, understanding which adults participate in the political processes and how they form their preferences toward education policy. The second half, Chapters 5 through 8, examine the often-negative consequences of these political processes on student learning. Chapter 9 ends with considerations about how to fix these problems.

THE CANCELLATION OF JAMES RAGLAND

I opened this book with the story of an attempted cancellation over a controversial social media post, and I will end this chapter with one, too. This second cancellation didn't involve the Pride flag or angry Armenians but it was successful – and resulted in an incumbent school board member losing his reelection bid. The story provides a fitting ending to this introduction and a great segue into the remainder of this book because it illustrates how local democracy empowers adult interests, and the extent to which adult political agendas – often organized around partisanship, identity politics, and employment concerns – can be weaponized to block efforts to improve education for public school students. It is a story about how James Ragland lost his elective office, and why I may have contributed to his downfall.

Ragland, who is Black, had been a rising star in the Franklin County Democratic Party. He began his career as a city council aide, before transitioning into education. He worked in a charter school and later helped start the Columbus campus of Cristo Rey, a network of Catholic private schools serving disadvantaged, minority students. His efforts were profiled in a 2014 article in the *Atlantic*. "The mission of the schools, as James Ragland described it, is to break the cycle of poverty through education," the article explained (Fallows, 2014).

Over the years, Ragland applied to fill vacancies on city council, always making it to the final round but never getting the nod. In 2015, Ragland ran for mayor. He came last, a disappointing fourth with less than 12 percent of the vote. But many political observers were impressed. When a vacancy opened up on the Columbus school board in 2018, he applied and was appointed to finish an unexpired term. That is when I entered the story.

Around the same time, I had stumbled upon publicly available state administrative data on teacher attendance. Looking at Columbus, I calculated the teacher attendance rates by school and made a disturbing discovery – in more than thirty Columbus schools, teachers' attendance was worse than students'! Many people complained about chronic student absenteeism, but no one was talking about chronic teacher absenteeism. I took the data to the leaders of the Columbus Education Association (CEA), the local teachers' union, and they offered a variety of plausible explanations. Toxic building principals, female teachers who were primary caregivers for young children, and several others. I took these hypotheses seriously and found other data to test them empirically, but none of the stories ultimately held up. I decided to share the numbers with Columbus school board (and the *Columbus Dispatch*).

When I described these patterns during public comment at a school board meeting, the board members stared blankly and said nothing. Except for Ragland. His face had a shocked expression and he addressed the superintendent: "Can we internally verify the data regarding teacher absenteeism? That is *astounding* to me!" A few weeks later, he appeared on a Black-themed *Dispatch* podcast and spent most of the time discussing the outrageous rates of teacher absenteeism. That was strike number one, as far as the CEA was concerned.

Although Ragland supported public schools, had graduated from Columbus public schools and sent both of his kids there, he also believed in options for parents who were being failed by their district. It was the reason he had gotten involved in Cristo Rey. In fall 2019, he accepted a position with School Choice Ohio, a statewide advocacy organization, in a role helping charter schools obtain access to underused public school buildings. That was strike two.

In early 2020, the school district released a 450-page external curriculum audit, completed by Phi Delta Kappa International, a highly respected professional association of educators. The audit was devastating, pointing out deficiencies in almost every dimension of the district's academic operations. Its most damning conclusions focused on the quality of Columbus teachers. Auditors had asked school principals for their honest opinions through an anonymous survey, and more than a third reported that at least 10 percent of the teachers in their schools were ineffective. In some buildings, principals rated nearly 20 percent of their teachers as below the bar. "That's the highest I've ever seen, I was shocked to see that!," the lead evaluator told the school board in her presentation of the findings (Kogan, 2020). Ragland was outraged and wouldn't stop talking about the audit – in particular, its criticisms of various provisions in the teachers' union contract that the auditors said tied the hands of principals and prevented them from improving building instruction. That was strike three.

Ragland had painted a target on his back, and on International Women's Day – March 8, 2021 – he handed the CEA a loaded weapon. "Happy Women's Day! Govern yourselves accordingly," he posted on his private Facebook page. The post also included images of two music albums, "Nice Girls Don't Stay For Breakfast" by Julie London and "Woman" by Raheem DeVaughn. The teachers' union pounced.

"It's bad enough that Mr. Ragland has a paid position advocating with [President Donald Trump's Education Secretary] Betsy DeVos for funneling our students' resources to charter and voucher schools," the union president said in its press release. "Now, Mr. Ragland has added insult to injury with a fundamental disrespect for the core values of Columbus City Schools. Our 50,000 students deserve board members who lead by example. Three-quarters of CEA members are women. Our Superintendent is a woman. By disrespecting and dehumanizing these leaders on a day set aside for honoring them, Mr. Ragland has demonstrated he is unfit to serve. He must resign immediately."

The press release described the post as containing "inappropriate and misogynistic" content and said it contained "a photo (now removed) with the text 'Nice Girls Don't Stay For Breakfast,'" without explaining that this photo was the cover of a hit jazz album.

I sent a text message with the link to the news story about the controversy to former Columbus school board member Stephanie Groce. "Anything for the children," she responded sarcastically.

Almost a decade earlier, Groce had also seen the teachers' union turn on her. After her initial election, Groce had become an outspoken critic of the school system and its performance. At the time, the district had a practice of displaying student art work at its downtown headquarters and in the board meeting room. Instead of the art work, Groce suggested at one point, the district should put up data on student achievement, so the board could be reminded of what was at stake. (This is where the idea for my June 2023 tweet had come from!)

When she ran for reelection in 2007, Groce initially won the endorsement from the Franklin County Democratic Party. But just weeks before the election, the party announced that it was withdrawing its endorsement at the request of the CEA. Groce would go on to win the election anyway, with the help of a group of grassroots parent volunteers. Eventually she would step down, and join the board of School Choice Ohio, the same organization that would later hire Ragland.

But many things changed over the interceding fifteen years. Education policy debates became increasingly nationalized, and the bipartisan consensus in support of reform evaporated. Although Franklin County was already Democratic in 2009, the county had become a blue wall after the election of President Donald Trump.

In 2007, the prominent Wolfe family owned the *Columbus Dispatch*, and they used its editorial page to name and shame local leaders. "Stephanie Groce was not the loser on Tuesday when the Franklin County Democratic Party kowtowed to the local teachers' union and withdrew its endorsement of her for the Columbus Board of Education," the newspaper inveighed. "The biggest loser was the county party and its top officeholders, who had a chance to demonstrate leadership by standing on principle for an independent-minded and highly qualified candidate. Instead those leaders caved cravenly. The other loser was the Columbus Education Association, which nakedly illustrated that the union's top priority is not the welfare of students but the protection of its members against any demand for accountability and fiscal responsibility within the Columbus City Schools" (*Columbus Dispatch*, 2007).

A decade later, the *Dispatch* had become a shell of its former self. The Wolfe family had sold it to a hedge fund and layoffs followed. In 2021, there were no editorials about CEA's efforts to oust an incumbent school board member. In fact, there was no coverage of that year's school board election at all.

In August, the county Democratic Party gave in to CEA pressure and voted not to endorse Ragland. That meant his name would not appear on the party "sample ballot" – listing all of the endorsed Democrats running for office, a death knell to his campaign. On Election Day, Ragland lost big, coming in fourth place, with less than 8 percent of the vote.

This book is not about what happened to James Ragland, but it is about what his defeat symbolizes. It is about the roles of teachers' unions, political parties, identity commitments, and the media all play in influencing what schools do. It is about how local democracy actually works in practice – not in some idealized Nirvana – and how politics affects our education system and its ability to effectively serve our kids.

2

Skin in the Game

> Student outcomes don't change until adult behaviors change.
> —School board governance coach AJ Crabill

The school board is, in many ways, the quintessential symbol of American democracy. With about 50,000 elected school board members making high-stakes policy decisions – covering everything from curriculum requirements and teacher compensation to disciplinary policy and school mascots – for the country's 14,000 or so school districts, it is the most numerous elective office in our country. Add up all members of Congress, the president, every cabinet secretary, and the Supreme Court justices and you will still get to a count that falls well below the number of elected school board officials in just one moderately sized state.

Many of the academic researchers who write about education governance begin with the premise that school boards are the natural default. They worry when local elections through which these boards are chosen are being undermined – by billionaire reformers and forces of nationalization (e.g., Henig, Jacobsen and Reckhow, 2019; Saunders-Hastings, 2022), by right-wing state legislatures (e.g., Morel, 2018), and by enrollment losses that might come by way of competition from charter and voucher-funded private schools (e.g., Buras, 2015; Lay, 2022). Some view proposed governance reforms, such as mayoral control or state takeovers, as fundamentally undemocratic power grabs that deprive local communities of say in how their schools are run. They begin, in other words, with a romantic, idealized view of how local democracy actually works.

One goal of this book is to provide for a more realistic description of local democracy. We have to understand how education governance actually works in practice, not how we wish it did. Although we might hope that school districts would serve as small Tocquevillian laboratories of democracy, bringing together diverse community stakeholders to engage in serious deliberation about important issues of the day, the data suggest that it is not what happens in most communities. At best, school board elections are extremely low-turnout affairs, in which a small and highly unrepresentative group of adults impose their parochial, self-interested, and often uninformed views on the rest of the community. Few of these adult voters actually have children enrolled in the local schools, and they seem to care little about student academic outcomes.

Which adults participate in local school board elections and how much these adults care about learning matters because almost none of the students public schools educate can vote themselves. The extent to which elected officials are motivated to take their interests into account thus depends on whether the adults who vote in (and perhaps vote out) school board members care about student learning. Their revealed preference, as reflected in aggregate election outcomes that I review in this chapter, suggests that they don't care very much at all.

One reason is that most voters who participate in these elections lack a direct personal stake in how public schools perform and, because of their age and other demographic characteristics, often have interests that are in conflict with students'. For these reasons, we should not expect local elections to be a particularly effective mechanism for holding public officials accountable for educational quality even under the most favorable conditions.

Unfortunately, the reality is often even worse. In many cases, school district governance devolves into an absolute clown show, where performative politics takes precedence over serious policy meant to serve the academic interests of students.

For one such case of buffoonery, just take a look at San Francisco. The city's school district has long had a reputation for political dysfunction, but things reached a new level of nuttiness during the COVID-19 pandemic. After schools nationwide closed in spring 2020, the San Francisco school board decided that reopening them would not be a major priority. Instead, the most urgent task in the aftermath of the murder of George Floyd was to review the names of district school buildings to purge, in the words of the board president, "white supremacy, racism, colonization, ties to slavery, the killing of indigenous people, or any symbols that embodied that" (Chotiner, 2021).

When a committee charged with reviewing school names met via Zoom that summer, out went George Washington (slave owner), Abraham Lincoln (horrible to Native Americans), and the city's first female mayor, Diane Feinstein (she took too long in removing a confederate flag that once flew on a city property). Then, the committee members got to Sanchez Elementary:

"Sanchez, this is another colonizer who – " began one school names committee member.

"Did you say colonizer? Meets our criteria!" another committee member interrupted, with apparent glee.

"Colonizer, California missions, blah blah blah, it's in the notes," the first speaker continued, referring to the group's shared Google document annotated with links to Wikipedia.

The notes did indeed show that José Bernardo Sánchez was a colonizer. A Spanish missionary, he had joined a military expedition targeting California's indigenous Native American tribes.

The problem was that Sanchez Elementary was not actually named after José Bernardo. Instead, it was apparently named after nearby Sanchez Street, which itself seemed to honor a native Californian who had died in 1846, before California had even become a state, and was buried in the area.

Sanchez Elementary was not the only embarrassing historical error. The committee also decided to rename Paul Revere Elementary because of its namesake's role in the 1779 Penobscot Expedition, which the committee proclaimed was intended to colonize the indigenous Penobscot peoples. (It wasn't. The naval expedition's goal was to seize back control of the Maine coast from the British.)

"Let's bring the same urgency and focus on getting our kids back in the classroom, and then we can have that longer conversation about the future of school names," the city's frustrated mayor, London Breed, pleaded in a statement her office released. For Breed, the issue was personal. The African-American mayor had grown up in San Francisco's troubled public housing projects and believed a high-quality education was essential to providing other disadvantaged youngsters a chance to succeed just like she had.

Although California teachers received priority access to the COVID-19 vaccine, the San Francisco teachers' union argued it was still unsafe for its members to return to work in spring 2021. As precondition for safe reopening, the union demanded that the district install toilet seat lids in every bathroom to prevent virus particles in feces from being aerosolized when the commodes were flushed. The board apparently agreed, delaying the reopening indefinitely. Eventually, the city government sued the school district, arguing that it had violated state law by failing to reopen the schools – all to no avail. Even as new assessment data showed that San Francisco's highest-risk students were falling dangerously behind, the schools stayed shuttered (Tucker, 2021a).

That was just the beginning. Soon, someone discovered a Twitter thread made by the school board's African-American vice president, Alison Collins, shortly after the 2016 election asking followers to provide examples of "anti-black racism in the Asian community" (Tucker and Egelko, 2021). Asian Americans, she went on, "use white supremacist thinking to assimilate and 'get ahead'." Later in the thread, she compared Asians to privileged slaves who got plum positions by cozying up to their masters. "Do they think they won't be deported? profiled? beaten? Being a house n****r is still being a n****r. You're still considered 'the help'."

The revelation couldn't have come at a more politically awkward moment: Week's earlier, the school board had overhauled the admission process at the city's premier high school, Lowell. Lowell was the district's crown jewel – it had graduated Nobel laureates and a sitting Supreme Court justice. Historically, the school used a selective-admission process that relied on test scores and middle school grade point averages. However, the system had come under attack because of the racial disparities it generated – leading to underrepresentation of Black and Latino students. The problem was that any change to increase enrollment for these groups would mechanically reduce the number of Asian students, who had been winning more than half of the spots at Lowell under the selective-admission system (despite representing less than 30 percent of the district's overall student population). Members of the Asian community were understandably enraged by the changes to admission criteria and viewed them as being motivated by anti-Asian animus.

When embarrassed colleagues voted to censure Collins and remove her from board committees, the vice president sued the district for violating her constitutional rights and demanded $87 million in compensation. It was money the school system didn't have, since it was facing a $125 million budget deficit the board had consistently put off addressing.

The district and the teachers' union did eventually agree to bring back high school students in spring 2021 for in-person learning. But only graduating seniors, and only for one day – apparently enough to qualify for $12 million in state funding Gov. Gavin Newsom had put aside to incentivize districts reluctant to reopen their schools to do so (Tucker, 2021c).

At his wit's end over the board's antics and apparent interest in every hot-button political issue except educating the district's students, district Superintendent Vince Matthews announced his retirement that spring. A month later, he reversed course and agreed to stay on. But only with a new contract in which the school board committed not to micromanage the district, promise to review the prepared background documents ahead of each board meeting, and not create any new programs until the city's schools were back fully in person. "It shouldn't be needed," a former school board member told the *San Francisco Chronicle*. "The fact that he had to put in his contract that the board had to follow the rules they wrote themselves and adopt every year is kind of crazy" (Tucker, 2021b).

This rest of this chapter will explain how local democracy created San Francisco – and why there is likely a school district similar to it near you.

MEASURING THE QUALITY OF DEMOCRACY

It is useful at this point to pause and more explicitly define the criteria by which we might evaluate local school board elections and the quality of democratic representation they produce. Contrast my pessimistic account in this book with a sunny depiction of education governance offered by political scientists Michael Berkman and Eric Plutzer in *Ten Thousand Democracies* (2005). Our disagreement ultimately comes down to measurement.

Berkman and Plutzer argue that school districts should be judged based on their ability to translate local public opinion into policy – a concept political scientists often call "responsiveness." In their book, they use sophisticated statistical methods to estimate the relative ideology of voters in each school district, then correlate these estimates with the level of school spending in each community, finding a high degree of responsiveness. In liberal districts, schools spend more per student than in more conservative ones – although perhaps not as much as their liberal voters would prefer in the absence of other budgetary constraints. "The empirical story shows that school districts are indeed democratic," Berkman and Plutzer conclude. "To a degree that surprised both authors of this book, there is a high correspondence between what citizens want and what they get" (p. 156).

Other empirical researchers examining local democracy have also relied on responsiveness as their outcome of interest and have tended to find similar patterns (e.g., Tausanovitch and Warshaw, 2014). For example, a recent study looked at the availability of books focusing on LGBT and racial topics, subject to considerable controversy over the past few years. Taking advantage of data from a common catalogue vendor used by thousands of school libraries across the country, the study found that books centering LGBT and minority characters and themes were far more likely to be available in school libraries in Democratic-leaning communities (Mumma, 2024). High responsiveness, in other words.

There are several serious – and arguably fatal – problems with this approach when applied to the study of representation, however. The first is that, in most applications, public opinion and policy outcomes are measured using different scales. In the previous example, for example, public opinion is defined by partisanship while policy is measured through book availability. As economist John Matsusaka proved formally many years ago (Matsusaka, 2001),[1] this makes responsiveness correlations difficult to interpret. Our intuition might be that better democratic representation – more fidelity in the mapping between what the people want and what the government does – should produce more responsiveness, but this not always the case. There could also be *too much* responsiveness, producing a form of "leapfrog representation" in which policy swings too much between ideological or partisan extremes even as public opinion remains fairly moderate. (As I show in Chapter 4, this is can be a real problem in education policy.)

To move beyond the hypothetical, consider a concrete example where just measuring responsiveness might lead us astray. Traditionally, public school districts have offered different course options in mathematics. Some students might choose to take algebra in eighth grade, putting them in the position to take calculus their senior year, while others could delay algebra until freshman year (or even later). Having a menu of options unfortunately often produced "tracking" – with higher-achieving students clustering together in advanced math classes and lower-achieving students taking other courses. Given the strong associations between achievement and student demographics, this tended to result in racial and

---

[1] The same point was made decades earlier by Erikson, Wright and McIver (1993) but largely overlooked.

socioeconomic segregation, even between classes within the same school, which struck many people as objectionable.

About fifteen years ago, some places – including the entire state of California – tried to address these issues by adopting an "algebra-for-all" policy that simply had *all* students take algebra in eighth grade. Although obviously well-intentioned, this proved to be a disaster. Unprepared students – again, disproportionately students of color – ended up failing algebra at higher rates, and test scores in mathematics declined (Domina et al., 2015). In response to the political backlash, some communities reversed course. Others went even farther and, in the name of equity, adopted an "algebra-for-none" approach in which *no student* would be able to take algebra before high school.

Although I know of no large-N research looking at local mathematics placement policies, given the connection to modern racial equity debates, it is a good bet that districts eliminating middle school algebra in the interest of de-tracking would be located in more political liberal communities. San Francisco, a progressive beacon where President Joe Biden won more than 85 percent of the vote in the 2020 election, was one of the first districts to eliminate eighth-grade algebra, embracing an idea championed by controversial Stanford education professor Jo Boaler (Loveless, 2022). Looking at the correlation between local partisanship and middle school math offerings – the definition of responsiveness – we might conclude that communities are getting exactly what they want.

But this would be the wrong inference. When San Francisco recently put its math policy to an advisory public referendum, 85 percent of voters opposed it and demanded a return of eighth-grade algebra (Napolitano, 2024). The lesson? Partisanship and ideology are not always great metrics of public opinion on individual education policies. And using such proxies in studies of responsiveness tells us little about the quality of representation local voters actually receive.

This point was made even more forcefully in a famous paper by political scientists Jeff Lax and Justin Phillips (2012) focusing on state government. Using very fancy statistical tools, Lax and Phillips constructed measures of public opinion in each state on dozens of different policy issues and collected data on the actual policies states had in place. First, the authors estimated "responsiveness" – the simple correlation between public opinion and policy. It was very high, consistent with Berkman and Plutzer (2005) and other earlier studies. Then, they created a new measure they called "congruence" – did policy in each state actually match what a majority of voters in that state wanted? Using this alternative metric, things looked very different. Overall, policy was congruent with public opinion only about half of the time. This is essentially the same as we would see *if we got rid of elections and just made policy by coin flip* – heads and abortion is protected, tails, and its outlawed.[2] The upshot was that high responsiveness did not mean effective representation.

There is also a second problem with the Berkman and Plutzer approach. Even if one believed that responsiveness was a good measure of representation, it *still* wouldn't tell us much about the quality of local democracy, as I showed in a chapter of my doctoral dissertation (Kogan, 2017). My research took advantage of a natural experiment built into the Supplemental Nutrition Assistance Program (SNAP), known colloquially as "food stamps," which provides vouchers that low-income families can use to purchase food at grocery stores. It is a national program with largely uniform eligibility criteria, but one administered by the states. In some states, it is run by a single agency that operates local offices in different locations where people can meet with case workers and get enrolled. In others, the state outsources the operations to county governments, which are run by locally elected commissioners.

In my dissertation, I first used a statistical approach similar to Berkman and Plutzer to create an estimate of voter support for government welfare programs such as SNAP in each county. Then, I used official caseload data to calculate what percent of people eligible for SNAP were actually able to get enrolled. Correlating the two, I was able to estimate "responsiveness" – and I found lots of it. In politically conservative areas, many low-income people were not getting the welfare benefits they were entitled to, and I found some evidence this was at least partly due to decisions made by case workers.

Most interestingly, I found no difference in policy responsiveness to local opinion between counties where the program was locally run by elected officials and places where it was administered by a single, statewide agency. Even in the latter case, we saw a lot of responsiveness – and variation in policy implementation across counties within a single in what was nominally a uniform program – despite not having any elections!

In retrospect, this was not such a surprising finding. The people who staff welfare offices are most likely to come from the same communities

---

[2] A second study, using different data and methods, found essentially the same thing (Matsusaka, 2010).

where they work, and as a result probably share the general political outlook of their neighbors. Even if they were unconstrained by elections, not at all accountable to voters, and simply imposed their personal opinions on welfare recipients, we would still see a great deal of responsiveness between the policies in place across communities and those communities' partisan and ideological leanings. Indeed, if we eliminated elections and simply picked people at random to make policy for their local communities – whether welfare policy or education policy – we would see a lot of responsiveness because, on average, those picked at random would share the preferences of people living each community. Analyses such as in the Berkman and Plutzer (2005) book can quantify the amount of responsiveness that exists, but they can't tell us how much the current system of local elected school boards contributes or whether we might see even a greater amount under an alternative governance system.

There is also a third and final reason not to treat responsiveness as our metric of interest: While it might tell us something about how elected officials respond to the preferences of adults who vote, it is not actually related to quality of the education that students in each community receive. If that is ultimately what we care about – and I argue in Chapter 9 that is what we *should* care about – it is time to look elsewhere. We need to find alternative barometers of democratic health that are related to the core function that public schools exist to carry out, which is educating students.

ASSESSING PROCESSES AND OUTCOMES

In the remainder of this chapter, my analysis will examine a variety of alternative metrics. The first set will focus on democratic *processes*. In particular, I will look at participation in local school board elections. What percent of voters actually turn out and cast ballots in local school board elections? And what do these voters look like – especially compared to the students that local schools actually serve? Political theorists have long argued that effective democracy requires widespread and inclusive electoral participation, so that government officials have strong incentive to be mindful of all segments of the political community, including those who may lack power in other domains (e.g., Dahl, 1971; Lijphart, 1999).

In the context of education, the composition of the electorate is particularly important, even more so than in other types of elections political scientists usually study. Only adults vote, because kids can't. The extent to which elected officials are incentivized to think about the interests of students thus depends on how much adult voters actually have their interests at heart. In thinking about voter composition, I will rely on the idea of "skin in the game" – whether (and how much) the personal interests and concerns of a given voter are aligned with the what is good for students educated in local schools. Who turns out to vote in local elections is important because it affects how much skin in the game the electorate as whole has – how much voters are invested in serving students well and rewarding elected officials for doing so. I will demonstrate more concretely how this plays out in the real world with two memorable – and disturbing – case studies at the end of this chapter.

Another prerequisite for fair democratic processes is contestation. If incumbents face no opposition when they stand for reelection, or if elections are completely uncompetitive (e.g., due to gerrymandering), public officials need not worry much about being accountable to their constituents. In the scholarly literature on comparative politics – focused on countries other than the United States – the key dividing line between democracies and autocracies is whether sitting incumbents can actually be replaced if they do a poor job, or whether they face little risk of losing future elections and can effectively retain their offices for life (Huntington, 1991; Przeworski et al., 2000).

Good processes are necessary, but not sufficient, of course. Where the rubber really hits the road is election *outcomes*. Specifically, I will quantify how much – or, as we'll see, how little – student academic outcomes seem to affect the decisions voters make on Election Day. As it turns out, whether school board incumbents lose or win elections is only very weakly related to the performance of local schools during their terms. When they choose to run, incumbents almost always win – and often by margins large enough to make dictators blush – regardless of whether learning has taken off in their district or whether academic outcomes fell far behind. There are several important exceptions to this general pattern, however. These exceptions help illustrate both the importance of voters having "skin in the game" and the types of reforms that may help strengthen the governance of public schools (a topic I will turn to in Chapter 9).

ILLUSTRATIVE EXAMPLE: SAN FRANCISCO

"Democratic processes," "interest alignment," and "contestation" are abstract concepts that mean different things to different people, so it's useful to apply them in a real-world case – the San Francisco example that opened this chapter. Why did local elections produce such a dysfunctional body? And, perhaps even more interestingly, what explains the electoral earthquake that shook the city's school district in February 2022?

One year earlier, local activists began organizing a recall petition to remove several sitting incumbents before the end of their terms. They collected enough signatures to get the recall on the ballot, and when San Francisco voters got their say during a special election in February 2022, it passed overwhelmingly. Three names appeared on the ballot – the vice president behind the offensive tweet storm accusing Asian's of being implicated in white supremacy and two other incumbents.[3] Mayor Breed campaigned in favor of the recall, and in each case, more than 70 percent of the voters marked the ballot to remove the incumbents from office. It was the first successful recall in the San Francisco since 1914.

Although everyone agreed about the numerical outcome of the vote, people differed in what they saw as the democratic implications. They read different motives into the decisions voters made – and even disagreed about who the voters were!

The write-up by the *New York Times* the day after the election, for example, asserted that the "recall was a victory for parents who were angered that the district spent time deciding whether to rename a third of its schools last year instead of focusing on reopening them" (Fuller, Netter and Stegemoller, 2002). Other observers also argued that parents played a pivotal role. One of the organizers of the recall campaign announced: "Parents have spoken, parents have been heard" (Tucker and Vainshtein, 2022). "The recall effort, while catalyzed by Covid, reflects deep discontent of the parent community with the state of the public schools," another claimed (Jacobs, 2022). A Hong Kong-born parent, who became active in the recall after seeing students struggling while working as an "address fraud investigator" for the district (see Chapter 8 for more on such investigations) and led the campaign's outreach to the Asian community, emphasized that people like himself were behind the ouster. "[P]arents were frustrated with elected officials' failure to lead through a crisis," he wrote an editorial in *USA Today*. "Elected officials are elected to serve their constituents instead of advancing their

---

[3] The other four were ineligible for recall because they had just begun the their term when the petition was launched.

own political agenda. They must sincerely listen to parents and prioritize children's education over adult politics" (Lam, 2022).

"It also appeared to be a demonstration of Asian American electoral power," the *New York Times* continued, "a galvanizing moment for Chinese American voters in particular who turned out in unusually large numbers for the election" (Fuller, Netter and Stegemoller, 2002).[4]

Collins, the recalled vice president had a very different take. "We now know what it costs to buy an election in San Francisco," she said, pointing to the $2 million in pro-recall campaign cash raised from various Silicon Valley personalities, including some prominent billionaires that previously supported right-wing causes. "This is a backlash against progress, similar to what we are seeing nationally" (Tucker and Vainshtein, 2022).

Her view was echoed by the president of the Board of Supervisors – as a combined city-county, San Francisco doesn't have a city council. He pointed out that all three recalled school board members were racial and ethnic minorities and their removal clear evidence of racism. "Trump's election and bold prejudice brought a lot of that out, even in our Democratic and liberal city," he told local reporters. "There are a lot of people who do not want people of color making decisions in leadership, even though the voters said that is what they want."

These interpretations have profoundly different normative implications. Was the recall an example of democracy in action, a parent power revolution in which the majority of families got what they wanted? Or was it a power grab by a small and unrepresentative minority motivated by white supremacy and bankrolled by plutocrats? Of course, many people had their own intuitions about which of these two perspectives was most plausible. One recall organizer known for his "Gaybraham" Lincoln persona – a rainbow drag version of the former president – laughed at the suggestion that support for the recall reflected prejudice and conservative ideology. "I knew they were going to say, 'Oh isn't it just a bunch of Republicans?' and I am like, 'Do I look like a Republican?'"

However, intuition is no substitute for evidence – the kind of evidence social scientists usually expect to understand political phenomena. Fortunately, we can extract falsifiable hypotheses from these accounts and test them against publicly available data to determine which view has the

---

[4] The article was published a day after the election and inferred the racial composition of voters based on precinct-level turnout at that time. However, more than 90 percent of the voters had cast their ballot by mail, and these ballots could be returned up seven days after the election as long as they were postmarked by Election Day. Once all ballots were counted, turnout proved to be 50 percent higher than the initial results indicated.

TABLE 2.1 *Comparing participation in three San Francisco elections*

	Gubernatorial recall (2021, %)	School board recall (2022, %)	District attorney recall (2022, %)
Election information			
"Yes" vote on recall	14	72	55
Turnout	68	36	46
Voter demographics			
Have children	21	22	21
Over age of 50	50	59	55
Voter partisanship			
Democrat	68	66	67
Republican	7	7	8
No party preference	22	23	21
Third party	4	3	4
Voter race/ethnicity			
Asian	36	38	36
Black	4	3	4
Latino	11	9	10
White	43	43	44

Note: Turnout statistics and election outcomes are from official election results reported by San Francisco Department of Elections. Voter age and partisanship are based on fields recorded in the county voter file. Presence of children in household is determined using commercial consumer data purchased from Info USA. Voter race is estimated using method described in Imai and Khanna (2016).

most support. Each points to a different set of observable implications – although we cannot directly measure *why* people voted the way they did (at least, not from one election alone), we do observe *who* voted, and how the composition of the electorate in the San Francisco recall compared to other recent elections there. As it happens, San Francisco held two other similar elections within a year of the school board vote – a statewide gubernatorial recall in August 2021 and a recall of district attorney Chesa Boudin during the primary election in June 2022 – providing a natural point of comparison.

Table 2.1 combines information on all three elections from a number of sources. First, it reports the turnout rates and election outcomes from official county reports. Second, I purchased the official voter file from San Francisco – although how someone votes is secret, whether someone cast a ballot is a public record and available in such voter files. In addition to recording whether each registered voter cast a ballot in prior elections, the voter file contains information, including each voter's date of birth and partisan registration information. To determine which voters have children, I also purchased a commercial consumer list containing household composition information from a vendor called Info USA, which combines a lot of proprietary data sources to build consumer profiles of every American that it sells to other companies. I appended this information to the voter file using each person's name and address, two fields available in both sources. Finally, I also estimated each voter's race and ethnicity – using a sophisticated Bayesian method that combines data about the distribution of last names across racial and ethnic groups and census information about the composition of each census block group (see Imai and Khanna, 2016). Although this method is not exact, it is widely used for many applications, including by the federal government to track racial discrimination in home loans.

Several important patterns stand out in the data. First, turnout in the school board recall election was very low – just 36 percent of eligible voters. However, this did not appear to produce any meaningful partisan skew. Democrats still made up two-thirds of the voters who recalled the school board members, nearly identical to the earlier election when over 85 percent voted against recalling Gov. Newsom. The claim that right wingers and closeted racists came out to remove minorities from office is difficult to square with this partisan breakdown.

On the other hand, the argument that parents drove the recall is also not correct. Only 22 percent of voters who cast a ballot in the election had children in their households – and that includes many who sent their kids to private schools.[5] Indeed, the average age of voters in the election was 54, and nearly 60 percent were older than 50 – not the demographic likely to be personally use or be affected by local education policy.

There is also no evidence that Asian voters were especially mobilized. Although the share of Asians in the electorate increased modestly during the school board recall, to 38 percent, this was only marginally higher than in the gubernatorial recall the fall before or in the district attorney election several months later (36 percent in each). White voters still represented the largest voting bloc, and their share of the electorate was virtually identical across all three elections.

Clearly, none of the narratives put forward in media accounts and by local officials – an Asian awakening, a parent revolution, and a

---

[5] Federal data showed that more than 20,000 students were enrolled in San Francisco private schools in 2022, compared to 49,000 in the public district.

right-wing power grab – seem helpful for understanding why San Francisco voters rebelled in 2022. Instead, it appears that very intense media coverage of the school system's various scandals and foibles temporarily increased the salience of the district's and board's performance, leading overwhelmingly elderly voters with little personal skin in the game to act. Before the pandemic, "school board elections in San Francisco have for decades been obscure sideshows to the more high-profile political contests," the *New York Times* noted (Fuller, 2022). The pandemic temporarily raised the profile of the sleepy elections in which voters previously cared little about what the district was actually doing. The recall represented a very notable exception from this historical pattern – a pattern that, as I will show in Lesson 2, seems to replicate what we see in districts across the country.

NATIONAL DATA

The example just described illustrates the more general methodology I deploy in the remainder of this chapter. Going beyond San Francisco requires a more scalable approach than the one I implemented in Table 2.1, including different data sources.

Specifically, my analysis draws on a massive new dataset collected with my colleagues Stéphane Lavertu and Zachary Peskowitz. Election administration in the United States is highly decentralized, with individual counties or townships administrating local school board elections and tabulating and reporting the results. Some states do provide some centralized repositories of these records, but many do not. Thanks to a generous grant from the Spencer Foundation, Lavertu, Peskowitz, and I spent many years filing public records requests for local election results and then had a large team of undergraduate assistants, overseen by our postdoctoral researcher Carolyn Abott, manually code these disparate records into a consistent electronic database that could be analyzed using modern statistical methods. Our final dataset includes sixteen states, and covers the years 2002–2017.[6] It contains more than 50,000 contest-level observations on local school board elections – the largest collection of school board election records that exists, to my knowledge.

In addition to information about the candidates running in each election and how many votes each of them won, we can combine these records with two other datasets. The first is the Stanford Education Data

---

[6] Not all states have coverage over the full time period.

Archive, a national database that puts disparate state achievement tests into a common scale and format and allows for comparison of student academic performance over time and between different districts. I will describe it in more details in Chapter 5, where I use it for a much more finer-grained analysis, but for now I should note that it includes test scores in math and English/language arts in grades 4 through 8.

The final source is commercial voter file data from a company called Catalist, a campaign firm that traditionally works with progressive candidates and political campaigns but also provides subscription access to academic institutions. Catalist has purchased voter files – just like the one I obtained from San Francisco County – from jurisdictions across the country. In addition to information about each voter – including their names and addresses, and turnout history – Catalist has developed proprietary machine learning models to predict each voter's race and ethnicity (similar to the method I use above), political ideology, and other important attributes. The firm has also purchased commercial datasets from other vendors (including InfoUSA) – providing a high degree of demographic information about each voter, including whether there are kids in the household. The Catalist data thus provides a highly granular information about who votes in each election, and how this varies across school districts.[7]

The San Francisco example I describe above examined only one election in one school district. This makes it difficult to discern why voters have cast their ballots in ways that they did. However, by comparing the results over multiple elections across school districts and within a given school district over time, we can get analytical leverage that can help reveal which considerations are relevant for explaining voter behavior.

For example, if voters care about student learning, conventional theories of retrospective voting (see Berry and Howell, 2007; Burnett and Kogan, 2017) would predict that incumbents would do better – and be reelected at higher rates – when students are learning more. A strong statistical relationship between academic outcomes on one hand and incumbent performance on the other would be clear evidence of voters holding incumbents accountable for educational quality, thus motivating them to do a good job while in office. By contrast, the absence of such a relationship would indicate that voters don't seem to care much about the quality of local schools when they decide who to support.

---

[7] Unfortunately, the Catalist data is not available for all of the states in our sample due to some differences in how school board elections are administered.

LESSON 1: VOTERS ≠ PARENTS

It turns out the San Francisco recall does not stand out in the extent to which adults without children dominate the electorate in school board elections.[8] Table 2.2 provides information about voters who cast ballots in local school board elections in eleven large and mid-sized states, based on the Catalist voter file. Because the data cover multiple election cycle, I combine all of the available observations for each district and report the average figure for each district. Note that the Catalist coding of parents is somewhat different and less precise than the one I constructed using purchased InfoUSA consumer data. To be as conservative as possible, the table include voters identified as "possibly" having children present in the household. Not all of these households actually have children, so the table almost surely overestimates the representation of parents.

Nevertheless, the numbers are striking: Across each of the states, voters with children account for between 20 and 35 percent of the electorate in the average school board election. Put another way, in most school board elections, the vast majority of voters don't have school-aged

TABLE 2.2 *Representation of parents in local school board elections*

State	Average parent share of voters (%)	Districts with majority parent electorates (%)
California	30	6
Illinois	29	1
Iowa	30	3
Louisiana	34	0
Michigan	30	1
Missouri	31	1
Ohio	35	2
Oklahoma	33	7
Pennsylvania	27	0
Virginia	22	0
Wisconsin	25	0

Note: Parents defined as having children "possible" or "likely" in their household according to Catalist records.

---

[8] In this section, I will use the term "parent" to refer to voters with children in the household for convenience. In some cases, voters in households with children may actually be older siblings still living with their parents, grandparents, or have other relationships, which suggests that the figures below may even overstate the number of actual parents in the active electorate.

children. In the right column, I tabulate the percent of school districts where voters with children represent for a majority of the electorate. In many states, not a single school district qualifies – and in the remaining, the number is vanishing small.

To be fair, voters don't themselves need to have children enrolled in local schools to care about the quality of public education. After all, student achievement affects broader social outcomes – including economic growth, technological innovation, and crime – in which even childless voters and those with grown kids have big stakes. And how local schools perform influences local property values (as I will discuss in Chapter 8). Nevertheless, parents have the most skin in the game in students' education, so their relatively limited electoral influence should give us some pause. At minimum, we can confidently conclude that it is a mistake to conflate "voters" and "parents" when thinking about who is determining the outcome of local school board elections, as both journalists and education policy researchers often tend to do.

In a published study using the Catalist data and focusing on the subset of states in Table 2.2 – the largest ones, with the greatest number of school districts and the most racial and demographic diversity among students served across these districts – we found other worrying patterns. Not only do most voters not have kids, but they look quite different in terms of their race and income from the students being served by schools. To be exact, voters are consistently much whiter and somewhat wealthier than the public school students in their local communities. The demographic divide is especially large in school districts that have the biggest achievement gaps between white pupils and students of color. Although this relationship is unlikely to be causal, it is important. As we note in the study: "If elected officials are motivated to respond to voter preferences, our results suggest that school board members face the least political pressure to address persistent racial achievement gaps in precisely the districts where these gaps are largest because minority populations are most politically underrepresented in these jurisdictions" (Kogan, Lavertu and Peskowitz, 2021, p. 1087). The reality is that mostly childless, overwhelmingly white, upper-income voters are ultimately in charge of electing officials to run local schools – creating what we call a "democratic deficit" in education governance.

How school board elections are organized likely contributes to this deficit. In most communities, school board elections are "off-cycle" – which means that they are not held concurrently with high-profile national elections in November of even years. This is a legacy of early twentieth-century Progressive reformers, who believed that scheduling local and national elections at the same time would encourage partisanship in what was nominally nonpartisan local government. The consequence, however, is that turnout in off-cycle is abysmally low – typically much lower than in San Francisco's recall election (when it was 36 percent of registered voters) and often even in the single digits.

The voters who participate when almost everyone else stays home tend to be unusual, which further exaggerates the disconnect between adults who elect school boards and the students these boards are charged with educating. In a separate paper leveraging differences in when school districts hold their elections, we found that off-cycle elections increased the percent of voters who were white, had higher income, and didn't have school-aged kids – and dramatically ballooned the share of senior citizens in the electorate (Kogan, Lavertu and Peskowitz, 2018). Put another way, choosing not to hold school board elections in November of even years might encourage voters to think more carefully about local issues – but it encourages even more of them to just stay home and is a great way to minimize the skin in the game that few remaining participants actually have in the operations of local schools.

LESSON 2: VOTERS DON'T CARE MUCH ABOUT STUDENT LEARNING

One of the biggest puzzles about San Francisco is not that the district's voters booted out the incumbents during the 2022 recall but that they tolerated their antics for so long. Although test scores in San Francisco were not horrible – the district has consistently outperformed the rest of the state – they were not outstanding either, especially considering the wealth of the families who could afford to live in the city and the district's level of spending. Before the pandemic, fewer than half of the district's students met state grade-level standards in math and reading, and the gaps between white and Asian students on one hand and Black and Latino students on the other were astronomical. Yet voters didn't seem to care very much.

This pattern, too, is not unique to San Francisco. Before diving into the data, I must pause to emphasize an important point – one I made in passing in Chapter 1 and will return to again and again throughout this book. How we define school quality has tremendous consequences. The most common metrics used in the real world are simply an aggregation of student test scores – such as proficiency rates or percent of students performing "on grade level." These metrics tell us a lot about how much students know, but they don't actually tell us very much about how much they learned in their school. Schools are only one factor that affects student achievement and what happens outside of school – the resources students' family have available, how much their parents are involved in their education, variation in genetic endowments, and the culture in which a child is raised all matter as well. Collectively, they matter much more than school quality, so the most popular measures of student achievement largely capture differences in the composition of students that schools enroll, not how well they serve them.[9]

To separate outstanding schools from horrendous ones, we need to be able to isolate how much of the differences in students' tested achievement is due to things their school districts can actually control, such as teacher quality. Fortunately there are ways to do this, and these metrics are now commonly used in state accountability systems in many places. I will dive into more details behind these measures later in the book, but for now I want to emphasize that when I discuss the relationship between school board election results and student learning, I am speaking about the differences in academic outcomes we can be fairly confident are due to variation in school quality.

The Stanford Education Data Archive includes a measure capturing such variation. Merging it with our school board election data leads to a depressing conclusion: In general, voters don't seem to care very much about student learning when deciding whether to reelect incumbent school board leaders for another term (Kogan, Lavertu and Peskowitz, 2025). We find only small differences in election outcomes between districts doing the best job improving student achievement and those at the very bottom.

Some might wonder whether this result simply shows that student achievement data is very hard to find and so most voters just don't know how well their schools are doing. Instead of looking at the relationship between test scores and elections, we can also use a more accessible measure – the official accountability rating that states assign to schools. Such ratings were first required under the No Child Left Behind Act nationally. They have evolved since then, but most states still use some variant of them, assigning schools a letter grade ranging from an "A"

---

[9] Some researchers try to account for this by statistically "controlling" for observable student characteristics, such as income. Unfortunately, many important out-of-school determinants of achievement, such as parental involvement, are not available in administrative data.

to an "F" or a star rating, similar to those found on Amazon or Yelp reviews.

In a paper using fine-grained election data from Ohio (Kogan, Lavertu and Peskowitz, 2016), we used several clever research designs to see if such ratings impacted voter decisions in school board elections. During our period of study, Ohio assigned school districts different performance ratings, ranging from "Academic Emergency" for the worst to "Excellent with Distinction" for the best. We examined whether changes in state ratings had any impacts on how incumbent school board members did when they stood for reelection. In addition, we leveraged somewhat arbitrary cutoffs separating districts receiving different ratings – a "regression discontinuity" design – to compare otherwise identical districts that differed only in the accountability rating they received from the state. Using both designs, we found absolutely no evidence that academic performance impacted school board elections or turnover rates, confirming what we found in the national data.

There are many reasons why voters might not put much weight on student achievement. Perhaps voters don't trust test scores. (Certainly many education researchers find them distasteful, although mostly for political and ideological reasons.) Perhaps they care more about student discipline, or whether local school boards faithfully follow parliamentary procedures, or whether they provide ample opportunities for public comment at their school board meetings (e.g., Collins, 2021). But it is important to think about the incentives these dynamics create.

Consider another study on Ohio school board elections. Shortly after our paper came out, we were contacted by economist Paul Thompson, who was also interested in whether school board elections created accountability for performance. He was also looking at state ratings of school districts – but different ones. While we examined academic performance, Thompson had written a series of papers on financial solvency. Ohio school districts that posted bad test scores received the "academic emergency" designation. Districts that couldn't balance their budgets received a "fiscal emergency" label. Thompson had found that these labels were serious business – causing taxes to increase, as districts sought new revenue to close their deficits, and housing prices to decline (Thompson, 2016).

As the logical next step, Thompson wanted to use the election data we collected to see if voters held school board incumbents accountable for allowing districts to become such a financial mess. And he found that they did. When a district was identified by the state as being in a "fiscal emergency," incumbent school board members were about 10 percentage points less likely to run for reelection. And those who did run were about 25 to 30 percentage points more likely to get defeated (Thompson, 2019), massive effects when we benchmark them against what political scientists typically find in the literature on retrospective voting and what we found in our national analysis of school board turnover and student achievement.

Consider the implications, putting our Ohio study side by side with Thompson's. Suppose you are a school board member who likes their job – either because you enjoy serving your community or because you view the school board seat as a stepping stone to higher political office. Your district is facing a budget crunch, and you have to choose between making devastating budget cuts – cuts you know will negatively impact students in the classroom – and digging deep into your reserves as you try to find a long-term solution. If your goal is to get reelected, the incentives are clear. If you make the cuts and student achievement plunges, you don't have to worry about losing your seat. If you don't make the cuts because you want to protect students, there is a good chance the voters will give you the boot. Rational incumbents will prioritize the financial considerations over learning – not because they don't care about students but because of the incentives voters have created through their decisions on Election Day.

Nearly all of the careful studies on the relationship between student academic achievement and local school board elections I am aware of find the same thing we did in Ohio: Voters don't hold incumbents accountable for school quality in a meaningful way.[10] There are, however, two exceptions that stand out and deserve discussion.

One is a paper by political scientists Chris Berry and Will Howell (2007), one of the earliest to look for "retrospective voting" in local school board elections. Specifically, Berry and Howell focused on South Carolina in the early 2000s, when the state first unveiled its school accountability and rating system. They collected precinct-level election data and examined the extent to which these new school ratings influenced the electoral prospects of incumbents. In 2000, Berry and Howell found that voters did seem to reward incumbents for recent improvements in achievement in the local schools, although voters cared only

---

[10] Note my focus is on studies that examine *election outcomes*. Research looking at turnout have found some evidence that signals about school performance can impact political participation (e.g., Holbein, 2016).

about how their local school buildings were doing, not achievement district-wide. In 2002 and 2004, however, they found no relationships between student outcomes and election results.

To explain these apparently contradictory findings, Berry and Howell argued that the key mediating variable was media coverage. In 2000, the school ratings were new, and local newspapers covered them extensively, raising the salience of this information in the minds of voters. "In the 2002 and 2004 elections, however, media coverage shifted to other issues such as the closing of schools, the racial composition of schools and boards, disciplinary problems, and sports programs," they noted. "Whereas 45% of the newspaper articles on the 2000 school board elections discussed student test scores, only 30 and 34% of articles on the following two elections did so. Thus, it is possible that test scores were not a factor in the 2002 and 2004 elections because the costs of learning about test scores increased due to fading media coverage" (p. 855). This is just like the San Francisco experience, but in reverse: A sudden wave of media coverage made student outcomes salient during the 2022 recall election in ways press attention never seemed to be before.

It is also important to keep effect sizes in mind. Even in the years and elections when incumbents were held accountable in Berry and Howell's data, the magnitude of the punishments and rewards voters meted out was small. For example, during the 2000 election, moving from the twenty-fifth statewide percentile of achievement growth to the seventy-fifth percentile – a very large change – was predicted to increase an incumbent's vote share in the next election by just 3 percentages points. With the average incumbent winning with 58 percent of the vote, this would not have made a difference for the outcome of most elections.

The second study was written by political scientist Julia Payson (2017) and examined school board elections in California. Like Berry and Howell in South Carolina and our work in Ohio, Payson focused on voter responses to changes in official state accountability ratings, known as the Academic Performance Index during this period in California. Payson's innovation was to examine school board elections separately based on when they were held. Most of the time, she showed that incumbent school board members faced no consequences for poor performance. However, she did find evidence of accountability for school board elections held in November of even years, concurrently with the presidential election. Recall these were also the elections we found had the largest share of parents voting (Kogan, Lavertu and Peskowitz, 2018). But even then, the effect sizes were tiny – with a one-standard deviation increase in achievement growth boosting an incumbent's vote share by just 1 percentage point.

The lesson from Berry and Howell (2007) and Payson (2017) is that school board elections encourage elected officials to care about student learning only when (1) a critical mass of voters have sufficient skin in the game and (2) academic performance is made salient through mechanisms such as media coverage. And even then, the effects are modest.

I stress the effect sizes because they ultimately shape incentives of office holders. Compare the relatively small changes in election outcomes in the studies just described to other research looking at the impact of teachers' union endorsements. Untangling cause and effect here is tricky – do candidates do better because they receive the union endorsement, or do unions tend to endorse strong candidates to begin with to curry favor with future office holders? The most convincing evidence on this question comes from a recent study by political scientist Michael Hartney (2022b). Hartney collected data on the same candidates running in multiple school board elections over time – comparing the electoral performance of the same people in years when they ran for school board with support from their local teachers' union to years when they ran without their support. He found that an endorsement increased the odds of winning the election by between 25 and 30 percentage points – an effect ten times larger than what Berry and Howell (2007) and Payson (2017) uncovered even under the best circumstances with regards to student achievement.

Again, put yourself in the position of a school board member who must choose between two alternative policies – one that dramatically improves student learning in the district but perhaps upsets the adult employees and one that makes the employees happy but compromises academic achievement. If your primary objective is political survival – winning the next election, so that you can return to office and hope to do more good in the next term – the incentives are clear. You're much better off sacrificing student learning to win the teachers' union support. Local democracy, in other words, stacks the deck against good schools when this goal conflicts with what powerful, well-organized adult interest groups want.

Elections may play a big role in what school board officials do in office, but they currently don't encourage them to put student learning front and center. When voters don't care about achievement, the message to elected officials is that they don't need to worry about it either. And we should not be surprised when they act accordingly, as we saw in San Francisco.

LESSON 3: SCHOOL BOARD ELECTIONS DON'T PROVIDE VOTERS MUCH CHOICE

In many communities, voters couldn't replace their school board members even if they wanted to. A prerequisite for electoral accountability is that voters need to have choices when casting their ballot. And it turns out they often don't have one.

In Table 2.3, I present some summary statistics drawn from our national database of school board elections (Kogan, Lavertu and Peskowitz, 2025). The table also provides comparable measures for state legislative and congressional elections from the same set of states and years as the school board elections in our data.

There are several noteworthy patterns. Congressional elections are contested nearly 90 percent of the time, meaning that voters can choose between two major-party candidates when voting. State elections are less likely to be contested, an alarming finding that political scientist Steve Rogers has emphasized in a recent book (Rogers, 2023). Nevertheless, the majority of state legislative elections include multiple candidates. But school board elections are even worse – more than half of all races go uncontested.[11] And even when voters do have a choice, the elections are typically uncompetitive. Although many have expressed concerns about the decrease in competition in congressional elections – blaming

TABLE 2.3 *How school board elections compare to other legislative contests*

Outcome	School Board (%)	State Legislature (%)	House of Representatives (%)
Contested election	45[1]	53	85
Margin of victory (ave.)	26[1]	27	33
Incumbent runs	59[2]	76	90
Incumbent wins	82[2]	96	95

Note: Calculated using election data from Arkansas, California, Illinois, Iowa, Louisiana, Michigan, Mississippi, Missouri, Nebraska, Nevada, New York, Oklahoma, Rhode Island, Texas, Virginia, and Wisconsin during the period 2002–2017. See Kogan, Lavertu and Peskowitz (2025) for details about original sources. Excludes states that cancel uncontested elections.
[1] Figures limited to single-member elections to make them as comparable to state legislative and congressional elections as possible.
[2] Calculated using elections held after 2007, when incumbency status can be inferred.

[11] This estimate is based on single-member elections. Contestation is harder to define for multimember contests that produce more than one winner.

the incumbency advantage, gerrymandering, and voter geographic self-sorting, among other factors – it is noteworthy that the margin of victory in a typical House of Representatives race is not much larger than in a typical school board election.

Given how lopsided many school board elections are, it is perhaps surprising that so few incumbents choose to run for reelection. We estimate that about 40 percent of sitting school board members retire in every election cycle – a substantially larger share than we see for either state legislative (24 percent) or national congressional elections (10 percent). This may be a testament to how difficult and unpleasant the job of overseeing local schools has become – a job that is filled by uncompensated volunteers in the vast majority of places.[12]

The surprisingly high probability of retirement among incumbents, combined with the high rate of reelection among those who do seek additional terms, points to another noteworthy fact: Approximately 80 percent of the school board turnover we observe is driven by the decision of incumbents to not stand for office, rather than by active decisions of voters to replace those who run again. Whether incumbents choose to seek another term thus matters much more for who governs our local schools than who voters choose to support on Election Day. In most school districts, the identity of the policymakers charged with making high-stakes decisions for local schools is determined long before the election and has little to do with what local communities might want from their schools. This isn't how we typically think about democracy, but it's the system we have created to oversee our public education system. Perhaps it shouldn't surprise us when it doesn't work very well.

WHY BROKEN ELECTIONS MATTER

In this chapter, I sought to synthesize the scholarly literature on school board elections and offer original data and measures to paint a comprehensive picture of what local democratic control of public schools looks like in most places and the often-perverse incentives it can generate. To recap:

- In the average school board election, most voters don't have school-aged kids, and in the districts facing the largest academic challenges,

---

[12] Another possibility is that these individuals use their school board office as a stepping stone for higher office.

the voters look quite different from the students actually attending the public schools.
- Most of the time, voters also don't care much about academic outcomes and don't use local elections to punish and reward performance. When achievement does matters, the effects are small – too small to motivate school board members to do a good job maximizing student learning and often more than offset by competing adult political pressures.
- For most voters, elections don't provide much of a choice. Many elections are uncontested, and the rest remain uncompetitive. Most of the turnover on school boards is driven by voluntary incumbent retirements, not election losses.

These patterns have important implications both for how we study local democracy and for identifying the reforms likely to do the most good. First, they suggest that focusing just on voter participation – on differences in turnout in districts over time and efforts to increase it – won't tell us much about how elections affect educational quality. What matters most is not how many people cast their ballots but how much those voters care about student learning.

Second, interest group influence in local elections is only part of the story. We should be concerned that so many school board members are effectively hand-picked by local teachers' unions. But trying to reduce their electoral influence (e.g., through campaign finance or collective bargaining reforms) is unlikely to be enough. If such reforms simply shift the heuristics voters rely on, encouraging them to cast their ballots more based on party endorsements, for example, it's not at all obvious that the incentives facing office holders would change for the better or that student learning would improve.

I close with two case studies illustrating why a dysfunctional governance system ultimately matters and how it affects the educational experience that students receive.

The first comes from the East Ramapo School District, a suburban community in New York. Two-thirds of the population of this district is white – but over 90 percent of the students enrolled in the public schools are either Black or Latino. The reason is that the white residents are overwhelmingly ultra-Orthodox Jews who send their kids to private yeshivas, a traditional religious Jewish school. Because white Jewish voters represent a numerical majority, they control who serves on the school board. And because their own kids don't attend the district, this shapes the priorities and goals of the school board members who win.

In recent years, the district has been embroiled in voting rights litigation related to these issues, and it was profiled in a 2014 episode of *This American Life* titled "A Not-So-Simple Majority." In the show, the reporter visits East Ramapo and finds a disturbingly dysfunctional district. As the show recounts:

> Once the Hasidic [Jewish] majority took control, at first many of the ways it started to remake the district were incremental – changes to personnel and administration here and there. Kind of quickly, though, restricting the budget and reining in property taxes became a preoccupation. The school board determines the property tax levy when it sets its budget. Controlling taxes meant trimming corners off the budget, dropping extracurriculars, sports teams, cutting music teachers in elementary schools. . . .
> It also changed its approach to special ed placements. It replaced the district's head of special education, who Hasidic parents had had a ton of beef with, and then the district started placing special ed students in private Jewish schools in very large numbers. . . .
> Also high on the priorities list for the new Hasidic majority was reining in property taxes. And with the levers of power now in its possession, it launched what's pretty much been a systematic defunding of the East Ramapo public schools.

As a result of the changes, kindergarten class sizes increased from twenty students to twenty-eight. Middle school athletics were eliminated, and the director of the award-winning band laid off. Relying on controversial projections predicting declining in enrollment in public schools in the coming years, the district closed several school buildings and sold them – to yeshivas, apparently at below-market prices (Powell, 2014).

"Is there something inherently uncomfortable about a system being governed by folks who don't use that system or wouldn't want to use that system?" the reporter for "This American Life" asked the school board president an interview for the show. "Is there something that's uncomfortable just about that?"

The obvious answer is yes. But if we're uncomfortable about the governance arrangements at East Ramapo, we should also worry what happens in communities all around the country. Although the magnitude of the "democratic deficit" in East Ramapo is unusual, the broader story is not. The root causes of this deficit – voters who have no skin in the game and care little about how much learning takes place in the public schools – are present in districts all around the country.

The second example comes from California. In 2013, the state overhauled its school-funding approach, consolidating a series of categorical programs into a single "local control funding formula." The formula is weighted, with more state dollars going to school districts serving a larger number of English learners, foster care youth, and impoverished students. Reflecting then-Gov. Jerry Brown's belief in the principle of "subsidiarity" – the idea that policy decisions are best made at the lowest level possible – the funds came with few strings attached, and local districts had discretion in allocating these resources to serve high-need students.

Although the reform was effective in channeling more state funds to districts serving larger numbers of disadvantaged students, post-implementation analyses and evaluations have found that only a fraction of these dollars ultimately reached schools enrolling the most disadvantaged students. Instead, a significant share was spent at the district level or divided equally across schools, regardless of how many high-need students – the state's intended beneficiaries – they actually enrolled. A state audit (Auditor of the State of California, 2019) concluded that the new policy "has not ensured that funding is benefiting intended student groups and closing achievement gaps."

There is little doubt that districts receiving the extra money used it to improve their educational offerings – with student achievement increasing, graduation rates improving, and student suspensions and expulsions falling (Johnson, 2023). But there is not much evidence that the disadvantaged student subgroups *within those districts* – the ones who generated the extra dollars under the funding formula – benefited the most. "Four years into California's ambitious funding reform – boosting K–12 yearly spending by $23 billion – little discernible progress in narrowing achievement gaps could be observed," one study concluded (Lee, Fuller and Rabe-Hesketh, 2021, p. 1257).

These results are not surprising, in light of political logic local democracy creates. "When disadvantaged groups are poorly represented in the political process," we wrote in the concluding sentence of our "democratic deficit" article, "local elected officials may not have strong incentives to make decisions with their interests in mind" (Kogan, Lavertu and Peskowitz, 2021, p. 1088).

When we first wrote about California's funding reforms and the problems they revealed with school governance in a blog post for the Brookings Institution, it received a frustrated response from Stanford education professor Michael Kirst, who requested a retraction. Kirst had been the intellectual mastermind behind the policy and Gov. Brown's top education advisor, serving as the president of the California Board of Education. He complained we did not do justice to the reforms and the impacts they've had for the districts that received a large infusion of new state money.

When we spoke a few years after our piece came out, Kirst stressed the context in California at the time. The state was just emerging from the Great Recession, which produced devastating budget cuts. State education funding was earmarked for all sorts of pet programs written into law by long-retired lawmakers. Local district leaders lacked the flexibility to spend the money in ways that reflected the needs of their communities.

I asked him if the local control funding formula put too much faith in local democracy. Did it wrongly assume that local officials would naturally do the right thing and prioritize the needs of their most vulnerable students – who were the reason the additional dollars flowed into their districts – in the absence of state-level accountability? Even if few voters in their communities were concerned about the academic performance of these student subgroups? Kirst conceded that critics like us made reasonable points.

"It's still to me a work in progress, and we benefited from the early feedback," he told me. "As you know, in public policy, you rarely get everything. You make trade offs. In the context we had – we were coming out of this deep recession, and they had cut really severely. We're going to sit there in Sacramento and tell [local district leaders] how to restore those cuts?"

In recent years, the reforms have been tweaked, with additional accountability and guardrails added to ensure that the money actually reached the intended students. Much of the credit for this change belongs to John Affeldt, the managing attorney at Public Advocates, an nonprofit advocacy organization in California long involved in school funding litigation. Public Advocates published a number of reports revealing how districts found tricks to divert new state money away from their most high-need students, the intended beneficiaries. The biggest loophole in the original legislation dealt with so-called carry over of funds. Although districts were required to spend new state money on disadvantaged students when they first received it, funds left over at the end of the year would carry over to next year's budget and become completely unrestricted in their use. Initially the money had some strings attached, but those strings essentially went away if districts just waited a year to spend it. Many school systems started intentionally banking the dollars, waiting for the legal restrictions to go away so they could divert the money meant to help disadvantaged students to other uses (Jongco, 2016). The state eventually closed the carry-over loophole – but not until years later.

"You know that the local school boards are going to serve the squeaky wheels, which are going to tend to be the more vocal, white, middle-class voters," Affeldt explained when I asked him if local political pressures made additional accountability for state money necessary. "Many of them, like myself, will profess that they want the [disadvantaged students] taken care of. But people also want their local schools beautified, and the best teachers, etc."

DEMOCRATIC MYTHS VERSUS REALITIES

America's system of public education is built on a beautiful premise: Local communities care about their students, and when left to their own devices, they will do whatever is necessary to provide those students a high-quality education. As aspirations go, this is a good one. But it's not a very accurate description of reality.

As this chapter has shown, how we govern our schools can create a big wedge between the interests of public school students and the priorities of adults who vote in local elections. It is adults who ultimately control public school districts through the ballot box, and what they want is often quite different than what public school students need.

In the remainder of the book, I will take a closer look at what it is adults actually want from public education. I discuss how voters form preferences on education policy questions, how partisanship affects the behavior of elected officials responsible for making these policies, and how concerns over employment and housing prices often cause public schools to prioritize adult concerns over student learning. The discussion will cover a great deal of ground, but the underlying theme will always be the same. We need a public school system that serves students, but we have created one that is governed at the behest of adults. We should not be surprised when it puts the interests of those adults first.

3

Adults Follow Partisan Leaders on Education Policy

> Don't like President Obama? Then you probably don't like the Common Core – or as some conservative critics call it, "ObamaCore".... The research confirms what many have long suggested: President Obama and the Common Core have become inextricably entangled.
> —Education reporter Matt Barnum (2016)

The COVID-19 pandemic proved to be an unprecedented shock to America's public education system. In early March 2020, reports from Northern Italy depicted a healthcare system on the verge of collapse, with hospitals overwhelmed by critically ill patients. Many Americans began to worry about a similar disaster here once the new virus inevitably spread through the population and state officials acted quickly to flatten the curve of infections to preserve hospital capacity.

As part of these efforts, Ohio Gov. Mike DeWine announced on March 12 that the state's schools would close early for spring break and remain closed for at least the next three weeks. Within days, every other state followed suit. In fact, almost all schools would remain shut through the rest of the academic year – and in many places, much longer – representing the first time in history that every school in the country, public and private, closed its doors (Zweig, 2025). But closing schools proved to be the easy part. Reopening them again would turn out to be much more difficult – and reveal the underlying mechanisms through which adult politics influence public education policy. Indeed, observing (and participating in) the public debates related to school reopening over the course of the summer and fall of that year greatly shaped my own understanding of how voters form their preferences over education policies and helped plant the intellectual seeds from which this book would ultimately bloom.

The empirical section of this chapter examines two statewide referenda in California – a proposal to fire homosexual teachers that appeared on the ballot in 1978 and an initiative to outlaw bilingual education in 1998. My argument is that the outcomes of both elections were greatly shaped by political elites, with a significant share of voters changing their minds in response to top-down messaging and persuasion. That we saw these dynamics decades ago – before the rise of modern partisan polarization – demonstrates that elite influence is a long-standing feature of how regular voters come to understand and think about education policy questions.

In 1978, the key opinion leader was former California governor (and future president) Ronald Reagan, whose decision to come out against the gay teacher ban dramatically reduced support among Republican voters, ultimately leading to the measure's unexpected defeat. In 1998, it was another Republican governor, Pete Wilson, who weighed in at the last minute, endorsing the effort to outlaw bilingual education for English learners. Ironically, Wilson's involvement only hurt the campaign, greatly reducing support for the initiative among the state's Democratic and Latino voters.

Before turning to these historical cases, it is useful to spend some time on the more recent past and understand the politics of school reopening during the pandemic. As we will see, the dynamics of public opinion during this period followed a strikingly similar pattern as in the two California referenda decades earlier. The COVID-19 case study provides important insights about my broader theoretical argument for why elite messaging plays such a significant role in shaping mass attitudes about education policies and the conditions under which we should expect such effects to be most pronounced.

Understanding how American voters form their opinions amidst contentious education policy debates is critical for thinking about what local democracy does – and does not – ultimately accomplish. As I discussed at length in Chapter 2, some scholars have argued that our evaluations of local school district performance should focus on "responsiveness" – the extent to which policies that school systems adopt match public opinion in each community. In this chapter, I provide further reasons to doubt this approach. Specifically, I show that attitudes are powerfully shaped by partisan elites, often for political reasons that have little to do with the educational needs or interests of public school students. Maximizing the extent to which policies matches adult opinions can often mean sacrificing the quality of the education schools provide – as the pandemic powerfully illustrated.

THE TRUMP EFFECT

Like many Americans, my memories of the first weeks of the pandemic are filled with terror. After seeing a viral social media post with a back-of-the-envelope calculation estimating how quickly our country would run out of hospital beds and ventilators, I became convinced that Northern Italy foreshadowed the devastation that would soon arrive on US shores. The weekend before Gov. DeWine's announcement of the school closures, I ventured to the local Costco to stock up on bottled water and food. (Toilet paper was not yet in short supply, but giant bags of rice were already being rationed.) On Facebook, I harassed Columbus school board members, who tried to reassure the public that schools remained safe, begging them to close the buildings proactively to protect area hospitals. My wife initially thought I had lost my mind but seemed persuaded when the Ohio State University, on spring break at the time, announced that in-person classes would be suspended once students returned and reluctantly agreed to my demand that we pull our kids out of school, which we did a week before the statewide shutdown.

By that summer, however, my perspective on schools had begun to change. Outside of New York City, which experienced a horrific early COVID wave, much of the country seemed to have escaped Italy's fate. Having bought time, many states set up field hospitals to increase capacity, so it seemed only obvious that it was time for kids to return to school. Sweden, which had forgone strict lockdowns and kept both primary and lower-secondary schools open during spring 2020, did not appear to have experienced dramatically worse outcomes than the United States.[1] When my wife asked in June if schools in Columbus might not reopen come

---

[1] The most rigorous research on the Sweden experience, which exploits the age cutoff between lower-secondary schools (which remained open) and upper-secondary schools (which closed) did find that parents of children who continued to attend in-person schools faced higher risk of infection, although the magnitude of the effect was quite small (Vlachos, Hertegård and Svaleryd, 2021). The authors found larger effects for teachers – roughly a doubling of both positive diagnoses and severe cases among teachers working in person, although that still put upper-secondary teachers in the middle of the pack in terms of occupational risks (see Figure 3 of Vlachos, Hertegård and Svaleryd, 2021). The Swedish experience provides a useful example of a policy question where the interests of teachers and students are not aligned, a difficult and inherently political trade-off that many activists try to assume away.

August, I laughed at her question – the suggestion seemed absurd. Little did I know. In fact, public schools did not reopen in Columbus, or in many other big urban school districts, that fall at all.

Although governors of all political stripes ordered school closures in the spring, their approach by the fall had shifted. It was up to individual districts to make the call, they announced, not for state officials to impose one-size-fits-all policies. And as several independent analyses have shown, which candidate local voters had supported in the 2016 presidential election – not community COVID-19 transmission or hospitalization rates – proved to be the single best predictor of the decisions made by local school districts (Grossmann et al., 2021; Hartney and Finger, 2022). Republican-leaning areas largely resumed in-person learning as the new school year began in August and September 2020, while deep blue districts like Columbus stuck with virtual instruction. This striking pattern sparked a furious debate among us commentators: Was politics (rather than science) driving district decisions? Or were local officials being faithful representatives, as we would expect in a democracy, and simply reflecting the partisan divide in opinion over schools that had developed among their constituencies? With cross-sectional, correlational data, it was impossible to tell.

In November, just days after the fall presidential election, the clinical trial for the Pfizer vaccine released its first public results, showing an impressively high efficacy against hospitalization and marking the beginning of the end of the crisis phase of the pandemic. In January, states began to roll out their vaccination programs, with educators moved to the front line in many places in an effort to get schools reopened. Yet, public opinion remained a key concern. As still-closed school systems announced plans for eventual reopening, emerging data from big-city districts in Chicago, New York, and Washington, DC, revealed striking racial disparities: Parents of white children appeared far more eager to return to in-person instruction than African-American and Latino families (Kogan, 2021*b*). This posed obvious equity concerns – especially with the murder of George Floyd and the racial reckoning that followed still fresh in everyone's mind. But it also provided a powerful talking point for big-city teachers unions that opposed the resumption of in-person learning.

In California, where officials had proposed financial incentives to accelerate the speed of school reopening, the state's largest teachers union, representing Los Angeles educators, asserted the plan was "a recipe for propagating structural racism." In Chicago, the teachers union sent a viral tweet (soon deleted) stating, "The push to reopen schools is rooted in sexism, racism and misogyny." The racial angle quickly attracted media attention. Freelance journalist Rachel Cohen highlighted big racial gaps in surveys of parents asking about their preferences regarding the mode of learning, and a number of high-profile outlets published articles on the divide, many attributing the reticence of parents of color to sharp racial disparities in COVID-19 deaths and hospitalizations in the early months of the pandemic. "Parents' decisions," *Axios* reported in a typical article, "are grounded in part in the personal experiences of a pandemic that has had stark and disproportionate racial differences" (Walsh, 2021).

I was immediately eager to understand the source of the racial differences in what I called "school hesitancy" – adapting the term from contemporaneous debates about differences in vaccine take-up rates across racial groups. As a social scientist interested in public opinion, this was an intellectual itch. But also as a parent and, increasingly, a school reopening activist, responding to the union argument that reopening would just cater to white families and potentially exacerbate racial achievement gaps was a political necessity.

My initial hypotheses largely reflected the conventional wisdom of the time. Families of color, I reasoned, were more likely to live in multigenerational households, where grandparents might be particularly concerned about children bringing the virus back from school. Rates of diabetes and obesity, two huge risk factors for severe disease, were also much more common among adults of color. Statistically "controlling" for such demographic covariates as well as subjective beliefs about how likely one was to become hospitalized or die if infected, I expected, would surely close the racial gaps in parent preferences for in-person versus virtual instruction. Much to my surprise, however, survey data were not at all consistent with these expectations.

The analysis I ultimately completed, published as a policy report by the conservative American Enterprise Institute, revealed three novel findings. First, using unusually rich public opinion survey data that asked parents of school-aged children about family composition, living arrangements, high-risk comorbidities, and subjective beliefs about COVID-19 risks, I found that adjusting for all of these factors (and many more) left racial gaps in opinions on schools largely unchanged. Clearly, the conventional wisdom was wrong. Second, whether local schools had already reopened proved to be a strong predictor of whether parents felt comfortable sending their children back to in-person learning. This held true not only cross-sectionally but also over time. When schools reopened, local parents *changed* their opinion and became much more comfortable with in-person instruction.

The policy and political implications of the second finding were profound. The position of teachers' union officials and many sympathetic activists was that urban districts lagged so far behind in getting their schools reopened because the families they served – disproportionately families of color – were scared to send their kids back. Democracy was working, in other words, with individual school districts responding to variation in local opinion. My analysis suggested the causal arrow was reversed. "The racial disparities in access to in-person learning options appear to be one cause (rather than merely a consequence) of continued disagreement among racial groups about whether it is safe for kids to return to school," the report concluded (Kogan, 2021a). Local school districts were not responding to local opinion but rather their policy choices were shaping it.

Given the sensitive nature of the topic and coming amidst a particularly bitter debate about schools, the report attracted considerable attention, including a mention in a front-page *New York Times* article (Goldstein, 2021). Reopening opponents and commentators were not pleased, some taking to social media to accuse me of racism. In their view, I had disrespected and infantilized Black and Latino parents, implying they had been so dumb as to be tricked by local school officials and could not think for themselves. Of course, this was a gross mischaracterization of my argument. The implications was not that parents of color were particularly susceptible to messaging – it was that parents of color whose kids were enrolled in urban schools had gotten the *opposite messages* from local school districts than their white, suburban counterparts.

And it certainly made a lot of sense for parents, regardless of their race, to defer to local officials. After all, school reopening decisions required careful consideration of data, epidemiology, and understanding of local HVAC systems – level of detail, knowledge, and complexity that few regular people surely possessed. If local officials, presumably acting on advice of subject-level experts, announced that they could not reopen schools because doing so would not be safe, it was quite sensible for parents to defer to their judgments. And when local schools did reopen, district leaders typically announced that their decision was based on sound science and assured parents it was safe for their children to return.

The issue was that different groups of parents, living in different districts, had received different messages. For example, while schools in many parts of the country had been open for many months, with few apparent issues, district leaders in posh, deeply blue Alexandria, Virginia, voted in January 2021 to remain virtual. In justifying the decision, one board member asked parents during a virtual board meeting, "Do you want your child to be alive or educated?" When the policy choice was framed in this way, it would not be shocking if some Alexandria parents concluded that returning to school might not be the best idea. Indeed, in a series of experiments conducted during summer 2020, a team of political scientists had found that parents viewed school principals and local superintendents – along with scientists and the Center for Disease Control and Prevention – as the most persuasive messengers about whether resuming in-person learning was safe (Green et al., 2020).

For present purposes, however, it is my third finding that is most important. Although whether local schools had reopened was a significant predictor of parent attitudes and helped explain differences across racial groups, it was not the only one. Political preferences mattered a great deal as well. Many polls showed that Republican voters and parents were far more likely to support a resumption of in-person schooling. Because Black and Latino voters were, on average, far more likely to be Democrats than white voters, partisanship was another important driver of the observed racial divide in parent views about their preferred modes of learning.[2]

Removed from the unique 2020 political context, it would have been far from obvious that support for in-person schooling was an inherently Republican or conservative position. As part of my research, I tracked down every available public opinion survey to try to identify *when* the partisan divide over school reopening first emerged. Given the impressive frequency of polling on the issue, I was able to identify the precise two-week window during which opinion polarized – at the beginning of May 2020. In late April, a poll commissioned by ABC News and Ipsos asked parents how willing they would be to send their children back to school. It found almost no partisan divide, with 10 percent of Republicans compared to 6 percent of Democrats saying they would be very or somewhat likely to do so. Two weeks later, the same organizations repeated the

---

[2] When I wrote my report, the earlier wave of the survey that asked parents about which candidate they had supported in 2020 election remained embargoed, so I relied on several proxies of partisanship. Once the vote-choice data was released, I replicated the analysis and found that partisanship proved to be an even larger explanatory factor than my original analysis had indicated.

survey, and at this point the partisan gap had grown dramatically to more than 30 percentage points.[3]

What happened during this two-week period that caused voters to polarize along partisan lines? Scouring media accounts, I could find only one explanation. At a May 12 congressional hearing, Dr. Anthony Fauci and Republican Sen. Rand Paul had a divisive standoff over schools. Paul had demanded that Fauci come out in favor of school reopening in the fall, noting that the age gradient of the virus made kids appear to be quite low risk. Fauci refused to make such an endorsement, warning that much remained unknown and the evidence base was evolving. The next day, President Trump was asked about the exchange by a reporter at an event. Although he answered in his usual stream-of-consciousness style, the message was clear: "Well, I think they should open schools, absolutely." Asked about Fauci's exchange with Paul, the president responded, "Well, I was surprised – I was surprised by his answer, actually, because, you know, it's just – to me, it's not an acceptable answer, especially when it comes to schools." In the coming months, over the summer of 2020, the president would come out even more vocally in favor of school reopening, including in a series of tweets.

I was not the only observer to attribute the sudden polarization of attitudes regarding in-person schooling to the president weighing in on the school debate. "If you had told me that Trump was doing this as a favor to the schools-must-not-open crowd, I'd believe you," Rick Hess, the director of education policy at the American Enterprise Institute, told a reporter. In California, the Democratic chairman of the state Assembly's education committee explained that the president's advocacy had changed the "political calculus in the solidly Democratic state," explaining: "When you create so much division, it's hard to build a bridge to a solution. It's a political hot potato now" (Shapiro, 2020).

OBAMA DERANGEMENT SYNDROME?

Some might wonder whether the partisan polarization in attitudes over in-person education was due to President Trump's unique divisiveness – a symptom of a so-called Trump derangement syndrome among those on the political left. In fact, however, this was not the first time that presidential efforts to promote an education policy would backfire, setting

---

[3] Although the wording of the schooling question changed somewhat between the two surveys, this is unlikely to account for the growing partisan divide.

off countermobilization among voters from the opposite party. A decade earlier, President Barack Obama's campaign on behalf of the Common Core education standards played out nearly the same way.

Common Core standards were developed in the late 2000s under the aegis of the National Governors Association and the Council of Chief State School Officers – two bipartisan membership organizations – with financial support from the Gates Foundation (Loveless, 2021). An important motivation for the effort was recognition that the No Child Left Behind Act, President George W. Bush's education overhaul, had created very perverse incentives. By putting schools on the hook of achieving 100 percent proficiency in math and language arts by 2014 under the threat of punishing sanctions but also letting individual states develop their own definitions of "proficiency," the law had created a proverbial race to the bottom – encouraging states to lower the proficiency bar to make the goal easier to meet (Adkins et al., 2007). The Common Core initiative sought to reverse this downward drift in state academic standards, developing a common national framework organized around college- and career-readiness. The effort was bipartisan and enjoyed strong support from prominent Republicans, including governors Jeb Bush and Chris Christie and wealthy education reformer Betsy DeVos, who would go on to serve as President Trump's education secretary.

The political problems emerged when the Obama Administration incorporated the standards into its broader educational agenda. Obama's education secretary, Arne Duncan, predicted that the Common Core standards "may prove to be the single greatest thing to happen to public education in America since *Brown vs. Board of Education*" (Loveless, 2021, p. 1). Without calling them out by name, administration strongly incentivized states to adopt the standards through the Race to the Top, a multibillion grant competition that was part of the stimulus bill enacted in the wake of the Great Recession, and in the eligibility criteria for receiving a waiver from No Child Left Behind sanctions, which had really begun to bite by this point. By 2011, more than forty states had signed on.

President Obama's support, however, would prove to be politically toxic. By 2014, what had once been a technocratic issue attracting almost no political attention or opposition had become a huge partisan controversy. Conservative critics derided the standards as "ObamaCore," and a number of red states, led by Oklahoma and South Carolina, that had originally signed on moved to repeal the standards – usually in name only, dropping the Common Core label but largely keeping the underlying learning objectives (Jacobson, 2014; Jochim and McGuinn, 2016).

The issue also featured prominently in election campaigns for governor and state superintendent, an elected post in many states (Murphy, 2014).

Although the grassroots opposition to the standards united strange ideological bedfellows, including conservative Tea Party activists and far-left parents opposed to standardized testing, it is clear that Obama's support was a major factor in prompting Republican opposition. "There is a great deal of paranoia in the country today," former Georgia Gov. Sonny Purdue, an original Common Core supporter, told a journalist in 2014. "It's the two Ps, polarization and paranoia" (Martin, 2014).

Perhaps the strongest evidence about the partisan nature of opposition to Common Core comes from the annual opinion surveys done by *Education Next*, a journal published by a group of Harvard University education researchers. For several years, the researchers fielded two versions of the survey. One asked voters about their support for Common Core standards. Another version of the same question dropped the label, asking whether respondents supported states adoptions of "standards that are the same." In 2012, the survey found overwhelming support, with nearly 90 percent of both Democrats and Republicans favoring Common Core regardless of the question wording.[4] By 2016, support for "Common Core" among Democrats had fallen to 60 percent – and an even more dramatic 40 percent among Republicans. But support for generic "same standards" remained well above 60 percent and quite similar among voters from both parties (Peterson et al., 2017). In other words, the Common Core brand – not the substance of the policy underpinning it – had become unpopular among Republicans.[5] Interestingly, the partisan divide over the standards in 2016 almost perfectly mirrored the gap in support for school reopening that would develop four years later.

A TOP-DOWN MODEL OF MASS PREFERENCES

The idea that parents would take their cues about a question as important and deeply personal as sending their children to school amidst a

---

[4] In this paragraph, I use the counting rules of the Harvard authors, who included everyone not opposing Common Core as supporters, although this 90 percent also included about 20 percent who didn't care either way.

[5] Importantly, all of the decline among Republicans took place *after* 2013, corresponding to a period of attacks from conservative commentators such as Glenn Beck. This means that state repeal efforts in Republican states preceded, rather than followed, the turn against Common Core standards among Republican voters. The masses were following the elites, rather than vice versa.

global pandemic from partisan political leaders might initially strike some readers as implausible. But starting with the path-breaking work of John Zaller (2012), a large body of public opinion research has documented the importance of top-down, elite-led influence on the formation of political preferences among voters. Indeed, Zaller argued that the most educated and sophisticated voters were actually more susceptible to messages from prominent political elites, both because they were more likely to pay attention to politics and also had enough background knowledge to understand the content of their rhetoric.

More recently, Gabe Lenz (2013) directly tested the prediction that voters change their minds on policies by adopting the positions of candidates they already support – rather than deciding which candidate to back based on shared policy priorities. Using panel surveys collected amidst high-profile presidential campaigns, he found that when unexpected developments raised the salience of previously low-key political issues, revealing to voters that their preferred candidates did not agree with them, voters were far more likely to change their mind about the issues, aligning themselves with the position of their preferred candidate, rather than switch their vote and support the party that had initially agreed with them on the issue.[6] And other survey experiments have shown that simply informing voters of a position taken by presidents from their own political party is often enough to change their mind on the issues, even when the message is devoid of any clear rationale or argument (Afrouzi, Arteaga and Weisburst, 2023; Barber and Pope, 2019). Politics, in other words, is a form of political identity, much like professional and college sports among avid enthusiasts. In the same way that fans don't choose which team to support based on which coach follows their preferred offensive strategy and instead are happy to cheerlead their hometown favorites – especially when the team is winning – voters tend to stick with their side and adjust their own views accordingly.

Interestingly, the experimental research described in the previous paragraph generally find that persuasion effects are concentrated among copartisans. That is, when prominent political officials take positions on issues, they bring their supporters along into the fold. Neither study finds that endorsements polarize opinion by driving up opposition among members of the other party, in the way suggested by both the COVID-19 school reopening debates and the Common Core controversies. I will

---

[6] These dynamics are not limited to the American political context, with research in other countries finding similar patterns of opinion change (Slothuus and Bisgaard, 2021).

return to this important issue in the empirical analysis that follows and in the concluding section of this chapter, since predicting *which* voters are likely to respond to elite messages has important implications for coalition-building strategies and our theories of presidential and executive leadership. It is important to note, however, that other research has found strong evidence that feelings of animus toward the out-party can impact both policy attitudes and behaviors (e.g., Druckman et al., 2021).

To be sure, the theories of elite-led preference formation associated with Zaller and Lenz have not been accepted by all public opinion scholars (see Fowler, 2020; Mummolo, Peterson and Westwood, 2019). As critics rightly note, there are almost certainly limits to partisan loyalty, and it would be a gross exaggeration to extrapolate from the empirical evidence to conclude that most voters are dittoheads who mindlessly do whatever political elites tell them. High-profile cases of party realignment, over issues such as abortion (Achen and Bartels, 2017, pp. 258–263) and civil rights (Kuziemko and Washington, 2018), provide powerful counterexamples of voters abandoning their parties over heartfelt policy disagreements.

Unfortunately, little work has been done to identify the conditions under which we should expect the dynamics of top-down opinion formation versus bottom-up partisan realignment to dominate. My intuition is that education is an area where we should expect elite-led preference formation to be particularly important, for two reasons. First, many education policy debates are inherently complex and technocratic. Seriously engaging the question of when to reopen schools during the pandemic, for example, required difficult trade-offs and an understanding of sophisticated epidemiological arguments and model parameters. It is not surprising voters may have looked to public officials they expected to be relative experts for guidance. Most education policy debates, in other words, implicate what Carmines and Stimson (1980) describe as "hard issues" – precisely the kinds of issues where we should expect political elites to lead rather than follow.

Second, as I documented in Chapter 2, most voters themselves do not have school-aged children, especially the subset of voters who participate in low-turnout, off-cycle local special elections. Although the quality of education clearly has broader societal impacts, affecting important outcomes including economic growth and crime, the lag between policy adoption and result is often long. Thus, for many childless voters, educational policy debates are quite abstract, implicating symbolic considerations rather than instrumental personal calculations. With little of their own skin in the game, partisan and other identity considerations can play a more prominent role.

A TALE OF TWO BALLOT MEASURES

As insightful and persuasive as I find the two case studies regarding Common Core and pandemic school reopening, they only go so far. First, both focus on public opinion survey data – which critics of elite-led polarization quickly dismiss as cheap talk. For example, some studies find that simply offering survey respondents modest financial incentives for giving correct answers to factual questions dramatically reduces the apparent partisan polarization (Bullock et al., 2015), suggesting that surveys capture expressive partisan cheerleading that is unlikely to impact real-world behaviors.[7] Second, both of the examples that lead off this chapter are relatively recent, from the second decade of the twenty-first century. This is a period of historically high levels of partisan polarization, so it is not obvious whether similar dynamics are likely to operate in less polarized times and contexts.

To address both sets of concerns, I now turn to my empirical analysis of California ballot referenda. By examining voting behavior on actual policy proposals – which have real-world impacts, unlike survey responses – we can see whether voters continue to follow the leader under higher-stakes conditions. And by examining two cases from decades ago, the 1970s and 1990s, we can see whether the opinion dynamics we find in the modern era applied during these earlier years, when polarization was more muted – particularly the kind of "affective" polarization that makes political debates so divisive today.

Before turning to the data, I will describe the two ballot items, the associated campaigns and the two men behind these efforts whose names have been historically linked to the policy proposals.

The Briggs Initiative

Proposition 6 appeared on the California ballot in November 1978, the same day as the state's gubernatorial election. To understand its historical origins, it is important to recognize two other earth-shaking events that preceded the election.

---

[7] See Bullock and Lenz (2019) for a full review of the debates on this topic.

Four months earlier, California voters had approved Proposition 13, a constitutional amendment that dramatically reduced and capped the state's property taxes. Proposition 13 marked the start of a national property tax revolt and demonstrated what political scientist Dan Smith has called the "power of direct democracy" (Smith, 1998) – the ability of self-interested political entrepreneurs to take advantage of public concerns to change policy through the ballot box (see also Martin, 2008). And a year earlier, in 1977, voters in progressive Miami had shocked the nation by overwhelmingly repealing a local ordinance that had extended antidiscrimination protections to cover sexual orientation.

The Miami election represented a dramatic reversal for the gay rights movement, which had been on a roll by scoring political and policy victories through the organizing efforts that had followed the 1969 police raid on the Stonewall Inn in Greenwich Village, a watering hole popular among gay New Yorkers. In 1973, gay rights activists had convinced the American Psychiatric Association to remove "homosexuality" as a mental health illness from the *Diagnostic and Statistical Manual*. The Miami ordinance was one of many similar efforts to expand civil rights protections to gays and lesbians through local government policy change (Martin, 2015).

In Miami, however, the efforts sparked a countermobilization led by Anita Bryant, a beauty pageant queen and official brand ambassador for the Florida Citrus Commission. She called her campaign against the Miami ordinance "Save Our Children" and warned that the new ordinance would specifically protect gay teachers. "Homosexuals cannot reproduce – so they must recruit. And to freshen their ranks, they must recruit the youth of America," she warned (Smith-Silverman, 2020, p. 88). After the unexpected success in Miami, Bryant took her campaign on the road, using public referenda to successfully overturn local gay rights protections in other progressive strongholds, including St. Paul (Minnesota), Wichita (Kansas), and Eugene (Oregon). In some conservative states, including Oklahoma and Arkansas, state legislators responded to the gay rights backlash by passing legislation specifically prohibiting gays and lesbians from teaching in public schools.

Bryant's efforts attracted the attention of California State Sen. John Briggs, a conservative from Orange County. Briggs had thrown his hat into the race for the Republican gubernatorial nomination in 1978. But far behind in the polls, he withdrew before the primary and redirected his ample war chest to a new passion project: A direct initiative to outlaw homosexual teachers in the classroom, just as Oklahoma and

Arkansas had done. Thanks to his financial support, which paid for petition signature collectors, the proposal qualified for the November 1978 ballot.

During the campaign on behalf of the measure, Briggs would prove to be absolutely unabashed in his homophobia. "If you look like a duck and you walk like a duck, my friend, you're a duck. If you have a proclivity for having sex with young boys or people of your own gender, then you ought not be put in a position where you are going to be tempted," he said in an extensive interview with the *Los Angeles Times* (Scheer, 1978). In another interview, he told a different reporter, "If you'd put a second-grade child with a homosexual, you're off your gourd. We don't allow necrophiliacs to be morticians. We've got to be crazy to allow homosexuals who have an affinity for young boys to teach our children" (McMillan, 1978).[8]

The campaign to defeat the Briggs Initiative, as it came to be called, was led by David Mixner, a veteran political operative and long-time gay rights activist. But things were not going well. In late September, the California's leading pollster, Marvin Field, released the results of a statewide survey showing that voters supported Proposition 6 by nearly a 30-point margin – with 61 percent planning to vote in favor compared to 31 opposed. Mixner complained he was having a hard time raising money, blaming a "climate of fear" that had caused most traditional gay rights supporters in Hollywood to not contribute out of worry they would be labeled homosexuals themselves (Cannon, 1978).

With less than two months to go, Mixner decided his only hope was a Hail Mary pass – an endorsement from a prominent conservative Republican. And he could think of no better person that fit the bill than the state's former governor, Ronald Reagan. Using his connection within the Reagan world – a close advisor to the former governor who was himself a closeted gay man – Mixner was able to secure a fifteen-minute face-to-face.[9] Always the strategist, Mixner thought his best bet was to appeal to Reagan's law-and-order instincts, warning that the measure

---

[8] Modern-day readers might be struck by the parallels to the charges of "grooming" that have characterized recent education policy debates related to sexual orientation and gender identity.

[9] Mixner would later recall that he and the advisor – "He was married in California; he was gay in Washington" (Kirchick, 2022, p. 366) – had met at Denny's located in heavily Hispanic East Los Angeles, where they knew they would not run into any other Republican who might recognize them.

would undermine classroom discipline. He later recounted the meeting in his biography:

Mixner: Governor, you know about this initiative that would allow any school child to file a complaint about any teacher that he thought was homosexual. This initiative would create anarchy in the classroom. Any child who received a failing grade or was disciplined by a teacher could accuse the teacher of being a homosexual. Teachers will become afraid of giving a low grade or maintaining order in their classroom.

Reagan: I never thought about that. It really could happen, couldn't it?

M: Governor, the kids will control the classroom. Teachers will be terrified of their students. It will be chaos.

R: You mean, *any* accusation by a student must be heard by the school board? (Mixner, 1996, pp. 149–150)

A few days after the meeting, Reagan released a statement formally opposing the initiative. "I don't approve of teaching a so-called gay lifestyle in our schools, but there is already adequate legal machinery to deal with such problems if and when they arise," he explained, warning that the measure "has the potential of infringing on basic rights of privacy and perhaps even constitutional rights" (Mixner, 1996, p. 347). And one week before the election, Reagan would dedicate his regular newspaper column to making the case against the ballot measure as well as Proposition 5, another initiative that sought to ban smoking in public places. "Whatever else it is, homosexuality is not a contagious disease like measles. Prevailing scientific opinion is that in individuals, sexuality is determined at an early age and that a child's teachers do not really influence him," he wrote. "Will California rewrite that old line, 'As California goes, so goes the nation?' Here's one heterosexual non-smoker who, where Proposition Five and Six are concerned, hopes the answer is 'no'" (Boyarsky, 1981, p. 181).

Reagan's statement and column attracted considerable attention from other media sources and featured prominently in radio and television advertisements run by the campaign to defeat the Briggs Initiative. In late October, a new round of polling had found sudden shift in public opinion, with a majority now planning to reject it. Although a number of other prominent conservatives had also come out against the measure in the weeks leading up to the vote, including actor John Wayne and Proposition 13 author Howard Jarvis, most observers believed that Reagan's outspoken opposition had been pivotal. "The Reagan endorsement had a devastating effect on the Briggs campaign," the director of the *Los Angeles Times* poll recalled. "I could see no other reason for it going that way except for the Reagan endorsement. I was stunned to see it going the way it was going" (Boyarsky, 1981, pp. 180–181).

On Election Day, the ballot measure secured support from only 41 percent of voters – a striking reversal from polls taken just weeks earlier. Mixner had become convinced that Reagan's last-minute intervention had been critical – and so had Briggs. "That one single endorsement – Ronald Reagan's – turned the polls around," the senator complained. "I can't believe the Hollywood crowd has gotten him to take that kind of position" (Boyarsky, 1981, p. 181).

The Unz Initiative

The second empirical case I consider in detail in this chapter is Proposition 227, which appeared on California's June primary ballot in 1998. The measure sought to ban bilingual education in the state – and to understand the unique politics of the issue, it is important to back up and spend sometime describing both its primary backer, Silicon Valley millionaire Ron Unz, and the broader political history of bilingual education.

In 1999, Unz's face appeared on the cover of the *New Republic* next to the banner, "This Man Controls California." The featured article focused on his role in the Proposition 227 campaign and another ballot measure, to reform campaign finance and redistricting, Unz had been working on. Describing his spartan, ramshackle living arrangements in a $1.5 million Palo Alto home, the author wrote: "The bathrooms are dirty, and the dust is thick. There's no one who comes in to clean, no photos on display, and no escaping the thought that a well-heeled businessman has to have a screw loose to live this way" (Miller, 1999). The author of the profile seemed on the fence – was Unz "a benevolent philosopher-king" or "some mad political equivalent of Dr. No who's turning California, and potentially the nation, into his policy plaything?"

The few readers who recognize Unz's name today probably know it from the *Unz Review*, his webzine that has been called a white nationalist publication by the Southern Poverty Law Center. Unz, a prolific writer, has made headlines in recent years for pieces he has written supporting David Irving, a Holocaust-denying historian, and for endorsing claims that the Israeli national intelligence agency, the Mossad, had been heavily involved in both the JFK assassination and the terrorist attacks on 9/11. (Unz is himself of ethnically Jewish background.)

However, it would be a mistake to caricature Unz and his writing. When I reached out to interview him, Unz encouraged me to read his voluminous written record – and within days, three books arrived at my home that Unz had apparently ordered via Amazon, compilations of his highest-profile articles, self-published by the Unz Press. Probably his most well-known piece, "The Myth of American Meritocracy," which came out in the paleoconservative *American Conservative* in 2012, was the first to make the argument that Ivy League universities were discriminating against Asian applicants and was cited repeatedly in *Students for Fair Admissions v. Harvard*, the lawsuit that would lead the Supreme Court to end affirmative action in college admissions. At the time of publication, however, what attracted the most attention about the article was his claim that Jews were massively overrepresented in elite universities, prompting a wonky but heated debate over the "Weyl Analysis," an algorithm Unz had relied on to identify the share of Jews among National Merit Scholarship semifinalists.

Indeed, the best adjective to describe Unz is "heterodox." In other articles, also published by the *American Conservative*, he had taken on orthodoxies favored on the political right, challenging the idea that IQ was genetically determined by comparing test scores of East and West Germans[10] and arguing that Mexican immigrants were not more likely to commit crimes than Anglos, as some had claimed. The correlation, he concluded, was a statistical mirage driven by differences in the age distribution across racial groups and the fact that criminality was concentrated among the young. During the pandemic, he apparently alienated many *Unz Review* readers by endorsing the consensus view in favor of vaccination.

Although I didn't read everything Unz sent me, I came away with the impression that he was a very intelligent and serious thinker who enjoyed engaging in arm-chair social science. Quirky, out-of-main-stream ideas clearly appealed to him – especially if they were buried as brief asides or tables in 500-page soporific scholarly tomes.

---

[10] In 1994, political scientist and demographer Charles Murray coauthored *The Bell Curve*, which documented big difference in test scores across racial groups and suggested that this might be in part due to differences in genetic endowments. The book set off a political firestorm and made Murray a *persona non grata* in polite progressive circles.

Unz had made his millions founding a financial software company that was among the first to repackage mortgages into securities after graduating from Harvard with a double major in theoretical physics and ancient history. In 2024, he would have easily fit the profile of a Silicon Valley tech bro straight out of central casting – smart, quirky, Stanford dropout,[11] and obsessed with his own idiosyncratic political passion projects. Think Mark Zuckerberg, Elon Musk, or Sam Bankman-Fried. Unfortunately for Unz, he came of age three decades earlier, when this type of thing was still viewed as an oddity.

Unz emerged on the California political scene in 1994, when the thirty-two-year-old launched a self-funded campaign for the Republican gubernatorial nominations, taking on the sitting incumbent. Unz styled himself as a more conservative alternative to fellow Republican Gov. Pete Wilson, who he accused of being a RINO ("Republican in name only.") Wilson easily captured the nomination, but Unz spent $2 million of his own money and came in second, with a third of the vote. The campaign prompted a number of articles about the curious Silicon Valley millionaire, which all stressed his apparent peculiarities. A profile had quoted Wilson's campaign spokesman who had called one of Unz's early employers and reported back that the young whizkid had listed his IQ on his resume – 214. One journalist even interviewed his mother, who had raised Unz as a single mom while relying on public assistance. She was puzzled by her son's hard-right turn, but nevertheless said she was confident he would make a great governor. "Now all I can hope for is he will have some time for extracurricular life. And get a girl," she told the reporter. "Because he's had so few in his life."

The 1994 gubernatorial election would prove to be important for the Proposition 227 campaign four years later. With California's economy mired in recession, Wilson was lagging in the polls behind his Democratic opponent, State Controller Kathleen Brown, the sister and daughter of two former California governors. In a desperate bid, Wilson decided to yoke his reelection to Proposition 187, a measure appearing on the same ballot as the gubernatorial contest that sought to deny public services to undocumented immigrants. The now-infamous ad for the measure, funded by the Wilson campaign, showed a video of families running down the freeway across the Mexican border. With intense music in the background, a dark voice warned, "They keep coming; 2 million illegal immigrants in California."

---

[11] Unz had enrolled in the physics PhD program in the early 1980s.

Both Wilson and Proposition 187 would win by surprising blowout margins – Wilson leading Brown by 15 points.[12] However, many observers now believe it was a hollow victory, marking a turning point when Latino voters in California began to abandon the Republican Party and in the process transform the state into the deep blue, one-party fiefdom it is today (Bowler, Nicholson and Segura, 2006). Importantly, Unz had vocally opposed Proposition 187 and even spoke at the largest rally against it. But the campaign and Wilson's divisive brand would cast a shadow over the subsequent Proposition 227 effort.

The 1994 gubernatorial primary also foreshadowed for the ballot measure campaign four years later. Although Unz was highly critical of Wilson's embrace of Proposition 187 – and generally worked hard to portray himself as the pro-immigrant candidate – he also attacked the governor for allowing bilingual education to continue in California schools. Indeed, criticizing bilingual education was one of the key planks of Unz's 1994 platform in his failed bid for the gubernatorial nomination.

Just like the efforts to outlaw homosexual teachers in 1978, the California bilingual education debate had its genesis in Miami.[13] After the Cuban revolution, the city had experienced a historic influx of Cuban refugees, and in the early 1960s Miami public schools begun experimenting with a program that taught students – both Cuban and American-born – in Spanish for part of the day. The program was well received (Crawford, 1989). After the immigration boom that followed the historic loosening of national immigration laws during this period, support for bilingual education was written into federal law,[14] on the theory that it was most effective to teach children core academic subjects in their native language, to ensure they could remain on track, while they learned English.[15]

---

[12] Proposition 187 would be later struck down by the Supreme Court as unconstitutional.

[13] As historians have noted, the earliest debates about the language used in schools date back even earlier, to the anti-immigrant backlash that followed World War I and the related effort to inculcate more "patriotic" education into the school system (Tyack and James, 1985).

[14] Because the law applied only to districts receiving funding from a specific federal pot, which remained limited, its actual impact was modest.

[15] In the 1974 case *Lau v. Nichols*, a unanimous Supreme Court ruled that the San Francisco school district had violated federal law by not providing supplemental language services to non-native English speakers. Although the court did not require bilingual education as the only allowable remedy, subsequent guidelines on complying with the ruling, issued by the US Commissioner of Education, imposed such a requirement under certain conditions.

What was an admittedly technical policy question that had attracted minimal attention gained prominence in 1980 when, on the eve of that year's election, federal education officials announced a new regulatory proposal to effectively mandate bilingual education nationally. The move was interpreted by some as a campaign stunt designed to help President Jimmy Carter court Hispanic voters but had the apparent effect of increasing the salience and partisan valence of the issue (Crawford, 1989). Carter lost in a landslide, and the new Reagan administration moved quickly to reverse his policy pronouncement. In the same election, voters in Miami's home county made English the official language, prohibiting the use of taxpayer money for "promoting any language other than English or promoting any culture other than that of the United States" (Wildermuth, 1986).[16] When William Bennett became Reagan's education secretary in 1985, he launched an all-out campaign against bilingual education. "Perhaps no aspect of education policy in the United States excites political passions more than bilingual education," a *New York Times* reporter wrote in a deep-dive on the issue that year. "With thousands of jobs and several billion dollars in federal and state funds at stake, bilingual education that has divided educators, produced unlikely alliances, and raised fundamental social issues" (Rohter, 1985). "Bilingual education has become a code word for larger social tensions in the nation as a whole," the president of a major education foundation agreed. "Schools are the battleground for the issue of whether the nation can once again embrace a new group of immigrants whose native language is not English" (Fiske, 1985).[17]

While some of the growing opposition reflected sincere concerns about the efficacy of the method – several rigorous evaluations had found scant evidence that bilingual education produced better academic outcomes than other alternatives, including the much-reviled "sink-or-swim" English immersion – the issue was also caught up in a brewing culture war over multiculturalism versus assimilation. Although originally sold to policymakers as a superior pedagogical method to improve academic achievement in math, science, and social studies, bilingual

---

[16] The ordinance came in the wake of the Mariel boatlift, which brought nearly 125,000 new Cuban refugees to the county. The measure would be repealed thirteen years later.

[17] Although Bennett was the public face of the opposition to bilingual education, the issue did not breakdown purely along partisan lines and sometimes made for strange bedfellows. For example, legendary American Federation of Teachers President Albert Shanker, a vocal critique of nearly every aspect of Reagan administration education policy, backed Bennett's call to end bilingual education.

education was also seen by many of its proponents as a broader political project, designed to help minority children remain connected to their native cultures and identities. For many militant multiculturalists, the purpose of bilingual education was cultivating ethnic solidarity, not English proficiency or success in traditional academic subjects (Ravitch, 1983, pp. 271–280). This is one reason why progressive educators, including "whole language" reading advocates (discussed more in Chapter 4), were vocal supporters. Viewed through the lens of cultural preservation, rather than merely effective content knowledge communication, it made sense to keep immigrant children (and maybe even US-born children of immigrants) in bilingual education as long as possible, even after they had achieved English proficiency.

In 1986, the national debate had reached California, which at the time had one of the strictest bilingual mandates in the country. That November, California voters overwhelmingly approved an amendment to the state constitution making English the official language of the state. Although much of the debate and campaigning surrounding the measure focused on other cultural issues, Republican Gov. George Deukmejian pointed to the referendum to justify his decision to veto a renewal of the state's bilingual education law, which had recently barely passed the state legislature on a tight, party-line vote. In practice, Deukmejian's veto had minimal impact. Entrenched deep within the state's education bureaucracy, which reported to an independently elected state superintendent, bilingual education enthusiasts continued to insist districts provide bilingual education on the threat of losing state funding.

After the 1988 presidential election, however, the issue lost its partisan edge almost as quickly as it had gained it eight years earlier. Republican President George H. W. Bush appointed a vocal bilingual education supporter as his education secretary, and much of the California political establishment had moved on.

But by all accounts, bilingual education had become a complete disaster in the state. With immigration numbers rising quickly, districts struggled to hire a sufficient number of native-Spanish speakers. As a result, only a third of students eligible for bilingual services were receiving them, and the quality of these programs was highly uneven. Another third were taught by English-speaking teachers with the help of minimally trained and educated Spanish-speaking aides. "The greatest sin of bilingual education was that the neediest kids in the classroom were taught by the least educated adults," long-time *San Jose Mercury News* education columnist Joanne Jacobs, who wrote about the issue at the time, told me.

"What a horrible thing to do to these kids, who needed to learn at school because their parents couldn't teach them at home." The remaining kids were stuck in English-only classes, mostly taught under the same "sink-or-swim" model bilingual education proponents so abhorred. Since most of the existing programs focused on Spanish, other immigrant children – Russians, Greeks, and Vietnamese – rarely received any specific language services at all.

Academic achievement among English learners remained abysmal, and a 1993 report from the state's Little Hoover Commission, an independent oversight body, was absolutely scathing in its assessment of California's efforts and the bureaucracy that oversaw it (Little Hoover Commission, 1993). Since districts received more state money for students identified as having limited English proficiency, the report noted, schools were actually financially incentivized *not* to teach children English! Once a "good-hearted but vague impulse," bilingual education had become "a multi-billion-dollar hog trough that feeds arrogant education bureaucrats and militant Hispanic separatists," the libertarian *Reason* magazine concluded in a cover story (Garvin, 1998).

Behind the scenes, a bipartisan group of lawmakers sought to broker a compromise. The state would continue to allow for bilingual education – but also provide school districts with legal flexibility to consider other options. Year after year, however, the bill would die in committee, the victim of intense lobbying from ethnic advocacy group, including the Mexican American Legal Defense and Educational Fund, and the legislature's increasingly powerful Latino Caucus, which remained ideologically committed to bilingual education. One leader of the compromise effort was state Sen. Dede Alpert, a former school board member from a beach community north of San Diego. Aware of the growing backlash, Alpert had approached the Latino Caucus to present her middle-ground plan. Afterward, she had noticed that the microphone had mistakenly been left on, so she could hear the caucus deliberate – which largely consisted of trashing her proposal. "They weren't going to support a compromise, they weren't interested in that," she recalled.[18]

This is when Unz reentered the story. Although he was skeptical of the broader 1980s English-only efforts, Unz always thought bilingual education was a crazy theory, imposed by activist groups and fringe academics abetted by out-of-control bureaucrats. After all, neuroscientists had long

---

[18] Defender of the status quo argued the state had never adequately funded the program. It was wrong to say bilingual education had failed if it had never been done the right way.

known that it is easier to learn a new language at a younger age. But bilingual education delayed English instruction for years, until kids were older, flipping the widely accepted conventional wisdom on its head.

Sitting down to read the *Los Angeles Times* on Valentine's Day in 1996, Unz was amazed by an article on the front page of the metro section: A group of 63 Latino parents had decided to boycott their central Los Angeles Ninth Street elementary school because it insisted on putting their children into bilingual classes instead of teaching them in English as the parents preferred, despite repeated letters, requests, and petitions (Pyle, 1996).[19] Like the majority of California children in bilingual programs by this point, many of the kids were American-born citizens, yet they were placed in Spanish-language classes simply due to their ethnicity. Unz knew the California bilingual education law had expired a decade earlier, thanks to the Deukmejian veto, but that Latino pressure groups had ensured that the legislature would not act on the compromise plan being pushed by Alpert. Only by going directly to the voters, via direct democracy, could the problem be solved. And so the idea for Proposition 227 was born.

After investigating the accuracy of the boycott story (it turned out to be true), Unz recruited some of the families involved and teamed up with Alice Callaghan, the Episcopalian priest-activist for homeless and immigrant rights who ran the downtown Los Angeles community center where the protest had been organized, to help him draft the language. They came up with a simple title for their measure: "English for the Children." Under the proposal, English learners would be placed into an intensive, one-year sheltered English immersion program and then into regular, mainstream courses after that. Parents who preferred to keep their kids in bilingual programs could do so, but only by applying for a waiver from the local district. Unz then used his own money to get the measure qualified on the ballot and began making the media rounds to sell the proposal to the voters. At almost every interview and debate, he would begin with the story of the Ninth Street elementary walkout.

Early independent polls, fielded even before the measure qualified on the ballot, showed it overwhelmingly popular, with support from over 60 percent of both Democrats and Republicans and – perhaps most unexpectedly – nearly two-thirds of Latino voters. Additional support

---

[19] Local officials disputed the parents' claims, arguing that they had not followed the proper administrative procedures.

came from other unlikely sources: In Los Angeles, which had the largest bilingual education program in the state and where bilingual teachers received a $5,000 stipend, a grassroots group of teachers pushed through a referendum among the general union membership on whether to support Unz's initiative. Despite heavy lobbying in opposition from the entire union leadership team, nearly 48 percent of Los Angeles educators voted to support the bilingual education ban.

However, the effort to pass Proposition 227 had come at an awkward time. The divisive-anti-immigrant legacy of Proposition 187 remained fresh in everyone's mind. And in 1996, California had lived through another bitter direct democracy battle over race – Proposition 209, a state constitutional amendment that outlawed affirmative action. Much of the television coverage was predictable: Here was another Republican with an immigration-related proposal trying to feed off the culture wars. Was Proposition 227 just the latest effort, a sequel to 187 and 209?

A television panel on the issue, part of a public affairs program on a Los Angeles-area station, that was aired in July 1997 captured the dilemma. The roundtable featured Unz, famed Republican political consultant Allan Hoffenblum, business strategist Rick Reidy, and Los Angeles League of Women Voters President Xandra Kayden:

Hoffenblum: There's a perception within the Latino community that the Republican Party is anti-Mexican, anti-immigrant. And you're dealing with bilingual education – where obviously we have people from throughout the world, multiple cultures and languages, but the dominant one is from Latino immigrants who speak Spanish. ... Why isn't a Latino out in front talking about this? Because I think surveys show the majority of them opposed to bilingual education. We need to make sure this is not another conservative Republican attempt to bash Mexicans.

Unz: I agree with you 100 percent. In fact that is my single biggest concern in the campaign, to make sure it's not perceived as anti-immigrant or anti-Latino. ...

Reidy: I sort of feel like we're sitting around the table – what Alan was saying. It's like a group of men talking about the abortion issue. There's nobody who needs bilingual education here. ...

Kayden: We've gone through several election cycles of very divisive – painful – separation of communities in California. ... I trust your intentions, I have no doubt about your good intentions, ... but I think the initiative process again, one after another, is absolutely deadly. It's going to be very difficult to take away the kind of rumor-mongering and demagoguery that we have seen.

In an effort to separate his initiative from the stench of Proposition 187, Unz made clear he did not want Wilson's support. And the governor, still bitter over the 1994 reelection campaign when Unz tried to rob him of his nomination, seemed happy not to help his former foe. To ensure that other anti-immigrant groups would not become the public face of the initiative, Unz wrote in a poison pill – a $50 million program to provide English tutoring for adults. (The adults, in turn, would have to promise to help teach children English – a clever workaround to comply with the one-subject rule for ballot measures.) Finally, he sought out prominent Latinos to speak out publicly against bilingual education. One of the people recruited by Unz to serve as honorary chairman of the "English for the Children" campaign was Jaime Escalante, the legendary East Los Angeles AP Calculus teacher whose story was the basis for the movie "Stand and Deliver." "It's good to have bilingual teachers who speak two languages. But if you teach the kids in Spanish, you're not preparing them for life," Escalante explained. "In this country, we negotiate in one language and you have to master that language to be successful. And it's English" (Skelton, 1997). The strategy seemed to work. Although many newspaper editorial boards came out in opposition to the measure, it continued to receive favorable coverage on the news pages and maintained a large lead in polls across parties and demographic subgroups.

At the same time, opponents of the measure were pursuing the exact opposite strategy. The name of their political committee – "No on Unz" – made clear their goal was to frame the measure in the context of broader political debates and highlight the measure's backer, a prominent Republican. A month before the election, they finally convinced President Bill Clinton – who had earlier indicated his plans to stay out of the campaign – to come out against the measure. However, his opposition was halfhearted. Acknowledging the problems with the existing programs, the president proposed an alternative plan to limit bilingual education to three years and transition children to English classrooms thereafter.[20]

Proposition 227 would appear on the same June ballot as the 1998 gubernatorial primary. In an unusual development, Spanish-language television channel Univision hosted a joint debate among all of the candidates from both major parties in late May, simulcast in Spanish. The company's chairman, A. Jerrold Perenchio, an Italian-American, had been a large Wilson donor four years earlier and had taken heat from

---

[20] For the few California children that received actual bilingual education at the time, it was not unusual to stay in the program for six years.

immigration activists, who accused him of hypocrisy – making his fortune off Latinos while bankrolling an anti-immigrant candidate. In 1998, Perenchio donated to nearly every gubernatorial candidate,[21] regardless of party, and had given generously to the effort to defeat Proposition 227.[22] Univision had run public service announcements against the measure multiple times per day. At the debate, each candidate was asked to state their position on Proposition 227. All – three Democrats and the one Republican, Attorney General Dan Lungren – said they opposed the measure. Their answers were quickly cut into a devastating campaign ad (also funded by Perenchio). "Candidates for governor disagree on just about every issue. But they all agree Proposition 227 won't teach kids English," the ad began, before splicing in each candidate's statement from the debate.

Unz, who had been closely tracking the polls, told me the damage was almost immediate. After maintaining strong bipartisan support for over six months, polls showed a large drop off among Democrats. The final shoe dropped just weeks before the election. With members of the Latino Caucus concerned about the polling numbers, Alpert's compromise bill final gained traction and moved quickly through the legislature, a last-ditch effort to show that the reasonable concerns about the existing bilingual education programs were being addressed without the initiative. Just days before the election, however, Gov. Wilson announced that he had vetoed the bill – and threw his support behind Proposition 227. Unz was not happy. "It is very unfortunate that the governor has chosen to endorse our initiative," he said in a terse statement. "It would be grossly opportunistic and deceitful if our opponents seized upon Wilson's endorsement to attempt to discredit those of us involved in the campaign who have worked so hard over the past year to improve public education of California's immigrant children" (Ingram, 1998).

On Election Day, Proposition 227 still won easily. But exit polls showed it had lost more than a third of its initial Latino support, and a large partisan gap had opened up among voters, with Republicans backing the measure by nearly 30 percentage points more than Democrats (Barabak, 1998).

---

[21] One wealthy Democratic candidate, Al Checchi, was self-funding his campaign and did not accept contributions.
[22] Perenchio's motivations were perhaps self-interested. If more Latinos became proficient English speakers, would fewer watch his Spanish-language channel?

Quantitative Evidence

If the theory of elite opinion leadership I introduced in the first part of this chapter is correct, the narrative accounts of both Propositions 6 and 227 yield clearly divergent empirical predictions. In both cases, a prominent Republican governor made a last-minute, unexpected endorsement. But the effect should have produced divergent results, muting partisan divisions on Proposition 6 and exacerbating polarization on Proposition 227. In this section, I provide original analysis to demonstrate that this prediction fits the data quite well.

Specifically, I have collected city-level returns for both initiatives and linked the results to voting behavior in the gubernatorial elections that took place on the same days. In 1978, the referenda appeared on the general election ballot, so we can compare the relationship between support for Proposition 6 to the share of votes cast for the Democratic and Republican gubernatorial candidates in each municipality. These data come from hand-coding the Supplemental Statement of the Vote released by the California secretary of state. In 1998, Proposition 227 appeared on the same ballot as the gubernatorial primary, so I add up the share of votes cast in each municipality in the Democratic versus Republican primaries. The data is aggregated up from census block-level files maintained by the UC Berkeley Statewide Database.

The results are summarized visually in Figure 3.1, which presents a binned scatterplot – combining cities with similar levels of Democratic candidate support into buckets – showing the relationship between votes in the partisan gubernatorial races and support for each ballot initiative. Overlayed on top of the scatter plot are two dashed lines estimated using Ordinary Least Squares regressions run on the raw (unbinned) data. Both measures did better in more heavily Republican cities, but the relationship was far stronger for Proposition 227 ($r = 0.85$) than for Proposition 6 ($r = 0.32$). The numerical results are even more striking: Although Proposition 227 outperformed the earlier initiative by nearly 50 percentage points in the most heavily Republican cities, opposition to the two measures was virtually indistinguishable in Democratic strongholds. In each case, the pattern in the figure shows an almost perfect reversal of the Field Poll results revealed just a month before each respective election.

When I shared these results, Alpert, the former state senator, was quite surprised, her perception still influenced by early polling showing strong bipartisan support for the bilingual ban. Unz, by contrast, had seen nearly similar patterns in the polling data. Both, however, pointed to the same

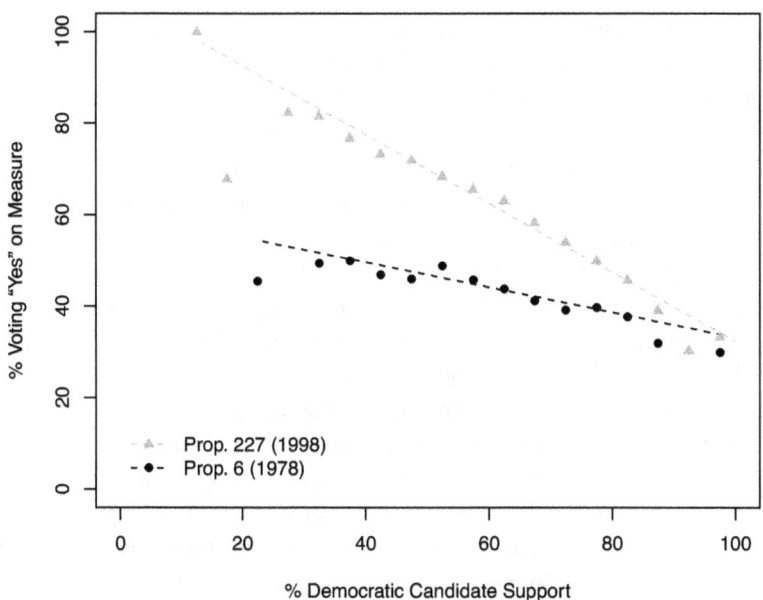

FIGURE 3.1 Relationship between city-level voter partisanship and support for two California education ballot initiatives

explanatory variable: elite partisan endorsements. "The other thing is that [Proposition] 187 proved to be a wake up to the Latino community. Saying, 'What is somebody doing here in in our state?' and getting more active, getting more people involved in office, probably putting more money into opposing or getting other Democrats to stand up to oppose this initiative," Alpert told me. Unz was more blunt when speaking about the effect of Wilson's endorsement: "It's sort of like if you're endorsed by Satan right before the election. That doesn't help your results with people who don't like Satan."

Yet other prominent Republicans, including the party's legislative leader and its gubernatorial candidate, had come out against Proposition 227. Why didn't this, and the Perenchio ads, reduce support among Republican voters in the same way that Wilson's endorsement turned off Democrats? "With Republicans, there was more of an even division of elite sentiment," Unz hypothesized, pointing to support the measure received from other high-profile Republicans, including Los Angeles Mayor Richard Riordan. The campaign may have also reminded both Democrats and Republicans of the partisan valence surrounding bilingual education, both in California and nationally, during the Bennett years, bringing voters from both sides back into their partisan folds. For Republicans, the strong initial support for Proposition 227 was entirely in line with long-run opposition to bilingual education. Among Democrats (and Latinos), the early support was a departure from prior eras, and the campaign reminded them of the "correct" side for their team.

This explanation echoes an argument made by political scientists Andrew Gelman and Gary King in a famous paper published three decades ago (Gelman and King, 1993). Polling during presidential campaigns is quite volatile, they noted, reacting to each gaffe, scandal, and development. Yet the outcomes of presidential elections are quite predictable based on a handful of variables – macropartisanship and economic fundamentals – known months before each election. The answer to this apparent paradox is that campaigns matter a great deal but do so in a predictable way – essentially reinforcing existing partisan loyalties and economic considerations. The consequence is that voters "com[e] home to their natural preferences" (p. 431). In the Proposition 227 campaign, coming home meant increasing opposition among Democrats.

A NEW ERA OF POLARIZED EDUCATION POLITICS?

The argument in this chapter has two important, practical implications for the future of education politics and policy. First, it suggests that partisan polarization is a top-down, elite-driven process. Prominent political officials stake out divergent policy platforms, and then their copartisans follow, not vice versa. Second, if this argument is correct, we are likely to see far more polarization over education among regular voters in the coming years than was the case during the first two decades of the twenty-first century.

In retrospect, the late 1990s through the years of the Obama administration were marked by a surprising bipartisan elite consensus on education, focused on standards, testing, and accountability. This consensus reflected an unusual alignment of interest groups – civil rights activists, long concerned about teachers' low expectations for poor students of color, and business groups focused on improving the quality of America's workforce (Rhodes, 2011). AEI's Rick Hass has called this halcyon time as the era of "Bush-Obama school reform," reflecting the bipartisan coalition that spanned the two administrations (Hess and McShane, 2018). Yet this reform coalition has largely unraveled since President Obama left office. One indicator, as journalist Jonathan Chait has written, is the evolving language regarding school choice policies written into the Democratic Party platform drafted as part of each presidential election contest (Chait, 2021). In 2000, the platform promised to "triple the number of charter schools in the nation." Twenty years later, it took a much more skeptical view: "Democrats believe that education is a public good and should not be saddled with a private profit motive, which is why we will ban for-profit private charter businesses from receiving federal funding. And we recognize the need for more stringent guardrails to ensure charter schools are good stewards of federal education funds."

This growing elite divide is increasingly filtering down to the masses, as my model of top-down opinion change would predict. In a recent study, for example, David Houston has shown that voters have begun to polarize on many major educational issues, with Democrats and Republicans increasingly sorting themselves along partisan lines (Houston, 2024).[23] Focusing on the subset of individuals surveyed repeatedly over time, he found the sorting "is overwhelmingly the result of individuals switching their issue positions to align with their party affiliations rather than switching their party affiliations to align with their issue positions," (p. 510), echoing the results of Gabe Lenz's research. However, the gaps Houston found in recent surveys are still relatively modest on most issues[24] – smaller than the divide among partisan elites – suggesting that polarization has only begun and is likely to get much worse.

The tendency for adult conflict over educational issues to coincide with broader partisan divisions represent a significant change. Although debates about the nature of public education – and the content of public school curricula – have always been political, school leaders were generally "successful in absorbing, co-opting, and deflecting" such challenges, historians David Tyack and Elisabeth Hansot have written. "One sign of their success in defusing conflict was that the major American political parties, unlike their counterparts in nations like England and Germany, rarely differed substantially about educational policy" (Tyack and Hansot, 1981, p. 3). This is no longer the case, and it remains unclear how well our existing political institutions of local democratic control of schools will fare as they face this new challenge.

---

[23] Similarly, Jensen et al. (2021) find that, aside from unions, education is the one policy area related to local economic development policy where voters are polarized along partisan lines. These authors specifically focus on attitudes toward charter schools and private school vouchers.

[24] For example, Houston found surprisingly little disagreement over annual testing and school vouchers.

Despite the overwhelming evidence of elite influence on public opinion, important puzzles remain. It is still much easier to document polarization after the fact than to predict the issues on which voters are likely to move apart. It is also unclear why elite endorsements sometimes move copartisans, such as Ronald Reagan's opposition to Proposition 6, but at other times seem to radicalize the other party, as with Wilson's endorsement of Proposition 227, Trump's support for school reopening, and Obama's advocacy on behalf of Common Core. Understanding when elite messages rally copartisans and when they mobilize the opposition has important implications for strategy, and the conditions under which presidential "leadership" is likely to help rather than hurt legislative efforts. This is the question I turn to in the next chapter.

The final implication worth considering is for broader, normative debates about how to evaluate the performance of public schools. As I discuss in the introductory chapter, many left-of-center academics and activists remain skeptical of standardized tests and measures of school quality based on student performance on these exams. Schools, they argue, exist to serve a broader range of stakeholders and should be evaluated by how well they channel vision and values of their community (e.g., see White et al., 2023). Proponents of this view assume, usually implicitly and but sometimes explicitly, that the relevant metric is fidelity to public opinion. Are school districts responsive to the preferences of the relevant stakeholders? And are local voters satisfied with the quality of the education they are getting?

The problem with this perspective, however, is that it largely sidesteps the question of where voter preferences come from, and why different communities prefer different policies. In other word, this approach treats public opinion as "exogenous," rather than itself the end product of the political process. The alternative account presented in this chapter, focusing on top-down opinion change, suggests that public opinion is often "endogenous," and this makes alignment between public policy and voter preferences a much less satisfying metric by which to judge whether public schools are doing a good job – particularly when public opinion and student interests and outcomes are not closely aligned.

4

All Curriculum Politics Is National

> When we do not have definitive research to answer a question about policy or practice, we can easily slip over the line and privilege ideology and belief over other evidence.
>
> —P. David Pearson, "The Reading Wars"

The first thing I noticed about North Dakota Rep. Corey Mock, as I read his biography in preparation for our interview, was his birthday – just two weeks before my own. But he had accomplished a lot in the first thirty-eight years of his life. Mock was elected to his state legislature in 2008, making him a seasoned veteran by the time we spoke more than a decade and a half later, and he had been an active participant in many education policy debates. Between 2012 and 2018, Mock was involved in Democratic leadership in his chamber, serving as the minority leader for the last two years, before founding a bipartisan leadership caucus.

I reached out to Mock because North Dakota, like many red states, has been riven by educational controversies in recent years. In particular, I was interested in two bills that had passed in the previous legislative session. Both sought to impose new curricular standards and regulate what teachers did in the classroom. But one had passed on a near-party-line vote, while other enjoyed large bipartisan majorities. I wanted to ask why Mock himself had voted yes on one bill (along with a majority of his Democratic colleagues), but no on the other (along with nearly all Democrats). A similar pattern had been playing out in state after state.

Chapter 3 demonstrated how the growing nationalization of American politics has contributed to the increasingly polarized public opinion on a variety of education policies. In this chapter, I shift focus from the *masses*, the regular voters, to examine the behavior of *elites* – the elected officials like Rep. Mock who actually write education policies at the state level.

Specifically, I focus on political conflicts over state academic and curricular standards – the topic of the two North Dakota bills. Adult disagreements about what American children should (and should not) be taught in our schools are age-old phenomena. Typically, these debates play out behind the scenes – in the pages of dense academic articles published in scholarly journals read by very few people and through concerted lobbying and advocacy efforts of particularly motivated "political entrepreneurs" who work to popularize obscure theories and subsidize the cost of translating these often abstract ideas into concrete policies (Mintrom, 1997). Occasionally, however, these conflicts capture national attention when they intersect with the most salient political issues of the day or when the relevant policy fault lines happen to fall along existing identity-based alliances. This occurred in the 1920s, with the famous Scopes Monkey Trial and a series of efforts by Christian fundamentalists to outlaw the teaching of evolution (Larson, 2003), and again in the early 2000s, surrounding efforts by the President George W. Bush to limit federal funding for sex education to curriculum that focused exclusively on abstinence (Irvine, 2004).

In this chapter, I zoom in on two other more recent curricular controversies and related state legislative efforts to regulate how American history and elementary reading skills are taught in the classroom, the topics of my conversation with Rep. Mock. The first debate, surrounding the extent to which so-called Critical Race Theory (CRT) along with diversity, equity, and inclusion (DEI) have infiltrated public schools, attracted particular attention among the political right since the publication of the *1619 Project*, a special 2019 edition of the *New York Times* Magazine that sought to reframe American history around the introduction of chattel slavery into the Americas and the broader contributions of African-Americans to our collective history. As I discuss in the next section, this was not the first time debates about history curriculum – and the extent to which it should celebrate the aspirations of America's founding principles or highlight the many shameful episodes when the country failed to live up to them – came to dominate policy debates.

The second argument, about the role that systematic phonics instruction should play in teaching early elementary students to read, has earned an even more prominent place in historical curricular battles. In his *Atlantic Monthly* article on the California "reading wars" of the mid 1990s, journalist Nicholas Lemann observed that "the two sides have one of the purest and angriest disagreements I've ever encountered" (Lemann, 1997, p. 129). Lemann quoted an anonymous lawmaker: "We're in the midst of a huge war." Another source used even more evocative language, telling Lemann, "This is worse than abortion."

In recounting how these once-arcane academic debates became the central focus of state education policy innovation in the early 2020s, I highlight the fascinating parallels between these two issues. Both include outsized roles played by two public media personalities – PBS documentarian turned conservative provocateur Christopher Rufo and American Public Media investigative journalist Emily Hanford – whose relentless (and some might say obsessive) focus on these curricular issues helped attract newfound attention from parents, activists, and ultimately state policymakers.[1] Both illustrate the challenging dynamics of translating complex – and often unsettled – scholarly debates about research methodology and epistemology into nuanced policy recommendations made amid heated national political campaigns.

Perhaps most interesting and revealing are the divergent political coalitions that have pushed through state legislation in these areas in recent years. Although both curricular issues raise broader normative and theoretical questions related to teacher autonomy and expertise and the desirability of political oversight of schools, efforts to use legislation to standardize both reading and history instruction have followed quite different paths. In reading, new "science of reading" laws have in most cases been adopted by overwhelmingly bipartisan coalitions, largely erasing the partisan polarization that characterized policymaking on this issue in the 1990s and early 2000s. By contrast, anti-CRT bills have been passed with almost exclusively Republican votes – often in the same states and during the same sessions as the reading legislation. North Dakota's experience, in other words, had been replicated in state after state.

In describing and ultimately helping explain these diverging dynamics, my account leverages a variety of information sources and modes of inquiry. I complement large-N, quantitative analysis of state legislative roll call votes with original interviews with a broad set of informants, including education scholars and researchers, prominent policy activists, and ultimately the elected officials themselves. As I discuss in the concluding section, the recent wave of state curricular policymaking also can

---

[1] In another fascinating parallel, Columbia linguist and *New York Times* columnist John McWhorter played a supporting role in both debates, harshly criticizing *1619 Project*-inspired history curriculum and repeatedly advocating in favor of phonics.

also inform theoretical models of federalism, presidential leadership, and the emergence of bureaucratic cultures – topics relevant in many policy spheres outside of education.

HONEST HISTORY OR POLITICAL INDOCTRINATION?

The country we know today as the United States of America was not founded in 1776, with the signing of the Declaration of Independence on July 4, but rather in August of 1619, when the first ship carrying enslaved Africans reached the colonies. So argued the editor's note leading off the special August 2019 issue of the *New York Times Magazine* titled the *1619 Project*. The note continued:

This is sometimes referred to as the country's original sin, but it is more than that: It is the country's very origin.

Out of slavery – and the anti-black racism it required – grew nearly everything that has truly made America exceptional: its economic might, its industrial power, its electoral system, diet and popular music, the inequities of its public health and education, its astonishing penchant for violence, its income inequality, the example it sets for the world as a land of freedom and equality, its slang, its legal system and the endemic racial fears and hatreds that continue to plague it to this day. The seeds of all that were planted long before our official birth date, in 1776, when the men known as our founders formally declared independence from Britain

In the lead essay of this issue, journalist Nikole Hannah-Jones argued perhaps even more provocatively, "Our founding ideals of liberty and equality were false when they were written. Black Americans fought to make them true. Without this struggle, America would have no democracy at all." Hannah-Jones would go on to win the Pulitzer Prize for Commentary for her essay, and the special issue of the magazine would fly off newsstands, with copies appearing on eBay at significant markups.

Almost immediately, however, the publication generated significant questions about the historical accuracy of some of its most controversial arguments – including the claim in Hannah-Jones's essay that the founders "believed that independence was required in order to ensure that slavery would continue." "Some might argue," she concluded, "that this nation was founded not as a democracy but as a slavocracy."

A group of prominent academic historians quickly challenged this claim in a letter written to the newspaper's top editors. Although the historians were sympathetic with the broader goal of making slavery a more central theme in the understanding of American history, they objected to what they described as clear factual errors in the piece. "These errors, which concern major events, cannot be described as interpretation or 'framing.' They are matters of verifiable fact, which are the foundation of both honest scholarship and honest journalism. They suggest a displacement of historical understanding by ideology," the historians wrote.[2] In a separate, blistering piece written for *Politico*, another historian, Northwestern University scholar of African-American Studies Leslie Harris, revealed that she had "vigorously disputed" the claim that the Revolutionary War had been fought to protect slavery during the *Times*' fact-checking process, only to see it remain in the published article (Harris, 2020b).

In response to growing criticism, the magazine's editor declined to issue a correction, writing: "Within the world of academic history, differing views exist, if not over what precisely happened, then about why it happened, who made it happen, how to interpret the motivations of historical actors and what it all means."[3] (However, the paper did slightly edit the introductory language of the online version of the magazine.)

The controversy may have remained limited to the pages of national news outlets and social media were it not for the decision of the *Times* to partner with the Pulitzer Center[4] to develop school curriculum organized around the magazine. The specter of a disputed historical account – depicting an unconventional theory for the causes behind American independence, written by an avowedly political journalist and challenged by a number of respected historians – being adapted for wide classroom use attracted considerable attention among prominent conservatives. In February 2020, Robert Woodson, an African-American economic development advocate, organized an effort he called "1776 Unites," featuring the voices of well-known right-of-center African-American academics and intellectuals writing in response to the *1619 Project*.[5] These efforts

---

[2] Although most of the criticism focused on lead essay penned by Hannah-Jones, some also found questionable assertions in other pieces in the magazine, including an essay by sociologist Matthew Desmond linking slavery and capitalism and claiming, incorrectly, that certain modern accounting practices have "roots [that] twist back to slave-labor camps."

[3] The *Times* published the historians' original letter as well as its response, and both are available at www.nytimes.com/2019/12/20/magazine/we-respond-to-the-historians-who-critiqued-the-1619-project.html.

[4] Despite the same name, the Pulitzer Center is not affiliated Columbia University, which awarded the Pulitzer Prize.

[5] The essays would be published in 2021 in a book titled *Red, White, and Black: Rescuing American History from Revisionists and Race Hustlers*.

would only accelerate in the aftermath of the murder George Floyd that May, which set off a wave of racial justice protests and a more general racial reckoning.

Over the summer of 2020, growing conservative criticism of the publication gave rise to political action. Arkansas Sen. Tom Cotton introduced legislation, "Saving American History Act of 2020," that sought to cut federal funding to schools that incorporated the *1619 Project* into formal instruction. Although the proposal quickly died, copycat bills were also introduced in several state legislatures.[6] The issue gained new political prominence when President Donald Trump, responding to anonymous tweet claiming that the *1619 Project* was being taught in California schools, announced that the federal government was investigating the matter. "Department of Education is looking at this. If so, they will not be funded!" he wrote in an early morning tweet on Sunday, September 6.

The president would return to the topic several times throughout the course of that fall's presidential campaign, including by issuing an executive order the day before the November election establishing a "1776 Commission." The order cited a "a series of polemics grounded in poor scholarship [that] has vilified our Founders and our founding" and claimed that, "[d]espite the virtues and accomplishments of this Nation, many students are now taught in school to hate their own country, and to believe that the men and women who built it were not heroes, but rather villains."[7]

The early criticisms of the *1619 Project* curriculum – perhaps fueled by the salience of the election and raw debates unfolding over the summer of 2020 – soon merged with broader conservative attacks on government and corporate diversity, equity, and inclusion efforts. This campaign was spearheaded by Christopher Rufo, a one-time documentary-maker and failed Seattle city council candidate. Working as a fellow at the right-leaning Manhattan Institute, Rufo had begun publishing exposés on controversial DEI trainings – starting with his home city of Seattle. Diving deep into the footnotes of some of the training materials, Rufo discovered that many of the ideas had been drawn from scholars advocating for a mode of legal and social analysis known as Critical Race Theory. This scholarship emphasized the importance of implicit (as opposed to

---

[6] A group of students in my American State Politics class interviewed the author of the Arkansas bill for a project in spring 2021. He specifically cited Cotton's bill as an inspiration.

[7] The commission issued its widely panned report, calling for "patriotic education," the following January, just days before the inauguration of President Joe Biden.

explicit) biases, examined how racial inequities were sometimes built into the structures and institutions of American government and society, and criticized the aspirational ideal of race-blindness associated with earlier civil rights leaders, including Martin Luther King (Wallace-Wells, 2021).

Rufo caught the attention of President Trump during one of Rufo's appearances on conservative cable television and soon incorporated criticisms of the *1619 Project* into broader legislative packages seeking to ban teaching that promoted "divisive concepts," encouraged racial resentment, or rejected the view that slavery and racism represented failures to live up to America's founding principles, rather than inherent motivations for the country's independence. The Rufo-inspired proposals became the basis for model state legislation and legislative efforts that would continue even after the change in presidential administrations.

History Conflicts, Old and New

That political backlash would come in response controversial history curriculum would not have surprised veterans of similar battles, which date back to at least the mid 1800s, when Northern and Southern states adopted markedly different approaches to teaching about the Civil War. The unique political sensitivity of history instruction should not be surprising. "The American people care deeply about the history their children learn. Study of the past, after all, embodies many of the most fundamental messages we, as a nation, wish to send to young citizens," a trio of distinguished historians wrote in a volume on the history of history wars (Nash, Crabtree and Dunn, 1997). "The past we choose to remember defines a large measure of our national citizens. The past we choose to remember defines in large measure our national character, transmits the values and self-images we hold dear, and preserves the events, glorious and shameful, extraordinary and mundane, that constitute our legacy from the past and inspire our hopes for the future" (p. IX).

The authors were speaking from personal experience: In the early 1990s, they became themselves entangled in a deep and highly partisan conflict over efforts to develop a model, nationally endorsed history curriculum. Under President Bill Clinton's signature education program, dubbed "Goals 2020," states were expected to develop uniform standards across many subjects and submit them for federal government review and approval. In 1994, a history center at UCLA released a list of proposed national history standards that quickly attracted conservative ire. Lynne Cheney, the former head of the National Endowment for the Humanities during several Republican presidential administrations and wife of future Vice President Dick Cheney, panned the proposed standards as providing "a very warped view of American history" and complained, "They make it sound as if everything in America is wrong and grim" (Associated Press, 1994). Republicans would win control of Congress a few weeks later and quickly defund the Clinton initiative, causing the issue to fade from the headlines.[8]

A similar controversy would arise exactly two decades later. In 2014, the College Board – which administers the Advanced Placement exams that high school students take to earn college credit – announced the first major reworking of the "framework" for the AP U.S. History exam in more than half a century. Although the revision reflected teacher demand for greater clarity and specificity of the topics and skills students needed to master for the test, decisions about what was included versus excluded as well as the choice of some politically charged adjectives used to describe figures such as Ronald Reagan quickly prompted a wave of criticism. In a resolution blasting the new framework, the Republican National Committee charged that the redesigned course "reflects a radically revisionist view of American history that emphasizes negative aspects of our nation's history while omitting or minimizing positive aspects"[9] Unlike the editors of the *New York Times*, who doubled down in the face of conservative criticism, the College Board quickly acknowledged the validity of some of the complaints and reached out to critics, inviting them to participate in further revisions. The deliberations and further changes seemed to produce what one initially critical historian described as a "an impressive middle ground" (Simon, 2016).

These were, however, only the most recent salvos in the history wars (for detailed overview, see Jost, 1995; Zimmerman, 2022). During the early decades of the twentieth century, for example, critics attacked what they saw an intentional rewriting of the history of American independence to provide a more favorable depiction of the British – America's newfound ally in World War I. During the 1920s, Chicago Mayor "Big Bill" Thompson led an organized effort to push out the city's superintendent and remove what he saw as "biased" history textbooks. "I will never

---

[8] Gearing up for his ultimately unsuccessful presidential campaign, Senator Majority Leader Bob Dole would echo Cheney's criticism the following year, telling an audience at a meeting of the American Legion that the proposed standards "disparage America and disown the ideas and traditions of the West" (Schoenberg, 1995).

[9] Available at https://prod-cdn-static.gop.com/docs/RESOLUTION_CONCERNING_ADVANCED_PLACEMENT_US_HISTORY_APUSH.pdf.

rest until the histories in use in the Chicago public schools are purged of their pro-British propaganda," Thompson had thundered (Zimmerman, 2022, p. 9).

Indeed, the record reveals three important patterns in the past battles over history curriculum. First, the political sensitivity of history instruction has, in previous eras, reflected the geopolitical climate of the times and tended to focus on the boogeyman of the moment. Thus, during the Cold War, much focus turned on rooting out what some had seen as anticapitalist, pro-Communist propaganda. Second, the geopolitical conflicts were most likely to escalate into curricular battles when they happened to coincide with broader activist movements within the academy. Many Progressive education reformers, for example, made little secret of their admiration of the Soviet Union – at least until Stalin's staged show trials to purge his political enemies. This made it easier for critics of Progressive pedagogy to accuse them of being Soviet stooges, a criticism that befell Progressive historian Harold Rugg, who had authored a widely used history text in the 1930s that included some passing critiques of American consumerism.[10]

Third, as the Progressive era illustrates, conflicts are particularly likely to arise when political activists attempt to use school curriculum as a tool in a broader campaign to promote what they view is unobjectionable, positive social change. In the late 1980s, for example, debates about history instruction were hijacked and co-opted by broader political conflicts over multiculturalism. Well-meaning and quite reasonable efforts to ensure that voices of racial and ethnic minorities found more prominent representation in the textbooks sometimes went overboard. For example, one such campaign to promote "Afrocentric" education that centered and celebrated the contributions and history of ancient African civilizations quickly crossed over into outright racism and anti-Semitism. A prominent advocate for Afrocentric education, City University of New York political scientist Leonard Jeffries, made national headlines when he claimed that the trans-Atlantic slave trade was a conspiracy organized by Jewish entrepreneurs and that Jews had partnered with the Italian Mafia to build "a financial system of destruction of Black people." World history, Jeffries argued, needed to be understood as a race war between the "Ice People" of European descent and the dark-skinned "Sun People," with

---

[10] A number of groups, including the American Legion, were outraged over what they saw as Rugg's "socialistic" slant and led a national campaign to have his textbook removed from schools around the country.

the amount of melanin in one's skin also correlating with physical and intellectual prowess (Taub, 1993).

Many of the same considerations shaped the political reception to the *1619 Project*. What some saw as a reasonable and overdue effort to more prominently center the history of African-Americans and popularize ideas from more recent (and still contested) historical scholarship others interpreted as just the latest effort by deranged activists in the mold of Jeffries to hijack history education to brainwash America's youth using fringy and debunked ideas.

READING WORLD WAR III

Just as with high-profile national arguments about social studies, debates about the proper way to teach reading date back almost to the very beginning of American public education (Mathews, 1966). For the first century, they surrounded the process and order in which reading skills should be taught – pitting supporters of the "ABC method," which focused on students first mastering the alphabet, against their arch-rivals, who argued that students should begin by memorizing whole words, with appreciation of individual letters to follow. The latter group enjoyed the support of one of the most prominent educational reformers of the nineteenth century, Horace Mann, the founding secretary of the Massachusetts Board of Education. Mann, who famously described letters as "skeleton-shaped, bloodless, ghostly apparitions," became an early and vocal advocate on behalf of the whole-word method. John Dewey, the father of the modern Progressive education movement, was another promoter, worrying that the skills-based approach associated with traditional "phonics" instruction put too much emphasis on dull and tedious drilling of students on letters and letter-sound correspondence, destroying children's innate love of learning.[11]

By the late 1950s, phonics appeared to have decisively won the debate. Growing American anxiety about falling behind the Soviet Union in the space race coincided with the publication of Rudloph Flesch's *Why Johnny Can't Read*, an unexpected 1955 bestseller that blamed poor

---

[11] Dewey was not particularly interested in curriculum for traditional academic subjects or in providing formal instruction in skills like writing, reading, or spelling, believing that "the true way is to teach them incidentally as the outgrowth of the social activities." However, his experimental school had to use *some* method of reading instruction, and he endorsed the whole-word method promoted by his University of Chicago colleague Francis Wayland Parker (Mathews, 1966).

reading proficiency of American children on the widespread use of whole-word instruction. As Harvard literacy researcher James Kim has written, "In the context of the cold war, Flesch's back-to-basics, phonics-first, message was embraced by many politicians and citizens who feared that the American educational system was losing ground to the Russians" (Kim, 2004, p. 91). Despite a growing research base of experimental studies providing empirical evidence for the superiority of the phonics method, the new consensus would not survive the end of the 1960s, however.

The second round of reading wars again pitted phonics against a newcomer, which came to be known as whole language. Although whole-language proponents lodged many of the same complaints about the drudgery of phonics instruction as advocates of the earlier whole-word method, they offered a fundamentally different vision of how reading should be taught. In the interest of space, I will not dive into the fascinating details behind the philosophical, methodological, and theoretical foundations of whole language – entire books could be (and indeed have been) written about this topic.[12] Instead, I will briefly summarize the key points of disagreement that divided whole-language and phonics supporters:

- A central tenet of phonics instruction is that reading is an unnatural act for which the human brain has not intentionally evolved. Thus, teaching children to master reading requires systematic and explicit, teacher-led instruction and individual practice, starting with basic skills including phonemic awareness (breaking down spoken words into individual sounds) and phonics (learning the correspondence between written letters and these sounds). Whole language rejects this belief, arguing that learning to read is as natural as learning to speak, and that students immersed in rich and authentic literature will naturally pick up the essential skills on their own, without explicit instruction.
- While phonics prioritizes teaching students the various letter-sound patterns that characterize much of the English language, whole-language proponents argue that English is far too complex – combining influences from many other languages, producing too many caveats, exceptions, and irregular spellings to be accurately summarized by a small set of simple rules of thumb. The extent to which

---

[12] Interested readers can find useful overviews in Kim (2004) and Pearson (2004).

most written English follows predictable rules and the impediment that exceptions pose to a rules-based approach to teaching reading remains a significant point of disagreement between the two camps.
- Given the importance of letter-sound correspondence, phonics-based instruction requires that students begin with appropriately sequenced decodable texts that limit the vocabulary to words following standard spelling and pronunciation conventions students have learned up to that point. Whole-language proponents find decodable readers too limiting and inauthentic – "linguistically vapid" (Strauss, 2005, p. 27) – preferring to expose children to richer, more traditional texts, including those using irregular spelling structures and letter combinations about which early readers may not have received systematic instruction (to the extent that they received any systematic instruction at all!).
- Perhaps more abstractly, the two camps also disagree about the purpose of reading instruction and the processes by which reading mastery is achieved. Although both sides acknowledge that the ultimate goal of reading is *comprehension* – understanding the messages and ideas encoded in the written word – phonics supporters believe young readers must begin by developing a toolbox to decode written texts and "attack" or "solve" unfamiliar words. Whole language begins with the end point, arguing that the purpose of reading is to construct meaning out of written texts and that decoding the structure of written language by breaking words down into the letters that compose them is only one of several strategies readers can use to extract such meaning.
- Ultimately, the core of the disagreement is about the essential ingredients in the recipe that leads to good readers. Phonics proponents believe these ingredients include set of learned skills that must be taught by a teacher and practiced repeatedly. Reading is a marathon, and before one can run, the child has to learn to crawl and then walk. Whole language proponents believe the essential ingredient is student motivation to find meaning in texts. Such motivation comes only from exposure to interesting and relevant texts, and boring skills-based practice only erodes it.

Most relevant to the present account, and to me the most fascinating aspect of this story, is that the scholarly debate about reading instruction that heated up again in the 1970s took on a strikingly partisan and ideological valence, spilling out of academic journals into political debates.

During my research, I interviewed many observers and participants of the reading wars, asking each the same question: How did phonics become seen as the Republican way to teach reading, while whole language come to be considered the Democratic method? Each offered a plausible answer to this question – but, strikingly, nearly every person's account was a different one!

Harvard's James Kim hypothesized that the ethos of student-centered pedagogy emphasizing teacher autonomy and empowerment that provided one of the philosophical foundations for whole language appealed to teachers and their unions, a core part of the Democratic political coalition. Reading researcher Tim Shanahan, who served on the congressionally mandated National Reading Panel (NRP) in the late 1990s – which I will discuss in more detail in the next section – pointed me to a 2000 *Chicago Tribune* article claiming that Republican presidential hopeful Barry Goldwater had written a pro-phonics plank into the 1964 Republican Party platform. A closer look at the actual platform, however, revealed nothing about reading instruction, although I did discover that the late conservative firebrand (and Goldwater supporter) Phyllis Schlafly was a vocal phonics supporter and had written her own book, the *First Reader*, extolling the method.[13]

Perhaps the most compelling account for the politicization of reading instruction was offered by Linda Diamond, a long-time phonics advocate in California and co-founder of the Consortium on Reaching Excellence in Education, which played a prominent role in legislative debates about reading instruction in that state in the 1990s. Many whole-language supporters, Diamond told me, had become enamored with *Pedagogy of the Oppressed* by Brazilian educator Paulo Freire. A foundational text in critical pedagogy, the 1968 book brings a stridently anti-colonial, Marxist lens to debates about education methods. Recounting Freire's experience teaching reading to indigenous peasants, the book "used a naturalistic approach, and that became very appealing in this sort of Progressive education world" that characterized much of the whole-language movement, Diamond told me.

---

[13] The website selling Schlafly-branded merchandise notes: "It is important to use *First Reader* before the child is taught wrong habits, such as pretending to 'read' by looking at pictures, guessing what is in the text or memorizing a story." As discuss in more detail (Section "'Phonics' to 'Science of Reading'"), this language mirrors recent arguments against the "three-cueing" method widely used in schools today and the target of recently passed "science of reading" bills.

Progressive educators had long complained that "traditionalists" – including phonics proponents – were too obsessed with promoting efficiency and workforce skills (e.g., Kliebard, 1995). This privileged the demands of capitalism and employers over student needs. And to many, teacher-led direct instruction, the preferred method in the phonics camp, felt too authoritarian and top-down. For this community of scholars and educators, whole language's philosophical commitment to student-centered learning was particularly attractive.

Regardless of the original reason for why scholarly debates about reading instruction became so intimately intertwined with modern American partisan politics, the connection was clear to all combatants in the reading wars. Summarizing this political ethos, one group of scholars has written that "whole-language instruction [was] seen as a means for advancing a political agenda descending from earlier Progressive movements in education. They [saw] education as a vehicle for individual liberation and the classroom as a model for an egalitarian society, in which each individual is free to develop at his or her own rate" (McKenna, Stahl and Reinking, 1995, p. 213).

The partisan valence – and the widespread view among activists that phonics was inherently a "conservative" approach to reading – clearly rankled many prominent phonics proponents, most of whom saw themselves as political liberals who believed helping disadvantage children master reading was essential to delivering both racial and economic equity. Cognitive scientist Keith Stanovich, who authored some of the earliest path-breaking empirical research on the psychology of reading starting in the 1970s, seemed clearly offended by the notion that phonics supporters were just Republican apparatchiks when I asked him about the partisan divide. "We were called right-wing by the whole-language proponents, but that was a strategy to discredit us among teachers," he told me. "The final irony here is that the teaching method that really supercharges social class differences in achievement is whole language!"[14]

---

[14] In a book compiling his highest-profile research, Stanovich criticized whole-language proponents for their dogmatic politics: "We must stop creating a progressive politics where to be of the left you must oppose science. We must stop expelling people from the progressive coalition unless they check their brains at the door.... The cleavage between progressive social policies and scientific research that the extreme whole language advocates have caused in the field has many negative effects, not the least of which is that it gives right-wing forces a club with which to attack teacher autonomy and progressive educational reforms" (Stanovich, 2000, p. 387).

"They all called us right wingers just because we were phonics people," Linda Diamond explained, emphasizing her own progressive bonafides – her mother had served as president of the Southern California Democratic Club and her father, a self-avowed Communist, had been hauled in to testify before the House Un-American Activities Committee during Sen. Joe McCarthy's Red Scare. P. David Pearson, a long-time literacy scholar and retired dean of the UC Berkeley School of Education who describes himself as a "moderate" in the reading wars, told me nearly all of the phonics supporters he knew were progressives ideologically sympathetic with the "Bernie Sanders wing" of the Democratic Party – a far cry from the right-wing stereotype associated with the approach.

California Dreams or Nightmares?

By the mid 1980s, whole language was clearly ascendant in the educational zeitgeist. Writing in 1989, Pearson seemed almost astounded by its takeover of the education world:

> The reading field seems to have a special knack for attracting wide-scale reforms – one after another, after another, after another. But never have I witnessed anything like the rapid spread of the whole-language movement. Pick your metaphor – an epidemic, wildfire, manna from heaven – whole language has spread so rapidly throughout North America that it is a fact of life in literacy curriculum and research (1989, p. 230).

As I discuss in the concluding section of this chapter, it should not be surprising that many educators – and, more importantly, professors teaching in the colleges of education that prepare future teachers – found much to like with the whole-language paradigm. It's focus on student-centered pedagogy and emphasis on having students "construct" individual meaning out texts aligned well with the dominant theoretical paradigms popular among education scholars. This is also one reason why many anti-racist texts, including those that would ultimately become targets in the CRT-debate, saw wide adoption on education school curricula several decades later.

As whole language gained new adherents, supporters flexed their political muscles – for example, pushing for laws that prohibited the use of state money for phonics-adjacent curriculum such as spelling books (Kim, 2004). California represented the first major political showdown, where whole-language supporters would win the battle but perhaps also lay the foundation for losing the broader war.

In 1982, California voters elected an energetic education reformer Bill Honig as state superintendent. The Democrat promised a "back to basics" overhaul of the state's education system and oversaw the development of several statewide "frameworks" to provide guidance to textbook publishers and local districts about curricular expectations. At the time, the social studies framework attracted the greatest attention and controversy – pitting advocates of multiculturalism who demanded greater focus on the perspectives and contributions of various underrepresented minorities and traditionalists who believed the history books underplayed the influence of Christianity on the country's history and traditions. Honig seemed to endorse both views, and the final framework called for a spicier approach to history instruction that required schools to "accurately portray the cultural and racial diversity of our society" while recognizing the "centrality of Western civilizations as the source of American political institutions, laws and ideology." When activists on the left remained unsatisfied, objecting that the additional focus on minorities was full of stereotypes and was still presented from a white perspective, Honig fired back, calling critics "tribalists," "separatists," and out-of-touch academics who "make a livelihood discrediting broader cultural ideas" (Reinhold, 1991).

On reading, however, Honig seemed to embrace whole language – by accident, he later claimed. Honig agreed with whole language's embrace of authentic texts in the classroom in place of monotonous worksheets, drills, and short, poorly adapted excerpts. The reading framework rejected dumbed-down textbooks and called on schools to have students read great literature. Conspicuously, the document spent little on basic reading skills, including phonemic awareness and phonics – lessons previously covered in the disfavored textbooks.

Whether Honig realized he had thrown his support behind whole language or whether he had been hoodwinked remains unclear. Writing in the *Atlantic*, Lemann described Honig as a "privileged idealist from San Francisco, tall, skinny, and enthusiastic to the point of obsession." When I spoke to Honig, now in his mid 80s, he seemed to have the same energy and passion. Honig had always understood the importance of phonics, he told me, and took for granted that it was regularly taught in schools without being explicitly singled out in the state framework. "We really pushed literature. We wanted all kids to have a good basis in humanities," he said. "Our framework really pushed that.... What we screwed up on – I just assumed everyone would be teaching phonics, so we mentioned it but we didn't really push it. I've never heard of whole language, but whole language usurped that framework and said, 'See, you don't have to teach phonics!'"[15]

Whatever the intent, whole language came to dominate California reading instruction. In a survey administered alongside the 1992 National Assessment of Educational Progress, a federal exam designed to track changes in student achievement over time, 87 percent of California teachers reported heavy reliance on literature-based readings (vs. 50 nationally) and 52 percent reported little or no instruction on phonics (vs. 33 percent in other states) (Kim, 2004).

The 1992 NAEP, the first to produce separate test scores for each state, shook California education politics like an earthquake. Long seen as a national leader in academic achievement, the newly released scores had put California neck-in-neck with Mississippi at the bottom of the pack. "State's Pupils Among Worst in Reading," a front-page headline in the *Los Angeles Times* proclaimed the day after the results were released.[16]

Honig, by then forced out of office in a conflict-of-interest scandal, channeled his limitless energy into a new effort to restore phonics in California schools, bringing the passion and zealotry of a religious convert.[17] He teamed up with Linda Diamond, the CORE co-founder I quoted earlier in this section, and Marion Joseph, a retired aide to a former state superintendent and grandmother of a struggling reader. Together, they lobbied the legislature to pass new laws overhauling reading curriculum and teacher preparation – the "purest and angriest disagreements" Lemann noticed when he arrived in California to write his article – firmly entrenching phonics into state law. Apparently just as shocked by California's slide in the rankings, other states also followed suit. By 1997, nearly three dozen states had passed their own legislation emphasizing phonemic awareness and explicit phonics instruction (Kim, 2004).

---

[15] Other observers have a different memory of the events. Honig "was extremely naive," Tom Loveless, a curriculum experts who used to lead the Brookings Institution's education policy center, told me. "He fancied himself a progressive and he really fell in love with whole language."

[16] Although state officials blamed California's high immigrant population, this didn't appear to explain the abysmal results. The national exam allowed states to exclude non-native speakers with insufficient English proficiency – and California dropped 11 percent of the students in its sample, the highest rate in the country. California's native English-speaking Anglo students also scored in the bottom fifth of the country.

[17] Not everyone agreed that whole language was to blame for California's poor performance. Some officials also pointed to the education funding cuts that had followed the adoption of Proposition 13 in 1978, reducing local property taxes and capping their future increases.

At the end, the California legislative package passed by nearly unanimous margins, with little or no opposition to the relevant bills. Although no systematic analysis of roll call votes has been done in other states, a number of contemporaneous observers interpreted the new phonics push through a partisan lens. In a 2000 article titled, appropriately, "The Politics of Phonics," curriculum scholar Frances Paterson found that more sixty-five percent of the sponsors introducing phonics legislation at the state level were Republicans, with the rate increasing in later years. Paterson, an apparent whole-language sympathizer, also examined state party platforms and identified provisions supportive of phonics in six Republican platforms. Finding higher rates of introduction of phonics legislation and more mentions in party platforms in states with larger and more active "Christian right influence," Paterson concluded that the "Christian Right is a substantial force in the prophonics movement and in the movement's efforts to translate its advocacy of phonics into state statute" (Paterson, 2000, p. 137).

At the turn of the new millennium, several developments worked both to accelerate the push toward phonics – moving the issue from individual state legislatures to the national stage – and reinforce its connection to the Republican Party. The National Institute of Child Health and Human Nutrition, a national research agency led G. Reid Lyon, channeled increased funding on applied research rigorously testing alternative instructional interventions. Lyon became convinced about the efficacy of phonics and worked with members of Congress to promote it. In 1997, a Senate committee instructed Lyon to assemble an expert panel to carry out a meta-analysis of research in reading instruction in elementary grades, and in 2000, the final report from the resulting NRP made headlines, giving a strong endorsement for systematic and explicit phonics instruction.

Whole-language advocates were unimpressed. Most of the panel members, these advocates complained, were psychologists, cognitive scientists, and academics, rather than teachers. (The single educator on the NRP wrote a minority report, calling the document "unbalanced" and "irrelevant.") The meta-analysis included only quantitative research utilizing randomized controlled trials, ignoring the qualitative ethnographic research popular among whole-language scholars. And the executive summary to the panel's report, the portion of document that attracted the greatest popular and media attention, seemed to overstate the strength of the evidence found in the more detailed and nuanced 400-page body. For example, while the executive summary offered a full-throttled endorsement of phonics, the full report suggested that studies found significant differences only in the youngest grades.[18] These benefits were much more pronounced for word recognition than reading comprehension, the ultimate goal of reading, and even then the effect sizes were relatively modest, corresponding to a few months of additional learning. Adding insult to injury, the report also threw shade on independent reading by students – often known by the acronym of "SSR" or "sustained silent reading" when I was in school – a beloved practice among many teachers.

The divided reactions to the NRP report would, in many ways, explain the polarized nature of the subsequent response. In Washington, the document was released amidst a heated presidential campaign, with education a major focus. Texas Gov. George W. Bush, whose brother Neil had struggled with reading as a child and under whose watch Texas had experienced impressive growth on state standardized exam, promised to launch a "Reading First" initiative if elected using only proven, effective programs. After the election, Bush brought Lyon on as an advisor to help write the legislative language for Reading First. Working with Republican staff in the House, Lyon developed a $1 billion per-year program to provide grants to local school districts to help ensure that NRP-endorsed principles were used in the classroom. The proposal was rolled into President Bush's broader educational overhaul, the No Child Left Behind Act, and specified that funding had to be limited to curriculum and programs aligned with "scientifically based reading research."

The federal government's formal embrace of phonics sparked an immediate backlash. Whole-language proponents were apoplectic, writing book-length jeremiads with titles such as *Reading the Naked Truth: Literacy, Legislation, and Lies*; *Resisting Reading Mandates: How to Triumph with the Truth*; and *Big Brother and the National Reading Curriculum*. It was no coincidence that all of these volume were published by Heineman, a company largely unknown outside of education circles but with a catalog heavy on whole-language curriculum and authors.

Other curriculum providers whose materials were deemed to be out of compliance with the Reading First requirement took direct action, lobbying powerful members of Congress and filing formal complaints accusing bureaucrats in charge of implementation with conflicts of interest (Stern,

---

[18] In addition to phonemic awareness and phonics, the NRP also emphasized the importance of fluency, vocabulary, and comprehension. But the latter three skills appear to be much less controversial.

2008). The resulting investigation by the Department of Education's inspector general uncovered e-mails from the Reading First program's top administrator using shockingly salty language. "Beat the shit out of them," he instructed another staffer, referring to a curriculum program he thought did not comply with the law, "in a way that will stand up to any level of legal and [whole language] apologist scrutiny. Hit them over and over with definitive evidence that they are not [scientifically based] never have been and never will be. They are trying to crash our party and we need to beat the shit out of them in front of all the other would-be party crashers who are standing on the front lawn waiting to see how we welcome these dirtbags" (Office of the Inspector General, 2006).

In retrospect, President Bush's personal embrace of phonics may have, in the long-run, saddled the effort with political baggage. Bush would go on to become the most polarizing president up to that date, with the sharpest partisan divisions in approval between Democratic and Republican voters (Jacobson, 2006). After the debacle of the Iraq War, opposing the president's education initiatives became a rallying cry for congressional Democrats, NRP member and veteran of both the Bush and Obama administrations Tim Shanahan told me. "It became, you know, 'This is one way we get the Bush administration.... You know we can't stand up to him on defense. But we can stand up on education. And even if we were for this, and even if this is a good program, we're going to knock it down.' And that's exactly how it has played out."

For some teachers, an overwhelmingly Democratic profession, the association with the Bush administration made the push for curricular reform a nonstarter. "Forget it, I wasn't going to do any of that," one Seattle-area teacher told Emily Hanford for an episode of her podcast, "Sold a Story." "And, you know, I wasn't necessarily rejecting the curriculum as much as I was rejecting Bush."

Perhaps the most devastating blow came from Russ Whitehurst, a psychologist appointed by Bush to serve as the inaugural director of the Institute for Education Sciences (IES), an agency within the Department of Education that oversees the collection of education data and provides funding for research. IES was charged with evaluating the Reading First program, and the final report was full of disappointment. The evaluation used a rigorous regression discontinuity design, exploiting sharp cutoffs within districts that separated schools that were eligible for Reading First funding from those that fell just short of qualifying. It found statistically significant but substantively modest improvements in decoding skills among students exposed to the program and no difference in reading comprehension in early elementary grades.[19] "The administration was aghast because No Child Left Behind was essentially a reading intervention and Reading First was that intervention," Whitehurst told me. "So you find a whole political enterprise is threatened by one particular study." To make matters worse, a growing number of experimental evaluations of "Reading Recovery," an intense intervention program targeting struggling first-grade readers based on work of Australian psychologist Marie Clay and popular in the whole-language community but detested by many phonics advocates, found it to be highly effective, including a major IES-funded scale-up study (Sirinides, Gray and May, 2018). Based on this evidence, the program won a coveted top endorsement in the Department of Education's What Works Clearinghouse, an effort to synthesize research evidence and promote adoption of effective interventions, giving it a higher rating than another program favored in phonics circles. ("The What Works Clearinghouse was almost shutdown because of that," according to Whitehurst.)

With President Bush's approval ratings further eroded by the botched response to Hurricane Katrina, Democrats took control of Congress in 2006. In 2008, Democratic President Barack Obama succeeded Bush, and the party quietly cut off future funding to the Reading First program, just as the Republicans had done with President Clinton's history curriculum push fourteen years earlier.

From "Phonics" to "Science of Reading"

Although education remained a top priority for the Obama administration, the president's focus was elsewhere – on improving teacher evaluations, increasing access to high-quality charter schools, and encouraging states to adopt more rigorous college and career-readiness standards (see Chapter 3). With the spotlight largely off reading instruction, the two sides of the reading war settled into an uneasy détente. Many schools embraced what they called "balanced literacy," combining phonemic awareness and phonics instruction – although much less structured and systematic than phonics proponents believed was necessary – with whole-language curriculum and approaches, such as guided reading and reading workshops. Many others continued to encourage struggling readers to use "cues" to solve unknown words they confronted in their reading –

---

[19] Phonics defenders complained the evaluation was too underpowered statistically, lacking sufficient precision to identify significant effects.

perhaps trying to sound them out, but also guessing the word based on the picture in the book or the first letter of the word, a practice anathema to phonics supporters who believed it instilled poor habits that would come back to haunt them later.

As I show in the next section, this uneasy peace would collapse by the early 2020s, with the third round of reading wars erupting in state legislatures after the pandemic. What ultimately caused this conflagration? Once again, many of informants I interviewed offered very different hypotheses, so I will do my best to briefly summarize the many separate developments that likely contributed to returning reading to the political agenda.

The first event was a rebranding of phonics as the "science of reading" by Kate Walsh, then-president of the National Council of Teaching Quality, a think tank established by the right-of-center Thomas B. Fordham Institute to advocate for better teacher preparation and merit pay. "It's kind of silly story, but when we were writing about reading twenty years ago, everyone was referring to good reading instruction as 'SBBR,' which stood for Scientifically-Based Reading Research – hardly a good way to engage the general public!" Walsh recalled. "I just said, 'We're just going to have to call this by something else and came up with the "science of reading.'" It stuck – for good or for bad" (Pondiscio, 2022).[20] In retrospect, this would prove to be a brilliant move. Amidst the COVID-19 pandemic in 2020, "follow the science" became a popular motto among anti-Trump liberals.

The second factor, according to many observers I interviewed, was increasing mobilization and advocacy among parents of dyslexic kids. Dyslexia is an umbrella term for learning disabilities affecting reading development. In the years leading up to the pandemic, many parents of dyslexic children became convinced that whole-language instruction had contributed to their child's difficulties and that more sustained and systematic phonics-based teaching would allow them to become skilled readers. "Their kids are really struggling, and they're probably going to struggle, no matter what kind of instruction they're getting," Shanahan told me. "But they're struggling and those parents want help, and they aren't necessarily getting that. And some of those folks are very political."

---

[20] Based on an extensive search of digitized books, Shanahan (2020) found that the term "science of reading" actually came into pedagogical use in the 1830s. However, more recent Google search trends data do confirm that the expression really took off in the second half of the 2010s.

Kareem Weaver, an award winning Oakland educator and long-time phonics advocate who now leads the education committee of the region's branch of the NAACP, also suggested that the pandemic itself helped mobilize parents around reading reform. "It was like crying wolf and people weren't paying attention. Then came the pandemic," Weaver recalled about his advocacy efforts. "And that's when it was all of a sudden people at home and you hear your kid in another room doing their reading lesson and the parents thought, 'What in the world what did that teacher say? Wait, wait, wait! You're supposed to *guess* the word, what's the context, what does it look like?' And all of a sudden parents say, 'Hold on, wait, that's not how I learned it. Baby, read this passage to me.'"

In spring 2022, another study also attracted a wave of attention in the education research community. The same team that had carried out the original "Reading Recovery" evaluation a decade earlier had gone back to examine how students had done several years after completing the program. What had originally been a big positive effect in first grade, however, had not only eroded over time but had actually flipped signs by the time students were in fourth grade (May et al., 2023). In other words, struggling first-graders who had received the intervention were doing *worse* three years later compared to peers who had not. Although the follow-on study had major limitations – including significant attrition in the sample and challenges harmonizing scores on exams used in different states – the results seemed to confirm many phonics advocates' arguments that the cueing stratagems taught to struggling young readers would lead them to develop bad habits and leave them poorly positioned to handle more challenging texts.[21]

Everyone I spoke with, however, agrees that Emily Hanford's podcasts through APM Reports, an investigative journalism spinoff from the Minnesota-based public radio broadcaster, played an important role in raising the salience of the issue. She released her first podcast in early autumn 2018, titled "Hard Words: Why aren't kids being taught to read?" The piece attracted attention among education policy nerds and some interest in trade publications such as *Education Week*. Although she would release several more follow-up pieces, her biggest hit would be

---

[21] Of course, "Reading Recovery" was not *just* a cueing intervention, so the negative impacts could have been driven by other parts of the program. But the same critique can be applied to research claiming to show efficacy of this approach, which often examine programs that bundle cueing with other interventions (e.g., Scanlon and Anderson, 2020).

an investigative series titled "Sold a Story," which hit the internet in fall 2022. In addition to explaining how whole language had come to dominate teacher education, Hanford's series revealed salacious details about the revenues Heineman made selling its whole-language curriculum to big districts and noted that one Heineman author – a retired education professor from my university – had purchased a Maserati with the profits she made from her materials. "Her reporting stood out. And at this stage, there have been a number of reporters around the country that are on that beat, and really kind of trying to do the same story in their local communities," Shanahan explained. "So it's multiplied."

Just as California's dismal performance on the 1992 NAEP set the stage for the state's reading battles, subsequent national tests also contributed to reframing narrative around how poor teaching has contributed to low student achievement. The 2019 release of the NAEP identified Mississippi – ranked forty-ninth in the country in 2013 – as leading the pack in terms of growth, and the only state posting significant improvements in fourth-grade reading. "What's up in Mississippi?" Hanford asked in a 2019 commentary about the so-called Mississippi miracle. "There's no way to know for sure what causes increases in test scores, but Mississippi has been doing something notable: making sure all of its teachers understand the science of reading" (Hanford, 2019).[22] In 2013, the state had toughened its reading accountability laws, including mandatory retention for third-graders whose reading fell short of grade level. In addition, the state allocated new funding to improve teacher training, ensuring that all teachers understood how to implement phonics-based instruction. Mississippi, and its legislative package, would become the template for many states as they would turn to retool their own laws after the pandemic.

CURRICULUM IN THE STATE HOUSE

The first part of this chapter provides the backstory for how and why CRT-related and reading bills achieved such high billing on education agendas in many states by the early 2020s. In this section, I turn to examining how these bills ultimately fared on their way through the legislative process.

---

[22] As with California in 1992, others challenged the idea that change in reading instruction were responsible for the "Mississippi miracle" (e.g., Thomas, 2019).

All Curriculum Politics Is National 121

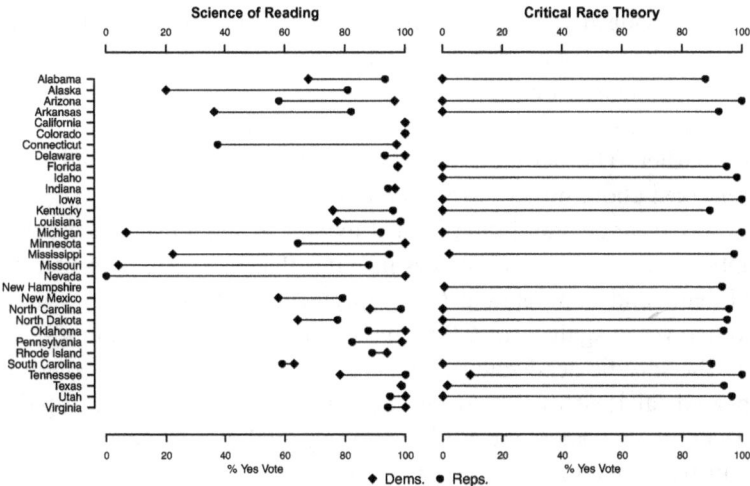

FIGURE 4.1 Legislative roll call votes on Critical Race Theory bans and "science of reading" legislation

The analysis focuses on final passage votes on all CRT and "science of reading" bills in lower (and larger) houses of state legislatures, regardless of whether these bills were ultimately signed into law. The data were collected from state legislative websites by my research assistants using lists of bills on each subject published and regularly updated by *Education Week*.

In several states, the anti-CRT bills passed with very large abstention rates from Democratic legislators, who apparently did not want to go on the record opposing them. For this reason, and to provide the most useful comparison, I focus on the share of legislators voting affirmatively on each bill, thus treating abstentions and "no" votes as interchangeable.

The results are presented in Figure 4.1, which plots the percent of each party's caucus voting in favor of each bill, with the distance between each point representing the degree of partisan polarization on the legislation. Several patterns stand out in this data. First, the CRT bans all passed by nearly perfect party-line votes, with almost no Democrats voting in support. Averaging across states, fewer than 1 percent of the Democratic legislators had voted in favor of these bills. By contrast, most reading bills were adopted by significant bipartisan coalitions, with 76 percent of Democrats and 83 percent of Republicans voting in favor on average. In half a dozen states, these bills passed unanimously or nearly so. The partisan divide that Frances Paterson found characterizing the reading debate in the 1990s had largely disappeared nearly thirty years later.

For me, the new bipartisan consensus behind the "science of reading" posed as big of a puzzle as the original polarization seen one generation earlier. The activists and researchers I spoke to seemed equally flummoxed about how to explain the recent developments.

To try to understand the political dynamics better, I reached out to a number of Democratic legislators in states that had recently passed both CRT bans and new reading laws. Specifically, I focused on lawmakers who had voted against the CRT legislation but in favor of phonics. Aside from the specific academic subject – history versus reading – these bills appeared (at least to me) to be quite similar, both involving top-down curriculum mandates and both imposing limitations on the autonomy and instructional practices of classroom teachers. Why did the legislators support one set of mandates but oppose the other?

Although most of those I reached out to did not respond, I was able to interview three Democrats who fit the profile above. None, it is important to note, served on their respective education committees in the relevant session, so could speak only from their perspective as rank-and-file members voting on legislation outside their area of policy expertise. Nevertheless, I found our conversations enlightening.

"I think a big part of it is the nationalization of politics," North Dakota Rep. Mock explained, pointing to the influence of conservative media such as Fox News in stirring up Republican anxiety about CRT even though there was little indication it had infiltrated his state's schools. "I think anytime you have the nationalization of an issue, in this case educational curriculum, you're having to oversimplify the content for the general public to be able to digest it, you lose some of the nuance."

Of course, Mock is a Democrat, so it would be convenient for him to believe the other party was overreacting to the issue. But his Republican colleague Rep. Cynthia Schreiber-Beck, the longest serving member of her party on the House education committee, agreed.[23] For Schreiber-Beck, there were a lot of parallels between Republican opposition to Common Core standards under the Obama administration – as I discuss in Chapter 3 – and current concerns about CRT issues. "It's totally a lack of understanding of the concept and the real meaning behind it," she said when we talked. In her view, many of her conservative colleagues believed that

---

[23] A self-described moderate, Schreiber-Beck had been passed over for chairmanship of the committee in the current session, they both told me.

schools were teaching kids that certain racial groups were more "special" than others, a perspective she did not believe represented the reality in her state.

When we spoke about the CRT bill, Mock told me he was quite frustrated with the state interference in curriculum decisions, which he thought would be best made at the local level. "We have overstepped our authority. We have micromanaged the education issues many times over." When I asked why this view did not prevent him from voting for the state's "science of reading" bill, which arguably raised many of the same issues, he paused to look up the legislation. Reading through the records, he noted that both sponsors of the reading legislation were chairmen of their respective chamber's education committees, with expertise in the subject matter. He also noted that many people across the ideological spectrum had come to testify in favor of the bill and praised the state's superintendent, a moderate Republican, for bringing both sides together.

Several Democrats in Oklahoma, another red state that has recently passed both CRT bans and reading legislation, offered quite similar explanations. Rep. Ajay Pittman, who had opposed the CRT effort but voted in favor of the reading, also noted that the authors of the reading legislation were chairs of their chamber's education committees, and one was a former teacher. "It makes a big difference for the trust factor," she explained. The other important difference was the political salience of the two issues. Many constituents had organized rallies and church meetings over the CRT bill, and her office was flooded with constituent calls. Reading, however, attracted very little attention.

Many of Pittman's Democratic colleagues were teachers themselves, elected in a wave in 2018 after teacher walkouts over low compensation in Oklahoma had made national headlines. One of them, Rep. John Waldron, was a high school social studies teacher and had previously served on the House education committee. He argued that the Republican push on culture wars issues – including the CRT bill – was part of a broader effort to discredit public schools and educators and pave the way for private school vouchers. "Recently the floor leader said, 'We love education, that's why we beat up on it so much,'" Waldron said. "He was tongue-in-cheek. But educators feel like they're in an abusive relationship."

Waldron also has personal familiarity with the reading wars – his mother had earned a master's degree in English in the 1980s, as the first major legislative battles over the issue were heating up. Most seemed to have forgotten about those conflicts, however, and even Waldron himself had no problem voting in favor of his state's reading legislation, saying "it was just a great idea and it was science-based." Like both Pittman and Mock, he noted the bill had been carried by respected education committee leaders, including an English teacher.

Of course, as Figure 4.1 shows, not all reading bills passed with bipartisan support. This appears to reflect important differences in the substance of the legislation. Although many of the "science of reading" efforts tend to include similar general language about teaching the five core elements highlighted by the NRP report – phonemic awareness, phonics, fluency, vocabulary, and comprehension – some also go further into more contentious domains, such as banning "three-cueing" guessing approaches. Most controversial, however, are requirements requiring the retention of third-grade students who fail to meet minimum achievement benchmarks, an important part of the Mississippi model. Inclusion of mandatory retention – and language related to open enrollment opposed by teacher unions – appears to be the main reason Democrat in Missouri overwhelmingly opposed that state's reading legislation, for example. By contrast, language *repealing* existing retention requirements in Nevada seems to explain why Republican legislators there voted against the proposal.

LESSONS LEARNED?

In this chapter, I have described how and why history and reading curriculum filtered to the top of state legislative agendas in recent years. Both issues raise important questions about the relationship between politics, schools, and instructional practices. To conclude, I want to briefly consider the broader implications – or, at least hypotheses – suggested by these recent developments.

One lesson is that the broader nationalization of American politics (Hopkins, 2018) has clearly impacted recent education policy debates. The ongoing financial decline of local newspapers, historically the primary source of information about both local and state politics, and the emergence of both national cable news and social media as the primary drivers of political narratives has resulted in both state and legislative policy efforts increasingly organized around the same national policy fault lines.

However, the precise mechanisms through which policies are nationalized, and the exact media sources involved in raising the salience of individual issues, are quite important. In the case of reading, it seems clear that Emily Hanford's podcasts played a pivotal role in elevating the salience of reading practices and getting "science of reading" bills on legislative agendas. Hanford herself makes this point in a recent bonus episode, which includes an interview with an Indiana legislator who describes introducing his state's reading bill after listening to her original podcast series. In this case, nationalization did not produce polarization – indeed, if anything, it may have helped *narrow* prior partisan divisions that dominated earlier reading debates. Partisan polarization, in other words, is not a one-way ratchet, and nationalization does not automatically lead to greater polarization.

As with the case of the Common Core standards discussed in Chapter 3, polarization over education policies does appear inevitable when it involves particularly partisan sources – either partisan news outlets or high-profile elected officials. During my many interviews, I put forward the same counterfactual: Suppose, I asked, that President Trump had decided to focus on reading rather than history, and had embraced phonics (rather than attacking the *1619 Project*) as his preferred method of teaching kids how to read, just as President Bush had done? Many chuckled at this question, but nearly everyone agreed the dynamics of both issues likely would have played out quite differently. "I have absolutely no doubt it would have," Shanahan told me. "And it wouldn't have to be phonics. Take any aspect of teaching reading – if [Trump] had embraced it, news media would be up in arms, there would be people trying to shut down school board meetings over this, and you'd be going, 'Boy, those crazy liberals!'"

"If a divisive figure like Donald Trump had come forward and was advocating for scientific-based principles, would those who believe in the scientific method now oppose the scientific method because of Trump?" North Dakota Rep. Mock pondered. After a pause, he concluded probably not. "But they may have questioned his ulterior motives."

The polarizing effects of presidential leadership challenge the conventional way many scholars of American politics have conceptualized executive power. In his famous book, *Going Public*, political scientist Sam Kernell (1997) argued that the bully pulpit was an important lever presidents could pull to advance their preferred policy agendas, using their public influence to pressure lawmakers and overcome gridlock. The actual effectiveness of the "going public" strategy was, at one time, a highly debated topic among scholars, although it seems clear Kernell's model does not work in our modern context of high partisan polarization. Indeed, it may be that presidential efforts to advocate for specific policies have the opposite effect – consolidating support among their copartisans but also mobilizing opposition from the other party by creating an opportunity to deny the incumbent president a political win and drive down public approval ratings. Some scholars have documented these dynamics in Congress (Lee, 2008), but recent policy debates also illustrate how they impact subnational politics, transforming America's system of federalism into many decentralized, simultaneous proxy wars infected by national partisan divisions.

Exactly this kind of polarization played out during the debates about Common Core. Michael Casserly, the long-time head of the Council of Great City Schools, a membership organization for big urban districts, remembered the great consternation many Common Core advocates felt about President Obama's embrace of the issue. He described a meeting he had with Obama's education secretary, Arne Duncan, in which Casserly encouraged the president to stay out of the issue. "We wanted Obama to stay as far away from this as we could," he recalled.

Of course, as the recent developments on phonics illustrate, polarization need not be permanent. I suspect one reason the partisan dynamics over reading have changed so quickly is that, even during the height of the reading wars, the conflict was driven by a small group of ideological warriors and policy activists, without penetrating deeper into public opinion. After all, the annual testing and strict accountability provisions of the No Child Left Behind Act attracted far more attention and criticism than the Reading First program. The only public opinion polling on the issue I could find, carried out in March 2020 by Phi Delta Kappa, asked voters if they favored phonics-based reading instruction, whole language, or a "balanced approach" combining both. More than 70 percent chose the balanced option.[24]

The same appears to be true with regard to public opinion on the most controversial social studies and history issues. Although opinion surveys show sharp partisan divisions about some topics – such as what students should be taught about the causes of current racial disparities – there is also overwhelming bipartisan consensus on many others. For example, in recent education surveys by researchers at the University of Southern California, over 80 percent of *both* Democrats and Republicans agreed that high school students should be taught about slavery and the contributions of people of color. And support for teaching about the successes of the founding fathers and about patriotism achieved nearly identically

---

[24] Unfortunately, the poll did not ask about partisanship.

high levels of bipartisan support. Most voters appear to reject – at least for now – the extreme policy views from activists on both sides, even though these views appear to structure much of the debate about curricular policy. As in the cases examined in Chapter 3, elites have polarized well before the electorate, which may eventually follow.

Finally, the recent debates about CRT and reading also reveal a great deal about the underlying socialization processes that shape the teaching profession. As James Q. Wilson (1989) famously argued, government agencies develop their own "organizational cultures" that, like personalities, influence and constrain their behavior. Although not a function performed out of a single federal agency, public education as a profession has its own distinct culture, reflecting both the selection processes affecting the types of people who are attracted to teaching and the influence of teacher preparation programs run out of university colleges of education.

From the research, interviews, and reading that informed the analysis and arguments in this chapter, I came away with a strong sense that teacher preparation and culture has played a major role in both the CRT and reading debates. For example, a number of systematic studies involving content analyses of course syllabi in the leading teacher preparation programs, carried by both academic researchers and various advocacy groups, have found that they tend to focus more on theory and less on application (Schalin, 2019; Steiner and Rozen, 2004). Overwhelmingly, these theoretical perspectives are rooted in concepts such as "constructivism" and multiculturalism – emphasizing students' lived experience and how it might affect their construction of meaning in the classroom. Many of these theoretical concepts are borrowed or inspired by critical analyses, and that may be one reason why authors such as Robin DiAngelo and Ibram X. Kendi – whose inclusion in corporate and government DEI trainings first attracted the ire of Christopher Ruffo – often feature prominently in college of education courses, including at my home university.

When I asked former IES Director Russ Whitehurst whether colleges of education were a barrier in getting teachers to adopt evidence-based reading practices, he couldn't help but laugh. "When I was IES director, I always needed an invitation, but I tried to go to the leading schools of education around the country," he explained. "And oh gosh I needed a stiff drink after most. ... Certainly leading schools of education had some faculty who are doing great work, but as an institution they always felt out of place, rowing against the tide."

During my interviews with education scholars and activists, I asked whether they thought that the predilection toward critical pedagogy that caused teacher preparation programs to embrace whole language in the 1980s also affects how teachers are trained to think about and teach US history and civics. Most of those I spoke to rejected the comparison. Reading is a real problem – just look at the percent of elementary students reading below grade level, many of them responded, while CRT is a manufactured crisis, promoted by conservative activists. But upon further discussion, some did agree that many of the controversial, and admittedly isolated, lessons that have attracted the attention of conservative activists – such having students complete "oppression matrices" and "privilege walks" – may grow out of ideas teachers confront during their training.

"What I think is really a mistake for liberals to is say, 'Oh, no, we're not doing anything like that!' They say, 'We don't teach Critical Race Theory, period.' Well, I don't care what you call it, you're teaching things that many would not agree with," former California Superintendent Bill Honig told me when I asked him about the CRT debate.[25]

Linda Diamond, who worked with Honig in California to promote phonics, argued that curriculum makers and textbook publishers are caught in the middle. Specifically, she mentioned one reading curriculum – highly rated by experts – that attracted criticism from both liberal and conservative states. In red states, the curriculum was attacked by some far-right groups on CRT-related grounds. But many progressives also accused the program of not being "culturally responsive" because it focused on building background knowledge that many viewed as too centered on the experience and history of whites. "I'm Jewish and I speak a little Yiddish," she told me. "The term we use is, 'This is *mishegas*.' *Mishegas* means insanity because there is nothing you can do to please everyone. There are these nutty people – on both sides. I think what we are seeing in the CRT debate, some are going overboard."

Keith Stanovich, the cognitive scientist who authored some of the early pivotal papers supporting phonics, also initially pushed back on my suggestion that the reading and culture wars debates were related. In our later conversations, he ultimately came to agree with some of my

---

[25] As the CRT debates played out nationally, California was undergoing its own version of the culture wars surrounding competing curriculum proposals for the state's new ethnic studies requirement. Honig was part of a moderate coalition supporting a compromise plan that was strongly opposed by a group of activists pushing a competing "liberated" curriculum seeped in CRT.

arguments – and unleashed his deep frustrations with teacher preparation programs. "I absolutely agree with you that CRT and the resistance to phonics ideas stem from the very same lack of intellectual diversity and monocultures within colleges of ed. I would wholeheartedly endorse that," he told me. "It's the same underlying problem, just manifest on different issues. ... Many of these ed schools are putting more effort into producing policy advocates than they are spending teaching early educators the role of syllable segmentation in an early reading curriculum. That class is training political advocates, not training teachers – and in a public institution, it is a betrayal of the taxpayers' trust."

Interestingly, whole-language defenders appear much more receptive to seeing parallels between the CRT and reading debates. Indeed, many criticize "science of reading" approaches precisely on CRT grounds – arguing that the obsession with quantitative, randomized studies excludes the kinds of reading research most likely to be done by scholars of color. A recent president of the American Educational Research Association wrote an entire article titled "Disrupting Racism and Whiteness in Researching a Science of Reading" (Milner, 2020). "[W]hiteness and maleness are at the very foundation of our understanding of the science of reading," he concluded (p. S252).

"I do see the reading wars as akin to or a particular version of the culture wars," University of Minnesota's Timothy Lensmire, whose research focuses on the intersection of reading and critical pedagogy, told me. Lensmire hypothesized that newfound support for reading reform among Democratic legislators might also represent a form of white liberal guilt or shame – or at least hope that better reading instruction might finally address long-standing racial achievement gaps, a perennial embarrassment in blue states like his.

Given the levels of attention and political capital that legislative battles over curriculum consume, it is perhaps surprising that the actual impact of these state-level interventions on student outcomes remains far from clear. There is a big difference between passing a new law and actually changing what is happening in individual classrooms. Teachers are the ultimate street-level bureaucrats, who exercise tremendous discretion with minimal oversight and top-down legislative efforts don't always succeed in significantly altering teaching practices.

That is certainly the lesson from many earlier curricular battles (e.g., Loveless, 2021; Polikoff, 2021). For example, in their book on debates surrounding the teaching of evolution in the early 2000s, Berkman and Plutzer (2010) included surveys of teachers, asking them to report how much time they spent on various topics. They then compared what teachers reported they did in the classroom every day to what the relevant laws and curricular standards in their states required – and found almost no relationship, particularly among more senior educators. On the other hand, more recent research leveraging the precise timing of when states changed their content standards on evolution do find long-run impacts among affected student cohorts, not only in terms of understanding of the relevant biological concepts but also employment in science-related sectors (Arold, 2024).

Researchers who have examined the implementation of the Common Core standards and curricula have also emphasized the slippage that can emerge in translating legislative pronouncements into actual practices. Consider Loveless (2021, p. 3): "Saying that standards depend on implementation is a bit like saying skydivers' enjoyment of the day depends on their parachutes opening. Fortunately for skydivers, the probability of the chute failing is infinitesimal. Not so for the odds of top-down policies encountering obstacles on the way to local sites of implementation." Or Polikoff (2021, p. 13): "If we know now, and have known for fifty years, that teaching is an isolating profession defined mostly by individual practice, how can a light-touch reform like standards possibly penetrate the classroom in any meaningful way?"

My sense is that state legislative efforts focused on overhauling curricula and content standards provide great position-taking and credit-claiming opportunities for elected officials, and allow various adults to score easy political points, engage in meaningful self-expression, or attain the satisfaction of seeing their preferred views written into state laws. At least among the researchers whose work provides the intellectual foundations for many of these debates, and among the policy activists and entrepreneurs who do battle on the front lines, almost everyone seems to be sincere in their belief that they are fighting on the side of the angels and that the policies they are promoting will be good for children. But for many advocates, it also seems that winning the political battle often becomes the end in itself, with adult political considerations ultimately explaining the policies that we see adopted. Whether reforms actually move the needle on academic outcomes remains a secondary concern – by the time definitive evidence on this question can be collected, the political attention has usually moved on to the next issue of the day.

5

Adult Culture Wars and Student Achievement

> It's negative, it's wasteful, it's not productive, it's sucking the energy out of the administration, the board, our staff, our teachers.
> —Mentor (Ohio) School board member Mary Bryner, on recent curriculum debates (Natanson, 2023a)

Darryl Adams, then-superintendent of the Coachella Valley Unified School District in Southern California, received an unexpected letter in November 2013. The correspondence was signed by the legal director of Arab-American Anti-Discrimination Committee (ADC), and the topic was the mascot of the district's lone high school – the "Arab." The image of the mascot featured a cartoon face of a bearded man with a pronounced hook nose wearing a traditional Middle Eastern head-covering. "All of these are examples of gross stereotyping, which must not be tolerated, and must immediately be addressed," the letter demanded. "ADC strongly believes the use of the word and such imagery perpetuates demeaning stereotypes of Arabs and Arab Americans. The 'Arab' mascot image is a harmful form of ethnic stereotyping which should be eliminated."

To be accused of racism came as a surprise to Adams, to say the least. The superintendent was an African-American man who had grown up in the deep South, reported to a majority–minority school board, and oversaw education for an overwhelming Latino student population. The "Arab" mascot was selected in 1921 as an honorific – to pay homage to Algeria and the Middle East as the original source of the date palm, one of the major agricultural crops first grown in the region. For the

(a) Original Mascot   (b) Updated Mascot

FIGURE 5.1 Coachella Valley High School "Arab" Mascot

next ninety years, it apparently never occurred to anyone that it might be offensive. The ADC said the group understood this history, but nevertheless expected action: "[I]n the 21st Century, such justifications for these actions are no longer tolerable."

The controversy immediately attracted national and even international attention – with prominent coverage in outlets including *Al Jazeera* and *Buzzfeed*. Graduates of the high school rallied behind their beloved mascot. The issue would come to occupy months of Adams' time, involving shuttle diplomacy to work out a compromise that both sides could ultimately live with. Eventually, they would settle on a new "Mighty Arab" mascot (see Figure 5.1). "It was a good lesson for the kids, for the adults, for the community," Adams recalled nearly a decade later.

But it is interesting to think about what Adams may have spent that time on instead. After all, school district administrators are very busy people and their time is arguably one of the scarcest resources in public education. Every minute spent negotiating a new high school mascot is a minute that could've been invested on improving instruction or revising curriculum with the goal delivering a better education in the classroom. When I asked about this type of zero-sum dynamic, Adams insisted that the controversy had not disrupted the district's academic performance – but did agree that similar distractions could have negative consequences on learning, particularly in places with more combustible racial relations.[1] "It depends on the leadership in the community," he told me. "I

---

[1] The year before the controversy, Coachella Valley had passed a bond measure that provided funding for a program to provide every student with an iPad. The initiative brought acclaim from the Obama White House, but within a few years, teachers began complaining about a botched implementation and inadequate training. I continue to wonder if, absent the mascot controversy, the iPad program roll out would've gone more smoothly. Adams would ultimately leave for medical reasons, and the board would

can see how, in some situations, it can be tough and can take away from the academic goals."

One such situation occurred in the Dover Area School District, located in a southern Pennsylvania. In 2004, the Dover school board majority adopted a change to the district's high school biology curriculum to include a statement describing "intelligent design" as an alternative theory to evolution and adopted the controversial intelligent design textbook, *Of Pandas and People*, as a reference text. The decision would lead to a lawsuit, and ultimately, a federal court case that would be nicknamed the "Dover Panda Trial" – a spoof of the famous "Scopes Monkey Trial" over evolution that took place in Tennessee nearly a century earlier.

The litigation became a circus – even Bruce Springsteen mentioned the case during a live performance – and turned tiny Dover into a center of media attention, fueling deep political divisions within the community. School board member Bill Buckingham, a pugnacious retired cop who led the charge on behalf of intelligent design, was transparent about the religious motivation for the policy change. "This country wasn't founded on Muslim beliefs or evolution," he told a local reporter. "This country is founded on Christianity, and our students should be taught as such" (Lebo, 2008, pp. 24–25). Yet at trial, he denied religion had anything to do with it. Confronted with his lies, Buckingham admitted he had been deep into an OxyContin addiction at the time of the policy change.

The school district would go on to lose the case and be ordered to pay the plaintiff's legal cost. (They generously asked for only $1 million, half of the actual expense, but a significant sum for a small school district.[2]) Amidst the controversy, voters booted out the anti-evolution incumbents, bringing in a slate of new board members, who immediately fired the superintendent, a man they accused of enabling the previous board majority,[3] and other top administrators, plunging the district deeper into chaos. "It was a huge distraction," Christina Kauffman, who covered the case for the *York Dispatch*, explained. "In terms of the kids, their educational experience was out there for the entire world. It wasn't just the media coverage of it, it was the fact that the adults – the ones who were

---

fire his top deputies – a lingering consequences of divisive salary negotiations with the district's teachers. "Union issues," as Adams described them.

[2] For context, the district's total spending was less than $40 million at the time.

[3] Like Buckingham, the superintendent had also testified that he never heard the board members discuss a religious motivation behind the policy change, although such discussions were clearly documented by local journalists who had attended the same meetings.

supposed to know what was going on – the adults were fighting. And much like a child growing up in a household where people are fighting, it's not conducive to learning."

I open this chapter with the controversies in Coachella Valley and Dover because they illustrate an important tension at the root of our public education governance institutions. In a well-functioning democracy, the decisions and actions of government officials must reflect the wishes of the governed.[4] Designing political institutions to achieve this goal, however, can require difficult trade-offs. What if increased responsiveness to public opinion results in the politicization of agencies that actually implement policies and impedes their performance (e.g., Gailmard and Patty, 2007; Lewis, 2008)?

Balancing political accountability with effective service delivery poses particularly difficult challenges in the context of public education. As I've argued throughout this book, the core democratic dilemma is that public schools exist to serve the educational needs of children but these students generally cannot vote in the elections through which key policymakers are chosen. Thus, dynamics that we would normally view as desirable in a democracy – elected officials' responsiveness to voter political preferences – could encourage school board members to prioritizing adult interests at the expense of student learning. For example, defending an offensive mascot or pushing through controversial curricular changes. This especially true when adults prioritize symbolic issues – be they cultural, religious, or identity-based – that are largely unrelated to the core academic functions schools are expected to serve.

This chapter examines how high-profile adult political conflicts ultimately affect student learning in the classroom. Traditional theories of democratic accountability do not provide clear expectations in this regard. On one hand, by bringing attention to the inner workings of the school system, high-profile controversies may pique voter interest in local school elections, increasing accountability pressures and diluting the corrosive influence of special interest groups who would otherwise play a dominant role in what are typically low-interest, low-turnout elections (e.g., Anzia, 2011; Berry, 2009; Moe, 2006). On the other, by shifting attention away from student outcomes to issues of interest to adults – including adults without children, the median voter in local

---

[4] There is considerable debate among philosophers about whether public officials should be most responsive to the (sometimes uninformed) *opinions* or to the *interests* of constituents (Pitkin, 1967).

school board elections – the controversies could distract teachers and district administrators and create unnecessary chaos and staff turnover, disrupting student learning.[5]

The evidence, I show, points firmly in toward the latter dynamics – and the mascot and evolution controversies help illustrate the likely mechanisms. In public schools, as in most government agencies, personnel time and financial resources – in the Dover example, literally $1 million in legal fees – are the ultimate constraints on the quality of public services. On the margin, a district must decide whether to spend a dollar on litigation or an artist to design a new mascot versus spending the same dollar in the classroom. In addition, divisive political conflicts can lead to churn both at the school board level and also among top district administration, and such turnover in itself can be highly disruptive. Certainly, the loss of both the superintendents and their deputies seemed to affect the operations of Coachella Valley and Dover. When superintendents are forced out, other district administrators usually go into a holding pattern, worried whether they'll still have their jobs once the next leader arrives, and avoid making any high-stakes decisions that could stir up controversy. School principals and teachers face the challenge of navigating difficult political terrain and dealing with the potential drama the political conflicts create among the families their schools serve.

The empirical analysis in this chapter combines a decade of data on high-profile "culture war" controversies in local public education that have been tracked as part of the Cato Institute's Public Schooling Battle Map with information on student academic achievement in grades three through eight from the Stanford Education Data Archive (SEDA) (also known as the Stanford Educational Opportunity Project). Unlike much of the analysis earlier in the book, which is descriptive, here I leverage variation in the timing and location of these controversies to estimate the plausibly causal effect of such conflicts. Specifically, the analysis implements what researchers describe as a "difference-in-differences design" – comparing the trajectory of student test scores in the affected districts before versus after the outbreak of each controversy to contemporaneous achievement trends in a "control group" of school districts that do not experience a similar controversy over the same time period.

---

[5] For example, Berry and Howell (2007) note that media coverage of student achievement plays an important role in making academic outcomes salient to voters and the weight voters put on achievement when deciding whether to reelect incumbents, as I discuss in Chapter 2. By making culture war issues more salient, controversies may cause voters to place less weight on academic achievement.

To preview the findings, I show that local political controversies hurt student performance on state exams, particularly in mathematics. The decline in achievement, on the order of 0.02 to 0.03 standard deviation units, is roughly equivalent to 10 days of learning out of a standard 180-day school year. Moreover, these effects persist for at least four years after the focal event. Examining potential differences both in the nature of the controversies and the students affected, I find that the learning disruption is particularly pronounced in the wake controversies related to racial issues and the teaching of evolution, which both reduce math achievement by between 0.06 and 0.07 standard deviations. However, I do not find evidence that the disruptions impact disadvantaged students more than their peers, leaving the magnitude of the achievement gap between low-income and other students largely unchanged.

MEASURING CULTURE WARS

The data on local education controversies comes from the Cato Institute's Public Schooling Battle Map, which was assembled by Neal McCluskey, the director of Cato's Center for Educational Freedom. McCluskey used a combination of Google News alerts, direct reports from individuals, and the ChoiceMedia.tv "Newswire," an aggregator website for education-related news. As such, the data is largely limited to sufficiently high-profile controversies that attract media attention and likely misses many smaller conflicts in districts with less media coverage. It is thus useful to think of the "treatment" that causes a district to enter the dataset as a bundle that includes both the controversy and the media attention that follows. While the database includes incidents dating back to 2005, it is most complete starting in 2011. Each controversy was classified by McCluskey into one of nine categories: (1) freedom of expression; (2) religion; (3) curriculum; (4) reading material; (5) race/ethnicity; (6) moral values; (7) gender equity; (8) sexuality; and (9) human origins.[6]

It is useful to highlight some of the specific cases, to illustrate the type of school district dramas these categories actually represent. One racial/ethnic controversy, for example, involved an Ohio district where

---

[6] Events are coded into categories based on the dimension of the controversy that is judged to be most central. For example, several cases in which districts prohibited students from wearing rosary beads are coded as "freedom of expression," although the expression in those cases is religious in nature. Similarly, complaints about books are coded as "reading material" disputes even if the specific books in question are controversial because they deal with racial or sexual topics.

middle school students sang "Cotton Needs Pickin" at the fall concert, to the outrage of many African-American parents in the audience. Another, from the same category, was the tragic case from a Southern California district that disciplined students who skipped school to attend an immigration reform rally. One of these students, apparently traumatized by his punishment, ended up taking his own life, prompting a high-profile lawsuit from his family. Many others dealt with controversial school mascots – in particular, the "Redskins," a popular team name that fell out of favor in recent years.

Freedom of expression controversies often involved school uniform or dress code infractions, including a female student disciplined for wearing a shirt that said "Twin Peaks" on one side and "Save the scenic views" on the other to raise breast cancer awareness. Another example was a school bus driver suspended for refusing to remove a Confederate flag from his truck, which he parked in the school parking lot. Critically, although the term education "culture war" often has an ideological valence in popular use – usually referring to conservative activism – my analysis includes controversies initiated by activists from both sides of the ideological spectrum. For example, many issues targeted by groups on the political left focus on equity and racial justice concerns, similar to considerations that motivated the ADC letter to the Coachella Valley superintendent. (The "Arab" mascot controversy is on one of the observations in the dataset.)

To examine how these controversies affect student academic achievement, I merge the Battle Map dataset with records from the SEDA (Fahle et al., 2021). This collection includes measures of student academic achievement based on test scores in math and English language arts in grade three through eight that states report to the US Department of Education.

Because this vintage of the SEDA data covers the years 2009 through 2018, I impose several data restrictions for technical reasons.[7] First, I exclude from the analytic sample districts that are "always-treated" – dropping all districts with a controversy observed in 2009 or earlier years. Second, I limit the sample to districts that experience only one controversy during this time period, excluding school systems with more than one event in the data.[8] In addition, I exclude state-level controversies

---

[7] Specifically, the motivation for these restrictions is to avoid bias due to treatment effect dynamics and heterogeneity.
[8] This is done for technical reasons, since we cannot assume that multiple controversies have an additive effect.

that are likely to affect all districts in a given state.[9] In effect, the analysis compares districts that experience one local controversy during the years included in SEDA compared to a control group made up of "never-treated" school districts that do not experience a controversy. The final sample includes approximately 520 such episodes. The total number of events ranges from 30 to 80 per year, and the most common type of controversy focuses on freedom of expression, which accounts for nearly a third of all of the events in the dataset.

EMPIRICAL STRATEGY

An obvious challenge to studying the effects of political controversies is that such events are unlikely to be random. For example, larger districts located in the core of their newspaper circulation area or television media market are probably more likely to see a run-of-the-mill, small-scale conflict escalate after attracting press coverage. In addition to district size, McCluskey (2019) finds that both student racial composition and the partisanship of each district's surrounding county predict the outbreak and frequency of events (see also Table 5.1).

My empirical approach directly accounts for such nonrandom patterns. Casual readers who are not interested in the technical details behind the analysis can feel free to skip the remainder of this section, which describes what is going on under the statistical hood in the analysis.

Specifically, I estimate a difference-in-differences model (Angrist and Pischke, 2009) that controls for time-invariant factors that could affect both the probability of an outbreak of a political controversy and student achievement. In most specifications, I use the following Ordinary Least Squares model:

$$Y_{dgst} = \alpha_d + \beta \text{Controversy}_{dst} + \delta_{st} + \varphi_g + \epsilon_{dgst},$$

where Y_{dgst} represents test scores of students in grade g in district d located in state s during year t. The model includes both district (α_d) and state-by-year (δ_{st}) fixed effects. The latter accounts for both potential changes in the assessments used by individual states over time as well as the impact of state-level policy changes and statewide education-related

---

[9] As discussed below, my statistical model controls for state-by-year fixed effects that absorb the effects of these statewide controversies.

TABLE 5.1 *Summary statistics, measured in 2010*

		Excluded from analysis		Included in analysis	
	Full SEDA sample	Always treated	Multiple events	Never treated	Treatment districts
Total enrollment (grades 3–8)	1,695.40	4,022.44	17,581.48	1,089.52	3,666.09
Ave. enrollment per grade	287.10	670.88	2,930.25	184.93	612.43
Attending urban schools (%)	0.06	0.15	0.34	0.04	0.14
Attending suburban schools (%)	0.20	0.40	0.40	0.18	0.35
Attending town schools (%)	0.17	0.20	0.06	0.18	0.20
Attending rural schools (%)	0.57	0.26	0.19	0.60	0.31
White (%)	0.75	0.70	0.60	0.75	0.69
Black (%)	0.08	0.12	0.16	0.07	0.11
Hispanic (%)	0.12	0.13	0.17	0.12	0.15
Econ. dis. (ED, %)	0.48	0.43	0.43	0.49	0.44
English learners (%)	0.05	0.06	0.08	0.04	0.06
Special ed (%)	0.14	0.14	0.13	0.14	0.14
Ave. math achievement (grade 5)	−0.00	0.07	0.09	−0.01	0.07
Ave. ELA achievement (grade 5)	−0.01	0.05	0.08	−0.01	0.04
Math Non-ED-ED achievement gap (grade 5)	0.48	0.55	0.64	0.47	0.53
ELA Non-ED-ED achievement gap (grade 5)	0.52	0.58	0.67	0.50	0.56
Districts	13,105	185	367	12,031	521

political controversies. I pool data across all tested grades and some specifications also include grade-specific fixed effects (φ_g), although the results are not sensitive to this choice. Controversy$_{dst}$ is a binary indicator that takes the value of one starting in the year of each controversy. The variable remains "on" in all subsequent years, although I also estimate more flexible event study specifications that examine the dynamics more carefully. All standard errors are clustered by school district to account for serial correlation (Bertrand, Duflo and Mullainathan, 2004).

The primary quantity of interest is the estimate of β. This can be interpreted as the causal effect of controversy on student academic achievement under the assumption that student performance in the affected districts would have followed trends parallel to those in districts not experiencing an event. To probe the plausibility of this assumption, I examine the trajectory of achievement in the affected districts compared to never-treated controls in the years leading up to the controversy using the following event study specification:

$$Y_{dgst} = \alpha_d + \sum_{j \leq -5}^{\geq 5} \pi_j \text{Controversy}_{dst} \cdot I(\tau_{dst} = j) + \delta_{st} + \varphi_g + \epsilon_{dgst}.$$

Given the staggered nature of the treatment and the relatively short duration of the achievement panel, I bin the event window end points, combining all years at least five years before and five years after each event into two categories.

Table 5.1 provides a summary of the full dataset as well as the analytic sample. While each district is observed for multiple years and test scores are reported across multiple grades, the table summarizes district characteristics in 2010 and student achievement in the fifth grade. Several patterns clearly stand out in the data. First, districts that experience a controversy attracting media attention are considerably larger, more urban, and enroll a smaller share of white students than districts that serve as the control group. On the other hand, treated districts are also somewhat wealthier, as measured by the share of students designated as economically disadvantaged, and have achievement levels that are modestly higher than for the districts in the control group. In addition, the treated districts have somewhat larger achievement gaps between higher- and lower-SES students. Second, districts that experience multiple events during the period of the study and are thus excluded from the analytic sample are particularly large – enrolling more than 17,000 students on averages in the tested grades – and are especially urban.[10]

CONFLICTS AND TEST SCORES

Table 5.2 reports the standard difference-in-differences estimates. The first two columns show results for math scores while the latter two columns present comparable estimates for English language arts (ELA) achievement. Overall, student math achievement declines by approximately 0.018 standard deviations in the years after a local political controversy. The estimates are the same regardless of whether the model includes grade-level fixed-effects. By contrast, there does not appear to be any impacts on ELA achievement. While the divergence between math and ELA scores may be surprising, it is consistent with other education policy research showing that student performance in math is much more sensitive to policy interventions than ELA achievement (see Fryer, 2014 for overview).[11] Although education scholars have offered a number of plausible explanations for this pattern, the most likely is that students acquire a much larger share of their mathematical knowledge inside the

TABLE 5.2 *Effect of local culture war controversy on student achievement*

	(1) Math	(2) Math	(3) ELA	(4) ELA
Controversy	−0.0183***	−0.0183***	−0.00557	−0.00556
	(0.00668)	(0.00668)	(0.00484)	(0.00484)
Observations	522,359	522,359	548,946	548,946
R-squared	0.035	0.037	0.041	0.046
Number of districts	11,215	11,215	11,252	11,252
Time FE	State-year	State-year	State-year	State-year
Grade FE	No	Yes	No	Yes

Robust standard errors clustered by district in parentheses.
***p < 0.01.

[10] Since these large urban districts are excluded from the analysis, caution is warranted in generalizing the findings to these types of districts.
[11] Nearly every analysis of pandemic-related learning losses has found much larger test score declines in math than in ELA, for example.

classroom, in contrast to activities outside of school that complement formal reading instruction.

It is useful to put the effect size into more intuitive units. Hill et al. (2008) provide national benchmark for typical learning gains in both math and ELA during each year of schooling. Focusing on math achievement growth in just grades three through eight – those covered by the SEDA data – student scores increase by about 0.39 standard deviations per year, on average. The estimated effect of 0.018 corresponds to roughly 5 percent of annual gains, which translates to about 10 days of learning assuming a typical 180-day school year.

Figure 5.2 presents estimates from the event study specification. The top panel reports results for math achievement while the bottom panel focuses on ELA scores. Encouragingly, there is no evidence that test scores begin to decline in the years prior to the outbreak of local controversy. However, math scores show a clear decline starting in the year after the event, and they remain significantly lower for at least four years. Although the individual point estimates are quite noisy, there is no evidence of a rebound in the short term – if anything, the impact appears to grow more negative over the first three years. The figure does find some evidence of pretreatment trends, raising some questions about the plausibility of the parallel trends assumption. I will return to this issue, presenting additional analyses and probing the robustness of the results, later in the chapter.

It is important to note that the Cato dataset records only the calendar year of each event, with no additional information about the precise day or month for most of the observations, while the test score data is reported based on academic years.[12] Thus, controversies that occur in the fall of calendar year t can affect achievement no earlier than the following spring, the first testing cycle after the event, which would show up as school year $t + 1$ in the SEDA data. That may explain why effects for year zero are relatively small and not significant and why the impact does not appear until the following spring testing window.

Which Controversies Affect Learning, and for Whom?

The results presented thus far focus on average achievement. It is important to consider whether the learning disruptions disproportionately

---

[12] The database began including full dates starting in 2017. For the available years, more than 60 percent of the events occurred in June or later, after the testing cycle had already concluded for that calendar year.

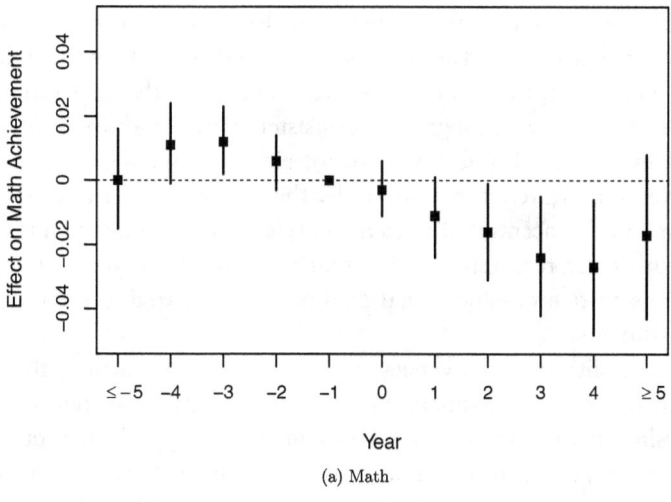

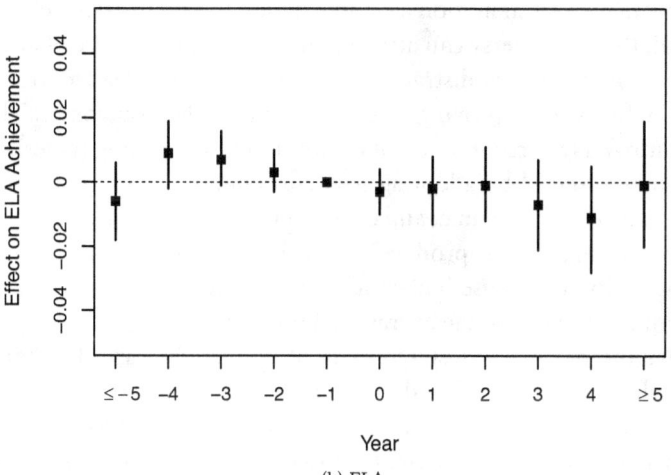

FIGURE 5.2 Event study plot for the effect of local controversy on student achievement

affect high-risk students. Because the SEDA dataset reports subgroup-specific achievement estimates only for subgroups with at least twenty students, it is not possible to examine race-specific data in most districts. However, many districts to enroll a sufficient number of economically disadvantaged students, proxied in most states by their participation in the federal free- and reduced-price meals program and family participation in cash welfare and Medicaid.

These results shows nearly identical declines in the math scores of both economically disadvantaged students and students not identified as such. As a result, there is no meaningful change in the achievement gap between these student subgroups. Consistent with the above results, there are no effects on ELA achievement for either group. When reestimating the effects separately for each grade, the declines in math achievement appear to be concentrated in elementary school grades, which is consistent with prior research showing that the learning of younger students is more sensitive to educational disruptions compared to the impact on older students.

Local political controversies can affect student learning through a variety of possible channels. First, school boards may replace senior leadership that becomes the focus of community opprobrium, producing turnover in administrative ranks and subsequent disruption in district operations. Voters may also replace current school board incumbents, which can also set in motion a chain reaction of other personnel changes. Second, the controversy can attract a disproportionate share of attention, energy, and resources, distracting school and district leaders from their primary focus on improving instruction and student outcomes. Third, if the controversy surrounds specific curriculum or teaching materials, districts may respond by adopting new curriculum, resulting in significant retraining needs, prep time, and transition costs for educators, which may negatively impact their productivity in the short term. Fourth, the negative publicity may cause higher-achieving students to leave the districts, mechanically reducing the average achievement.[13]

That the decline in test scores is of comparable size for both economically disadvantaged and wealthier students – who are much more likely to have the resources necessary exit the public schools for private options or to move to a different district – provide some evidence against the last explanation. I examined several other outcomes that speak to this question as well. Focusing on total enrollment, I found no evidence that enrollment declined in the districts after a political controversy. In fact, total enrollment actually increased by between 2 and 3 percent after each event.[14] There were also no changes in the demographic and

---

[13] The version of the SEDA data I use in the analysis includes charter schools located within the geographic boundaries of districts, so students switching from public to nearby charter schools would not affect the results above.

[14] It may be that growing districts, which experience a large influx of new families unfamiliar with local cultural norms, may be particularly likely to have small issues escalate enough to attract media attention.

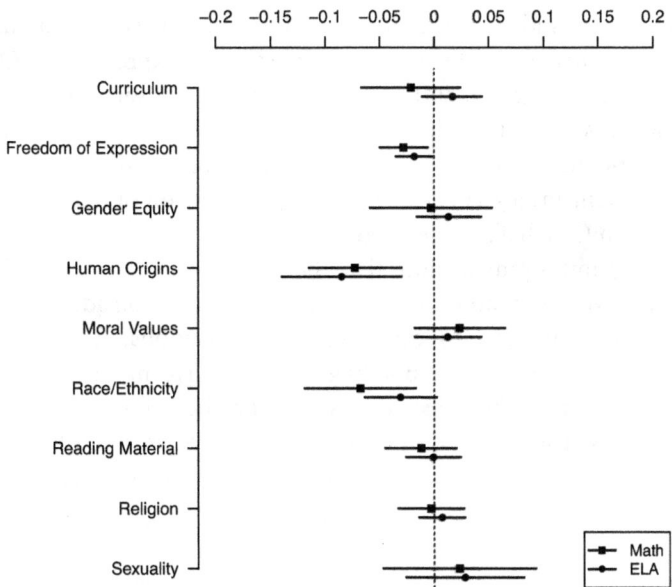

FIGURE 5.3 Student achievement impact by the topic of controversy

socioeconomic composition of students served that would explain the changes in achievement.[15]

Unfortunately, there are no national data on staff, administrator, or school board turnover nor on curricula used by individual school districts, so it is not possible to directly test the remaining three possibilities. However, estimating separate effects for each type of controversy can provide some suggestive evidence about what's actually going on inside school districts.

These results are presented in Figure 5.3. Interestingly, most types of controversies appear to have little if any effect on student learning. Importantly, this is true for controversies surrounding instructional curriculum and those related to reading materials, suggesting that transition costs related to changes in pedagogy or teaching materials are unlikely to be driving the overall findings. Instead, large negative effects appear only for two types of controversies – those dealing with human origins and evolution and disputes surrounding race. As I noted above, that the latter category mostly includes fights unrelated to the actual content of

---

[15] Although there is a marginally significant decrease in the share of white students, the absolute magnitude of this decline is very small – less than 1 percentage point – and so cannot explain the decrease in test scores.

instruction. In addition, there are smaller but still significant declines following controversies dealing with freedom of expression.[16] Overall, these results suggest that staff turnover and/or the diversion of attention and resources away from learning and day-to-day instruction are likely to represent the most plausible explanations for the observed declines. These mechanisms are consistent with my impression of the aftermath of the events in Coachella Valley and Dover.

It is also important to note that the point estimates for the declines linked to evolution and racial controversies are considerably larger, on the order of 0.06 to 0.07 standard deviations. These are substantively significant, corresponding to nearly 1.5 months of learning in mathematics in the affected grades. For these types of controversies, there is also evidence of declines in ELA scores, although the point estimates is considerably smaller for ELA achievement for racial controversies.

GETTING MORE IN THE TECHNICAL WEEDS

The estimates discussed above come from what is known as a two-way fixed effects (TWFE) regression. A flurry of recent papers in economics have shown that TWFE approaches can breakdown when estimating treatment effects with staggered timing – precisely the application in this chapter. In this section, I address this concern and show that the main results are robust to alternative modeling approaches that address the problems with TWFEs. I also discuss other evidence to support the validity of my findings. As before, readers not interested in the technical details should feel free to skip to the next section.

I begin by replicating the event-study results using an alternative approach developed by de Chaisemartin and D'Haultfœuille (2020). These results are presented in Figure 5.4. Although these estimates are noisier – as we would expect, since the de Chaisemartin and D'Haultfœuille (2020) method uses fewer observations – they are qualitatively quite similar to those produced by TWFE. The figure also shows less noticeable pretreatment trends in the years immediately before each controversy, providing additional support for the parallel trends

---

[16] Although the decrease is much smaller than for racial and human origins controversies, there are far more events in this category, so the aggregate impact on achievement is nevertheless substantial.

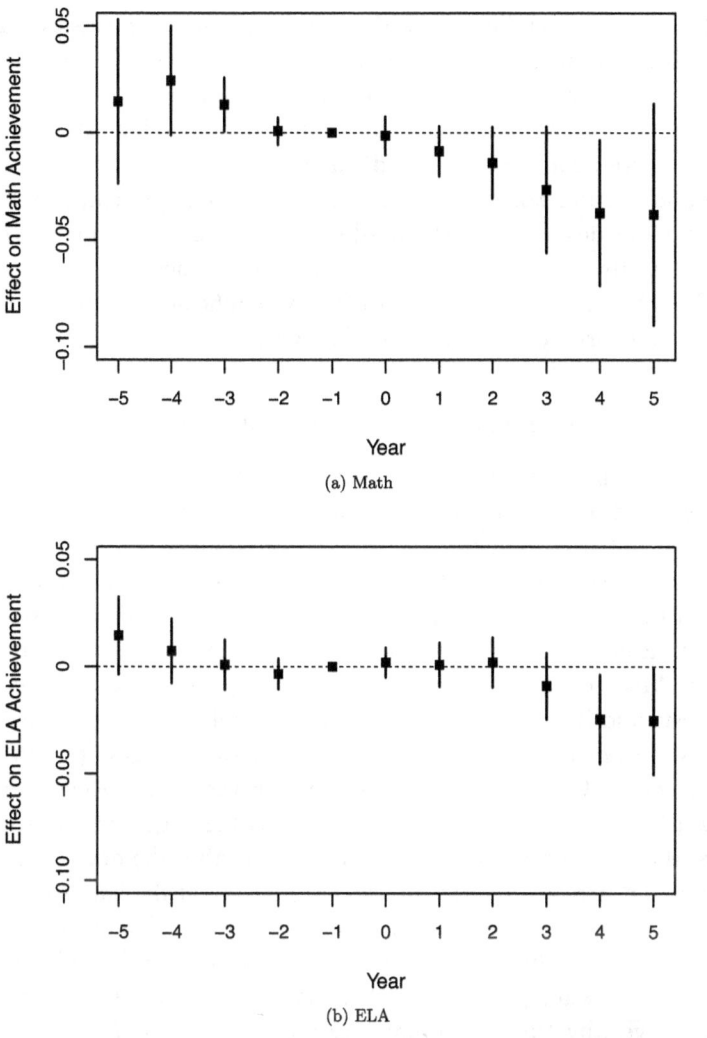

FIGURE 5.4 Alternative event study estimates for the effect of local controversy on student achievement

assumption necessary to interpret these results as causal effects (rather than mere correlations).

Nevertheless, skeptical readers may still have doubts about whether parallel trends hold. As I noted above, districts hit by a scandal tend to be growing faster than their counterparts in the years immediately prior to the controversy. Maybe there are some unobservable (time-varying) differences between districts with versus without controversies that confounds the results? One way to address this concern is to examine only districts that experience a controversy and leverage the differences in the *timing*. In other words, we can use "later-treated" school districts as the control group for "earlier-treated" districts, and vice versa (see, e.g., Harvey and Mattia, 2024).[17] Using this alternative approach, I find nearly identical results – a 0.02 standard deviation decrease in math scores in the years after each controversy. In addition, the negative point estimate on ELA scores also becomes statistically significant, corresponding to a 0.015 standard deviation decrease in scores.

IT SHOULD BE ABOUT THE STUDENTS, STUPID

To summarize, this chapter documents that high-profile political controversies dealing with issues only tangentially related to education have a small but persistent negative impact on student learning. For many readers, these results are probably not surprising. After all, a growing literature in other policy domains examining how political controversies affect the quality of public services at the local level tends to find the same thing. Much of this work focuses on policing and has found that public protests and investigations in the wake of high-profile police shootings of civilians can reduce officer effort and proactivity, resulting in higher crime rates (Campbell, 2024; Devi and Fryer, 2020; Rivera and Ba, 2023; Shi, 2009). This finding is known as the Ferguson effect, named after the city that experienced a rise in crime after the death of Michael Brown, an African-American eighteen-year-old, at the hands of a police officer. To my knowledge, this chapter provides the first evidence of similar dynamics in the context of public education. In one media interview about these results, I described them as the "Loudoun County effect" – after a wealthy Virginia community whose school system was thrown into turmoil over sexual assault allegations some parents attempted to link to the district's transgender bathroom policy (Homans, 2023).

These findings have broader implications for debates surrounding educational governance and policy. On the policy front, they should make activists cautious about well-meaning efforts to push local schools to confront important social justice concerns. Although the most salient current

---

[17] Note that this is the exact opposite of the de Chaisemartin and D'Haultfœuille (2020) approach. That all three methods – standard TWFE, de Chaisemartin and D'Haultfœuille (2020), and earlier- versus later-treated districts – produce substantively identical estimates provides strong evidence for the robustness of the results.

educational policy controversies – including debates about Critical Race Theory and instruction about sexual orientation and gender identity – have a conservative bent, many of the conflicts in the Cato database originated from progressive complaints and umbrage. Such forms of activism may be counterproductive. In recent years, for example, many have raised objections over racial disparities in student discipline (e.g., Liu, Hayes and Gershenson, 2022) and the presence of armed school resource officers in school buildings (e.g., Weisburst, 2019). I have little doubt that advocates working on these issues are sincere and genuinely concerned about student interests. However, it is important to consider the unintended consequences and learning disruptions produced by local controversies that can arise surrounding debates over such issues. Even if the advocacy is ultimately successful, it is not obvious that the net effect for students is positive in the end.

In this chapter, I have offered what I hope is convincing evidence that when adult political conflicts cause school district leaders to take their eye off the ball of educating students, learning suffers. The statistical analysis admittedly offers much less direct evidence of the underlying mechanisms, and so I want to close with two additional case studies that I think help illustrate these mechanisms. As it happens, both caught my attention just as I was finishing this chapter.

In June 2023, PBS "Newshour" ran a segment titled "School boards become battlegrounds for nation's divisions." It featured another rural Pennsylvania school district, Penncrest, and deep conflict within the community over the school board's recent decisions to ban sexually explicit books from the school libraries and also require that transgender athletes to participate in sports teams that match their biological sex. This was explosive stuff for this small, tightly knit community – and it immediately reminded me of the drama in Dover nearly twenty years earlier. Near the end, the segment quoted Penncrest school board member Jeff Brooks, a military veteran and life-long Republican who had opposed both policies. "The biggest effect that [the policy controversy] had is that it has taken time away from our administration being able to focus on the classroom," Brooks said.

Brooks' argument – adult culture wars are taking time and attention from learning – is exactly the point I wanted to make in this chapter, so I reached out to him to learn more. He graciously agreed, and our conversation helped illustrate the kinds of dynamics I worry about most.

When we spoke a few weeks later, I asked Brooks to walk me through specific examples of how the controversies surrounding the new policies had negatively affected the district's students. He had plenty of receipts. "Every minute that we're spending on something outside of the classroom is time that we could be spending on a curriculum, on teacher development, on classroom observations, on improving literacy skills," he explained. "We don't pay the administration to cater to the board. ... Back in old times, when I went to college, one of the things that stuck from one of my economics classes was opportunity cost." For example, to implement the district's new book policy, six building principals, three assistant principals, and three librarians had to spend two weeks going through every book in the district's libraries – time they could've directed to something else.[18]

And Brooks told me the latest controversy was just a continuation of other adult drama. Penncrest was once rated in the top 10 percent of the state for achievement but had dropped precipitously as a result of budget cuts, poor administration, and political dysfunction on the board. "Mostly it was just the lack of focus on education, the focus being on every other thing," Brooks said regarding his frustrations with the board. "We've been manufacturing different nonsense drama for a while. ... With a school board like ours, you can't tell from month to month what the next controversy is going to be." And the dysfunction had other consequences. When the district last tried to fill its superintendent position, only two qualified candidates applied because of the district's reputation. Each of the applicants had their own baggage from prior districts. Uncertain about how long he would have the job, the district's prior superintendent didn't even bother moving in and instead lived out of a hotel.

Brooks had decided not to run for reelection himself. He was tired of being called a "groomer" for speaking out on behalf of LGBT students. As a public official, he did not feel like he could respond with the decorum and restraint an elected office required.

I found the Penncrest example illuminating. It had all of the pieces – misguided priorities, misallocation of scarce staff and financial resources, administrative turnover, negative impact on recruitment, school board member turnout – that I believe helps explain why adult political conflicts like these ultimately filter down to the classroom and negatively impact students.

---

[18] Another school district, in Virginia, estimated that it took a staff of eleven working forty hours a week all school year to respond to complaints filed by a "serial" book challenger upset about sexually explicit content (Natanson, 2023b).

Just a few days before my interview with Brooks, another LGBT-themed school controversy broke out on the other side of country. In Temecula, a wine-growing region in Southern California, a conservative school board majority had just voted against adopting a new social studies textbook because the supplementary material mentioned Harvey Milk, a murdered San Francisco County supervisor who had been the first openly gay elected official in US history. The school board president had called Milk a "pedophile" at the meeting – in apparent reference to Milk dating a sixteen-year-old – and the story blew up. It even attracted the attention of California's publicity hungry governor, Gavin Newsom, who called the board president ignorant on Twitter and announced the state would step in to buy the rejected textbooks and bill the district for the cost. The governor's spokesman noted the move was unusual but pointed to a little-noticed law that allowed the state to intervene when districts faced textbook "shortages." Because the lack of approval of the textbooks meant the district was stuck with old, outdated materials that did not comply with the most recent standards, the administration argued, the law applied.

Despite the attention focused on the social studies controversy, the chaos and dysfunction Temecula was much deeper. A few days after the textbook vote, the conservative board majority fired the district's superintendent. A few months later, the majority disintegrated – one member resigned to move to Texas for work, another lost a recall election by just a few hundred votes. The community seemed evenly divided and the conflict was playing out in the district. However, various political interests were happily to milk the controversy to for political gain.

In an insightful article, veteran California education journalist John Festerwald noted that Gov. Newsom seemed eager to wade into the culture war issue playing out in Temecula. Oddly, however, the governor had not taken similarly proactive action to address outdated reading curriculum – including those using the controversial "three-cueing method" I discuss in Chapter 4 – which arguably had a much bigger impact on the state's students and affected many more school districts. "An unknown number of districts are also using outdated textbooks or early literacy curriculums with disproven reading techniques," Festerwald noted dryly in his piece. But a spokesman for the governor said "the administration doesn't intend to respond similarly to them" (Festerwald, 2023).

The Temecula story seemed to be an uncanny repeat of the Penncrest experience. Adult culture wars were sucking all of the air out of the room, and strategic politicians were taking advantage of the situation to score political points. All of the media publicity and attention was turning up the volume and the emotions. No one seemed interested in student learning.

But the recent LGBT debates also illustrate why these kinds of battles are unavoidable, given the incentives all of the key actors face. Consider the book *Gender Queer*, which has been the focus of much of the recent controversy over school book bans. The graphic memoir tackles the issue of gender dysphoria and has won wide critical acclaim. Trans rights activists insist it is important to make it available to students struggling with their gender identity, a long-overlooked and disadvantaged population suffering particularly high rates of suicide. However, several of the pages in the book are very graphic, including one depicting a scene in which a character wearing a strap-on gets a blowjob. Conservative activists believe the material is inappropriate for younger (e.g., elementary grade) children.

Certainly there seems to be room for good-faith disagreement – people who want to make the book available to trans kids are not "groomers," and parents concerned about age appropriateness are not "transphobes." Yet a decision has to be made, and there is no room for compromise – either the book is available in libraries serving younger children or it is not. One camp has to win and one has to lose. The more one side advocates for their position, the more the other feels like it must countermobilize. "Nothing enrages parents more than the idea that their children are being turned against them, and few things worry a partisan more than the fear the opposing party is using schools to inculcate its beliefs in the young," journalist Jonathan Chait summarized presciently in a recent article (Chait, 2023).

In some cases, it may be difficult to separate the (adult) political dimension of conflicts from reasonable disagreement about (student) academic goals. For example, disputes over Critical Race Theory and history instruction (discussed in Chapter 4) and evolution are fundamentally tied to content standards. How these disputes are ultimately resolved may impact student performance on tests aligned with those standards. Deciding whether or not to teach about intelligent design ultimately impacts how students perform on science exams (see Arold, 2024). In the real world, it may not always be possible to separate purely political arguments from legitimate academic or pedagogical considerations. But even in such instances, it is worth taking trade-offs into account. The benefits of adopting better curriculum, to take one example, must be weighed against the learning disruptions and operational dysfunction the associated advocacy campaigns on behalf of such adoptions may cause.

Unfortunately, asking one side in a culture war to show some forbearance while other pushes full steam ahead can feel a lot like unilateral disarmament. And the Cold War analogy is actually quite appropriate. During this fraught period, both the US government and the Soviet Union had to choose between investing scarce resources in guns to retain parity in the arms race or in "butter" – other public services essential to social welfare. Both obviously preferred to spend less on guns and more on butter – but only if they believed the other side would do the same. As long as one side kept buying more guns, the other side had to do the same. Some observers have argued that the Soviet Union ultimately collapsed because it simply ran out of money – it could not spend as much as the arms race demanded while maintaining sufficient investment on other government services. Similar dynamics plague today's education culture wars.

6

The Color of School Employment

> In a war, there must be some casualties, and perhaps the Black teachers will be the casualties in the fight for equal education of Black students.
> —Attributed (perhaps apocryphally) to U.S. Department of Health, Education, and Welfare staff attorney in 1965

In 1897, an African-American man by the name of Gabriel Jones was elected as a Republican to the Indiana state legislature. Originally born in Tennessee, Jones had moved to Indiana two decades prior and had built an impressively diverse resume – working as a police officer, a federal tax collector, and a deputy county recorder. Indeed, an obituary after his death would describe Jones as "one of the most widely known colored men in the state" (Indianapolis News, 1915). His real passion, though, was education. Jones had been both an Indianapolis teacher and an assistant principal – and once in the legislature, where he would serve only a single year, Jones turned his attention to schools, particularly for the state's Black children.

At the time, Indiana did not have an enviable track record on this score. It had not updated the state law on public education to provide schooling for non-white children until 1869, becoming one of the last Northern states to do so. Even then, the reform was half-hearted – allowing school districts that did not have enough "colored" children living within a "reasonable distance" to fill a racially segregated school to provide "other means of education for said children," while being mindful of taxpayer expense (Thornbrough, 1957). By the last decade of the nineteenth century, when Jones had ascended to state office, different parts of the state had implemented the mandate in different ways. Most rural areas, which had few minority children, simply allowed them to attend white schools. However, a handful of larger urban school systems, including Indianapolis, were operating separate, legally segregated schools. Concerned that this was producing huge inequities in educational quality that short-changed students of color, Jones put forward a bill to integrate the education system in his hometown and the other areas of the state that were operating separate schools for minority children.

Initially, the bill seemed to have a smooth path to passage. The House education committee reported favorably on the legislation, and when it reached the floor, an amendment to continue to allow racially segregated schools was defeated. Indeed, other adopted amendments actually strengthened Jones's initial language, expressly permitting Black children to attend the school located in closest proximity to their residence and making discrimination against them a misdemeanor offense subject to a fine. The amended bill passed out the House.

However, before it could become law, the legislation faced an unexpected mobilized campaign of opposition, from surprising quarters. A petition, signed by thirty Black Indianapolis teachers, arrived at the statehouse, urging state senators to vote against it in the legislature's upper house. "If such a Bill becomes a Law, we believe that it will be detrimental to the colored people of the State," the petition read, noting that the city's Black schools also provided an important source of good-paying jobs for educated African-American teachers.[1] "[I]t will deprive not only ourselves but many colored men and women of their livelihood; and that it will remove the opportunity that colored men and women now have to strive after and obtain honorable employment in our public schools" (Thornbrough, 1957, p. 338). In response, a group of some of the most highly educated Black residents of Indianapolis filed their own *counterpetition*, in support of the Jones bill. "Indiana alone of all of the northern states keeps this discrimination against colored children," they wrote. "We ask no special or class legislation, but simply that the class legislation on our statute books be removed."

The dueling petitions presented a dilemma for white Indiana state senators. Who really spoke for the interests of the Black community? And, with competing arguments made on each side, how should they vote on

---

[1] Across the state, some "colored" schools employed only Black educators, while others employed a mix of both Black and white teachers. However, schools for white students and integrated schools employed almost no Black teachers, as was the case in much of the country.

the bill? For advice, they turned to George Knox, the publisher of the *Indianapolis Freeman*, one of the country's leading African-American newspapers. Knox's message to legislators was clear – prioritize the good-paying jobs, not the educational interests of school children. "He spoke against the adoption of the law," one historian wrote, "because its enforcement would put so many Negro educators out of work" (Lyda, 1953, p. 87). Knox's counsel apparently had great effect. The Senate killed Jones's bill, and Indiana would not take legislative action to integrate its schools for another five decades.[2]

I begin this chapter with the story of Jones's failed integration efforts because it clearly illustrates several political realities that make improving public education is so difficult, particularly in low-achieving urban districts. First, although many commentators like to pretend otherwise, the interests of students and those of school employees are not always aligned. Time and time again, when the choice is between good jobs for adults and good schools for children, the political process stacks the deck on behalf of adult employment interests, just as happened in Indiana.

Second, if choosing between adult employment concerns and student learning was not already difficult enough, the politics becomes even trickier when these trade-offs take on a racial dimension, which we will see is often the case. This reflects America's unique political history that has resulted in racial minorities being employed disproportionately in the public sector. In many urban centers, such as Baltimore, Washington, DC, and Atlanta, local schools have long been an important source of good-paying, middle-class jobs for African-American residents and the preservation of these jobs a major priority for prominent Black elected officials and other community leaders. Unfortunately, this means that any decline in public sector employment often produces disparate racial impact, creating yet another political impediment to making difficult but sometimes necessary decisions that put the interests of children first – with the resulting costs often borne by disproportionately low-income children of color. (I examine how these dynamics play out in debates surrounding school closures in Chapter 7.)

More than a century after Jones was elected to the Indiana state legislature, another reformer focused on improving education for Black children

---

[2] Knox's warning would prove prophetic. Although the 1949 Indiana law integrating schools specifically outlawed discrimination "in any way in hiring, upgrading, tenure, or placement of any teacher on the basis of race, creed, or color," Black educators nevertheless lost their jobs en masse (Lyda, 1953, p. 88), previewing the dynamics that would play out in the South two decades later.

learned this lesson the hard way. In 2007, Michelle Rhee was appointed to lead the Washington, DC, school system by newly elected Mayor Adrian Fenty.[3] Tapping Rhee, of Korean descent, to run a majority-Black school system was a politically fraught move. "The racial politics will kill you," she had been warned before accepting the job (Whitmire, 2011, p. 128). During Rhee's three-year tenure, DC schools underwent dramatic changes, among them a major reform of teacher pay and the adoption of a highly regarded teacher evaluation system that researchers have shown has substantially improved the quality of city's teacher workforce (see Adnot et al., 2017; Dee and Wyckoff, 2015; Dee, James and Wyckoff, 2021). Indeed, a rigorous evaluation carried out by the research consultancy Mathematica found that the Rhee-era reforms produced dramatic improvements in the achievement of DC students, far outpacing the gains made by most other big-city districts during the same period (Dotter, Chaplin and Bartlett, 2021). However, Rhee's tenure would not survive long enough to see the praise. In 2010, Fenty was voted out of office in a landslide widely seen as a referendum on Rhee's leadership, and she would subsequently resign.

Ultimately, Fenty argued that the political costs were worth it. "If it's a war," he explained in a televised interview after the election that swept him out of office, "someone's got to be at the front of the line, and they've got to get killed first. That's how you win a war, is by going forward" (DeBonis, 2010). An alternative interpretation, however, is that Fenty's loss and Rhee's defenestration illustrate the political difficulty of sustaining educational reforms that prioritize students ahead of adult employment in a system where elections drive policy and mostly childless adults cast the votes. In retrospect, it is not obvious that Fenty and Rhee martyrdom really did much to win a war, or that the war was even winnable.

Many observers attributed the political backlash and subsequent downfall to Rhee's decision to layoff several hundred educators in October 2009, almost all of them Black, in response to a budget shortfall. "In cities around the country, like in D.C., the Black middle class are educators, they're teachers, they're principals. So when you have a tough economy they are impacted in a disproportionate amount," explained Rhee's future husband, Kevin Johnson, a former NBA player and himself

---

[3] The city's school board had just been stripped of its decision-making authority, handing the power to the mayor.

a rising African-American politician.[4] "I think that parlayed into a race issue. Whether it was right or wrong, it became real because you're talking about people's livelihoods in a real way" (Whitmire, 2011, p. 199).

This theme seemed to repeat itself throughout Rhee's tenure. Consider the case of Sousa Middle School, a long-struggling building in the city's disadvantaged southeast side. Before Rhee's appointment, the school had an abysmal reputation and even worse academic achievement. One teacher from a different school told a reporter that Sousa was a "dumping ground" ground for checked-out educators – "a place toxic with low expectations, where students roamed the halls and fought" (McCrummen, 2010). Rhee decided to clean house, fixing up the building and installing a dynamic new (Black) principal who fired most of the teachers, infuriating their union. Student test scores in Sousa soared, posting the largest middle-school gains in the district.

On Election Day in 2010, however, Fenty won less than 15 percent of the vote in the precinct that contained the school. When journalist Richard Whitmire went to interview voters and parents in the neighborhood for his book *The Bee Eater*, they acknowledged that the school had improved dramatically but were still upset about the teacher firings. Intrigued, Whitmire commissioned a professional survey, which compared public opinion among residents of the neighborhood to voters citywide.[5] Although Sousa parents were more likely than their peers in the rest of the district to report that DC schools were moving in the right direction, most disagreed that the teacher firings had been necessary to achieve the improvements in their middle school and more said Fenty's education policies had caused them to oppose his reelection than to vote for him. If education reform was a net vote-loser among parents in what was previously one of the worst-performing (and now fastest-improving) schools in one of the nation's most dysfunctional urban school districts, it's hard to imagine how it could be a politically winning strategy anywhere else.

In this chapter, I zoom in on two fascinating historical case studies – the desegregation of Southern schools after *Brown v. Board of Education* and the dramatic education overhaul in New Orleans after the destruction of Hurricane Katrina – that illustrate the challenge of improving

---

[4] Johnson would go on to serve as the mayor of Sacramento, California.
[5] The survey was carried out by Clarus Research Group in late September 2010, shortly after the mayoral election.

education when adult jobs at stake. Although both are stories with an arguably happy ending – student interests prevailed, and student outcomes subsequently improved – they are also exceptions that prove the rule. In each case, it would take extraordinary political interventions and erosion of local democratic control of schools, made possible by threat of losing federal funding in one case and a horrific natural disaster in the other, for policymakers to ultimately prioritize student needs. Such interventions are quite rare – representing outcomes that game theorists would describe as "off the equilibrium path." But by providing contrasts with business (and governance) as usual, they illustrate how the political process normally stacks the deck in favor of vested interests opposed to institutional change and reform (Moe, 2015). In the context of education, this often means protecting adult employment – even if the jobs come at the expense of public school students and their education. The desegregation and New Orleans success stories are so powerful because they are so rare, giving us a glimpse for what might be possible if adult politics didn't get in the way.

RACE AND GOVERNMENT EMPLOYMENT

To fully appreciate how race and politics intersect to shape many debates about education policy, there is a crucial piece of historical context: To this day, racial minorities – and especially African-Americans – are more likely to work in the public rather than private sector (Laird, 2017). This statistical regularity is both a legacy of the racism that shaped America's economy during much of its history and intentional efforts to redress historical wrongs through government action.

One often overlooked reason for why minorities have been hired disproportionately into government jobs is the impact of civil service reforms that swept through much of the public sector in the first half of the Twentieth Century. By requiring that open positions be filled based on objective criteria, such as performance on civil service exams, these reforms sought to limit the extent to which elected officials could pad government rolls with their political supporters. In addition to preventing political and partisan patronage and favoritism, however, these efforts also limited the extent to which other irrelevant considerations – including racial prejudice – entered into hiring and promotion decisions.[6] In

---

[6] Given the historical importance of civil service exams in limiting racial prejudice in government hiring and promotions, it is ironic that many civil rights activists today object to these same exams because of racial disparities in passage rates.

addition, efforts to eliminate discrimination in employment began first in the public sector, through a series of presidential executive action. Such discrimination was not banned in the private sector until the Civil Rights Act of 1964, decades after similar efforts began in the context of government employment.

Finally, starting in the 1960s, politicians at all levels of government implemented affirmative action programs that sought to specifically boost the employment and contracting opportunities for racial minorities (Collins, 1997). At the local level, minority hiring and contracting efforts were a key campaign plank of newly elected African-American mayors, such as Tom Bradley in Los Angeles (Sonenshein, 1993). Indeed, rigorous economics research has shown that the election of Black mayors continues to have a causal effect on labor market outcomes, disproportionately increasing Black employment in the government sector (Nye, Rainer and Stratmann, 2015).

I suspect many readers find such efforts unobjectionable in the abstract. Government jobs, after all, tend to provide better security, more generous health-care and retirement benefits, and opportunity for promotion to occupations with greater authority and autonomy (Wilson, 1997). Policies designed to provide greater access to these perks for disadvantaged and underrepresented groups seems a small down-payment on righting a long history of systemic racism and government-sanctioned injustices (e.g., Rothstein, 2018).

The problem with thinking about policy in the abstract is that obscures difficult trade-offs and overlooks important questions of distributional justice. Famed Harvard African-American sociologist William Julius Wilson made the latter point in his critique of government affirmative action programs, noting that they disproportionately benefit relatively well-off, highly educated African-Americans (Wilson, 1978). The problem, he noted, is that the benefits of such programs rarely reach more disadvantaged, lower-income African-Americans who have suffered job losses and economic dislocation from outsourcing of low-skilled jobs and automation in recent decades. Putting lots of energy into affirmative action government hiring programs for the middle class uses scarce up fiscal resources and political capital that would be better invested in helping the urban underclass, whom Wilson called the "truly disadvantaged."

While Wilson was most concerned about how the costs and benefits of government programs are distributed across economic classes, in the case of education, we should also consider distributional consequences across generations. What if government jobs meant to lift up economically disadvantaged adults mean a worse education for their children, leaving them less competitive in the labor market when they grow up and creating yet another generation of economically disadvantaged people in need of government support? From my conversations with many activists and school board members, well-meaning progressives almost instinctively reject the idea that such a trade-offs exists. One common refrain is that we can walk (provide good education) and chew gum (provide good-paying jobs) at the same time. Sometimes they throw out academic jargon, like the "scarcity mindset," or blame racism, "neoliberalism," and "privatization of public education" for the lack of resources. If only corrupt politicians fully funded public education, if only we spent a fraction of what we allocate toward the military on our schools, if only we redirected some of the wasteful fossil fuel subsidies to invest in our children, we could provide *both* a good education and good-paying jobs. Over many years of asking this question, I have heard every silver-tongued, pass-the-buck dodge and excuse in the book. Yet in the real world, trade-offs are unavoidable because resources are scarce and there is never enough to accomplish all of the desirable goals we might have. That does not mean that the goals are not admirable, only that we can't achieve them all. At the end, some prioritization is necessary, and in education, many questions come down to choosing between adult jobs and education for children. My argument is that the incentives created through democratic control stack the deck in favor of adults.

Washington, DC, provides a illustrative example of this dynamic. In 1978, civil rights activist Marion Barry was elected as the city's mayor. Although he is best known today for his downfall a decade later, when he purchased crack cocaine in an undercover sting operation – his exclamation at the time of the arrest, "Bitch set me up!" has become infamous – he remained highly popular among the city's Black community. Getting more African-Americans into government jobs and contracts was a major part of Barry's agenda. Initially, Barry pledged to give a quarter of all city contracts to minorities, a figure he later bumped up to 35 percent. This included the city's schools, and the minority contracting mandate immediately caused costs of school meals to balloon. Since the district didn't suddenly have more money to cover the additional costs, this necessitated making offsetting cuts.

The superintendent of schools at the time, a Black man named Vince Reed, went to the mayor to complain about the unintended consequences of the minority contract quota. "I understand that you want to give contracts to Black companies. But when you tell me to take food out of a

Black kid's stomach so some Black dude can get rich, I have to ask what's your rationale?" Reed reportedly asked the mayor. "Black entrepreneurs are at the top of my agenda,' Barry responded. "We have to do it this way. It's the only way to get them into the mainstream" (Jaffe and Sherwood, 1994).

Many other scholars and commentators have noted how clientalistic racial politics often get in the way of serving students. In a pathbreaking book, titled *The Color of School Reform*, political scientists Jeffrey Henig, Richard Hula, Marion Orr, and Desiree Pedescleaux offer a fascinating study of four urban school districts, Atlanta, Baltimore, Detroit, and the District of Columbia.[7] All served overwhelmingly kids of color and all were staffed by Black superintendents, administrators, and teachers. Yet, despite ample descriptive representation, all struggled to meaningfully improve. "The politics of jobs can be – and often is – an impediment to systemic school reform, but the power of education professionals rests on more than the votes and campaign contributions they can muster from within their own ranks," the authors concluded. Employment concerns can motivate broader political activism and lobbying – including among Black clergy, a historically powerful political block, whose middle class congregants often work in local government. As a result, "community mobilization around school issues often takes the shape of protecting jobs and their incumbents instead of demanding higher levels of performance and structural change," they noted (Henig et al., 2001, p. 27).

Another political scientist, Wilbur Rich, reached a similar conclusion in his in-depth study of Detroit, Gary (Indiana), and Newark (New Jersey), three cities where Black leaders and elected officials have overseen the school systems since the 1960s. In each city, he discovered a "cartel" of school administrators, activists, and union leaders largely incapable of improving the achievement of their overwhelmingly Black students. "Our role," one former Detroit school board member recalled, "was more than just to educate but to give Blacks positions and jobs, so that they can hire other Blacks in the future" (Rich, 1996, p. 145). A board member from Newark agreed, explaining that "urban boards of education are conducive to becoming the community employment agency. The primary mission is not to educate the kids but find employment for the community" (p. 209). Rich came away quite dejected about the future prospects for meaningful change. "I must confess a new admiration for those who

---

[7] The title of this chapter is adapted from the title of their book.

kept the faith that American schools can be reformed," he wrote in the preface to his book. "I have gone from being a true believer to an athiest" (Rich, 1996, p. xii).

This chapter departs from this admittedly depressing scholarship by instead focusing on two success stories – historical cases where serious employment concerns were ultimately overcome. The end result was significant improvement in educational opportunities for students, especially students of color. In both cases, however, reform was accompanied the loss (or lack) of local political control and accountability, and I argue it was the absence of electoral accountability that made the reforms possible. This suggests a normatively difficult trade-off – just as we must decide whether we want to prioritize adult jobs or students, we must sometimes choose between democracy and educational quality. Not all good things go together.

UNTOLD STORY OF SOUTHERN DESEGREGATION

When people think about the desegregation of public schools, the narrative that usually comes to mind is something like this: In the Jim Crow South, African-American children attended decrepit, overcrowded, underfunded schools under a system notionally "separate but equal" – but in fact a much more separate and unequal. The US Supreme Court overturned nearly 100 years of precedent in 1954, ruling that "separate but equal" violated the Equal Protection Clause of the 14th Amendment in *Brown v. Board of Education* and ordered de jury segregation to end. This prompted an organized effort by racist Southern whites, dubbed "Massive Resistance," to thwart the school integration efforts. Eventually, the advent of court-ordered busing would effectively (but temporarily) integrate the schools, leading to overwhelming political opposition among white families and the election of conservative Republican presidents, the appointment of conservative jurists to the Supreme Court, and ultimately the end of busing (see, e.g., Hannah-Jones, 2019).

Although there are important grains of truth in this popular narrative, it also gets a lot wrong. Start with the claims about the dire state of segregated schools prior to *Brown*. It is true that, historically, Southern states provided much less funding for Black schools than they did for their white counterparts. Ironically, however, this had begun to change in the years leading up to the 1954 Supreme Court case – in large part as an effort to head off to the looming legal threats. The best evidence we have comes from the work of journalist Harry Ashmore, an editorial writer for the *Arkansas Gazette* who carried out painstaking research on the state of Black education in the South for the Ford Foundation in the early 1950s. In 1940, Southern states spent just forty cents to operate Black schools for every dollar they spent on schools for white kids, and the gap was even larger in terms of capital funding. Teachers working in Black schools were paid about half of what educators in white schools made and had nearly a year less of formal education, on average (Ashmore, 1954). By 1952, two years before the *Brown* decision, Ashmore found that the gap in funding had shrunk dramatically. Teacher education levels across both types of schools approached parity and educators in Black schools now made about 87 percent of average salaries in white schools. In his 1951 inaugural address, for example, South Carolina Gov. James F. Byrnes called for greater funding for schools serving African-American children: "It is our duty to provide for the races substantial equality in school facilities. We should do it because it is right. For me that is sufficient reason."[8]

Nor was *Brown* the first Supreme Court case to strike down educational segregation. The earliest cases – decided nearly two decades earlier – dealt primarily with higher education. Southern states could not afford to maintain segregated programs for every college major and professional degree program, which made the defense of "separate but equal" untenable. Missouri, for example, had only one law school, and it did not accept Black students. Like many other states at the time, Missouri officials offered to pay out-of-state tuition for Black students to pursue their studies elsewhere, in places that did not insist on segregating their programs. One consequence, as pointed out by Fenwick (2022), is that many African-Americans in the South received a better education than their Southern white counterparts, attending elite universities such as Columbia and Harvard at taxpayer expense. Many returned to work as teachers in all-Black Southern schools, where pay for Black educators was increasing rapidly in the pre-*Brown* years thanks to the concern about ongoing litigation. Despite such out-of-state opportunities, however, the Supreme Court struck down the Missouri system as unconstitutional in *State of Missouri ex rel. Gaines v. Canada et al.* decided in 1938. When states responded by trying to build new all-Black

---

[8] In other parts of the speech, Byrnes anticipated the coming litigation and explained that "separate but equal" could only be defended if Black schools were, in fact, equal. "Whatever is necessary to continue the separation of the races in the schools of South Carolina is going to be done by the white people of the state. That is my ticket as a private citizen. It will be my ticket as governor," he said in the same address.

law schools and graduate programs from scratch, subsequent decisions struck these down too, arguing that upstart programs were inherently unequal.[9]

Not only did *Brown* build on decades of precedent, it did not produce much by way of integration, despite the reverence many have for the decision today. The court tempered its repudiation of "separate but equal" with instruction that integration proceed with "all deliberate speed" in a follow-on opinion. This meant that, outside of a few border states, it did not proceed at all. In 1964 – an entire decade after the original *Brown* decision – more than 98 percent of African-American children in the South were still attending segregated schools (Orfield, 1969). Much of this reflected entrenched opposition among racist whites – but some also reflected the divisions among Black elites and interest groups, including concerns about the employment impacts.

One underappreciated fact is that, just as in Indianapolis half a century earlier, segregated schools in the South provided an important source of good-paying jobs for highly educated African-Americans. According to the 1960 census, teaching accounted for an astounding 41 percent of all jobs held by college-educated Blacks in the South – with no other occupation exceeding 5 percent (Thompson, 2022, p. 962). It was clear to many observers that integration of students would result in the loss of well-paying, middle-class jobs for Black educators. Getting Southern whites to accept Black students in their schools was already a heavy lift. Allowing Black teachers was going to be a political nonstarter. "While many southern localities were prepared to tolerate a few Negro students in the white schools, the general popular assumption was that there were no Negro teachers competent to teach in white schools and that white teachers would absolutely refuse assignment in Negro schools," legal scholar Gary Orfield (1969, p. 69) noted.

Whether school integration was worth the cost of the likely job losses divided prominent Black leaders and intellectuals, just as once it had in Indiana. One integration skeptic was Oliver Cox, a sociologist at the segregated, all-Black Lincoln University in Missouri. Cox had seen firsthand

---

[9] In the 1950 case *Sweatt v. Painter* case, striking down an effort by Texas to start a new law school for Black students while keeping the University of Texas segregated, Chief Justice Fred Vinson wrote: "What is more important, the University of Texas Law School possesses to a far greater degree those qualities which are incapable of objective measurement but which make the greatness in a law school. Such qualities, to name but a few, include reputation of the faculty, experience of the administration, position and influence of the alumni, standing in the community, traditions and prestige."

how the integration of higher education that preceded the *Brown* decision had resulted in massive job losses among Black college professors. Now, he warned a similar fate was about to befall elementary and secondary teachers. "If Negro teachers must face unemployment as the price of the abolition of discrimination in education, the bargain is unacceptable," he argued in a 1953 article published in the *Nation* and titled, "Negro Teachers: Martyrs to Integration?" After all, what would be the point of a better education if it meant fewer good employment opportunities to actually make a living using the skills Black children learned in their integrated schools? "Freedom to work is at least as sacred as the right to non-discrimination in education," Cox wrote. "Indeed, education itself will have a decreasing value if the occasion to employ it is increasingly limited. ... Anti-segregation legislation is important, but its proponents must remember that their real purpose is to enhance the welfare of a people" (Cox, 1953).

Cox was not alone. Writing in his Ford Foundation report, Ashmore noted that opposition to school integration did not come exclusively from racist whites. "For entirely different reasons, it appears that there has been at least as much tacit opposition to the move on the part of Negro teachers who are afraid of losing their jobs through discrimination or direct competition with better-trained whites," he noted (1954, p. 80). In some cases, local officials made the threat explicit. In a message to Black educators, the superintendent of the Topeka school district – the defendant in the *Brown* case – warned that an unfavorable outcome might affect their employment. "Due to the present uncertainty about enrollment in schools next year for Negro children, it is not possible at this time to offer you employment for next year," the superintendent stated in a letter to one teacher. "If the Supreme Court should rule that segregation in the elementary grades is unconstitutional, our Board will proceed on the assumption that the majority of people in Topeka will not want to employ Negro teachers next year for white children. ... If it turns out that segregation is not terminated, there will be nothing to prevent us from negotiating a contract with you at some later date in the spring" (Fenwick, 2022, p. 5).

Other prominent Black leaders spoke up in defense of integration, however. This included Charles Henry Thompson, a dean at Howard University. Writing in a 1951 "editorial comment" in the *Journal of Negro Education*, which he had founded, Thompson highlighted a recent decision by the University of Louisville to close its "Negro branch," the Louisville Municipal College for Negroes, as part of the integration process, and similar job loss concerns in an Illinois school district Thompson had visited the summer before. "I have gone into this situation at some length because some uncertainty as to the status of Negro teachers when segregated schools are outlawed has played and is playing a silent but important role in our present fight to eliminate this undemocratic practice," Thompson explained. The Louisville example "makes it appear that Negroes are faced by the dilemma either of acquiescing in the maintenance of segregated schools with Negro teachers, or of obtaining admission of Negroes to white schools with the consequent elimination of Negro teachers" (Thompson, 1951).

Nevertheless, Thompson downplayed the employment risks, arguing that there was simply not enough white teachers to replace all of the Black educators. "I might add, however," he went on, "that even if they were faced by such a dilemma, the elimination of legally-enforced segregated schools should outweigh in importance the loss of teaching positions even by a majority of the 75,000 Negro teachers who might conceivably be affected." In the two decades that would follow, Thompson's *Journal of Negro Education* would be on the forefront of reporting on the employment impacts of school integration.

Powell Amendment

As I mentioned earlier, the *Brown* decision itself accomplished little in terms of actually integrating schools. What ultimately did the trick was an act of Congress – and the tenacity of one legislator, Rep. Adam Clayton Powell. The backstory of how Powell brought about the integration of Southern schools also explains why the effort resulted in so many Black educators losing their jobs in the process.

Powell, who was elected to Congress after a stint as the first Black member of the New York city council, was a larger-than-life character. President Truman once banned him from the White House for insulting the first lady. When he came under fire for taking two young women (neither his wife) on a foreign trip at taxpayer expense while chairing the House education and labor committee, Powell replied incredibly, "I wish to state very emphatically ... that I will always do just what every other Congressman and committee chairman has done and is doing and will do." His colleagues voted to expel him from the House – only to have Powell reelected by his constituents![10]

---

[10] The Supreme Court would ultimately rule that the expulsion was unconstitutional.

Frustrated by the Southern foot-dragging in complying with the *Brown* decision, Powell began putting forth amendments to all sorts of federal spending legislation making qualifications for funding contingent on school integration. When Congress had proposed appropriating federal funding for school construction in 1956 – the first major effort to include education funding in the federal budget – Powell tried to attach his amendment, requiring that local districts receive federal dollars only if schools were "open to all children without regard to race in conformity with the requirements of the United States Supreme Court decisions," a clear reference to *Brown*. Political scientist William Riker argued that opponents of federal funding had used the Powell amendment as a poison pill – voting in favor of adding it to the legislation, knowing that the amendment's inclusion would cause enough Southern Democrats to vote against the final bill to defeat it (Riker, 1986, Chapter 11).[11]

The politically divisive history of the Powell amendment had a profound impact on debates about education policy, shaping the strategies of key interest groups. For example, while the American Federation of Teachers (AFT) quickly came out in support of the 1954 *Brown* decision, its larger competitor, the National Education Association (NEA) said little. Part of this reflected differences in the internal politics of the two organizations. A union made up of teachers in primarily large urban Northern cities, the AFT had little to lose in supporting the decision. The NEA, by contrast, represented many teachers in Southern states and indeed operated segregated affiliates in those areas (Urban, 2000). Perhaps more importantly, at the top of NEA's legislative agenda was pushing through federal funding for public education. Having seen how efforts to attach the Powell amendment to appropriations bills led to their failure in the past,[12] the NEA adopted a position of "calculated silence" on the issue (see Schultz, 1970, p. 76).

For years, Powell's campaign was a lost cause – a symbolic effort doomed to failure. But the politics changed on November 22, 1963, with the assassination of President John F. Kennedy. In the months before, the Kennedy administration had been working to shepherd a civil rights

---

[11] Fearing that the Powell amendment would effectively derail federal funding efforts, the 1956 Democratic presidential nominee Adlai Stevenson opposed it (Orfield, 1969, p. 26). More recently, however, other scholars have challenged Riker's interpretation (see Gilmour, 2001).

[12] The *NEA Journal* reminded its members: "Keep in mind, however, that the adoption of the Powell Amendment prevented Southern members who favored the [1956 school funding] bill from voting for it" (cited in Schultz, 1970, p. 80).

package through Congress. Taking advantage on the nation's shock after Kennedy's assassination, his vice president, Lyndon Johnson, pushed through the legislation, which became known as the Civil Rights Act of 1964. Crucially, the law included the language requiring an end to legal segregation as a condition for receiving federal money that Powell had long sought to get passed.[13]

Initially, Powell's amendment did not have much teeth, since the federal government spent little on education, so segregated districts didn't leave much money on the table by not complying with the *Brown* decision. This changed dramatically in 1965, with the passage of the Elementary and Secondary Education Act (ESEA). Under Title I of the law, the federal government for the first time became a major contributor of funding to local schools. Critically, the formula for allocating Title I aid was based on poverty – and as a result, the impoverished South stood to gain the most. With so many federal dollars on the line, the calculus facing local education administrators had changed. "The interaction of these two laws," Orfield has written, referring to the Civil Rights Act and ESEA, "confirmed the worst fears of Southern leaders and prompted revolutionary change in Southern schools" (Orfield, 1969, p. 4).

But there was a wrinkle. The Powell amendment dealt exclusively with the integration of *students* – it said nothing about the integration of school faculty, who were just as segregated in the South. While Title VII of the Civil Rights Act outlawed employment discrimination, language added by the Senate Republican leader, Everett McKinley Dirksen, expressly limited federal enforcement efforts in this area.[14] Lawyers advising the federal Department of Health, Education, and Workforce (HEW), in charge of enforcing the Powell amendment, concluded that their ability to do anything about faculty integration was circumscribed by Dirksen's language (Orfield, 1969).[15] Ultimately, an intentional decision was made to prioritize students over teaching jobs, as summarized in the quote that opens this chapter.[16]

---

[13] Importantly, the law also gave the attorney general power to enforce these requirements through litigation.

[14] See Kenworthy (1964) for a detailed account of Dirksen's role in coming up with the compromise language.

[15] Some *court* school integration orders – as opposed to directives from federal bureaucrats – did include requirements for faculty integration.

[16] Although this quote appears in many journalistic and scholarly accounts of school integration, I could not ultimately verify its authenticity. The first mention I could locate was in a 1979 article written by NEA official Samuel Ethridge published in the *Negro Educational Review* (Ethridge, 1979). Ethridge's citation is "*Washington Post*, September 21,

Decline in Black Teacher Employment

How did the integration of Southern schools affect the employment opportunities of Black educators? It turns out this is an incredibly difficult question to answer, since it involves quantifying not just how many teachers were dismissed as a result of integration efforts but also how many were not hired (but would have been otherwise). The scholarly research on this question is mixed and largely anecdotal. In 1965, for example, the NEA released *Report of Task Force Survey of Teacher Displacement in Seventeen State* based on interviews with hundreds of teachers in the affected areas. Many claimed they had been dismissed or demoted as a result of integration efforts. Other reports (e.g., Hooker, 1970) uncovered similar examples, but they were based on unrepresentative and perhaps cherry-picked samples. By contrast, an informal survey of placement directors at leading Black teacher-training schools reported that recent graduates faced "little difficulty" finding employment (Campbell and Richardson, 1968). Others have offered more dramatic figures. For example, Upchurch (2016) argues that nearly 30,000 Black educators lost their jobs – a substantial share of the roughly 84,000 Black teachers who were employed in 1954, at the time of the *Brown* decision.

The most careful and credible estimates come from the work of economist Owen Thompson (2022), who collected detailed district-level data on both teacher employment levels and the precise timing of local integration efforts. By focusing on staffing changes in the years immediately following student integration, he is able to more directly link the two trends. The results from Thompson's analysis are sobering – suggesting that the typical Southern district reduced employment of Black teachers by more than 40 percent during the transition from full segregation to full integration, representing both the dismissal of some existing teachers and a reduction in new hiring.

1965." However, a careful perusal of that day's edition – or any surrounding dates, or similar dates during surrounding years – revealed no trace of the original article. Nearly every subsequent mention I have found uses the same vague citation as Ethridge, apparently lifting it from him (or from each other) without confirming the original source. By contrast, Fenwick (2022) attributes it to a 1970 "US Department of Health, Education, and Welfare Report" without providing any additional information. None of the academic authors who have used this quote in their writing responded to my e-mails for more information. Education journalist Greg Toppo, who quoted it in a 2004 *USA Today* article, did respond but could not recall where he had found the quote. Several research librarians who helped me in my quest also ultimately had no luck tracking down the original source, if it exists.

The Color of School Employment

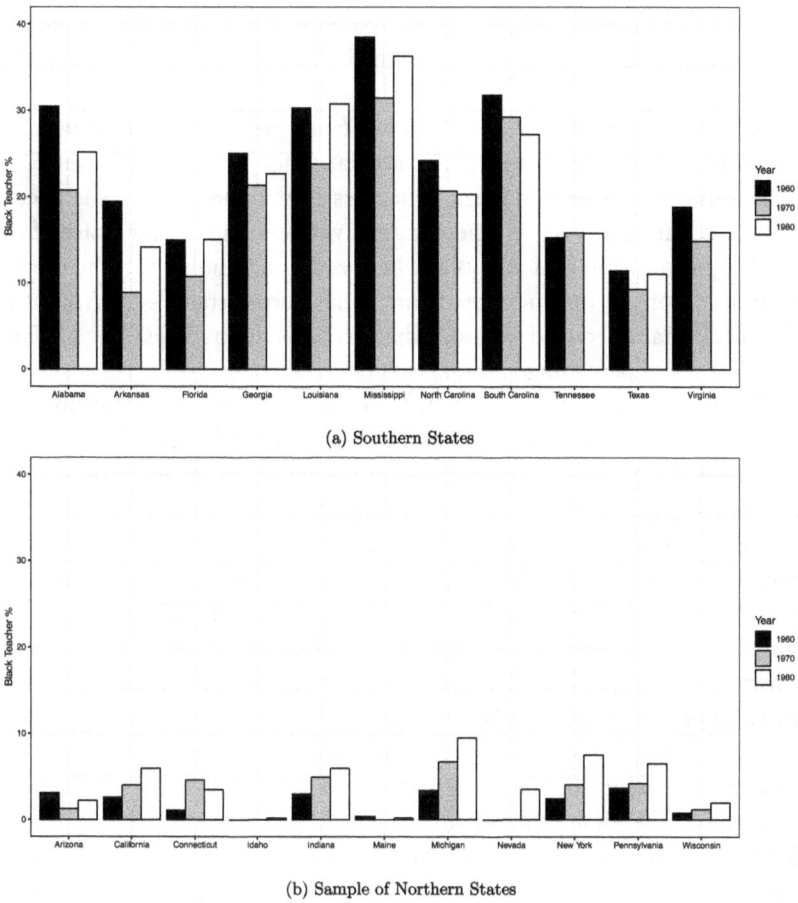

FIGURE 6.1 Trends in Black teacher employment over time

In this chapter, I present a different look at the impact of school integration efforts – moving beyond individual districts and short-term effects to understand how these developments changed the overall racial complexion of the teacher workforce over the course of three decades. Specifically, I rely on micro-data from the 1960, 1970, and 1980 censuses.[17] For each census, I identified respondents who reported their occupation as a teacher and then calculated the *share* of each state's teacher workforce that was made up of African-Americans. The results are presented in Figure 6.1, with panel (a) representing the former

---

[17] For 1960 and 1970, the data are from the 1 percent sample of the full census, meaning that they include a random sample representing 1 out of every 100 people enumerated as part of the national count. For 1980, the data are from the 5 percent sample.

Confederate states in the South and panel (b) providing similar figures for a sample of states in the North, which did not have *de jure* segregated schools.

Several important patterns jump out from the figure. Consistent with other accounts, we see clear evidence that school integration resulted in substantial job losses for Black educators in the South. With the exception of Tennessee, every Southern state saw a reduction in the share of the teaching profession that was Black between 1960 and 1970. The precise magnitude of the decline varied somewhat across states – in Arkansas, the Black share declined by more than half, while in Texas, the decrease was just a few percentage points.

But two other patterns, which have received far less attention, also appear. First, the initial decline was quickly reversed in nearly all Southern states. By 1980, the share of Black educators increased substantially across the South and – with the exception of the Carolinas – strongly rebounded from the nadirs of 1970. Indeed, in a number of states, the racial composition of the teaching force by 1980 looked at least as racially diverse as in the 1960s, prior to the *Brown* decision. Many of the initial declines found by researchers like Thompson appeared to be transitory and the lack of modern day diversity among the Southern teaching force does not appear to be due to the whole-sale dismissal of Black teachers that followed in the wake of school integration efforts, as some modern commentators have suggested.

Second, the figure highlights how much *more* diverse segregated Southern schools were compared to their Northern counterparts. In 1960, Black educators accounted for at least 15 percent of the Southern teaching force in every state. In none of the Northern states highlighted in the figure did figure exceed 5 percent. Although the Northern teacher force became more diverse over the next two decades – moving in the opposite direction of the South between 1960 and 1970 – Black educators still represented a far smaller share of the teacher workforce in the North by 1980, even compared to the reduced numbers seen in the South a decade earlier, in the wake of mass unemployment resulting from integration.

The painful reality that school integration came with a substantial – albeit apparently temporary – mass displacement of Black educators poses a deeply uncomfortable question: Was integration worth it? Increasingly, some revisionist scholars have argued that the answer may be no. This includes the late Harvard law professor Derrick Bell, one of the founders of Critical Race Theory (see Chapter 5 for modern political debates about "CRT" in the context of education). As a young lawyer, Bell had worked with the NAACP Legal Defense Fund on hundreds of desegregation cases. Later in his career, however, Bell had become disenchanted with these efforts. Forced integration had backfired in many cases, fueling white flight to the suburbs, and too many civil rights activists were obsessed with the narrow objective of achieving numerical racial balancing in school enrollments – not with the ultimate goal of improving educational opportunities for Black children. Perhaps, he suggested in a law review commentary in 1980, a better strategy would have been the "creation or preservation of model Black schools." He acknowledged this risked returning to the pre-*Brown* era of "separate but equal" but wondered if it would have still been a better alternative. "Some Black educators, however, see major educational benefits in schools where Black children, parents, and teachers can utilize the real cultural strengths of the Black community to overcome the many barriers to educational achievement," he wrote (Bell, 1980).

In his book *Pyrrhic Victory: The Cost of Integration*, Daniel Upchurch (2016) made a similar argument. "Once schools became integrated, Black students received equal funding and supplies, but lost the benefit of having teachers and school officials who were interested in their success," he concluded. "Many white teachers and administrators, whether due to personal prejudice or resentment of the system changes following *Brown v. Board of Education of Topeka* (1954), simply were not as dedicated to teaching Black students as white students" (p. 8). Others have made somewhat different arguments – suggesting that integration gave rise to ability tracking, with Black students disproportionately assigned to lower-tier, less rigorous classes. Over time, this gave rise to the stereotype that doing well academically amounted to "acting white," creating a culture that undervalued academic excellence in the Black community (see Buck, 2011; Fryer and Torelli, 2010).

Regardless of the empirical validity of these critiques, the evidence suggests that the net effect of integration was overwhelmingly positive for Black students – at least in the South.[18] Careful economic analyses have found that after integration, Black dropout rates in the South declined and, over the long-run, Black students exposed to integrated schools went on to have better labor market, criminal justice, and health

---

[18] In the North, where school segregation was driven primarily by housing patterns rather than legally separated schools, the evidence about the impacts of integration on Black student outcomes is much more mixed (see Melnick, 2020).

outcomes (Anstreicher, Fletcher and Thompson, 2022; Guryan, 2004; Johnson, 2011). This does not mean that the decline in exposure to Black teachers had no negative impacts on students but rather that other improvements in school quality as a result of integration, including higher per-pupil spending and better facilities, more than offset these effects, leaving students better off academically overall.

It should go without saying that it would have obviously been better to have brought about school integration *without* the loss of Black teaching jobs. But as the historical record makes clear, this was not a politically plausible counterfactual during the 1960s. Given the reality at the time, political leaders had to choose between doing what was best for Black students and preserving Black employment opportunities in public schools. They chose the former, to the long-term benefit of students.

Most importantly, we might wonder why the political process ultimately led local leaders make this choice. In particular, did the majority of Black voters ultimately agree with Charles Henry Thompson that the loss of Black teaching jobs was worth it if it meant better schools for Black children? Unfortunately, I know of no survey data from the relevant era on this question, although what little polling does exist might give us some doubts. In particular, in 1969, Gallup commissioned a survey of Black respondents, with a number of questions focused on schools.[19] When asked in the abstract, 80 percent said they would prefer to see their children to attend schools with white children. But when asked about trade-offs – specifically if they'd be willing to have their children bused across town to attend integrated schools – support declined to just 46 percent.[20] It is possible that if other questions asked about employment trade-offs, support would also be mixed, with many African-Americans taking the side of Cox rather than Thompson.

As it turns out, however, what Black constituents thought about the manner probably didn't matter all that much. We know that during the 1960s, the South had not only segregated schools but also used all sorts of stratagems – literacy tests, poll taxes, and intentional racial gerrymandering to dilute Black voting power – to keep political control in the hands of whites (United States Civil Rights Commission, 1968). Thus, tempted by the promise of federal ESEA funding, Southern elected officials had

---

[19] Gallup/*Newsweek* Poll: "Negro Survey," 1969. https://doi.org/10.25940/ROPER-31089332

[20] Among respondents, 36 percent said they would not support busing and another 18 percent reported they were unsure.

little to fear electorally from pursuing integration policies that involved mass layoffs of Black educators.

The integration of Southern schools happened to precede the mass enfranchisement of Black voters in the South by just a few years, with enfranchisement accomplished primarily through the enactment of the Voting Rights Act of 1965 (VRA). The law banned many of the outrageous practices previously used to disenfranchise African-Americans and, for the South only, created an aggressive system of federal oversight requiring "preclearance" to change any aspect of the electoral process. Considerable research has shown that the VRA dramatically increased Black voter registration rates and turnout in elections, leading to the election of more Black officials to state and local office. The 1982 amendments to the law, which reduced the evidentiary burden for proving VRA violations, were particularly important, requiring the adoption of by-district (or ward) elections that greatly increased minority political representation in elective office (see Marschall, Ruhil and Shah, 2010; Sass and Mehay, 1995).[21] Indeed, it is possible that the resulting political empowerment of Black voters explains why Black teacher employment shares rebounded in many Southern states between 1970 and 1980, as can be seen in Figure 6.1(a).

HURRICANE AND REFORM IN NEW ORLEANS

The success of school integration in the aftermath of the Civil Rights Act poses a deeply controversial question: Was the effective disenfranchisement of African-American voters in the Deep South in fact an important reason for why local officials had little trouble prioritizing the educational interests of Black students over the job concerns of Black school employees? In other words, is the loss of democratic control sometimes necessary to do what is right for kids – particularly when adult jobs are at stake?

In the case of integration, it is of course impossible to answer this question since we don't know the counterfactual – how would have school integration proceeded if Black voters had the ability to exercise their political power. But another, more recent example suggests that perhaps there is indeed an inherent tension between maximizing local

---

[21] Other studies found that VRA led not only to more descriptive representation but also substantive policy influence and access to greater government financial resources (Cascio and Washington, 2014; Schuit and Rogowski, 2017).

democratic control and improving student achievement, especially when adult employment concerns are a big part of the mix. Consider what happened in New Orleans.

In late 2005, powerful Hurricane Katrina hit the city head on, causing the levies to breach and flooding many areas, including the heavily African-American Lower Ninth Ward. The hurricane represented a perfect storm of both natural disaster and government dysfunction – from mixed messages about whether an evacuation was necessary beforehand to a botched federal response afterward. Chaos and looting followed, and more than a thousand residents ultimately lost their lives.

With several important exceptions that I will discuss in more detail (Subsection "Responding to Critics"), both the fans of the New Orleans educational governance reforms that followed in the wake of Katrina as well as its most bitter critics agree on the basic facts. The two sides acknowledge (perhaps begrudgingly) the dysfunction and disarray that characterized the city's public school district before the storm. They also generally accept the district's dismal academic performance – with both test scores and graduation rates among the lowest in the state (Harris, 2020a, p. 80) – while disagreeing about about the fundamental causes of low achievement. And (nearly) all also agree that achievement improved dramatically in the years immediately after the hurricane, although there is again some dispute about what the numbers mean. I parse these debates because understanding which narrative is most consistent with the facts has important implications for what lessons we ultimately take away from the New Orleans experience.

Start with dysfunction. Several months before Katrina hit, the Associated Press had run a story about the city's school system titled "New Orleans Schools a National Horror Tale."[22] In the previous decade, the school district's top leadership had been a revolving door – each superintendent lasting less than a year on average. Financial mismanagement was so bad, the district could not prove that federal funding intended for low-income students had actually been spent on them. So many district officials were under investigation for corruption that the FBI had literally set up shop inside the district's headquarters, with nearly a dozen leaders ultimately facing indictment. School buildings were in disrepair and lacked basic amenities, with students bringing their own toilet paper to

---

[22] This was the headline that appeared in the *Lakeland Ledger*, a newspaper in Florida. The original wire story had a modestly more subdued headline – "New Orleans' School System Is a 'Train Wreck.'"

school. And academic achievement was abysmal – in one high school, the valedictorian could not graduate after failing to pass the state's high school exit exam, despite taking it five times.[23]

No one disputes these basic facts, although they disagree about the root cause. "Most teachers knew as well as anyone that the pre-Katrina schools failed too many of the city's children," journalist Sarah Carr (2013) acknowledged. "And all but the most extreme would concede that, in some cases, subpar educators were to blame" (p. 121). Yet Carr ultimately blamed taxpayers and state officials for "starving" the district of resources. Similarly, education scholar Kristen Buras has argued that the woeful underperformance in New Orleans schools ultimately reflected "white supremacy and state neglect of Black public schools" (2015, p. 3).

The problem with pleading poverty is that ignores the actual data. To start, spending in New Orleans schools was roughly at the Louisiana statewide average before Katrina. Much of the district's achievement issues, to be sure, reflected socioeconomic factors, compounded disadvantage, and tough home environments over which the schools had little control and for which they deserved no blame. But focusing on student *growth over time*, which strips out time-invariant factors such as poverty, parental involvement, and systemic racism, still left New Orleans at the very bottom of the pack, ranked sixty-sixth in the state out of sixty-eight districts. "This means New Orleans used its resource inefficiently, so simply adding more resources, without reforms, probably would not have helped as much as in other districts," economist Doug Harris (2020a) concluded (p. 94).

At the state level, the woeful conditions in New Orleans schools distressed many education reformers, including state superintendent Cecil Picard and state board of education member Leslie Jacobs. They believed that much of the blame fell on the locally elected school board and the district's powerful teachers' union, which made any meaningful reform a political nonstarter. For them, Katrina presented an opportunity. With the city's schools flooded, power out, and much of the student populations displaced, reformers and Louisiana's Democratic governor, Kathleen Blanco, passed a surprise expansion of an existing law allowing the state to take over academically underperforming schools. With nearly every New Orleans schools meeting the newly expanded takeover criteria,

---

[23] This account is based on Harris (2020a) and Moe (2019).

operational authority was transferred from the local school board to a state entity, the Recovery School District (RSD).

Several subsequent decisions in the coming months set the stage for the dramatic reforms to come. First, local education leaders – having lost control of most of the district's buildings and unable to quickly reopen the few that still remained under their purview – terminated all of the district's teachers, the largest mass firing of educators in history (Moe, 2019). This also effectively dissolved the city's teachers' union. Second, RSD officials realized they lacked the capacity to directly run more than 100 schools and instead announced plan to contract with private charter school operators to take over individual buildings.[24] With interest and investment from national education reformers and foundations, the city attracted a number of very high performing charter operators – such as Knowledge is Power Program (KIPP) – which in turn hired nontraditional educators, including many Teach for America corps members. The new teaching force consisted largely of young, white recent college graduates from outside of New Orleans, and indeed, outside the state. In short, New Orleans had become a testing ground for nearly all of the policies long advocated by prominent education reformers.[25]

Impact of NOLA Education Reforms

Two things make New Orleans highly unusual in the history of urban education reform. One is the unprecedented scale and magnitude of governance changes that followed in the wake of Hurricane Katrina. As political scientist Terry Moe has argued, "Katrina was a unique event in modern American history. The new school system that emerged in its wake is also unique, a stunning institutional transformation that goes well beyond what reformers in other cities and states have been able to achieve. ... What Katrina provides, as a result, is a rare natural experiment. It allows us to observe what no one in in this country has ever observed before, at least during the modern era of American education reform: a reform process in which the power of vested interests

---

[24] As part of this reform, school attendance boundaries were largely eliminated, giving families the ability to apply for admission to programs located outside of their neighborhoods.

[25] The new system closely approximated a "portfolio model" of school governance – involving the decentralization decision-making to individual school buildings combined with strong accountability requirements – popularized by education researcher Paul Hill and his University of Washington-based Center on Reinventing Public Education (see Hill, Campbell and Gross, 2013).

has mostly been removed, and policymakers are largely free to pursue institutional reform without obstruction by the core political opponents that, under normal circumstances, are the most formidable barriers to change" (Moe 2019). The second is the careful and rigorous independent evaluations of how these reforms ultimately impacted student outcomes, much of them carried out by a newly founded center at Tulane University run by Harris.

The results from this work are summarized in Harris' book, *Charter School City* (2020), and they paint a picture of a remarkable academic turnaround in New Orleans. Between 2005 and 2015, achievement of New Orleans students saw substantial growth, corresponding to a 10- to 15-percentile point boost for the average student or nearly an entire year of additional learning.[26] Test scores improved across the board and for the most disadvantaged students, with achievement gaps by race and income shrinking relative to the rest of the state.

Moving beyond test scores, which some might dismiss as the product of teaching to the test, the city's students caught up with the Louisiana average in terms of high school graduation and college attendance rates by 2010, after lagging statewide performance by large margins for many years.[27] In the most recent longer-term follow-up, Harris and his coauthor, Matthew Larsen, found that these effects persisted as students continued through higher education, with college graduation rates of former New Orleans students improving by almost 30 percent, albeit from a very low baseline. "The effects of Katrina, including all of its direct and indirect effects, were clearly large. We find that that the storm had large positive effects on both the quality and quantity of education New Orleans students received," the authors concluded in their usual understated, careful language (Harris and Larsen, 2023a, p. 1639). Although unpacking the precise mechanism responsible for these gains is more difficult to do, Harris and Larsen were ultimately convinced that the school governance and operational reforms implemented after Katrina "are likely the main cause."

Responding to Critics

One of the most surprising aspects of researching the New Orleans story for this book is the deep sense of ambivalence that some folks in the

---

[26] This conversion is based on estimates from Hill et al. (2008).
[27] Both graduation and college attendance rates declined somewhat after 2010, however.

education policy community have about the remarkable New Orleans academic turnaround. Many seem downright skeptical that the academic gains were real – rather than a statistical artifact reflecting a change in the socioeconomic composition of the city's school system as a result of the mass displacement following the hurricane. "I don't know exactly what to make of New Orleans, to tell you the truth," Michael Casserly told me. "The change in the population of the city makes that so difficult to figure out what was improvement and what was just change in the demographics." When I interviewed him, Casserly had just retired from heading the Council of Great City Schools, an organization of large urban school systems.

I heard the same reaction from A. J. Crabill, a school board governance coach and former deputy education commissioner in Texas. In 2005, Crabill was serving as the president of the Kansas City school board, which was living through its own near-death experience and wave of reform after decades of dismal achievement. (I discuss the Kansas City story in Chapter 7.) After Katrina hit, Crabill traveled to New Orleans with a group of volunteers to help the city rebuild. "It was very apparent to me that the population that was there when I was there was radically different than the population that was there before the hurricane. That to me is inescapably an element of this," he told me. "There is probably a ton of selection bias in who was able to make it back and who wasn't."

Many academic researchers also appear to believe that compositional change has contributed to the achievement rebound in New Orleans, which is why Harris and his coauthors have found it necessary to address this point and stress-test their results accordingly in their publications. They provide three pieces of evidence that convincingly rule out demographic change as a major driver of their results.

First, Harris has access to pre-Katrina test scores for the students who used to attend the city's school system, allowing him to compare the baseline achievement of students who left the city permanently after the hurricane to those who ultimately returned post-reform. He found that students who had returned to New Orleans schools had actually had *lower* test scores and *higher* rates of poverty prior to Katrina compared to classmates who never came back. In academic-speak, the returning students were negatively selected – suggesting that compositional change alone would cause average achievement to *decline* after the hurricane, not improve.

Second, New Orleans was not the only Louisiana city that suffered mass displacement during the 2005 hurricane season.[28] However, it was the only one to see major governance reforms and also the only one to have recorded such a sharp positive shift in the academic trajectory of its students. Finally, Harris and his coauthors carefully matched returning New Orleans students to a "control group" of peers who had similar pre-Katrina achievement. Before the hurricane, both groups of students had followed parallel achievement trends. Their academic outcomes were moving together, in the same direction, at the same rate. After the Katrina, the New Orleans students' saw their achievement take off while their matched controls did not.[29]

A different argument emphasizes that spending on New Orleans schools increased significantly – on the order of nearly 15 percent – after Katrina and the governance reforms. Under the most cynical view, the stingy state that had starved New Orleans schools when they were under local (Black) control suddenly opened up the spending taps to help their out-of-town (white) friends who came to run and staff the new charter schools. Had the same funding been available to the local school board before the hurricane, the argument goes, student achievement would have also improved earlier.

There are several problems with this argument. As noted by Harris earlier, New Orleans was incredibly inefficient in translating each marginal dollar into academic improvements before Katrina. There is little reason to think that an extra 15 percent in spending would have delivered major gains – and certainly not anything comparable to the magnitude of improvements that have been realized. More importantly, much of the new spending appeared to have been spent on administration, reflecting diseconomies of scale under a new, decentralized administration model. Instructional expenditures in the classroom, which we would expect to have had the largest impact on student outcomes, actually declined after the reforms.

---

[28] Hurricane Rita followed Katrina that year, with a quarter of Louisiana students ultimately displaced (see Pane et al., 2008).

[29] Harris and his coauthors have also carried other additional analyses, including comparing students who had moved into New Orleans before versus after Katrina, and examining whether better schools that students attended during their displacement could explain the results. All of these additional analyses suggest the gains are real, rather than illusory. Both Casserly and Crabill said they have read all of the Tulane studies but remain unconvinced.

The final critique shifts the focus from objective outcomes – such as test scores and graduation rates – to subjective measures, such as voter and parent satisfaction. That is the approach taken recently by political scientists Domingo Morel and Sally Nuamah (2020), using surveys carried out by Tulane's Cowen Institute. Analyzing a poll of New Orleans residents from March 2013, Morel and Nuamah find that a majority of white respondents believed that New Orleans schools had become better after Katrina – in contrast to a plurality of Black respondents reporting they had been better before the hurricane.

The problem, however, is that Morel and Nuamah don't tell the whole story. Although their article was published online in 2019, they oddly do not include other Cowen Institute polls done after 2013. This is a major oversight. By the 2015 survey, the result Morel and Nuamah highlighted in their paper had gone away – the plurality of Black respondents now reported that schools in New Orleans had become *better* after Katrina, with the racial gap shrinking sharply.[30] And even on the earlier 2013 survey, other questions – not analyzed by Morel and Nuamah – painted a very different picture. For example, nearly 60 percent of Black respondents agreed that bringing in a charter to take over a failing school – the strategy pursued by the state after the hurricane – created the best chance of improving student achievement. Only 34 percent disagreed.

To be sure, the governance reforms did not come without their own problems and implementation challenges. With attendance boundaries largely eliminated, families had to navigate a complex and foreign school application and admission process. Some schools found ways to weed out "undesirable" students during admissions or used exclusionary disciplinary practices to push them out afterward. Some students found themselves assigned to distant buildings requiring long bus rides. These issues and the admittedly imperfect efforts undertaken by RSD officials to address them – including the creation of a centralized, single-application process and more standardization and oversight of disciplinary practices – are described in detail in Harris' book. Many critics rightly point to these serious issues but then ignore the main lesson from Harris's research: *Although the new system created after Katrina was hardly perfect, it represented a major improvement on what existed before.* Most

---

[30] See the Cowen Institute for Public Education Initiatives, "K-12 Public Education through the Public's Eye: Parents' and Adults' Perception of Public Education in New Orleans," May 2015.

local parents – black and White – and even many skeptical researchers have themselves said so much.[31]

Jobs and Votes?

Morel and Nuamah are right to point to the significant racial divides in public opinion in New Orleans – especially on the issue of the state takeover. The specter of mostly white state officials seizing control of a school district where the students were 93 percent Black did create horrible optics, particularly in our current era of increased sensitivity to racial injustice. Many critics of the New Orleans governance reforms most object to the loss of local political control by the city's Black community. Some likened it to the mass disenfranchisement in the South during the era of Jim Crow.

Two recent articles (Jeffers, 2024; Jeffers and Dixson, 2024), for example, attempt to trace the intellectual history of the New Orleans state takeover and the choice-based education reforms that followed to slavery and what the authors describe as a "plantation complex" – a system of ideologies, beliefs, and practices designed to impose domination on the Black community in Louisiana.[32] "In our view, *the plantation complex has been even more effective in New Orleans largely because the comprador bourgeoisie welcomed and ushered in a network of disrupters who set their sights on the total upheaval of all aspects of public infrastructure and social safety nets*," Jeffers and Dixson (2024) wrote (italics in original). "This upward distribution of fiscal and public education resources and the erosion of democratic education is a hallmark of how neoliberalism manifests in education policy. ... Post Hurricane Katrina, the neo-plantation bloc, with support at the national level, stripped public assets and dissolved local democratic institutions, such as public schools." Morel and Nuamah similarly argue that the loss of local political power is what soured many Black residents on the state takeover and the subsequent reforms.

---

[31] An illustrative example is a book by Tulane University political scientist Celeste Lay (2022). After describing the New Orleans education reforms as a type of "racial oppression" and cataloguing the many grievances and complaints of New Orleans parents about the new system, she noted in passing: "That is not to say that they" – the parents – "were happy with the system before Katrina, and they certainly do not want to go back" (p. 10).

[32] Elsewhere, Jeffers and Dixson (2024) describe these as an "anti-Black ontological order."

For many other observers, the main grievance is the loss of well-paying teaching jobs. Before Katrina, more than 73 percent of the educators were African-American. They were all fired after the takeover and were largely replaced by young white teachers from out of town.[33] "The firing of New Orleans school employees was an attack on the city's Black middle class, even if not intended as such," journalist Sarah Carr argued in her book on the city's education reform, which struck a position somewhere between skepticism and outright criticism. Many teachers were the first in their family to reach this level of economic prosperity, and "their success represented the culmination of more than a century of battles fought and freedoms won, starting with the abolishment of slavery and continuing through the decades as a African-Americans attained the right to attend public schools, the right to vote, the right to hold public office, and the right to live, travel, and move throughout the country as they chose. ... [Few] paid attention over the following months as the school board and state dispossessed much of the city's Black middle class – ironically the more invisible class in this instance – of their livelihoods and any remaining sense of security" (2013, p. 121). Similarly, Buras (2015) claims that the "mass termination of Black veteran teachers in New Orleans is one of the most striking instances to date of accumulation of dispossession" (p. 138).

Echoing Derrick Bell and Oliver Cox, who warned about the social consequences of the loss of Black educators a generation earlier, Jeffers and Dixson (2024) argue that Black schools, staffed by Black educators, serve an important cultural role. They "symbolize expressions of where Black people's ways of knowing and being in the world [had] persisted" but were lost in New Orleans with the mass teacher layoffs and displacement. And this argument is supported by a growing body of evidence showing that students of color do better academically and behaviorally when "matched" to teachers that look like them (see Egalite, 2024 for overview of the research on this topic) – on average.

The problem is that, pre-Katrina, New Orleans was not the average. It wasn't anywhere near it. In reading the criticism of the reforms, one is struck by how numerous authors and commentators romanticize the pre-Katrina Black-run schools as sites of Black liberation. They echo many of the ideas espoused in the later writings of Bell and are heavily influenced

---

[33] About 32 percent of the former teachers were rehired in New Orleans in 2007, and 18 percent found teaching jobs in other Louisiana districts. By 2013, only 22 percent of the pre-Katrina teachers were still employed in New Orleans (Lincove, Barrett and Strunk, 2017).

in trendy (in academic education policy circles) "-isms" in the tradition of postmodernism, postcolonialism, and critical studies. Yet this romantic view has almost no relationship with the dire reality of public education and student achievement in New Orleans before the hurricane. The bottom line is that if education for New Orleans was so great when schools were staffed by veteran Black educators, their achievement and attainment would not have gone up so dramatically after the schools were taken over and the teachers replaced by overwhelmingly inexperienced, young, white educators.

"Before Katrina, New Orleans was a *profoundly* corrupt city," Casserly told me, emphasizing the word "profoundly." "The use of the school system by and for the administration, the mayor, city council, state government, et cetra, to hire people to boost the middle class in the city was part of their economic model. ... [Today] New Orleans schools is not the job bank that they used to be." Indeed, Casserly noted that many other once-struggling cities – such as Boston, New York, Washington (DC), and Chicago – all used to be places where schools became the "hiring place of last resort." Things have gotten better in recent years, Casserly believes, with increased employment opportunities in the private sector for minorities allowing these cities to dramatically overhaul their hiring practices with the goal of improving student outcomes. Yet in New Orleans, it seems clear that Katrina provided the key catalyst for these changes.

Upon closer inspection, one is struck by how many critics of various educational reforms – not just the dramatic overhaul in New Orleans – tend to focus on the employment impacts. Before his work with Nuamah, Morel authored a book highly critical of state takeovers of urban school districts, inspired by his experience in Newark, New Jersey. Many of the most salient community concerns about state control of local schools highlighted in the book focus on jobs.[34] In Newark, in the run-up to the state takeover, "hiring community members to work in the district, a practice that had developed as an *essential* part of the city's economic

---

[34] Morel also argues there is little evidence that state takeovers improve student outcomes on average, a finding that has been confirmed by rigorous research (Schueler and Bleiberg, 2022). However, we should expect the main benefit to arise from the *threat* of state takeovers – by changing the incentives of local elected officials and encouraging them to prioritize student academics over adult political concerns, such as employment – not the takeovers themselves. This is similar to arguments made by political scientists about the benefits of direct democracy, which can act as the "gun behind the door" to influence the behavior of state legislators without actually having to go off (Gerber, 1996). Finding null effects of takeovers tells us little about the effects of the threat.

development for decades, came under political attack" (2018, p. 26, emphasis added).[35] After state officials enacted "drastic layoffs," the decline in the "school-related workforce in the city had the most severe consequences for the city's Black community" (p. 31). "The job cuts were devastating to many Newarkers who relied on the school district for employment. ... An examination of the Newark school district's professional employment data show that African Americans were the most negatively affected by these layoffs." (p. 33). "In sum, the state takeover of the Newark schools had a significant effect on the community, which depended on the jobs the district provided" (p. 35). I could provide many more examples.

Scholars such as Morel seem to reject the very premise for this chapter – that the interests of students attending local public schools and the interests of adults employed in those schools may sometimes conflict. In July 2023, for example, Morel appeared on a panel on state takeovers as part of a virtual conference organized by Harvard University. How should we think about policies that require trading off what may be good for students from what local adult political interests might want, including employment concerns, I asked him from the audience. "I think I would like to hear what are some specific examples of tradeoffs between student outcomes and, 'community' or 'adult politics'," he responded. "I think that genuine community-centered politics are politics that are about the kids, right? So there may be people who might say that they're community-centered but I think that the community itself would question that. And so I don't really see a tradeoff in that."[36]

AN IMPOSSIBLE TRINITY?

On April 19, 2019, I sat in the back of the room as the twice-monthly meeting of the Columbus school board was about to begin. It was a high-stress time for the district. The year before, Columbus had received an "F" rating on the state report card, which under the Ohio law at the time started an ominous clock. The board had just a few years to turn things around before the state took over and replaced it with an appointed "Academic Distress Commission" – with the ability to throw

---

[35] "I understand that parents need jobs, so if they are going to do the job, give them a job. ... That is not patronage, that is community," the district's one-time superintendent explained.

[36] The video from the conference is available at www.youtube.com/watch?v=UMGPK m7cXIk and our exchange takes place around minute 35.

out local collective bargaining agreements. Just months before, the board had brought on a new superintendent, who had previously served as principal of the city's highest-ranked, selective-admission high schools.

Columbus school board meetings always began with public comment, which usually consisted of some combination of parents coming to request special consideration related to their own kid and crazy gadflies (like myself) raging and raving about various topics. On this day, however, the first speaker was Nana Watson, the president of the Columbus chapter of the NAACP. Wow, I thought to myself, the head of our nation's foremost civil rights organization was finally here, to advocate on behalf of students – majority Black in Columbus – who had been let down by adults for too long!

During her comments, President Watson said she wanted more information about an item on that night's consent agenda – a contract for $175,000 with the Columbus convention center to host the district's "Re-Imagine Me" conference. The funding, Watson noted, was coming from a restricted federal fund earmarked to pay for efforts to improve the effectiveness of teachers and principals. Why, she asked, was the district going to spend it on a conference? Officials responded that the purpose of the conference was to lay out the superintendent's vision for the district and get the staff excited and on board. With nearly 10,000 employees, only the convention was large enough to host the event. I sat up a little straighter in my chair, eager to hear Watson lay into the district for wasting precious dollars on such obviously dumb programming instead of using the money to actually help students. Her response shocked me.

"I learned from the convention center that they outsource business," she began. "I want to know: How will you *ensure* that Black businesses get a piece of this $175,000. Thank you." That was it. No discussion of students, no discussion of learning, no discussion of education at all.

In retrospect, and as I hope this chapter has shown, I should not have found Watson's comments so surprising. Employment concerns – and the racial dimension to this employment – have long characterized debates about public education, especially in America's declining big cities. Gabriel Jones learned as much in 1897 when he tried to desegregate Indianapolis schools, and so did Michelle Rhee in DC more than a century later. This dynamic is closely connected to what political scientists have described as the "hollow-prize problem" – the reality that minority groups have achieved political power precisely in jurisdictions that have suffered through white flight, trade- and technology-driven employment losses, and an erosion of their tax base, leaving too few resources to be allocated through the political process (see Kraus and Swanstrom, 2001). Education, however, has been largely spared, thanks to state-level finance reforms that have greatly increased the amount of state funding flowing to high-poverty, lower achieving districts over the past three decades. In many of these cities, the public schools now remain one of the last remaining sources of political patronage and relatively well-paying government employment.

Of course, as the literature cited throughout this chapter has shown, I am hardly the first person to make these points. My contribution (I hope) is to link these perverse dynamics to the electoral pressures that shape the incentives of public officials. One big reason why local democracy pushes public officials to prioritize adult jobs over student learning is because adults can actually vote while students can't.[37] It is thus perhaps not surprising that the two most disruptive examples of reform that prioritized students at the expense of jobs – the desegregation of public education in the South and the overhaul of New Orleans schools after Katrina – took place in contexts of limited political accountability and democratic participation.

At the risk of saying the obvious, I am not endorsing the disenfranchisement of minority voters that characterized much of the South during the desegregation period. I am also not advocating for dumping local democracy as the primary mechanism for shaping education policy. For one, it is not obvious there are better options that can be implemented at scale with fidelity. The New Orleans model, as many observers have noted, would be almost impossible to replicate in a different context absent the unique set of crises that led to its creation. And even there, despite overwhelming community agreement that schools improved under the state-run, mostly charter model, political pressure ultimately led the state to return day-to-day oversight of the system to the local school board.

Nor am I arguing that the interests of students and school employees need *always* be in conflict. For example, the evidence suggests that increasing teacher salaries – at least under certain circumstances – is an effective way to improve student achievement, particularly if the compensation changes are tied to clear evaluation systems and designed to

---

[37] Another, as other scholars have pointed out, is that public employees are well organized and their associations actively engage in electioneering, further increasing the incentives for office holders to put their priorities first (see, e.g., Anzia and Moe, 2015; Moe, 2006).

incentivize the best educators to take positions in the hardest-to-staff schools.

Rather, my point is that the three things community members might want and expect from public schools – a quality education for students, democratic accountability to local voters, and good-paying employment opportunities for local residents – can sometimes come into conflict. When this happens, it is usually the quality of education that receives short shrift, with local democratic control and adult employment prioritized, because politically this is the path of least resistance that produces the lowest electoral backlash and minimizes the political risks for public officials.

This argument in some ways borrows from the idea of the "impossible trinity" in research on international economics. Countries might want to have three desirable policies – a fixed foreign exchange rate, free movement of capital, and an independent monetary policy. The idea behind the "impossible trinity" is that it is not possible to have all three at ones. Accomplishing two of the goals necessarily requires letting go of the third. Perhaps a similar dynamic is present in education – at least in the large urban districts that serve their communitie's largest employers – with educational quality ultimately paying the price?

7

Bootleggers, Baptists, and Building Closures

> There are many reasons why the United States has lagged in the realm of education but one of the things holding us back is that sometimes our educational bureaucracy puts kids in the middle or even at the back of the line; on the policy level, they can fall behind teachers, administrators, politicians, and sometimes even the men and women who run the school *buildings*. We as adults love to say that children always come first, but too often that's simply not the case.
> —Former Sec. of Education Arne Duncan (2018)

Just as tree rings provide a running record of historical climate patterns, school enrollment figures reveal a great deal about the ups and downs in the health of the local public education sector. And in many ways, the story of Linden-McKinley High School tracks the complicated educational politics of my adopted home town of Columbus.

The school, originally built in 1927, is located less than three miles east of the Ohio State University in a troubled neighborhood called Linden. Until the late 1960s, Linden was a thriving working-class, majority white area, and Linden-McKinley a well-regarded school. By the 1970s, however, white flight and the erosion of nearby manufacturing employment began the neighborhood's long decline. Linden's older housing stock, owned largely by absentee slumlords, fell into disrepair, crime began to increase, and Black enrollment grew to become a majority of the school's student body. In 1971, a small group of students inspired by the Black Power movement and encouraged by a controversial OSU professor who chaired the university's new Black Studies Department organized a Black Student Union to advocate for changes. Responding to their demands, the school introduced the district's first Black history curriculum, but growing racial conflict among students, protests and marches, and a violent altercation with the police temporarily closed the school that year.

Although Linden-McKinley reopened the following fall, things continued going downhill for the school – and for the Columbus school system as whole. After peaking at 110,000 in the year of the shutdown, the district's enrollment began to shrink. In response to court-ordered busing to achieve racial integration and undo racially gerrymandered school attendance boundaries, white families fled for suburban and private schools in growing numbers, with enrollment falling below 65,000 by the mid 1990s. By this point, the district's student body had become majority Black, a transition that had occurred at Linden-McKinley two decades earlier. In 1998, Linden-McKinley was placed on the latest list of schools slated for closure in an effort to rightsize the district, prompting an outpouring of community opposition that ultimately saved the school.

Soon, the school caught a lucky break. The new Columbus superintendent, Gene Harris, was a Linden-McKinley graduate from the class of 1971. Although the district continued to close schools as enrollment declined steadily, Linden-McKinley appeared to be protected. When a nearby middle school was shuttered, the high school added grades seven and eight to its configuration. In 2011, the district completed a $34 million renovation and expansion – turning the Linden-McKinley building into a "palace," as one former school board member described it, with world-class sports facilities – and rolled out an innovative STEM curriculum in the school. Build it, the district seemed to believe, and the students would come.

Unfortunately they never did. And in 2012, Harris was forced out in a shocking data scrubbing scandal a decade into her tenure. (By this point, district enrollment had fallen to just above 50,000.) Facing pressure to raise Columbus test scores, district officials had leaned on principals to temporarily unenroll and then reenroll students with poor attendance and low achievement, a trick that would remove them from the denominator used to calculate the district's state accountability rating. Linden-McKinley's principal was identified as one of the worst offenders in the scandal – accused of not only fudging attendance data but also replacing failing student grades with passing ones on a massive scale. And despite the new building and programming, kids from the Linden neighborhood overwhelmingly avoided the school – with more than 70 percent of those zoned to attend it enrolling elsewhere. State data showed that just 50 percent of Linden-McKinley freshmen graduated within four years in 2016, the same year two students were injured in a drive-by shooting while waiting to be picked up outside during dismissal time. When I went on a police ride-along in the neighborhood a few years later, the officer who accompanied me shook his head as we drove by the campus. Student violence was so bad, he told me, cruisers were stationed outside of the school every day around dismissal to break up fights.

In the wake of the data scandal, Columbus voters rejected the district's latest property tax levy, exacerbating the fiscal squeeze from declining enrollment and adding new urgency to close more school buildings. As it had done previously, the district assembled a task force of parents and community members to objectively assess the data and identify which buildings to shutter. In October 2018, the deeply divided task force voted narrowly to add Linden-McKinley to the closure list and move its remaining students to another half-empty high school four miles away that had recently been renovated as well.[1]

With district enrollment down by more than half since the peak, it was clear *some* schools had to close. And it certainly seemed like Linden-McKinley – a violent dropout factory that was shunned by the majority of the students living around it – was an obvious choice. Combining the two high schools would also create a critical mass of students needed to improve extracurricular programming and course offerings, dramatically increasing the number of available Advanced Placement courses.

Yet, surprisingly, when the school board met to vote on the task force proposal, they faced a packed room of community members demanding the school, and the others on the proposed closure list, stay open. Some were proud Linden-McKinley alumni who celebrated the school's legacy.[2] Some were outraged that East High School, chosen to receive the students currently attending Linden-McKinley, was a football and marching band (and perhaps gang) rival. Some worked for the community partners that were responsible for the STEM curriculum and were upset that they had not been consulted, in apparent violation of the contract with the district. As each speaker pleaded their case at the microphone at the start

---

[1] Under the plan, Linden-McKinley would remain open as a middle school, keeping its lower grades and absorb students from another nearby middle school, which would then close completely.

[2] The district's closure plan recognized of the community's attachment to the school and the pain its closure was likely to cause, noting: "Linden-McKinley High School has a significant history/legacy in the Linden community. Though the school will remain open [as a middle school] and serve the neighborhood, the change will require the community to alter its perception of the school and its continued support for middle-school students/student activities."

of the meeting, the room would erupt in applause. The loudest cheer came about an hour later, when the board voted against closing a single building. The decision was a surprise to many observers – including, apparently, one of the board members, who had not been consulted on the pre-written resolution rejecting the task force recommendations and who resigned in protest just a few weeks later. But perhaps it shouldn't have been. Two years earlier, the same thing had happened to another list of proposed school building closures.

As I would learn later, similar dynamics have played out across the country over the past twenty years, especially in other big-city districts that have undergone dramatic enrollment decline. Although some did manage to close a few buildings, nearly every effort would engender overwhelming community push back. Even when such opposition did not completely derail the closures, it generated steep political costs for sitting school board incumbents (Nuamah, 2023), sending a message to their successors. In national politics, House Speaker Tip O'Neill famously described Social Security benefit cuts as the "third-rail" of politics – incinerating the career of any politician who dared to suggest it. In education, it seems, school closures are that third rail.

Yet, just as many community members object viscerally to the idea of losing their neighborhood schools, many education reformers believe such closures – especially of chronically underperforming schools – represent one of the most effective strategies for improving educational outcomes for students. One such reformer is Arne Duncan, who served as President Obama's Secretary of Education. Duncan grew up in Chicago, where his mom ran an after-school program in the city's struggling South Side. After college, Duncan played professional basketball in Japan for several years but ultimately returned to his hometown. Duncan's childhood friend had by then become a wealthy investment banker and hired him to mentor a cohort of students at one of the city's worst performing schools, Shakespeare Elementary. "The first surprise had nothing to do with these kids' personal lives and everything to do with the school they attended in sixth grade," Duncan would later write. "We went in thinking our students would have a basic level of academic rigor, but in truth there was none. There were no expectations at Shakespeare. Not low expectations – no expectations" (Duncan, 2018, p. 20).

Shortly after Duncan's program began, the school district ended up shutting down Shakespeare, scattering the group he was supposed to mentor across other public and private programs all around the city. Much to his surprise, despite the resulting transportation headaches and the stress of moving to new schools, the students thrived. "One of the lessons learned here – good schools are infinitely better than bad schools – seems blatantly obvious, but its corollary is somewhat counterintuitive: sometimes closing a school is the best thing that can happen to a group of students," Duncan recalled later. "These were the lessons I'd come back to time and time again in my career" (p. 22).

This chapter makes an effort to reconcile these perspectives. On one side are district administrators pushing to close schools, who argue that the cost savings from shuttering half-empty buildings and programmatic economies of scale that such consolidation unlocks ultimately benefit students across the entire school system. On the other are opponents, who charge that school closures are just the latest indignity pushed by a blatantly racist system that disproportionately target children of color. Both argue they are on the sides of the students, yet their narratives cannot both be right.

After doing my best to steelman the arguments from each camp, I put their claims to the test using real-world data. Specifically, I examine whether districts intentionally target school closures in disadvantaged communities of color (as critics claim), or whether they focus their closure efforts on the most academically laggard buildings (as district leaders insist). The reality, it turns out, doesn't fit neatly into either of these accounts. After identifying the *causes* of school closure, I then turn to examining their *consequences* – quantifying how the shuttering of school buildings affects student achievement (neither positively nor negatively, on average), student enrollment (which declines), and school district employment (which falls even more).

The analysis points to clear if controversial conclusion: When it comes to the politics of school closures, it really does seem like the interests of teachers, politicians, and even "the men and women who run the school buildings" ultimately drive policy narratives and, to a surprising degree, the policy outcomes themselves, just as Duncan's quote in the opening epigraph of this chapter suggests. Efforts to close schools mobilize adults much more than they seem to ultimately affect the educational outcomes of students.

In researching this chapter, I couldn't help but notice a striking parallels between how school closures play out in the communities I profile and the "bootlegger and baptist" model of politics associated with economist Bruce Yandle (Smith and Yandle, 2014). In Yandle's likely apocryphal telling, many modern laws regulating alcohol distribution and consumption – including bans on Sunday sales – came about through an unusual political alliance. It included bootleggers, who sought to create a profitable monopoly by pushing legal retailers out of business, and Baptists, who believed that booze was the devil's drink and sought to leverage the full force of the state to try to reduce its consumption. Critically, the bootleggers provided the behind-the-scenes financial and organizational resources to mobilize for policy change, while the Baptists served as the movement's more sympathetic and earnest public face.

Many analysts, especially libertarian cynics, see similar dynamics behind a number of public policies, especially costly regulations that can allow incumbent firms to protect themselves from up-start competitors. In this view, a "bootlegger" is "any individual, group, or organization that seeks favors for financial gain." By contrast, the "Baptists" are "individuals or groups that seek political favors for loftier reasons" (Smith and Yandle, 2014, p. 30). In the closure debates discussed in this chapter, school employees – including teachers, custodians, and cafeteria workers – appear to play the role of the bootleggers. They can push to keep academically distressed, under-enrolled buildings open because their own jobs depend on it. But they rarely make these employment concerns explicit in their arguments. Instead, employee interest groups help recruit and subsidize the advocacy of other closure opponents, including alumni, parents, and students, making them the public face of the campaign, and develop and popularize poignant narratives that attribute the efforts to close neighborhood schools to some combination of anti-Black racism and historical underfunding. These groups include teachers' unions – but also those representing blue-collar school employees who work outside of the classroom and who are far more likely to live in the affected neighborhoods.

Although the interviews and analyses I present in this chapter are retrospective, focusing on closure debates of yesterday, they foreshadow the political battles that appear likely to play out in many communities in the coming years. Prior to the pandemic, enrollments in public schools were already on the decline, especially in large urban districts. Part of this reflected changing population dynamics and part an increase in alternative schooling options, including homeschooling, private school voucher, and charter schools. The COVID-19 pandemic only accelerated these trends, with enrollment in many urban areas plummeting. Indeed, a recent analysis by the Brookings Institution found that nearly one in ten elementary and middle schools around the country saw their student numbers fall by at least 20 percent between the 2019 and 2022 academic years (Burtis and Goulas, 2023). With the American school-age population projected to shrink in the coming decades, enrollment losses will continue, and the financial pressure to close schools will only increase. Debates like the ones surrounding the future of Linden-McKinley in Columbus will take place in many communities around the country, and if the recent history is any guide, considerations most relevant to student learning will not take center stage.

COMPETING NARRATIVES

Given some of the findings in Chapters 3 and 4, which documented strong partisan and ideological dimensions to conflicts over school curriculum and other education issues, one might expect similar dynamics to shape the politics of school closure. This does not seem to be the case, however. Political fights over school closures – at least in the heavily Democratic urban districts where these have attracted the most national attention[3] – are entirely internecine wars within the progressive community. Both sides see themselves as good Democrats – socially conscious anti-racists looking to do right by overwhelmingly disadvantaged students and families of color. To begin to understand why, despite similar commitments to social justice, these advocates have landed on opposite sides of the school closure issue, it is useful to let each side articulate their views in their own words.

The Case for School Closures

In 2014, Shanthi Gonzales was elected to the Oakland Unified School District as a progressive, pro-labor candidate opposed to school closures. Oakland is located across the bay from San Francisco and, like much of the Bay Area, is a Democratic stronghold. Gonzales had written a graduate thesis on the labor movement and efforts to organize low-wage workers. She herself had worked as an organizer of home health-care aides for the Service Employees International Union. So many were surprised when Gonzales, elected board president by this point, voted to close eleven school buildings in 2022 – amidst a tumultuous and chaotic period marked by protests and hunger strikes. Shortly thereafter, she announced her resignation from the board, in the process heaping

---

[3] Building consolidation efforts have taken place disproportionately in Democratic areas because urban districts that have experienced the most significant enrollment losses are overwhelmingly Democratic.

opprobrium on the Oakland teachers' union. Two other closure supporters also retired, deciding not to run for reelection in light of the backlash; the next elected board majority would almost immediately reverse course and keep the buildings open.

Gonzales's resignation letter went viral in education policy circles and was ultimately reprinted in *The 74*, a nonprofit education website funded by many prominent philanthropists active in education reform. It read, in part:

[Oakland Unified] is not a jobs program, or a social justice organization, or a small business incubator, or a housing organization, although those things are important. Our city is full of brilliant people who care deeply about our students and have many ideas about how to serve them better. However, I believe that as long as we are struggling to ensure that students can read at grade level, it is a disservice to our students and families to spend so much time on issues that are not central to our core mission. ... It is not enough to say that there is poverty and that is why students aren't doing well, or that the state doesn't provide enough funding. These things are true statewide, and yet other districts with similar levels of poverty and/or funding are achieving much greater results. One reason is that our teachers' association has consistently resisted efforts to address school quality, and organized others against such efforts as well.

School closures were one such effort, and the union's opposition to them a sore point. "When I ran, I didn't think I would ever, ever, *ever* support a school closure," Gonzales told me when we spoke a few weeks after her resignation. "But I saw us doing other things to balance the books, year after year of budget cuts, year after year of layoffs, hundreds of layoffs. I saw that we had used all of our other strategies, there was only one strategy left."

A key turning point came in 2018, when Gonzales voted to close a middle school located in a neighborhood she represented. The school happened to be the lowest-performing in the district. It was colocated with another program, the Coliseum College Prep Academy (CCPA), one of the highest-ranked in the city. Interest CCPA was high, but the number of available spots limited, so the waiting list to get in was long. Closing the colocated middle school would allow CCPA to expand into the whole building, admitting and serving more Oakland students. "It was morally wrong to have the chance to expand opportunity and not do it," Gonzales explained, recalling her 2018 vote. The decision would cause an irreversible rupture with the Oakland teachers union, which saw school closures as part of a neoliberal, capitalist privatization agenda. The union would never endorse her again and would work behind the scenes in the Alameda County Democratic Party to try to deprive Gonzales of the party's endorsement as well, a near-certain political kiss of death in a deep blue community.

In subsequent years, Gonzales came to believe that the teachers' union opposition to building consolidation was not only bad for students but also for the teachers themselves. When we spoke, she compared Oakland to the Fremont Unified School District, located thirty miles away. Fremont enrolled nearly as many students as Oakland – 35,000 versus 37,000 – but operated fewer than half as many schools. Thanks to the resulting operational efficiencies and economies of scale, Fremont teachers made approximately $20,000 more per year on average – but the district also employed about a third fewer of them. "If a school gets closed, that's going to impact those 200 or 100 students," Gonzales said, walking me through the math. "But all 37,000[4] students [in Oakland], whether they realize it or not, are experiencing the impact of the maldistribution of resources" that results from trying to keep so many under-enrolled buildings open.

I heard a similar explanation from A. J. Crabill, who I introduced in Chapter 6. Crabill first got involved in local education advocacy after becoming disturbed by the developments in Kansas City – in 2000, it became the first school system in the country to lose its accreditation, and like Oakland and Columbus, had seen its enrollment plummet since the 1970s. Crabill eventually recruited a group of candidates to take on the incumbents in the 2008 school board elections. When one ended up withdrawing from the race, Crabill stepped in at the last minute and ran himself. He won and was eventually appointed to chair the school board.

To fully grasp the events and decisions that followed, it is also important to understand the unique history of Kansas City. Like many other big-city districts, Kansas City had spent a decade under a federal court order focused on increasing racial integration. Its experience, which is chronicled in Joshua Dunn's fascinating book *Complex Justice*, was unusual, however. The legal arguments focused not on disparities in student racial composition between schools within the district, as was the case in most other cities, but rather on segregation caused by white flight to the suburbs. The intricate legal ins and outs of the case are beyond the scope of chapter (interested readers should see Dunn, 2012), but the

---

[4] This figure excludes approximately 8,000 students who were attending charter schools in Oakland.

upshot was that federal court pursued a very different integration strategy in Kansas City than was the case anywhere else in the country.

Instead of busing, the court ordered the district to turn most of the city's schools into magnet programs and imposed significant spending increases, funded through a mix of local tax hikes and greater state aid. Ultimately, Kansas City would end up spending several *billion* dollars on its desegregation efforts. These included building world class facilities and creating new specialized academic and extracurricular programs. Among the enhancements were a new swimming complex with an underwater viewing area and a model United Nations facility with simultaneous language translation technology. The district even hired the former Soviet Olympic coach to oversee a high school fencing team – all with the goal of convincing white families from the suburbs to return. It was a version of the "build it and they will come" model Columbus tried in Linden-McKinley. And, just like in Columbus, it failed.

"In Kansas City we had some amazing, amazing facilities, just gorgeous, that would rival the facilities in the suburban areas," Crabill recalled. "Their idea was that the way to fix urban education is to convince white kids to be in the same room as Black kids. We tried that experiment, and it failed. And the idea that we'd improve education by having better facilities and really nifty programs, and that this would bring white kids back and rich white kids – all of that was a failure."

In 1995, the US Supreme Court stepped in to end the desegregation case by a 5–4 vote. Despite the increase in funding that accompanied a decade of court-ordered integration efforts – the trial judge had increased local property taxes two-fold, and by the mid 1990s, Kansas City had become one of the highest spending big-city districts in the country – the academic performance remained woeful. Middle-class Black families had also begun to leave the district for the suburbs and many others took advantage of increasing charter school options. Having built new facilities with state aid, the district was now stuck with buildings it could neither fill nor adequately maintain.

Between the early 1970s and the mid 1990s, when the case ended, the district's enrollment shrank from more than 60,000 to approximately 35,000. By 2006, it had declined to under 26,000 and, a decade later, to fewer than 15,000 students. Despite the closure of dozens of schools in the preceding decades, Crabill's board majority faced some very difficult choices if they had any hope of balancing the budget and making meaningful progress on academics.

"We were willing to blow up everything on the Kansas City school board and just start the governance system over. Basically accept that everything we're doing as a school board is just failing children," Crabill explained to me. "It's impossible to conceive the district could be in this state if the board hadn't radically failed at its job. So we just started from that as a premise: We failed. This is a failed institution, full stop."

Reflecting the dire state of the district, in 2010, then-Superintendent John Covington unveiled one of the most radical school consolidation proposals I've ever seen. It included the closure of *half* the district's remaining schools. In some communities, the initial school closure lists are used as an opening gambit to jump start the negotiations – superintendents make long lists knowing that, in navigating the local political process, some buildings will inevitably be removed and remain open. Ask for a full loaf, knowing that you will get half if you're lucky. This was not the case in Kansas City. Covington actually intended to close all thirty schools. Surprisingly, the school board green-lighted the proposal. Even more shockingly, the incumbents were reelected after doing so, and Crabill returned to his position as board chair.

As I noted in Chapter 6, things went less smoothly in Washington, DC. By all accounts, the political backlash to Chancellor Michelle Rhee's decision to shutter about a dozen school buildings – just a third of the number of schools closed in Kansas City, which had a smaller number of buildings to begin with – helped cost Mayor Adrian Fenty reelection and ended Rhee's tenure leading the district. I spoke with two of Rhee's aides who had overseen the school closure effort, and like both Crabill and Gonzales, they made clear their overriding motivation had been to improve the educational experiences of students.

Eric Lerum moved to DC in 2000 to attend law school, where he became a Marshall-Brennan Constitutional Literacy Project fellow. The position involved working in local high schools to engage students in constitutional law and oral advocacy. He saw the public education system's injustices and inequities playing out in the lives of his students every day. "And it was there that my interests in constitutional law and civil rights and social justice all sort of just gelled and became really clear in terms of what I wanted to do and who I wanted to work for," he said.

To Lerum, right-sizing the district was itself a civil rights and social justice imperative. Every building, no matter how many students attended it, needed to be heated and air conditioned. Every building had to be regularly cleaned. And every school required some minimal staffing level in order to offer a viable educational program. As a result, the fixed costs of operating a school were high and the total costs did not scale linearly with student enrollment. As fewer students attended, the per-student costs increased dramatically, sucking up more and more resources that might otherwise be used to improve the educational experience for other students.

Although the basic idea seems intuitive, the aggregate financial impact of operating under-enrolled school buildings is difficult grasp. As a real-world recent example, consider Chicago's Frederick Douglass Academy High School, located on the city's West Side, which enrolled just thirty students during the 2023 school year, according to state data. This was less than one-twentieth of the citywide high school average (which was 730 students). The per-student expenditures at Douglass totaled more than $69,000 per year – almost three times the citywide average and more than the tuition at the most exclusive private schools. Closing the school and moving its students to a typical building would free up $1.3 million per year, money that could be reinvested to improve programming and education for both current Douglass students and kids attending their receiving schools. That's just one high school. Chicago had more than a dozen high schools enrolling fewer than 150 students that year. If every one of them closed, the savings would exceed $4.5 million.[5] And that's just the high schools – start doing the math, and the numbers really start to add up!

This was the kind of reality Lerum had seen firsthand in DC. "In a public system, resources are always limited," he explained. "So if we want to serve students the best way we can, it behooves us to use them efficiently and to concentrate the resources where the kids actually are."

To help Rhee execute her closure plan, Lerum worked with Abigail Smith. Like Rhee, Smith's foray into education began in Teach for America, a competitive national service program that recruits college students to work in understaffed urban schools, and was rooted a deep commitment to progressive social change. After teaching in a small town in North Carolina, Smith moved to DC and eventually served as the deputy mayor for education for Fenty's successor, Vincent Gray.

Smith told me she regularly saw DC principals with half-empty school buildings struggling to make the finances work, forced to choose between things that would normally be seen as must-haves. For some, it meant

---

[5] Even this figure is likely an underestimate, since the *marginal* cost of educating the displaced students in other buildings with open seats would likely be below the *average* costs.

having to decide between hiring a social worker to help students deal with the trauma they experienced in their communities and a teacher to staff an additional Advanced Placement course. In low-enrolling schools, "the limitations on resources in terms of what you can deliver for kids and families are real," she explained. "What we did was the quintessential ripping off of the band-aid. Do I think that needed to happen? Yes, I still think that needed to happen, and I'm not sure there was really a way to do it nicely."

The Case against School Closure

On the opposite side of the school closure debates are people just as passionate, just as well meaning, and just as confident in the righteousness of their agenda. They also see themselves as fighting for social justice and students – but they offer very different accounts of the forces that brought their schools to the brink of closure and the likely consequences. Many of their arguments are summarized in a report titled "Death by a Thousand Cuts: Racism, School Closures, and Public School Sabotage" that was published by the Journey for Justice Alliance, a national umbrella group made up of local anti-closure advocates. The report came out a decade ago, but it lays out the familiar talking points frequently cited by closure opponents today.

"We write this report because we need the American people to know that the public education systems in our communities are dying. More accurately, they are being killed by an alliance of misguided, paternalistic 'reformers,' education profiteers, and those who seek to dismantle the institution of public education," it begins. The report blames decades of disinvestment, compounded by enrollment losses to (nonunionized) charter and private schools, and specifically calls out prominent education reformers including Bill Gates and the Walton family – heirs to the Walmart fortune – for pursuing a "privatization" agenda. "The real, underlying cause for these school closures is that there has been a realignment of political forces. Right-wing conservatives have long sought to eliminate public goods such as public education, and dismantle organized labor, especially teachers' unions."

Reformers, the report continues, confuse the "symptoms of the problem" – low attendance and dismal academic achievement – "with the problem itself, which is that our public schools have been persistently under-resourced, under-supported, and undermined for decades, including by many of the same people that now purport to 'fix' them. The harsh reality is that the equitable education of our children has never been a priority for education policymakers."

Some claims in the report are obviously at odds with the facts. For example, complaints about disinvestment and underfunding certainly hold little water in Kansas City, where one of the desegregation-era high schools was so grand, it was nicknamed the "Taj Mahal." Just ask the Soviet fencing coach! Few could credibly argue that $69,000 per student that Chicago spends each year to keep Douglass open is a case of underfunding. And many other urban districts that have experienced large waves of closure, including New York, spend far more than the national average per student and in many cases more than some of the surrounding suburbs. While urban schools *were* underfunded in previous eras, when school districts relied primarily on local property taxes, several waves of finances reforms since the 1960s that dramatically increased state spending and targeted it to lower-wealth areas mean this is largely not true today (Lee, Shores and Williams, 2022).

Other arguments have more merit. For example, it is true that the growth of charter schools has significantly contributed to enrollment losses. In some cities, including Washington, DC, and Detroit, charters educate nearly half of the students, increasing financial pressure on the public schools. Yet these enrollment shifts are driven by decisions of families who find the local education options unsatisfactory, not a secret right-wing plot to starve the public education system. While reformers do indeed promote policies to increase choice options, no one is forcing local families to exercise them.

The most political sensitive questions, however, deal with community perceptions around race and school quality. While many closure opponents recognize that enrollment in some schools is disturbingly low, they argue that decades of racist policies are to blame. They point to the "red lining" practices surrounding home loan financing during the 1940s, federal policies – such as funding for the national highway system – that subsidized white flight to the suburbs, and in cities such as Chicago, the mass demolition of high-rise public housing during the 1990s, which displaced a large share of school-aged kids in neighborhoods that used to host these developments. Such policies hit the Black communities in these cities hard, and now school district officials only want to double down on the pain by closing their schools, depriving these neighborhoods of some of the only remaining community institutions and the good-paying, blue-collar jobs they offer!

In his ethnographic research on community opposition to school closures in Philadelphia, urban studies scholar Ryan Good has argued that "declining enrollment can be understood not as the *cause* of closures but as the *outcome* of decades of underinvestment in public schools" (emphasis in original). And recent closures have occurred in the "same neighborhoods that have for decades endured the consequences of racial segregation, job loss, private disinvestment, and underfunded public facilities and infrastructure" (Good, 2019, p. 362).

Many closure proponents readily acknowledge some of these points. It *is* unjust that the most disadvantaged communities – especially the adults employed in the schools in those communities – must bear the burden and disruption, after suffering for decades. But what are the alternatives? As Kansas City shows, spending even more with the hope of enticing white and middle class Black families to return rarely works. And keeping under-enrolled buildings open means having less money to spend on other high-impact programs and support services to improve kids' future lives. In their calculus, closures may not be fair but they represent the least bad of the available options.

"All those statements are completely accurate. There is in my minds no dispute over any of those assertions," Crabill told me when I ticked off the arguments made by closure opponents who blame decades of systemic racism. But then he offered his response:

We now are requiring today's adults to bear the burden for tomorrow's children. And anyone who is not for that, I'm sorry we just are at cross purposes. Because my expectation is today's adults *will* bear the burden for tomorrow's children. That is what it means to be an adult, that we make sacrifices so that our children don't have to. Because anyone who's experienced the ravages of systemic oppression and racism and their horrors understands this: It's coming. And now the real choice that we have as adults is: Do we take the hit or do we step out of the way and let our children take the hit? Show me the folks who willfully step aside and let our children take the hit so that adults don't have to? I couldn't find many of those folks [in Kansas City]. I found folks who didn't like it, but I couldn't find many folks who said, "It's OK for these kids to suffer so these adults can keep their jobs."

Lerum agreed. "We absolutely need to address and to rectify the systemic racism and the injustice that's been perpetrated on these communities for decades and centuries, we have to address those. At the same time, kids only get one third grade and they only get one fourth grade," he told me. "To me, the worst violence that you can perpetrate on a community is the eighth grader that you've got in the back of the room who's looking around and realizes that all of his peers can read and he can't and now he has to figure out what's he gonna do with his life. ... We're throwing away entire populations of kids, because we know that they go into these buildings as three-, four- or five-year-olds. They're all three-and-a-half, four feet tall, they're bright-eyed, bushy-tailed, ready to learn, bright futures ahead of them. And they come out of these buildings with very different futures and opportunities, based on the color of their skin and the wealth of their parents. You have to do something about that building that they're in and stop that."

Lerum's last point – school closures are often a last resort for schools that have failed to educate kids for decades – often gets far less attention in school closure debates. While enrollment declines usually trigger the decision to close buildings, *which* schools ultimately shutter is an important question. In many districts, public officials at least claim that academics are one of the important considerations. (This is ultimately an empirical question, and one I will turn to later in this chapter.)

In recalling the first round of school closures in Chicago, early into his tenure as the chief executive of the city's school system, Arne Duncan described a series of town hall meetings he attended in the impacted communities. Many parents accused Duncan of racism for wanting to close their neighborhood school. At one meeting, Duncan walked an angry mother through the data about the abysmal academic performance of her child's school, year after year, all of which seemed to be news to her. "If I were a racist, then I would leave this school exactly as it is," he told her. "That's not what I want. They're children; I believe in them as much as you do. They can't wait for things to improve any longer" (Duncan, 2018, p. 63).

In Duncan's telling, the data were persuasive. "In time, some of the angriest parents from these three closures became some of our staunchest allies," he claimed. "They partnered with us and helped us communicate with other schools that we closed in the following years."

My sense, however, that such arguments are rarely effective and that few closure opponents can be won over by pointing out how bad the neighborhood schools are for their kids. In New York, parent and long-time education justice activist Zakiyah Ansari helped organize community opposition to the school closures carried out during the tenure of Mayor Michael Bloomberg. Among education reformers, Bloomberg and his education chancellor, Joel Klein, are celebrated for their efforts to take on vested interests and improve student achievement. However, Ansari told me she remembers Bloomberg's time in office as a reign of terror against Black families – with school closures a particularly sore point. She recalled organizing a meeting with stakeholders and education leaders during a round of consolidations. There, a top district official berated the closure opponents, arguing that the parents were trying to keep open "failing schools." "It was almost like they were blaming us, not listening and acknowledging the pain that people were sharing," she remembered.

Many activists such Ansari reject the idea that test scores – or other metrics divorced from the lived experience of local community members – are the right basis for evaluating school quality. Most parents love their teachers – and when the data suggest maybe they shouldn't, they are far more likely to dismiss the data then update their beliefs.

I saw many of these arguments echoed at Columbus board meeting, when the district decided to spare Linden-McKinley and the other schools on the closure list. "Everything is data driven. Let's talk about the human interest part," a prominent African-American pastor pleaded. "Look at the whole picture. Look at what's happening in the human heart." Sociologist Eve Ewing makes a similar argument in her recent book decrying school closures in Chicago. For many policy choices, hard data on school enrollments and test scores have their value. But for high-stakes decisions surrounding closure, "it seems inappropriate to rely on them so heavily, to the exclusion of other forms of knowledge or insights or subtlety, as the basis for a decision that will have a huge impact on hundreds of people's lives" (Ewing, 2018, p. 102).

More pragmatically, some also stress that low test scores may be a small price to pay if it means keeping kids safe. A frequent worry in urban areas is that consolidating buildings may mean bringing together students in rival gangs or requiring displaced students to travel to school through rival gang territory. "You're talking about gangs, you're talking about fighting, and nowadays you don't settle arguments with your fists, you settle them with powder and lead," the same Columbus pastor warned about the consequences of moving Linden-McKinley students to East High.[6]

At least as importantly, the reality in many places is that academic concerns are just not at the top of the priority list for many community activists fighting closures. In their minds, schools don't exist just

---

[6] All of the closure supporters I interviewed acknowledged that the safety concerns are real, especially in the shorter term. "It's crazy that you're going to let neighborhood crews define your school boundaries," Lerum said when I asked him about the violence concerns. "At the same time, it's wrong to dismiss it. It is a legitimate concern."

to educate students, and school buildings are valued for more than just the quality of the education they provide. School closures hurt so much because they seem to symbolize something far greater.

"But if the schools were so terrible, why did people fight for them so adamantly?" Ewing asked in the introduction of her book. She returns to this question again and again, never quite providing a concrete answer. Finally, she offers this: "We see that this community's choice to resist a school's being characterized as 'failing' is in fact about much more than the school itself: it is about citizenship and participation, about justice and injustice, and about resisting people in power who want to transform a community at the expense of people who live there" (Ewing, 2018, p. 17).

COALITION MERCHANTS AND NARRATIVE CONSTRUCTION

Reflecting on their time in DC, both Lerum and Smith acknowledged that they underestimated the strong emotional connections many neighborhoods and communities have not just with their local schools but also their local school *buildings* – even if those schools have a long record of providing a lousy education to their students.

"We in the ed policy realm would like to think that, 'Student achievement, that's gotta be the most important thing on your mind!'" Lerum recalled. In reality, some parents may legitimately place value on other considerations – not just safety, but travel time to a more distant campus, or the intrinsic value of having their children attend school with other kids living in the same neighborhood.

"That's a lot of what I think we learned in in this process. Coming in like a bull in a china shop, but now recognizing that there needs to be a little more nuanced," Smith agreed. "Everybody's gone to school, so we consider ourselves experts on school. In the case of school closures, in many situations, parents of the current students went to that school. Maybe their grandmother went to that school. So there is a legitimate, strong, emotional connection. 'How are you going to close this building? This is where I came to learn to read. This is where I played basketball. I come back and I watch the football games and this is my high school Alma mater.' Like who the fuck cares right? But they care. They care because that is part of their identity, part of their community."

Perhaps the most puzzling fact is that much of the opposition to school closures comes from people who do not actually send their own kids to the schools whose fate is at stake – and in many cases actively made the decision not to do so. As I noted in the introductory section of this chapter, in the context of Linden-McKinley in Columbus, the vast majority of the students zoned for the building chose to go elsewhere, and similar patterns are present in other cities. It is hard to reconcile the community's stated symbolic and emotional attachment to particular schools with how the same community members vote with their feet when given choices about where to educate their own kids.

Some activists have attempted to square this circle. In debates surrounding the closure of Germantown High School in Philadelphia, one local pastor acknowledged that "as a parent, based on the way the school district is run now, I would not have sent my child to Germantown High. ... [T]o me, it's less than standard." Yet he demanded that the school remain open anyway, apparently because of the its rich history and the neighborhood's emotional attachment to the building. "So, take away this building, if you will, you know, that's a big deal for [the community]. Even if it wasn't good to them" (Good, 2017, p. 872).

We should not doubt whether these attachments are real, nor is it productive to question the sincerity of critics who attach significant political symbolism to building closures. At the same time, it would be a mistake to conclude this is a whole story (as many sympathetic scholars seem inclined to do). Although far less salient in public debates, self-interested instrumental and pecuniary considerations also play a role. As discussed at length in Chapter 6, one reason why schools are often valued so highly as community institutions is because of the jobs they provide to the adults they employ. And school closures put those jobs at risk.

This is true regardless of whether financial or academic decisions drive closure decisions. In the cases of fiscal pressures and enrollment losses, the arguments about efficiency and economies of scale implicitly assume some amount of job loss. Although district officials often point to savings from building maintenance and heating and air conditioning, these are usually strategic arguments. Unlike teachers, custodians, and cafeteria workers, the local utility company seems to provoke little sympathy or solidarity from community members. But the truth is that education is a highly labor intensive business, with more than eighty cents of every dollars spent on people. Building closures cannot provide significant cost savings if they don't also produce a substantial reduction in headcounts. Reducing the number of school employees is the primary goal when districts talk about consolidating their footprint to save money.

In Kansas City, the district's decision to close half of the school buildings also reduced the number of teachers employed in the district by a shocking one-third over a period of just a couple of years. Crabill told me district officials used the reductions as an opportunity, offering targeted financial incentives to less effective teachers to encourage them to leave. Indeed, when it comes to academics, some researchers have long argued that school closures and major restructuring – involving the replacement of school principals and a majority of teachers – are often the strategy of last resort for fixing chronically underperforming schools. The No Child Left Behind Act included school closures on its menu of options required for buildings that could not escape "program improvement" status through other means (although this option was rarely exercised in practice). And President Obama's School Improvement Grant (SIG) program, which required states to intervene in their most academically distressed buildings, also encouraged the replacement of teachers. While evaluations of the SIG programs have produced mixed results, those finding positive effects on achievement almost always linked them to interventions that resulted in the mass replacement of existing teachers (see, e.g., Carlson and Lavertu, 2018; Dee, 2012).

Quite naturally, the employees who face the prospect of losing their jobs as part of the school consolidation efforts – even if the end result is an improvement in educational quality for students – are strongly motivated to resist them. It is quite clear from existing case studies that unions representing these employees play a central role in organizing and subsidizing much of the broader community opposition to school closures. In addition to providing important organizational resources and capacity, employee groups also serve as what political scientists Hans Noel (2012) has described as "coalition merchants" – intellectual thought leaders who help articulate and popularize broader policy narratives, develop talking points, and provide a shared language used in such campaigns. Indeed, the role school employee unions play in shaping the narratives surrounding school closure debates – including framing them as yet another example of structural racism – is not altogether different from the opinion leadership provided by activist Chris Rufo in debates about Critical Race Theory (e.g., Bertrand, Lyon and Jacobsen, 2024) and journalist Emily Hanford in the promotion of the "science of reading" (see Chapter 4, where I discuss both campaigns).

While nearly all of the scholarly literature on school closures that I have reviewed – much of it generally sympathetic to closure opponents – recognizes the involvement of school employee unions, they are generally described as supporting actors, just one of many groups involved in the coalitions. There is one exception, however. In her book about school closures in Chicago, *Closed for Democracy*, political scientist Sally Nuamah (2023) begins by acknowledging the pivotal role of community organizations and unions in mobilizing people to participate but argues that "they are not the focus of this work" (p. 26). Yet, throughout her account, unions appear again and again, always playing a key role. During the 2012–13 closure process, the city's teachers' union "promoted multiple narratives that ran counter to the race neutral one promoted" by district administration (p. 51). After alerting the affected communities, the "next step was typically for community organizers, including union leaders, to mobilize the local media to raise public awareness of potential school closures and the activities to protest them" (p. 93). Indeed, in comparing community mobilization against closures in Philadelphia and Chicago, Nuamah argues differences in the strength of each city's teachers' union was the key explanatory factor that made the difference in Chicago. The "bootleggers and Baptists" theoretical framework I propose in this chapter is entirely consistent with Nuamah's account, although it provides a much more cynical interpretation of the same basic facts than one would get form reading her book.

To be clear, one should not equate union involvement in anti-closure activism with the more incendiary claim that opposition to school closure is all a form political "AstroTurfing" or that unions hoodwink community members. (I myself have been guilty of thinking this in the past.) There is little doubt that local attachment to schools – even chronically underperforming schools – is real and the emotional pain in the face of school closure deeply felt. Unions elevate the voices of closure opponents, providing them resources to make their advocacy more effective, and help develop shared policy frames. They don't manufacture opposition where none exists.

When I asked Ansari about the supporting role teacher and custodian unions played in opposing school closures in New York, she argued against drawing any sort of cynical conclusions. The employees and community members were allies, united by a common interest. "I don't see anything wrong with that," she said about the union support. Labor help was an invaluable counterbalance against out-of-town billionaires pushing reform agendas. "If it's from the community, if the community wants to save [the schools], you find allies to help you fight. And [you need] a powerful ally, because the big money was real."

But just as we cannot fully understand the politics behind anti-alcohol blue laws by focusing only on the fervent efforts of religious activists, ignoring the support provided behind the scenes by bootleggers, we cannot understanding the politics of school closures by focusing only on grassroots community activists while ignoring the aid provided by teachers' unions and other employee interests. While Baptists are sincere and passionate about the cause, they would be far less politically successful without the pivotal support provided by the bootleggers.

WHAT WE KNOW

As the preceding two sections should make clear, when it comes to school closure, there is fundamental disagreement about the ground truth – about why some buildings are selected for closure (and other spared) and regarding the consequences of closures for students and surrounding communities. The remainder of this chapter will offer new empirical evidence to help sort fact from fiction. But before turning to my analysis, it is useful to review what other researchers have found on these questions.

To date, only one high-quality study has examined the predictors of school closure using national data (Harris and Martinez-Pabon, 2023).[7] Written by economist Doug Harris and his graduate student, Valentina Martinez-Pabon, it provides fodder for both sides in the closure debate. On one hand, the authors find that both low enrollment and poor academic performance predict which buildings are ultimately selected for intervention, suggesting that district decisions are driven largely by legitimate and objective considerations. On the other, they find that student race and socioeconomics also matter – even among schools with similar enrollment and achievement levels – supporting the contention that the burdens of closure are borne disproportionately by communities and neighborhoods of color.

For my purposes, the insights from their study are somewhat limited, however, because the sample in the analysis covers not just school closures but also interventions the authors describe as "major restructuring" – "where the school buildings remain open, but under different educational personnel and/or governance" (p. 33). This is obviously a related but conceptually distinct interventions. Restructurings account

---

[7] An earlier 2017 study Stanford's Center for Research on Education Outcomes (Han et al., 2017) looked at school closures in two-dozen states, but examined predictors of closure one at a time, without being able to separate them and speak to predictive power of each. Another recent study, Greene-Bell and Perlman (2024), does try to disentangle different factors predicting closure but largely leverages differences across districts. As a result, it cannot identify which are most important considerations for closure decisions within a district – why officials close one school but keep another open.

for nearly half of the events analyzed in the study, and the statistical model assumes the same decision-making calculus applies to both sets of decisions. Removing the restructuring events and focusing only on closures, I find somewhat different results in the next section.

The evidence base on the effects of school closure is much larger, but also quite mixed, allowing advocates to pick and choose the findings that best fit their preferred narrative. For example, the "Death by a Thousand Cuts" report focuses on Chicago, where several studies have showed that achievement declined both among the students displaced by closures and among those attending the receiving schools that displaced students switched to afterward (Gordon et al., 2018). What the report doesn't mention is that the declines among displaced students occurred the year *before* their schools actually closed, when the plans were first announced – suggesting that the political drama and community advocacy surrounding the closure debates, not the closures themselves, were responsible.[8] While research from other places has also sometimes found evidence of negative academic effects (see Larsen, 2020), some evaluations have shown that student achievement can actually improve after moving to a new school (see, e.g., Carlson and Lavertu, 2016; Kemple, 2016). And focusing only on students enrolled at the time of the closure, who end up paying the transition costs, ignores the potential benefits for future cohorts diverted to schools with better opportunities and outcomes (Bifulco and Schwegman, 2020).[9] Short-term academic pain – often the focus in studies finding negative effects – may still bring longer-term academic gains for future generations of students.

Indeed, the fairest read of the empirical literature on school closure is that, in terms of impacts on student learning, it depends. When building closures and consolidations result in students attending *better* schools, academic outcomes improve – often quite substantially (Bross, Harris and Liu, 2023; Brummet, 2014; Chin et al., 2019; Engberg et al., 2012; Steinberg and MacDonald, 2019). The problem is that closures don't always produce such gains in quality. One reason is that achievement concerns are just one consideration when choosing which schools to shutter. Another is that the kind of metrics of quality that may be most salient to policymakers – average test scores or proficiency rates – don't actually

---

[8] The negative impacts on students attending receiving schools appear to be due to the closures themselves. However, research in other cities has not consistently found similar disruptions elsewhere.

[9] In communities where schools are also the epicenter of juvenile crime, closures may have other positive spillovers as well (Steinberg and MacDonald, 2019).

isolate school "value added," or how much a given school itself impacts student outcomes.[10]

As I noted earlier in this book (and will discuss again in Chapter 8), differences in average test scores across schools almost always tell us much more about differences in the composition of students they serve and are not actually a reflection of school quality. In Chapter 9, I discuss how this can often lead parents to make bad choices – selecting schools that *appear* to be better, mostly because they enroll wealthier students, over schools that actually *are* better, but whose success is masked by a disadvantaged student body. It turns out that district leaders can make the same mistake. Ultimately, however, whether officials accurately identify and focus on low-performing schools as part of the closure process and, probably more importantly, whether displaced students actually secure spaces in better schools are ultimately empirical questions – ones I will turn to now.

CAUSES AND CONSEQUENCES OF CLOSURE: NEW EVIDENCE

So far, I have focused on giving voice to the different perspectives that frame the debates surrounding the closure of public schools. Understanding why well-meaning people of good faith may disagree is important – but ultimately not that helpful, from a real-world practical standpoint. Some of the policy considerations really are question of values – such as how to allocate scarce public resources and how to trade-off academic performance against other things communities might want from their local schools – on which reasonable people really can disagree and no consensus is likely to be possible. But other questions – Do closures disproportionately affect schools in minority neighborhoods? Does academic achievement increase or decline after closure? – are questions of fact where, at least in principle, there should be right and wrong answers.

The lack of consensus largely reflects the fragmented nature of the empirical scholarship. Rigorous analyses of school closure typically focus on one of a few large urban school districts, where administrative data are available to researchers and where it is possible credibly and precisely estimate causal effects. While this research may paint an accurate picture of individual cities' experience, it tells us little about the impact

---

[10] Some studies, including Carlson and Lavertu (2016), find evidence that moving to a higher achievement school can improve student outcomes, perhaps through exposure to a more favorable mix of peers. Most of the research on school closure, however, shows that academic gains are achieved only when students move to higher *growth* buildings.

of the *average* school closure, which almost certainly happens in school districts that have not been included in existing studies. And, for communities pondering their own closures, it is not always obvious whether they should look to cities like Chicago (where closures reduced tests scores) or instead to districts like New Orleans (where closures increased them) as the most relevant benchmark.

This section presents the results of a new national analysis drawing on the experiences of hundreds of school districts to address exactly these issues. I begin by constructing a panel of all public schools and school districts spanning a two-decade period between 2000 and 2022. Drawing on the National Center for Education Statistics' Common Core of Data (CCD), I identify every public school in the country that closed during this period.[11] In a typical year, between 800 and 1,000 public schools close nationally. This is not a trivial number, but it means that in a given year, only about 1 percent of the existing public schools close their doors. The federal data also include information about each school, including the racial composition of students it serves as well as total enrollment numbers, and details about each school's parent district.

I combine the CCD records with information about academic outcomes from the Stanford Education Data Archive (SEDA), the same source I used in Chapter 5. As a reminder, SEDA provides information about test scores in math and English language-arts in upper elementary and middle school grades from the 2008 through 2019 academic years. This is available both at the school district level, allowing me to examine the broader academic spillovers produced by the closure of individual schools, and at the building level for most (although not all) schools that enroll students in the tested grades.[12] The district-level achievement measures vary over time, while the school-level estimates are based on the pooling of all tested years and provide a single measure that does not vary over time.[13] The lack of information on how achievement in a particular school changes across school years is a significant limitation that likely introduces measurement error. This may cause me to underestimate

---

[11] I rely on the building closure codes in the CCD data, excluding temporary closures and buildings that reopen within three years of initial closure. I have also created my own coding based on schools that simply drop out of the federal government's panel, and my measure is highly correlated with the formal CCD codes. The analysis focuses only on traditional schools run by public school districts, excluding charter schools. Unlike Harris and Martinez-Pabon (2023), I do not examine private schools.

[12] In particular, very small schools that do not have a minimum number of tested students necessary for inclusion in SEDA.

[13] For schools that close, the achievement data all comes from the pre-closure years.

FIGURE 7.1 Student demographic composition and school closures in selected cities

the impact of academic considerations in school closure decisions. Note, however, that it cannot explain one of my key findings – that achievement *levels* appear to be a much more potent predictor of closure than achievement *growth*, as both measures cover the same years and are constructed using data on the same student cohorts.

I begin by trying to understand which factors drive school closure decisions, following the same general approach as Harris and Martinez-Pabon (2023) with several important changes. First, I include more years of data, examining all years between 2009 and 2018, but focus only on school closures, not restructuring efforts. Second, I compare the schools that close only to other schools that remain open *within the same district* in the year of the closure – not to schools in other districts that don't close any buildings of their own. Formally, this is done by including "district-by-year" fixed effects. Finally, when looking at racial and ethnic composition of schools, I construct separate percentages for Black and Latino students, without combining them into a single "students of color" category.

The first question I examine is the extent to which school closures disproportionately affect non-white communities, as many critics have argued. One example is Figure 7.1, an infographic created in 2013 by the Schott Foundation, a progressive organization that worked closely with the Journey for Justice Alliance on its advocacy and mobilization efforts. The infographic is titled "The Color of School Closures" and compares the racial composition of schools that closed in three large districts to the overall student population in those cities as a whole. "School closures across the country disproportionately hurt Black and low-income students," it concludes.

If one models school closures solely as a function of student racial and ethnic composition, the claim made in the figure does appear to be true nationally: When a district chooses to close at least one school building, it is disproportionately likely to shutter schools attended by Black and Latino students. But this does not prove that districts close schools *because* of their racial composition. It is possible, for example, that districts might unintentionally close such schools even if they prioritize racially neutral considerations – including enrollment levels and academic achievement – if schools with declining or low enrollment and disappointing achievement are disproportionately located in heavily non-white neighborhoods. (Unfortunately, they are.) Of course, unintentional racial impacts would not let districts off the hook – theories of "structural racism" focus precisely on the unjust impacts of plausibly racially neutral policies. But they would require tough conversations about difficult trade-offs that claims of blatant racism largely sidestep. Understanding whether the racial disparities are intentional is important on both normative and practical grounds – and doing so requires a more sophisticated method that can account for other differences between school that may be correlated with the racial composition of their student body and independently affect district closure decisions.

Figure 7.2 presents the results of such a multivariate model. As noted earlier in this section, my model includes district-by-school-year fixed effects and incorporates additional attributes that could put individual schools at risk of closure. In addition to enrollment levels, I include two measures of school quality taken from the SEDA database. The first is a measure constructed from average student performance on standardized tests, which I call a metric of "achievement levels." This is a highly salient measure but also a very problematic one, since it largely captures differences in the type of students schools serve, not differences in the quality of the education the schools they provide. The second measure captures how the performance of the same cohort of students changes across grades, which I call the "achievement growth." In the absence of student-level data, which are not available on a national scale, this is the closest we can get to calculating true school value added.[14] If school leaders really

---

[14] In an important validation exercise, Reardon et al. (2019) use student-level data from Massachusetts, Michigan, and Tennessee to show that this cohort-based learning

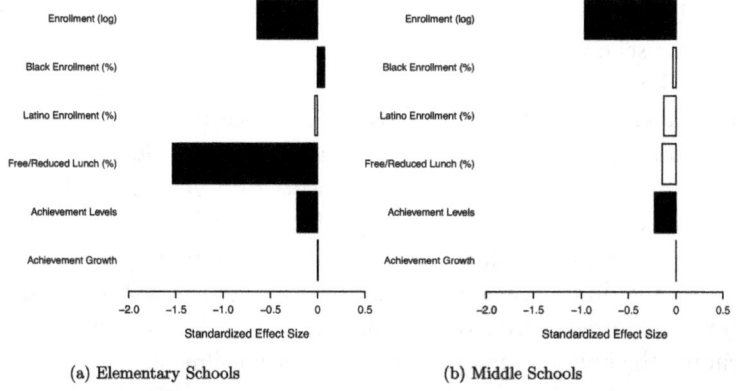

FIGURE 7.2 Predicting school closures
Note: Figures show effect of a school-level standard deviation increase for each variable on the probability that a building closes, estimated via a linear probability model that includes school district-by-year fixed effects. Solid bars indicate statistically significant effects.

wanted to use closures as a mechanism drive improvements in educational opportunities for children, they would prioritize closing schools with low achievement growth, since these are precisely the buildings that are failing children academically.

My analysis focuses only elementary and middle schools, both because these are the buildings most likely to be shuttered and also because achievement data are not available for high schools. I estimate separate models for each level and present results in the two panels in Figure 7.2. To make the regression results more intuitive, the figure plots the predicted percentage point change in the probability that a building closes in a given year for a standard deviation[15] increase in each variable. Solid bars indicate effects that are statistically significant at the usual 95 percent confidence interval, while hollow bars indicate estimates that fall short of significance. While only about 1 percent of schools nationally close in a given year, my model leverages information only from district-years when at least one closure happens, so the baseline probability is

rate measure is highly correlated with more conventional student-level value-added estimates, especially at the school district level.

[15] The standard deviations are calculated by examining the school-level distribution of each predictor. This may cause some confusion, as the SEDA variables are scaled to be in student-level standard deviation units.

higher. It is closer to 25 percent for elementary schools and 32 percent for middle schools.

Three key findings stand out. First, after accounting for other observable differences, there is no consistent evidence that schools enrolling more students of color are disproportionately likely to close. While Black enrollment does increase the odds of closure for elementary schools, the effect size is very small, and the sign flips for middle schools. Latino enrollment is negatively correlated with closure for both types of schools, although the differences are not statistically significant. Second, one of the most important predictors of school closure is the number of students attending the building. Increasing a school's enrollment by one standard deviation reduces the odds of closure by about 0.6 percentage points for elementary schools and nearly a full percentage point for middle school. This corresponds to a reduction of 3 percent relative to relevant baseline risk.

Third, school quality matters much less[16] and, to the extent that districts consider academics at all, they appear to focus on the wrong measures. Schools posting lower test scores are modestly more likely to close. But these test scores don't reflect poor educational quality, which is much better captured by the achievement growth variable. Unlike average achievement levels, which seem to influence decision-making on the margin, progress in raising scores does not seem to matter at all. Perceived school quality, in other words, affects closure decisions more than actual quality (to the extent that either matters at all).

Interestingly, districts are also far less likely to close high-poverty elementary schools – proxied by percent of students who qualify for free and reduced-price lunch – compared to other similar buildings. Indeed, poverty is even more predictive of closure decisions than student enrollment levels for elementary schools. For middle schools, on the other hand, the socioeconomic composition of students is not a significant predictor of closure.

While there are multiple ways to interpret these relationships, in my view they undermine key arguments of both school closure supporters and opponents. On one hand, they debunk the argument that school

---

[16] One alternative interpretation is that low enrollment levels may reflect parents' revealed preferences – which might, in turn, incorporate academic performance information. As a result, enrollment might be considered a "post-treatment" variable that itself absorbs some of the effects of the academic factors. My results are consistent with this view but still suggest that district leaders put little independent weight on school quality beyond the impact flowing through families' enrollment choices.

closures are driven by racism. It is true that schools in minority neighborhoods are more likely to close, but this appears to reflect the fact that such schools tend to have the lowest enrollment and also lower levels of achievement. It is hard to imagine a rational school consolidation process that does not focus on the most under-enrolled schools – and once one accepts this reality, there is no way to avoid racially disparate impacts of closures. On the other, the claim that closures are motivated primarily by academic concerns – as Arne Duncan argued about the efforts he oversaw – also don't quite fit the data. If districts truly wanted to shutter failing schools, they would focus on building doing the worst job improving student performance from one year to the next. The data show that they fail to do so – at least for the average school district. Academic considerations receive far less weight than student enrollment number, and when districts take student performance into account, they seem to focus on the wrong measures. Put another way, closures seem to be driven more by fiscal considerations and a desire to achieve operational economies of scale, not academics.[17]

The latter finding, of course, does not prove that closures are bad for students. It is possible that the financial savings realized by shuttering low-enrolling schools are reinvested to improve programming – both for the displaced students and for the rest of the school district. To see whether this actually happens, I now turn to modeling the effects of closure on a variety of outcomes.

Unlike the previous analysis, which is conducted at the school *building* level, I now focus on outcomes at the school *district* level. One rationale for doing so is that closures may affect student subgroups differently. For example, student displaced by a closure may suffer some academic harms, but other students – including younger cohorts that are diverted from an under-enrolled building with threadbare academic opportunities – may benefit. While these distributional consequences are definitely important, policymakers ultimately want to know the net effect on the district as a whole.

Before turning to the results, I want to address some important challenges to credibly estimating the causal effects of closures. One is that different districts close buildings in different years, which creates a staggered "treatment" that complicates the use of standard econometric

---

[17] The variables I observe explain only some of the variation in closure probability. Other difficult to quantify considerations, such as the age and state of individual buildings, are not doubt important as well.

techniques. I discuss this issue in more detail in Chapter 5 in the context of the empirical analysis presented in that chapter and use the same solution here, implementing a newer statistical method developed by de Chaisemartin and D'Haultfœuille (2020) designed to address bias due to staggered timing.

Second, some districts may close schools in multiple years. Without clear theoretical expectations about when we might believe the effects of a particular closure to begin and how long such effects should last, it is not obvious how to separate the impacts of earlier closures from subsequent ones. To sidestep this complication, the analysis focuses on the first year in which districts close a school.[18] However, the results are quite similar if I simply exclude districts that undergo multiple rounds of closure.

It should be noted that the typical district experiencing a school closure looks a bit different from the very largest school districts such as Chicago and New York. Among the school systems in my estimation sample, the average district that decides to consolidate elementary schools operates about twenty-six total schools on average (and seventeen elementary schools) prior to consolidation and enrolls roughly 20,000 students. The student body of such districts is 59 percent white, 15 percent Black, and 14 percent Latino on average. These districts shutter about 1.5 schools during the closure process, and these schools enroll about 15 percent of the respective district's student body. Consolidations involving middle schools happen in districts that are somewhat larger in terms of total enrollment but have comparable student bodies in terms of racial composition.

Figure 7.3 plots the "event study" coefficient, comparing the trajectory of achievement in the relevant districts before and after closure relative to a control group of unaffected districts. It presents separate estimates for standardized math and ELA test scores, and I limit the analysis to the period 2008 through 2019, the years covered by the SEDA achievement data. In the years before schools are closed, there is no evidence of a significant differences in the trajectory of student achievement. There is also no evidence of large impacts – either positive or negative – afterward. While districts do experience small but statistically significant declines in achievement the year after they close a school, the longer-term impacts are not consistent. After the closure of elementary schools,

---

[18] I exclude districts that open a new school in the years immediately after closing one. These types of closures are likely to be quite different.

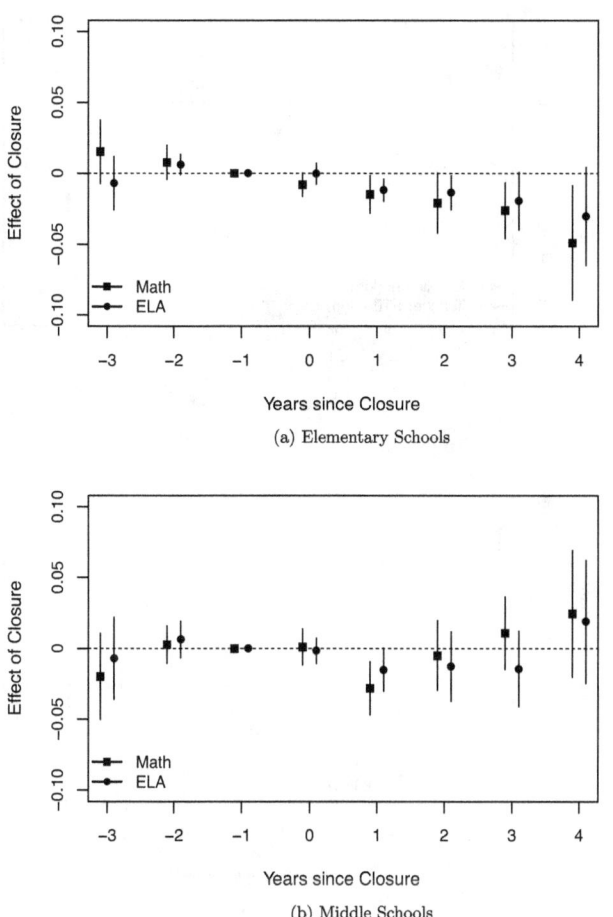

FIGURE 7.3 Effect of school closure on student achievement (in standard deviation units)

the achievement remains somewhat lower in future years. For middle schools, by contrast, the medium-term effects become positive (although not statistically significant). For both types of closure, the estimates are precise enough to rule out effects larger than 0.05 (student-level) standard deviation units in the first three post-closure years, near the floor of what most education researchers would consider substantively meaningful. On average, closures appear to neither deliver the academic benefits we might expect from more efficient allocation of resources nor the academic harms that the resulting disruption are often claimed to cause. With about one in six of the districts' students displaced by the typical

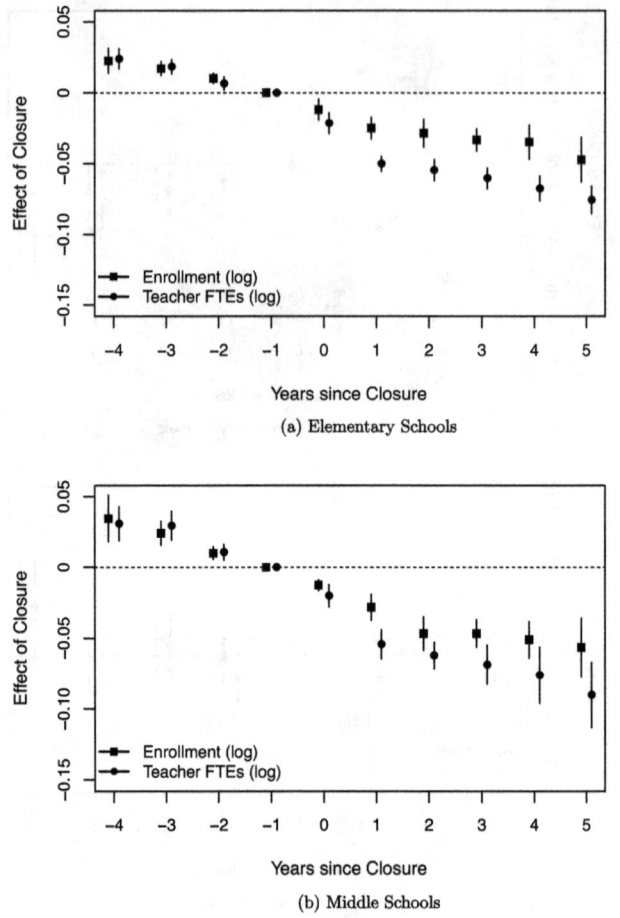

FIGURE 7.4 Effect of school closure on district enrollment and staffing

closure in my sample – and many more affected through their attendance in one of the receiving schools – these results cannot be chalked up to a lack of statistical power or focus only on overall, district-level average achievement.

Figure 7.4 examines how school closures affect student enrollment and teacher employment levels in the affected districts. These outcomes are available back to 2000 and I include the earlier years in the analysis to maximize precision. In contrast to achievement, both of these outcomes show some negative pre-trends in the years leading up to closure. This is not surprising, in light of the earlier finding about the importance of building enrollments for closure decisions, and suggests that enrollment declines at the district level is one factor that triggers school consolidation efforts.[19] However, the loss of students accelerates somewhat after buildings are closed, with districts losing between 2 percent (for elementary) and 3 percent (for middle schools) of their student bodies. Since the closed buildings enroll about 20 percent of each district's students in earlier years, that suggests that about one in ten students who are displaced by a closure ultimately end up leaving the district for other options. The vast majority, however, seem to remain and transition to one of the other available buildings.

One potential concern is that the students who leave are disproportionately high- (or, less plausibly, low-) achieving, changing the composition of remaining students in ways that distorts the observed test scores in subsequent years. Losing higher-achieving students would mechanically depress average achievement, perhaps masking real gains among the students who remain. Although I cannot completely rule out this possibility, it seems unlikely for two reasons. First, the district-level achievement estimates in the SEDA data include charter schools located within the geographic boundaries of the school district, not just students attending traditional public schools. So if students leave the public schools for charters, they would still be included in the achievement estimates. (That is not true for students leaving for private schools or homeschooling, however.) Second, Figure 7.3 shows that student enrollments decline fairly steadily in the years after a closure cycle. To produce no net change in achievement each and every year, the timing in the test score improvements among the remaining students would need to match precisely these outflow dynamics – not impossible, but unlikely.

The figure also shows significant declines in teacher workforce after closure. After accounting for the pre-trends, the number of teachers employed in the affected district declines by between 5 and 8 percent, depending on the level of the school closed and how many years have passed since, and student–teacher ratios increase by between 0.3 and 0.5 on average. These results are not surprising – if budgetary efficiency is a primary motivation for building consolidation efforts, meaningful savings cannot be achieved without staffing reductions. But they help explain why teachers' unions and other school employee interests are so active in opposing school closures, and why employee unions play

---

[19] It may also be that news is announced several years prior to the actual closure, prompting some families to leave, and that districts may close a school gradually, eliminating one grade a time. In my data, I observe the closure only after a school's terminal year.

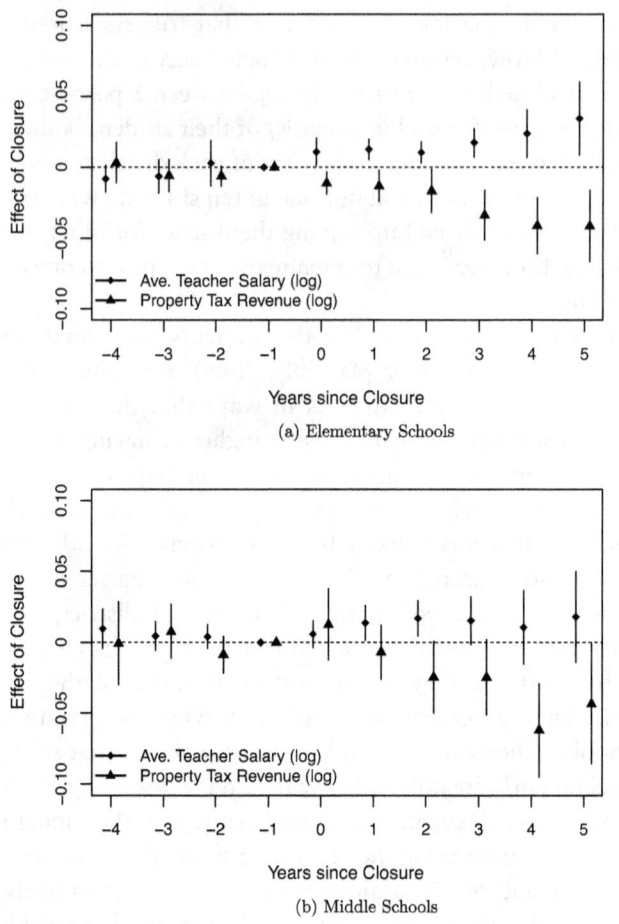

FIGURE 7.5 Effect of school closure on teacher salaries and local revenues

such an important behind-the-scenes role in mobilizing and organizing like-minded community members to serve as the public face of the opposition. Federal staffing data do not breakdown blue-collar occupations such as custodians, bus drivers, and cafeteria workers but the support worker category that includes these occupations also sees significant declines of roughly similar magnitude as impact on teacher employment.

The analysis also confirms that school closures generate significant efficiencies. Overall, annual per-pupil spending falls by between $500 and $1,000. Most of this decrease appears to be driven by reduced staffing levels, especially teachers. While expenditures on plant operations and maintenance also declines, this explains less than 15 percent of the total observed decrease. As Figure 7.5 shows, districts appear to use the savings for two things: (1) reducing property taxes (which decline by about 4 percent over the medium term) and (2) higher teachers' salaries (which increase by about 1 to 2 percent on average).

Two caveats are in order. It is possible that property taxes decline as a result of falling property values, with school closure becoming capitalized into home prices (see Chapter 8). It is also possible that higher average salaries are driven by districts retaining more experienced and thus higher-paid teachers as they downsize rather than through changes in the salary schedules. But regardless of the precise mechanisms, the evidence establishes that closures reduce total spending even as the compensation of teachers increases, just as Oakland's School Board President Shanthi Gonzales had hoped.

MYTHS AND (POLITICAL) REALITIES

To summarize, my national analysis reveals three important new findings about the causes and consequences of school closures:

- Although such closures do appear to disproportionately affect communities (and neighborhoods) of color, the disparities are explained by school enrollment patterns and differences in achievement that are correlated with the racial composition of students. When comparing otherwise similar schools, buildings enrolling more Black and Hispanic students are closed at similar rates as those enrolling fewer such students.
- In the average school districts, building closures neither improve nor reduce average student performance substantially on math or ELA exams in elementary and middle school grades. (We lack data to know what happens in high schools.) This likely reflects the fact that districts do not appear to prioritize academic growth and progress when deciding which buildings to shutter, leaving potential for significant learning gains that could be realized through better targeted closures on the table.
- School closures modestly accelerate student enrollment losses, perhaps undermining districts' stated right-sizing and fiscal goals. But teacher employment levels decline even more, and closures do ultimately unlock some degree of budgetary flexibility.

These insights can help provide important context for evaluating the arguments that often come up in the context of school closure debates in many communities. Overall, they largely debunk most of the worst-case predictions made by school closure opponents, with the important caveat that I examine only academic outcomes. Other concerns, dealing with student behavior and violence, cannot be evaluated rigorously with the available national data. Individual district case studies in the existing literature paint largely a mixed picture on these fronts and many of the practitioners I spoke to for this chapter insisted that, while real, such issues can be managed and generally fade over time as displaced students are successfully integrated into their new schools.

My results also undermine some of the arguments made by closure supporters. School consolidation efforts do not, at least in the aggregate, appear to do much to move the needle on academic achievement. This too is unsurprising, given evidence in the existing literature. Nearly all previous studies find that school closures improve student tested performance only when they produce a substantial improvement in school quality, as measured by school contribution's to student growth. Because high-growth schools tend to have few vacant seats, it is difficult to use closure as a policy lever to shift students to these buildings at scale. The fact that districts do not appear to prioritize building value added when deciding which schools to shutter makes achieving meaningful improvement in student outcomes even less likely.

These null results do have one important upshot – for policy debates about school choice. I began this chapter by arguing that school closures represent the third rail of education politics, but choice comes a close second. The two are interconnected – in many urban areas, the proliferation of charter schools and, in some places, private school vouchers have accelerated the loss of public school enrollment, contributing to the pressures to close of public schools. The effect of attending a school of choice on the children whose families take advantage of these options – what researchers often describe as "participant" effects – is generally mixed and depends both on the types of schools these families choose and the quality of the neighborhood school they leave behind. But that is only part of the story. School choice could also affect the education quality experienced by rest of the students who remain behind in the neighborhood schools. Supporters of school choice argue that options benefit these students, too; even if individual students don't exercise choice, the mere threat of them leaving forces public schools to up their game. This is often described as the "competitive" effect, and I summarize the empirical findings from the relevant literature in more detail in the concluding chapter, which focuses on policy solutions to the political problems I document in this book.

Some skeptics question the purported benefits of competition. They argue that existing research on competitive effects focuses only on very local and short-term effects, ignoring how enrollment losses over time force districts to close schools, displacing students and harming their learning. My findings help put this contention to the test. Although I examine all school closures, not just those prompted by enrollment losses brought about by greater choice options, the results suggest that school consolidation efforts do not appear to cause major academic harm to students who continue to attend public schools, strengthening the empirical case for greater choice.

As declining student enrollments and resulting financial pressures force more communities to begin their own consolidation efforts, do my results offer policy recommendations they should consider? The obvious answer is that, when deciding which schools to close, districts should put much greater weight on academic considerations, and focus on metrics that capture differences in schools' contribution to student learning, not crude differences in achievement driven mostly by student demographic composition. Prioritizing academic growth would also have the added benefit of reducing the apparent racial disparities – a serious political impediment to school closures, particularly in era since the death of George Floyd, when claims about racial disparities have particular resonance. This is because school value added is much less strongly correlated with either school-level socioeconomic status or race than average achievement levels.

Implementing such a recommendation will be difficult, however. Putting more weight on growth also means putting less weight on school enrollment and size. And if balancing the budget and right-sizing are the ultimate goals, closing buildings based on value added rather than enrollment will require closing more of them to achieve the desired budgetary savings and economies of scale. In addition, there is a chance that in closing schools based on measures such as value added – a metric few parents understand – would cause even more families to leave the local public schools than I found in my analysis. After all, low-enrolling schools have very few students for a reason. Closing *other* schools with the hope that parents move their kids to these buildings seems pretty unrealistic. Since school closures are already a heavy political lift, increasing the number of buildings to be shuttered and justifying the closures based on measures no one can understand makes the politics even more treacherous.

Fortunately, there is another alternative. School closures can allow districts to use their resources more efficiently precisely because they reduce the number of adults employed in the districts, something my empirical analysis confirms. In chronically low-performing systems, this could be a feature rather than a bug – if implemented the right way. When reducing the teaching staff, for example, district leaders could offer financial inducements to target the least effective educators, even if they don't work in the buildings selected for closure, as Kansas City did.[20] In many cases, this will require changes to existing collective bargaining agreements that require districts to rely strictly on seniority when implementing layoffs. And even in places where seniority is not a binding rule, identifying least effective educators requires a robust and well-implemented teacher evaluation system – something few school systems currently have.

For me, the main lesson from this chapter is that school closure is unavoidably a political rather than technocratic process, one driven largely by the concerns of various adults and much less by the academic interests of kids. It is a process greatly shaped by powerful narratives linking current policy debates to real historical injustices. Employment considerations loom large, and school employee unions provide much of the organizing power that mobilizes and sustains community opposition to consolidation efforts and helps develop and popularize racially inflected narratives. Changing the criteria district leaders use to decide which schools to close and doing a better job of ensuring that closure efforts improve (rather than impede) student learning will not change this political reality. A more effective and equitable approach to closure might change the identity of the "Baptists" who show up at school board meetings to oppose these efforts. But as long as closures result in job losses, the "bootleggers" will be the same and ready to fight, regardless of whether doing so is in the interest of the children local schools serve.

---

[20] To avoid the fight, some districts just rely on normal attrition – not replacing teachers who retire or leave for other reasons – to produce the savings, making it even less likely the end result will be an increase in average teacher quality.

8

Housing Markets Create Educational NIMBYs

> No one is paying attention to the scandalous system that determines a five-year-old's educational destiny based on his or her address. If education is the key to the American Dream, millions of children are being issued defective keys.
>
> —Former California State Sen. Gloria Romero (2014)

There is a good chance this book would not exist were it not for a kind act of an elderly manager of a small apartment building in Northern California more thirty years ago. Let me explain.

In June 1993, my parents and I left Moscow, Russia, where I was born, to move to the United States. We were the lucky beneficiaries of recently passed legislation allowing groups historically persecuted in the Soviet Union – in my family's case, Jews – to come to America as long as they had relatives here.[1] Our family's sponsor was my mother's great uncle, who had settled in Northern California several decades earlier, and we moved into a two-bedroom apartment in Castro Valley, a small unincorporated community in the East Bay known for the quality of its schools. Just days after our arrival, I enrolled in summer school at Castro Valley Elementary, my zoned campus located down the street, and started third grade when the academic year began that August.

---

[1] The legislation is known as the Lautenberg Amendment after New Jersey Sen. Frank Lautenberg, who added it to the 1990s appropriations bill. It flipped the usual burden of proof for refugees by creating the presumption that religious minorities from the former Soviet Union faced a well-founded fear of persecution.

A month into the school year, however, my parents sat me down to share some bad news. During our first three months in the country, my family received assistance from local Jewish resettlement agency. But that aid was ending, and with my father still looking for employment and my mother – a mechanical engineer in Russia – enrolling in beauty school to earn a cosmetology license, my parents applied for government assistance. In addition to food stamps, we were eligible for Aid to Families with Dependent Children, a joint state-federal welfare program that provided cash assistance to low-income families with kids. The total aid was just over $600 per month – the same as our monthly rent, leaving nothing to pay for utilities or other bills. We had to move to a cheaper apartment right away, my parents announced.

Within a few days, we had found a place we could afford. It was a one-bedroom unit – I would sleep in the bedroom, and my parents in the living room – and cost $500 per month. And it was only two miles away, less than a ten minutes' drive. But it was located in a different school district, San Lorenzo, and I would almost certainly have to switch schools. This was not ideal, but it was the only option we had. My parents signed the lease and put in a thirty-day notice at our current apartment complex.

That's when the kind apartment manager entered the story. A few days after my parents had notified him of their intent to move, he knocked on our door one evening. Although my parents spoke very limited English, he was somehow able to explain to them his concerns. The schools in San Lorenzo were considerably worse. If they moved, he warned, my education and my future could be impacted. And then he made them an amazing offer: If they downsized to a one-bedroom apartment in our existing building, he would lower the rent to match what my parents had agreed to pay in San Lorenzo. I would be able to stay at Castro Valley Elementary. Surprised by this unprompted and unexpected proposal, my parents agreed immediately.

To this day, I wonder how my life would have turned out without the manager's intervention, if I had ended up attending schools in San Lorenzo instead of Castro Valley. In 2003, the year I finished high school, the graduation rate in Castro Valley was 15 percentage points higher than in San Lorenzo – 95 versus 80 percent – and a substantially larger share of my graduating classmates had completed the coursework that made us eligible to attend the California public university system, where I enrolled. The same year, Castro Valley Elementary had scored nearly 100 points higher on the California's Academic Performance Index, the state's official school accountability rating system, than the elementary school I would have attended in San Lorenzo.[2]

There are two key lessons reflected in my childhood experience. First, a small kind act of a selfless stranger can have profound, even life-changing consequences. Second, one of the most inequitable and least defensible aspect of America's public education system is how it links educational opportunities to housing markets. Although many venerate the idea of the local "neighborhood" school that serves students living in close geographic proximity, the consequence is a system that relies explicitly on housing costs to ration access to the most desirable schools.

Ironically, many of the same progressive activists and teachers' union leaders who bemoan the influence of "neoliberal" ideas in education and complain about capitalist exploitation and the oppressive power of markets passionately defend neighborhood schools and disparage alternatives – such as selective-enrollment programs and open-enrollment charter schools. Yet they don't seem at all bothered by a system in which the quality of the education children access is determined by the ZIP Code in which their families can afford to live.

One person who does understand the blatant inequities created when we use home addresses to define school attendance boundaries is former California State Senator Gloria Romero, a Democrat who has long bucked her party and its teachers' union allies. "In California and mostly throughout the nation school assignment is largely based on ZIP Code – a geographic boundary. Five simple, arbitrary digits become the basis of separation from the American Dream for millions of children who, through no fault of their own, happen to live on one side of the tracks or the other," she has argued (Romero, 2014). "I ask you, where else in American life do we restrict opportunity and movement to geography? We have struck down racially restricted covenants in the purchase of homes, and we can move into any neighborhood. We can choose to worship at the church or temple of [our] choice. Imagine if you tried to visit a park and were asked for your papers at the entrance to the park and were informed, based on your ZIP Code, that you could not enter because you were from the wrong side of town. Imagine if you could only choose to visit a dentist or a doctor or shop at a mall in 'your neighborhood.' We wouldn't stand for it. So why do we do this in education?"

---

[2] Unfortunately, California did not roll out its school accountability system until the late 1990s, so data from 1993 is not available.

A few months before I began writing this chapter, a group calling itself the No More Lines Coalition launched a publicity campaign in support of legislation to eliminate school attendance boundaries across the country. The idea seems popular – a 2023 YouGov poll commissioned by the group found super-majority support for "making it possible for students to access any public school in their state regardless of where they live." More impressively, the question elicited no partisan divide, with 66 percent of Democrats and 65 percent of Republicans favoring the proposal.[3]

Although I know and respect many of the individuals involved in this campaign, I won't spend much time on it here because it has almost no chance of success. The reason school boundaries exist is because spots at the most desirable, high-quality public schools are limited. (Just as limited as spots at elite, high-price private schools.) There needs to be *some* mechanism to distribute these highly coveted seats, and it's hard to think of an alternative system that would be less arbitrary and more politically viable than geography – and one that would not create its own set of perverse and unintended consequences. The central problem is the scarcity of high-quality educational options, not the mechanisms that we use to ration the limited opportunities that are available. Eliminating attendance zones does little to address the root causes of the problem – the various adult political interests and forces I described in Chapters 2–7 that conspire to impede the effective governance of schools in so many communities and make a great public schools such a precious and scarce commodity.

Perhaps more importantly, the campaign to eliminate attendance boundaries almost certainly will not succeed, despite the popular support found in survey data, because it takes on yet another well-organized vested interest: homeowners. They are one of the most powerful interest groups in local politics. Even if they don't themselves have school-aged kids, people who own homes in desirable school districts – and desirable school attendance zones within those districts – have paid a premium for that privilege. School quality – or, as I will argue in this chapter, *perceived* school quality – is capitalized into home prices. Any effort to eliminate attendance zones will mean imposing substantial haircuts on the value of houses located in the desirable areas by doing away with the premium currently attached to the these homes. In America, home equity is the primary savings mechanism families use to build their wealth, so we should

---

[3] The poll was conducted in September 2023 by Arc Insight.

not be surprised that any effort that threatens housing prices prompts vicious and well-organized counter offensives from affected incumbent homeowners.

The idea that real estate interests advocate for narrowly self-interested policies, often at the expense of the most disadvantaged members of our society, is not new. For example, there is a large literature documenting how incumbent homeowners predictably advocate for land-use policies designed to increase the costs of housing development and prevent the construction of affordable housing units in of their neighborhoods (e.g., Einstein, Glick and Palmer, 2020). In the context of housing policy, such efforts are often described using the derisive acronym of "NIMBYism" – "Not In My Back Yard."

Yet NIMBYism is not limited to housing policy. In this chapter, I bring together findings from several different academic fields to make the case that NIMBY forces also play an active role in education policy. Unlike other adult interests I have focused on throughout this book, the cause of educational NIMBYism is not people lacking skin in the game. In some ways, it is the opposite – just as with school employees, homeowners may have *too* much of it. For many people, the bulk of their life and retirement savings is tied to the equity of their home, which in turn gives them particularly strong incentives to follow and participate in policy debates that may affect housing prices. And, at least in principle, there is nothing wrong with homeowners having a voice in education policy. Their pecuniary self-interest strongly incentivizes homeowners to pay close attention to local education policy, to remain informed, and to serve as watchdogs who demand that public dollars are spent most effectively (see, e.g., Lastra-Anadón and Peterson, 2023).

The problem is that homeowner activism and advocacy are not unalloyed goods, and this chapter focuses on the downsides. First, I show that homeowners punch above their political weight in raw numbers. Part of this reflects the fact that homeowners are more likely to vote in local elections – especially when such elections are held off-cycle and almost everyone else stays home. Second, I argue that homeowners focus on only a subset of educational policies that impact student learning. In many cases, they overlook less salient measures – including achievement growth over time – because these are not capitalized into home values, even though growth provides arguably the cleanest metric of "school quality" among those available. At other times, homeowners focus on the demographic composition of students because this, too, affects the resale value of their home. Together, the political overrepresentation of homeowners and the imperfect overlap between what influences home prices and what affects educational quality leads to a variety of perverse outcomes, with homeowner activism often creating pressure on local districts to pursue what are downright racist, classist, and unjust policies. The educational opportunities available to our most disadvantaged kids – those who need good schools the most – suffer as a result.

POLICING THE BOUNDARIES OF EDUCATIONAL OPPORTUNITY

NIMBYism in housing policy may be a familiar concept for many readers. Both the academic literature and popular accounts of this phenomena are replete with ridiculous case studies. Neighbors who show up at the local planning board meeting to oppose a new development because it would – they claim – impact the habitat of some little critter no one had ever heard of before. Born-again preservationists who argue that the decrepit and long-abandoned eyesore property down the street cannot be torn down to build apartments because it is a rare example of an architectural style that absolutely must be saved for posterity. And cringy, explicitly racist comments warning that the "invasion" of "undesirables" will cause local property values to plummet.[4]

Educational NIMBYism, by contrast, is less well known, so I will begin by providing four concrete examples. The first involves my childhood friend, Sherry, and Mr. Morrison, one of the vice-principals at our high school. I met Sherry when we took karate classes at the same dojo. Although she was different from most of my friends – with bright pink hair and facial piercings – we got along well, and when I started a Russian club at my high school, Sherry and her cousin joined as members (even though neither was Russian). I never asked about the details, but I had the impression that Sherry's family was not the wealthiest – at least relative to the advantaged background of most of the kids in my high school. It was an open secret that her house was located outside of our district, in the less desirable town next door. Apparently, Sherry had registered to attend our school using a relative's address.

As I said, Sherry's housing situation was an open secret – and Morrison was one of the people who knew about it. But he couldn't quite prove it. One of four vice-principals, Morrison had reputation for being

---

[4] The HBO miniseries "Show Me a Hero," based on a nonfiction book of the same name by Lisa Belkin, provides a powerful example of such NIMBYism in action by recounting the story of the Yonkers, New York, housing desegregation case.

the hardass disciplinarian. One of his responsibilities, apparently, was ferreting out students who were attending our school despite not living in the school district, and he and Sherry were constantly playing a cat-and-mouse game. One day, Sherry told us that Morrison had called the sheriff to her relative's house, in an effort to prove that she didn't actually live there, so he could get her unenrolled.[5] (The effort failed, because she continued to attend our high school through graduation.)

I thought of Sherry's predicament recently when reading an outrageous story about the Hazelwood School District, a suburb outside of St. Louis. The local NPR affiliate and the Center for Public Integrity had obtained public records piecing together the district's aggressive campaign to track down students who were committing residency fraud by attending its schools (Mansouri and Grumke, 2023). Hazelwood had apparently assembled an entire team of staff whose job was to show up at the homes of families suspected of committing "educational larceny" to collect evidence, including digging through their clothing and personal effects. Over a five-year period, the district had carried out 300 home visits, as part of nearly 4,500 housing investigations. During the most recent one-year period, nearly 12 percent of the district's student body had at some point been placed under investigation.

In a job posting, the district advertised the position of a "residency investigator." Among other responsibilities, the investigator was charged with conducting "surveillance in the community at bus stops," to detect kids trying to sneak into the district to attend school. Some of the investigations were apparently prompted by reports made using an anonymous phone tip line created just for this purpose. In one case, a parent appealing the district's determination that the family lived outside of the district e-mailed officials pictures of the child's pet guinea pig and stuffed monkey, to prove that the child really did sleep at the grandparent's house in the district, the one they had listed as their home address.

"Residency investigations in themselves are not unusual," the news story noted. "School districts around the country use them to ensure families actually live within their boundaries and can rightfully attend school and access resources there." Hazelwood attracted attention only because of the volume and visibility of its efforts.

The Center for Public Integrity documented similar campaigns at other upscale school districts, including several outside of Philadelphia

---

[5] As an unincorporated area, Castro Valley did not have a police department, with the county sheriff providing law enforcement service.

(DiPierro and Mitchell, 2023). In many cases, the families and children caught in the residency enforcement dragnet were among the most vulnerable and precarious – those doubling-up with family or couch-surfing, just one step removed from living on the street or a homeless shelter. Although federal law provides special protections for homeless youth (see American Bar Association Commission on Homelessness and Poverty, 2018), requiring district officials to allow them to continue attending the same school and providing free transportation if necessary, what counts as the type of homelessness that triggers federal protections seems to be a gray area where districts exercise tremendous discretion. If a family is displaced when their landlord did not renew a release, and they could find no other affordable housing in the district, that does not qualify, according to some of the school systems profiled by the Center for Public Integrity.

"I'm appalled!!" one woman wrote to her local district after learning that her grandson had been unenrolled after the district rejected the family's request for homeless protections and deemed him to have stable housing outside of the district. "How does sleeping on someone's sofa and your children sleeping on air mattresses or paying your last dollar at a hotel considered stable living conditions. I believe having a permanent address would be stable living conditions."

Education larceny is not only an actual crime in many states, but one that can come with serious penalties. In 2013, for example, the prosecution of a Connecticut woman Tanya McDowell made national news. McDowell was sentenced to five years in prison after pleading guilty to larceny and other charges (DeRoche, Korman and Hinds, 2023).[6] Homeless at the time and living in Bridgeport, McDowell had enrolled her son in Norwalk, a much more desirable district, using her babysitter's home address. The backlash over the charges led to a bipartisan campaign in Connecticut to end the prosecution of parents for address sharing, although it remains a criminal offense in other states.

Not all NIMBYism involves educational larceny. Consider the case of the Normandy School District north of St. Louis. In 2014, the district – 97 percent Black in terms of student enrollment – was struggling mightily. Its academic achievement was so horrendous, the state board of education ultimately stripped it of its accreditation. This created a big question – where were the kids zoned for a now-unaccredited district

---

[6] Although originally arrested only for larceny, the guilty verdict involved some drug charges as well and the sentence reflected all of the crimes to which she pled guilty.

supposed to go instead? Eventually, the case reached the state supreme court, which ruled that students living in Normandy were allowed under existing state law to attend another district while theirs got its act together.[7] Nearly 400 families took advantage of the ruling to enroll in the nearby Sir Francis Howell School District, one of the best in the state, with only 15 percent of students qualifying for free or reduced-price lunch and 84 percent white.

The prospect of Normandy students being bused in created a panic. When the district scheduled a town hall at Sir Francis Howell High School to discuss the developments, hundreds of community members showed up. Emotions were raw, and many of the comments – captured in a video of the event by the local news station – were deeply offensive and hurtful. "I deserve to not have to worry about my children being stabbed, or taking a drug, or getting robbed – because that's the issue," one irate mother told the crowd. "I grew up with *this*. I will not have *this* for my son," another mother announced. "So will this district send my son to a better school when this one goes down?"[8]

After playing the above clips from the meeting, the local newscast zoomed out, doing in-depth profiles of the people organizing the opposition to the Normandy kids. "Why are we taking unaccredited school children and moving them to an accredited school?" one of the parent leaders and a former district teacher, Jocelyn Swan, asked the camera. "I chose this district because it was safe environment and a good district for my daughter. I didn't choose to have her walk through metal detectors." Then she turned to the topic of the Normandy children who were transferring: "It's going to be shocking for them. They're going to feel unwanted and uncomfortable." (Swan was apparently oblivious to how her own words and advocacy might contribute to the transferring students' discomfort.)

To be sure, one could interpret some of these conflicts as being driven by purely fiscal considerations. Public schools are funded partially by local property taxes – although to a much smaller extent than was the case half a century ago. Residents who pay these taxes to maintain local schools may reasonably argue it's unfair to allow those who

---

[7] Specifically, students could transfer to any district in the same or neighboring county.
[8] Not everyone in attendance opposed the new students. "I'm totally appalled that we have gone back to 1954," an African-American mother responded, referencing the year of the *Brown* decision (see Chapter 6), to loud applause.

don't contribute financially to nevertheless access their programming.⁹ But taxes is only part of the story. Housing markets play an even bigger role, as my final example helps illustrate.

Note that education funding, whether from local property or state sources, is pooled at the school district level. Although families live within districts and pay the same property tax rates regardless of which school their children attend, they typically cannot choose to attend just any building. Instead, they are usually assigned just one option based on their address. If fiscal concerns were at the heart of education NIMBY-ism, we'd expect political conflicts over enrollment and attendance to end at the school district boundaries. Changes in attendance zones across schools located *within* districts – which don't directly involve any fiscal redistribution or property tax changes – would not be controversial. Yet they are, as recent events in Florida show.

In May 2023, the Tampa school board voted to shutter one of the district's worst elementary schools – the only one to receive an "F" grade on the state accountability scale. Even before the decision, many families had voted with their feet: The majority of those zoned for the building chose to attend elsewhere, leaving the school less than half-full. The good news was that there was another school just two miles away – one whose academic outcomes were far better. The bad news was that redrawing the attendance boundaries to absorb the students previously assigned to the failing school was a nonstarter (DeRoche, 2023).

The Tampa superintendent had already learned this lesson. A few months earlier, he had proposed a major building consolidation initiative district-wide, designed to save millions of dollars (see Chapter 7) and an accompanying rezoning plan that would shift attendance boundaries to reflect the reduction in the number of school buildings. When word of the proposal got out, many families – especially those whose homes would be rezoned for lower-ranked schools – nearly lost their minds (Schecker, 2023). Many were worried about how the changes would impact their home values. Some said they had purchased their homes precisely *because* they were located in the attendance area of a desirable school and were now having their hard-earned privilege at risk of being stolen from them. "We did our homework when we bought out house," one complained.

---

⁹ In the case of Sir Francis Howell, the students' home districts was required to compensate their new one.

"That was kind of the reason we bought the property here," another agreed.[10] The superintendent ended up resigning shortly thereafter.

I first heard about the Tampa controversy from the writings of Los Angeles-based author and consultant Tim DeRoche, who has a long history of involvement with Democrats for Education Reform. In recent years, DeRoche has published articles in a variety of national outlets trying to increase the salience of educational NIMBYism – although he doesn't use the label – and explain to a broader audience why housing markets are at the root of inequality in public education. In 2020, he published an entire book on the subject, a searing indictment of geographically based attendance zones titled *A Fine Line: How Most American Kids Are Kept Out of the Best Public Schools* (DeRoche, 2020).

DeRoche told me he became interested in the topic after seeing a Facebook group for local moms in his northeast Los Angeles neighborhood blow up in a thread about how to get kids into the highly desirable Mt. Washington Elementary School, even as another lower-achieving building located nearby remained half-empty. Many believed the traditional (and outdated) narrative that educational inequities were the result resource disparities created by a reliance on local property taxes. The bad guys were the conservative white Republicans who fled to the suburbs to escape school integration.

DeRoche's neighborhood was not in the suburbs, the local schools were not reliant on property taxes – a legacy of California's Proposition 13, which reduced and froze local property taxes in 1978 – and his neighbors were young progressives with Black Lives Matter signs in the front yard. Yet, when DeRoche asked them at a cocktail party about opening up Mt. Washington to lower-income, Latino students who couldn't afford the houses in his neighborhood, the suggestion was not well received.

"Those people just go apoplectic. They just can't handle it because they're like, 'I've already paid for this school'" by buying a house in its attendance zone, he recalled. "The great irony is that these people are very progressive in their politics, and yet here they are segregating themselves into this school, which is less than a mile from other communities that are completely boxed out. So it highlighted to me that this issue cuts across party lines."

---

[10] Defending his plan, the superintendent also pointed to property values. "What that does is increase [our] property values the more we continue to address our high-quality education within every one of our schools," he argued, describing his efforts to reduce the number of low-rated schools in the district (Muller, 2023).

This chapter builds on DeRoche's observation, with a slight amendment: Education NIMBYism *is* political – but it represents a different kind of politics, one that operates largely independently of the liberal-conservative divide that characterizes much of American political discourse.

POLITICAL POWER OF HOMEOWNERS

As with other kinds of NIMBYism, the educational variety is driven by the disproportionate political influence of homeowners. Some of this reflects homeowners' higher propensity to engage actively in local politics, particularly when it comes to costly forms of participation. In their research on housing politics, for example, political scientists Katie Einstein, Max Palmer and David Glick digitized the minutes of zoning and planning commissions in the greater Boston area. Combining the record of participants with the Massachusetts voter file and other administrative sources, they found that residents who showed up and spoke at these meeting were quite different from the population of each town and city. On average, they were older, more likely to be male, have lived in their communities for longer – and were more likely to be homeowners (Einstein, Palmer and Glick, 2019).[11] Subsequent studies replicated this pattern in other cities in Texas and California (Sahn, 2025; Yoder, 2020). The homeowners are far more likely to be concerned about protecting their home values than ensuring that their communities have enough affordable housing, and their political advocacy influences policy to make development less likely, reducing housing supply and making it too expensive for those of limited means.

Our research team has found similar patterns in school board elections. As I discussed in Chapter 2, we worked with a company called Catalist – which specializes in maintaining updated voter files for use by progressive political campaigns – to assemble detailed records about voters who participate in school board elections in a number of large states around the country. One of the variables Catalist appends to each voter record is information about whether they owns their own home. Combining these records with aggregate data from the 2010 census, which tracked the percent of families with school-aged kids who own vs. renting, provides a comparison of voters and students on this dimension. We've assembled this data for approximately 4,000 school districts in 11

---

[11] Homeownership information was available for one community, the Town of Arlington.

large states and I rely on this sample in some of the descriptive analyses and calculations in the next section.

Overall, more than 80 percent of the electorate in the average school board elections is made up of homeowners. This is higher than comparable rates of homeownership among families with children in those communities. Indeed, the voters in the average school board election are about 10 percentage points more likely to own their own home than are the families of students – similar in magnitude to the gap that Einstein, Palmer and Glick (2019) found in their zoning and planning data. And even this is likely to underestimate the extent to which homeowners play an oversized role in local elections. One reason is that the census data includes all families, regardless of whether their children attend public schools. Given the costs involved, families who enroll in private schools are almost certainly wealthier and disproportionately made up of homeowners.[12]

There are at least three reasons for why people who own their home are more likely to participate in local school board elections than are renters. To start, homeowners tend to be wealthier, older, and have resided in their communities for longer periods of time – all factors widely known to themselves directly increase political participation (e.g., Verba, Schlozman and Brady, 1995). But this is not the whole story. Several recent papers by political scientists Andy Hall and Jesse Yoder find compelling evidence that the act of buying a house itself increases turnout in local elections (Hall and Yoder, 2022; Yoder, 2020). Similar to our approach that used Catalist data, Yoder and Hall took official voter files and combined them with data on real estate transactions, identifying precisely *when* voters purchased their homes. They found that turnout in local elections jumps by nearly 20 percent in the first election after a voter becomes a homeowner and increases further in subsequent years. The effect is largest among those buying the most expensive homes and most pronounced when issues likely to affect home values – such as changes to local zoning rules – appear on the ballot. Finally, the modal school board election is held off-cycle – meaning not in November of an even year,

---

[12] In addition, the Catalist variables on housing tenure are imprecise, and a significant number of voters are coded as "unknown" in terms of their housing tenure. In the estimate in Figure 8.1, I assumed that all of the voters with unknown tenure are renters, to be conservative and err on the side of underestimating the number of homeowners. Alternatively, we can remove them from the denominator and examine only voters with known housing tenure status, which increases the share of homeowners in the electorate by between 10 and 15 percentage points and roughly doubles the gap between voters and families with school-aged children.

when congressional and presidential races also appear on the ballot. This not only reduces overall turnout but also increases the share of voters who own their home by about 5 percentage points (Ornstein, 2018).

WHAT AFFECTS HOME PRICES – AND WHAT DOESN'T

Emerging evidence that homeownership mobilizes political participation surely does not surprise economist William Fischel. More than two decades ago, Fischel wrote a book titled *The Homevoter Hypothesis* (2001a) arguing that "mercenary concerns with property values, especially that of homeowners, motivates citizens to organize and make personal sacrifices for such things as public schools and amenable environments." The book is unusually accessible and well written for academic treatise, and his arguments are not subtle. For example, Chapter 4 contains a section titled "Homeowners Rule (and Renters Do Not)." This section analyzes the survey evidence that was available at the time and concludes that "the largest and most active group of voters in all but a few cities consists of homeowners" while renters "participate in local affairs in disproportionately low numbers" (p. 80). This is exactly the pattern that Hall and Yoder have confirmed in recent years with more complete voting and property tax records and sophisticated statistical modeling.

Fischel's starting point is the same one I make earlier in this chapter: For most people, a home is not just a place to live but also a long-term store of value and a way to build up savings. But housing is a particularly risky asset class. Most homeowners have only one property, preventing the type of diversification that hedges risks in other investment contexts. And houses are fixed in place, making them particularly vulnerable to localized calamities that might destroy them physically or erode their value in other ways. These might include natural disasters, such as hurricanes and tornadoes but also other geographically concentrated problems such a crime spike and environmental pollution.

The realization that they have put a lot of their financial eggs in one delicate basket encourages homeowners to pay particular attention to local policy debates and become active in the political process. If the local city council is considering building permits for a polluting industrial development, the neighbors have strong incentive to mobilize and fight the project. Not only because no one wants to live next to a toxic waste dump but because having one next door is likely to reduce property values. Similar concerns motivate a lot of opposition to affordable housing – for incumbent homeowners, such housing brings only downside in the form of more lower-income neighbors who might make the neighborhood less exclusive and attract crime and other undesirable elements.[13] Fischel noted these dynamics decades ago in an article titled "Why are there NIMBYs?" (Fischel, 2001b). (Answer: Because there are homeowners, and they care about their home values.)

In his account, the existence of "homevoters" – home-owning voters motivated by property values – is a wonderful thing for public education. The desire to protect the value of their real estate investments gives these constituents strong incentive to care about the quality of local schools even if they don't themselves have kids enrolled – because the people who will one day buy their home may have kids. "Homeowners who have no children in the public schools nonetheless have some incentive not to trash their local schools at the ballot box. To do so would reduce their net worth," he notes (Fischel, 2001a, p. 266). Even if information about the operations of the local school district is costly to obtain, encouraging free-riding, only a small number of homevoters need to pay attention. Their knowledge is transmitted to everyone else via market signals reflected through changes in housing prices, a process economists call "capitalization." The connection between school quality and home prices also provides incentive for homeowners to raise their own property taxes – at least when they are confident the additional dollars will be invested wisely and productively. While no one wants to pay higher taxes, improvements in school quality that result from higher spending should increase home prices, and thus homevoters' equity.

Here is how Fischel summarizes his argument:

> The reason that local governments perform better is that the benefits and costs of local decision making are reflected in the value of property in the jurisdiction. The homevoter hypothesis holds that homeowners, who are the most numerous and politically influential group within most localities, are guided by their concern for the value of their homes to make political decisions that are more efficient than those that would be made at a higher level of government. Homeowners are acutely aware that local amenities, public services, and taxes affect ("are capitalized in") the value of the largest single asset they own. As a result, they pay much closer attention to such policies at the local level than they would at the state or national level. They balance the benefits of local policies against the costs when the policies affect the value of their home, and they will tend to chose those policies that preserve or increase the value of their homes (p. 4).

---

[13] That hypothetical future tenants of such affordable housing don't live in the neighborhood yet and may not even be eligible to vote in local elections only exacerbates the asymmetry in mobilization.

There is powerful logic in this argument, buttressed by compelling evidence that at least some dimensions of apparent school quality are indeed capitalized in home prices. The most well-known research on this question is a study by economist Sandra Black (1999). Using data from Massachusetts, Black compared the sale prices of otherwise identical homes located *within* the same school districts – an important innovation, which holds constant many other factors that may impact prices, including property tax rates – but located just on different sides of attendance boundaries defining the catchment areas of local elementary schools. She found that homes zoned for better schools sold at a premium – about $4,000 (or 2.5 percent) more for every 5 percent increase in test scores.

Another study, by economist David Figlio and a local school district administrator in Florida, found something quite similar using a different research design. Specifically, Figlio and Lucas (2003) examined repeat sales of the same Florida homes over time – before and after the roll out of a new school accountability system introduced by Gov. Jeb Bush. Under the rating system, each school received a letter grade corresponding to the achievement of its students. After the state began grading schools, the sales prices of otherwise identical homes diverged. And as school ratings changed over time, so did school prices. The authors found that home buyers were willing to pay about 20 percent more for a home zoned for an "A" elementary school compared to a "B." A home assigned to a "B" school, in turn, sold for about 16 percent more than one located in a "C" attendance area.

The problem is that when it comes to school quality, perception and reality often don't match. As I have emphasized throughout this book (and especially in Chapters 2 and 7), differences in end-of-year test scores between schools tell us little about the quality of the teachers they employ or the actual amount of learning taking place inside. Mostly, they just capture differences in the composition of students – based on things like demographics and parental involvement – that schools serve. What we ultimately care about is school "value added" – how much more a given student learns by attending one school compared to how much she would have learned in another.

While test scores are indeed capitalized into home prices, it turns out that value added is not. About fifteen years ago, the *Los Angeles Times* obtained individual student data from that city's school district through a public records request, then teamed up with a researcher to estimate value-added ratings for individual schools and teachers. The newspaper released its ratings in August 2010, generating lots of publicity and controversy – especially after a teacher who received a low score ended up committing suicide. Yet when economists Scott Imberman and Michael Lovenheim (2016) looked at the local home sales records, they saw no significant changes. Home buyers in Los Angeles were still willing to pay more for houses zoned for higher-achieving schools, as defined by the state's official Academic Performance Index, although this was driven largely by differences in student composition. But they were not willing to pay more for homes that were actually doing a better job teaching students! A recent meta-analysis reviewing the broader literature on schools and home prices showed that this result was not unique to Los Angeles: "In the midst of the ... disagreements among studies, there is at least one point of agreement: value-added measures of school quality appear less powerful in capitalization than other measures" (Turnbull and Zheng, 2021, p. 1127).

There are many reasons for why home buyers might value schools that enroll higher-performing students but be unwilling to pay a premium to live near a school that actually grows student achievement from one year to the next. One may be peer effects – if academic achievement is contagious, a hotly debated empirical question (see Sacerdote, 2011), parents might have good reason to prefer to send their children to schools where they are likely to be in class with other smart kids, even if the school is not what made them smart. And families may put weight on other outcomes they perceive to be correlated with peer achievement – recall the Sir Francis Howell parent's concern that admitting Normandy students would increase the risk of her child "being stabbed, or taking a drug, or getting robbed."

Another explanation is differential salience.[14] After all, average student achievement ratings and other measures based on them, such as proficiency rates, are widely accessible and feature prominently on real estate websites such as Zillow. Most people have an intuitive understanding of what having 10 percent more students reading at grade level means. By contrast, value-added models are generally harder to find and even harder to understand. Even education policy wonks struggle

---

[14] Biasi, Lafortune and Schönholzer (2025) provide compelling evidence that salience conditions the extent to which different dimensions of school quality are capitalized into home prices. Specifically, they find that prices go up when school districts make highly visible investments in sports facilities (which don't actually improve student achievement) but not when they upgrade basic, less visible infrastructure such as HVAC (even though such investments improve learning).

to explain how to interpret the metrics value-added statistical models produce to regular people.

The reality that housing markets seem to value schools that enroll high-achieving students but not necessarily schools that produce such high achievement has profound consequences for Fischel's argument. Homevoters focused on maximizing the value of their investments should use their political voice to put pressure on local school leaders to *enroll* advantaged students – and to keep out those who would bring down test scores. They do not, however, have much incentive to prioritize and reward student learning, because housing markets don't reward it.

It turns out the evidence bears out this with this intuition. To examine the relationship between homevoter political power – the percent of voters in local school board elections who own their residences – and academic outcomes, I combine our Catalyst voter demographic information with data from the Stanford Data Election Archive, the same source I used in Chapters 5 and 7.[15]

If Fischel's homevoter hypothesis is correct, we should see higher achievement in districts where a larger share of the electorate owns their own home. As Figure 8.1(a) shows, that is precisely what we find. The figure plots the relationship between student achievement levels on the y-axis and homevoter electorate share on the x-axis, after statistically adjusting for a variety of other observable differences. (The "rug plot" at the bottom of the figure shows the distribution of homeownership rates for the school districts in my sample.) Importantly, the analysis holds constant the percent of families residing in the district who own their own home, ensuring that it is capturing the effect of having more *voters* who are homeowners rather than simply enrolling more *students* from home-owning families.

Overall, there is a statistically significant relationship between homevoter political power and average achievement. Increasing the share of school board voters who own their own home by a standard deviation – about 13 percentage points – predicts an improvement in student achievement of about 0.01 standard deviations. This is admittedly a very small effect as far as educational interventions go, but two caveats are in order. First, as the figure makes clear, the relationship is not linear.

---

[15] In Chapters 5 and 7, the analysis uses achievement data aggregated at the geographic district level, to include students who may leave the public school district for charter schools. Here, I instead focus on achievement outcomes only for students attending district-run schools.

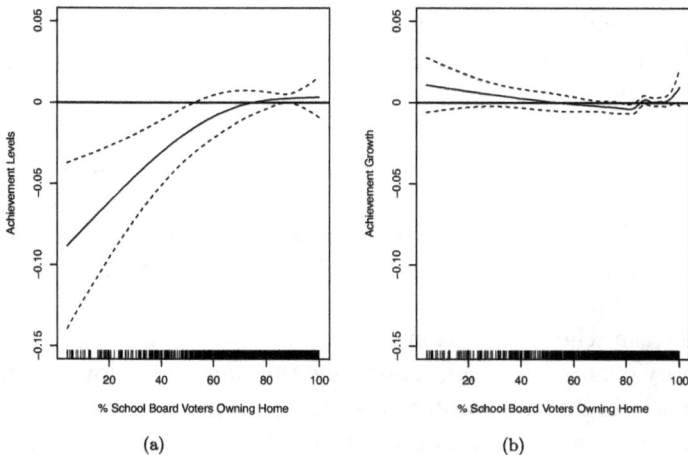

FIGURE 8.1 "Homevoter" political power and student achievement
Note: Figures show relationship between average share of homeowners in local school board elections and student academic outcomes at the school district level. Estimates are based on models that statistically control for state fixed effects, school district urbanicity, student racial and ethnic composition, the percent of students who are economically disadvantaged, a composite measure of socioeconomic status, and percent of families with school-aged children living in the district who own their own home. To account for potential nonlinearities, the effect of "homevoter" share is estimated using a generalized additive model with cubic spline. The outcomes are based on student test scores in math and English/language arts in grades three through eight.

More homeowners predicts higher achievement in districts where relatively few voters own their home, but the relationship flattens out almost completely in districts where more than 60 percent of voters own rather than rent. Second, recall that the figure holds constant other demographic characteristics of students. To the extent that these also impact achievement in ways that are capitalized into home values, homevoters should not "control away" these demographic determinants of achievement as I do in my statistical model.[16] Indeed, the bivariate relationship (comparing only school districts within the same state), is ten times larger, with a standard deviation increase in the share of homeowners in the electorate

---

[16] As I discuss later in this section, keeping low-income and minority students out of local schools is indeed one lever homeowners use to protect their property values. Thus, controlling for student demographic composition in my statistical model almost certainly causes posttreatment bias, artificially attenuating the relationship between achievement and homevoter political power.

associated with a 0.10 standard deviation increase in test scores. This corresponds to about a quarter of a year of learning in the tested grades, a substantively meaningful difference.

More important is Figure 8.1(b), which shifts focus from achievement *levels* to achievement *growth* – as I explain in Chapters 1 and 2, the best publicly available measure of school "value added." Here, we see no relationship: When homevoters have more political power, they do not seem to push districts to do a better job educating students and accelerating their learning.

How can school districts increase average achievement without actually providing a better education? By enrolling fewer lower-achieving students to begin with! In other words, by engaging in educational NIMBYism. In my account, what drives this NIMBYism is not explicit racism or classism but rather entirely rational concerns about property values among people who view their home as their primary store of long-term wealth. The problem is not that homeowners are selfish, but rather that housing markets reward the wrong thing – enrolling higher achieving peers rather than improving the quality of the teaching in local classrooms. When home values reflect *perceived* rather than *actual* school quality, school districts face strong incentives to find ways to keep lower-income and minority students out of the local schools (see Collins and Kaplan, 2022; Kane, Riegg and Staiger, 2006; Stemper, 2022).

I raised these issues with Fischel during a recent interview – suggesting that perhaps homevoters may not be as salutary for public education as his book had implied, at least from the perspective of lower-achieving and lower-income families. Although he pushed back gently on some aspects of my arguments, noting, for example, that some people may value diversity in their community and thus pay a premium to live in school districts that are not so exclusive, he was not surprised that housing markets didn't seem to care much about school value added.

"Put yourself in the position of a real estate agent trying to sell a house. You can say two things about the house," he explained. "You can say, 'Look at those fabulous SAT scores, better than all of the surrounding communities!' Or, 'Look at that value added! You took low-income kids and increased their scores more than any other school in the state.' If the buyer is upper-middle class, that may not be too important for them."

But then he walked me through another related implication of the homevoter hypothesis that I had not considered. Recall that local school districts historically relied on local property taxes to fund their operations. This produced sharp inequities in resources across schools – both due to differences in the size of the property tax base and in willingness of communities to pay high property taxes.

Starting in the 1970s, state courts struck down school funding models so heavily reliant on local property income. One of the most famous cases was *Serrano v. Priest*, a 1971 decision by the California Supreme Court that effectively forced the state government to increase its own contributions to local education to equalize resources across school districts of varying wealth and tax capacity. The end result was a more centralized system that limited the ability of local communities to increase their own taxes to fund schools. Fischel has been highly critical of this ruling and others like it, arguing that delinking tax effort from school quality – and thus home values – contributed to California's taxpayer revolt in the form of Proposition 13, a state constitution amendment referenced earlier that cut property taxes and dramatically limited local governments from increasing them in the future (Fischel, 1989).

The argument that *Serrano* led directly to Proposition 13 remains hotly debated among researchers, and not everyone agrees with Fischel. But in our conversation, he pointed out another unintended result of school funding reforms designed to equalize resources across districts: Taking variation in local property tax rates off the table has actually increased incentives for homevoters to engage in educational NIMBYism, since shaping the demographic composition of students now remains one of the last remaining ways in which they can increase the (apparent) quality of local schools and thus their own home prices.

"If you take the fiscal off the table" – in other words, reduce local control over school financing by relying less on property taxes – "people become more interested in sorting and so the zoning becomes more restrictive," he told me. "The clearest case was in California. They switched from fiscal zoning to personal zoning." The lesson is that housing markets and local politics interact with well-meaning reform efforts in complicated ways. When property value concerns and homevoters enter the picture, policies we think will increase equity could actually backfire and make things worse.

RESIDENTIAL SORTING VERSUS GERRYMANDERING

The kind of zoning Fischel referenced in his comment deals with local land-use policies. Historically, suburbs relied on such regulations – ranging from minimum lot size and setback requirements to outright bans on the construction of apartments – to keep low-income and minority residents out (Trounstine, 2018). This continues to be an important cause of student segregation between school districts to this day.

But such land-use rules are unlikely to explain segregation within school districts, particularly in big urban school systems that were largely built out before restrictive zoning became popular. For that, many observers have blamed the intentional gerrymandering of school attendance boundaries – the same boundaries Sandra Black used to study the capitalization of school quality into home values.

Tim DeRoche's book provides many outrageous examples, with the zigs and zags demarcating school catchment areas in ways that reveal careful and deliberate efforts to ration access to good schools and keep out less desirable populations from the most coveted ones. Other researchers have documented large racial and economic disparities among people living just across the street from each other, separated by nothing more than an invisible line defining school attendance zones. Many of the boundaries date back to the 1930s and correspond to the "redlining" maps used by federal housing agencies to determine which homebuyers received access to government home loan guarantees during those years (Monarrez and Chien, 2021). Yet there is also compelling evidence that historical "redlining" maps just followed preexisting neighborhood boundaries, reflecting existing housing disparities rather than creating new ones (see Fishback et al., 2020). So any similarity between those maps and school attendance boundaries is not dispositive evidence of intentional gerrymandering.

So to what extent have school attendance boundaries been gerrymandered, perhaps as a result of political pressure brought to bear by homevoters trying to increase the value of their properties? The clearest answer to this question comes from a fascinating recent study by Urban Institute economist Tomás E. Monarrez.

Monarrez began by taking residential addresses as given and then simulated what school attendance boundaries would look like if students were simply assigned to the school building that is nearest their home. This provides a neutral baseline of a world without gerrymandering. Then he compared these hypothetical attendance areas with the actual boundaries used by approximately 1,600 school districts – almost all of the ones with enough schools to require defining catchment areas. If gerrymandering was rampant, we would see that schools are much more segregated in reality than would be the case if students simply attended the building closest to their house.

To the surprise of many people, Monarrez found no evidence of gerrymandering. In fact, schools would actually be modestly *more* segregated in terms of both race and socioeconomic status if students simply attended their closest school. As in the context of partisan gerrymandering (see Chen and Rodden, 2013), much of what appears to be the intentional carving up of territory actually reflects residential sorting. The upshot is that housing markets and affordability constraints faced by disadvantaged families, not policies defining school attendance zones, are the primary culprits behind the within-district segregation we see today.

There are several important caveats to this finding, however. As DeRoche notes, school attendance boundaries matter only for the relatively few schools that are popular enough to fill up. In many districts, schools that have available capacity are willing to enroll students who live outside of the building's catchment area. By looking at all attendance zones, Monarrez's analysis may mask serious gerrymandering among the much more limited number of schools where the attendance zones actually matter.

"I would say that when you look at the elite schools, it's hard not to conclude that some of them have been gerrymandered to include the wealthier parts of town," DeRoche told me. Attendance boundaries "also encourage segregation over time, because then people buy into the zone. They distort the real estate prices, and then people are kept out. Nonwealthy people, immigrants, people of color, low-income folks, working-class folks are kept out of those areas."

And saying that current attendance zones don't increase segregation does not mean that these zones couldn't be tweaked to counteract it. There is some evidence, for example, that small changes to existing school catchment areas could boost integration and even reduce travel times (Gillani et al., 2023). But only theoretically. Such exercises in counterfactual line-drawing hold students' residential locations fixed. In reality, changes in school attendance boundaries would filter through the housing market, and households would simply move to sort around the new lines, undoing some of the intended benefits (Stemper, 2022).

HOW HOUSING MARKETS UNDO EDUCATION REFORMS

So far, I have focused on how the capitalization of perceived (but not actual) school quality into home prices combines with the political power of the homevoters to create and preserve the deep inequalities we see in the public education system. But there is another important reason to take housing markets into account when thinking through education reform proposals: They can undo intentional policy interventions designed to improve education for the most disadvantaged, lowest-income children. Once again house prices – and how they change in response to perceived school quality – are to blame. The sorting of households in responses to changes in attendance boundaries provides one example, but it turns out there are many others.

One reason why low income families tend to be concentrated in neighborhoods zoned for underperforming schools is that undesirable schools is what helps make the housing in these neighborhoods affordable to begin with.[17] Suppose policymakers find a way to improve these schools. They adopt and faithfully implement a basket of reforms, and student achievement goes up. These improvements cause home prices to go up in turn. As housing becomes less affordable, low-income families face displacement to other neighborhoods, where the schools are bad enough to keep the neighborhoods undesirable for wealthier families less constrained by house prices. So improving the school, paradoxically, means the benefits end up bypassing the very children policymakers may have hoped to help because of residential sorting that follows – and is indeed caused – by improvements in educational quality.

The dynamic I just outlined may seem far-fetched, but it is reality, not merely a theoretical hypothesis, as two studies help demonstrate. The first focuses on the School Improvement Grant (SIG) program, and Obama-era initiative that resulted in $7 billion being invested in the lowest-performing schools in the country over a period of about eight years. Although the details of the program are beyond the scope of this chapter, the most important thing to know is that the bulk of the SIG funding was targeted to schools ranked in the bottom 5 percent of each state. A number of careful analyses have evaluated the SIG-funded interventions, and many found substantial positive effects on student outcomes – particularly in schools that pursued the most dramatic turnaround efforts that included replacing a substantial share of teachers in the targeted school buildings (see Carlson and Lavertu, 2018; Dee, 2012; LiCalsi et al., 2015; Sun et al., 2017).

---

[17] Of course, education is not the only amenity that influences housing costs. Neighborhoods where housing is affordable tend to have not only low-quality schools but also high crime, more pollution, and all sorts of other disamenities that help depress the housing values.

That SIG worked to improve school quality (at least under certain conditions) is great news, and provides compelling evidence both that turning around chronically underperforming schools is possible and that actually doing so requires dramatic intervention – precisely the kind of intervention that adult politics and entrenched school employee interests often prevents. But a fascinating recent paper by economists Cameron Friday and Tucker Smith provides another important lesson.

In their study, Friday and Smith (2023) focus on Nashville, and examine what happened to the local housing market in neighborhoods zoned for schools that were part of Tennessee's SIG program. They use a very rigorous design – comparing changes in housing prices over time in areas just inside the relevant school attendance boundaries to neighborhoods located just outside of them, and thus zoned for different schools that were not part of the intervention. By design, the schools that became part of the SIG program were the very worst in the state, and this was reflected in the real estate market: Homes located just inside these schools' attendance boundaries were about 15 percent cheaper before the intervention, compared to identical houses located just a few blocks away and assigned to the neighboring school buildings.

After the rollout of the SIG program, the cost of housing in the attendance boundaries of the targeted schools went up, increasing more than 10 percent faster than homes just outside of these attendance zones. And the people buying homes in these neighborhoods also changed – with average incomes increasing and a substantially larger number of new home buyers becoming white. Evictions in the attendance zones also increased – by a dramatic 35 percent. Not surprisingly, the composition of students attending the schools also changed – with enrollment figures for white students increasing significantly and the number of students of color falling. The schools may have become better, but this caused the neighborhoods to gentrify and the most disadvantaged families to be pushed out. We don't know where they ended up moving to, but it's a good bet the schools in those areas were not great.[18]

Texas provides another example of how efforts to increase equity in education can become undone because of housing markets. Until the mid 1990s, the most prestigious public universities in Texas used some form of affirmative action by taking race into account in their admission

---

[18] In addition, a large literature shows that moving itself usually harms student achievement, so the displacement triggered by SIG program and resulting residential sorting probably made the displaced students even worse off academically.

decisions to increase the number of underrepresented minorities attending these campuses. Eventually, however, the federal courts struck down these programs. Eager to find a race-blind alternative, Texas adopted a new policy that guaranteed admission at elite public universities for the highest 10 percent of each school's graduating class based on high school grade point averages – effectively making admission criteria relative to the distribution of student performance in each neighborhood, rather than absolute and uniform statewide. A number of other states have similar policies as well.

The laudable intent of the "Top 10 percent" plan was to increase the number of underprivileged students, attending the state's underperforming schools, who could get a shot at upward economically mobility that a degree from the best Texas universities offered. But parents had other ideas.

Imagine, for example, that you were a relatively well-off family in a decent school. Your kid is pretty smart – but perhaps not quite high-performing enough to meet the flagship universities' high admission standards. And her classmates are also high-performing, meaning there is a good chance she would not be among the top 10 percent of her class and thus not eligible for the guaranteed admission program. Some parents might double-down on test prep, but others might decide to move their daughter to a worse performing school on the logic that she would have better odds of graduating near the top her class. It's easier to be a big fish in a smaller pond.

The idea that parents might intentionally chose to send their child to a *worse* school just to increase their chances of being admitted to a good university might strike many readers as far-fetched. But that is exactly what happened.[19] And school enrollment choices are not the only thing that changed – property values did too. In particular, homes zoned for the bottom 20 percent of the schools in the state (based on median college admission test scores) increased in value by about 5 percentage points, relative to housing zoned for slightly better schools (Cortes and Friedson, 2014). Compared to home prices in areas zoned for the

---

[19] Cullen, Long and Reback (2013) estimate that about 0.5 percent of students in the top four deciles of the statewide achievement distribution ended up attending a different school than they would have otherwise as a result of the policy change (see Table 6 of their paper). However, not all of these necessitated moving. In many cases, students opted into a lower-ranked zoned school that they would have otherwise not attended in favor of a higher-ranked choice option, such as a magnet school.

very best schools in the state, the prices of properties assigned to the bottom-ranked schools grew 10 percentage points faster.

Once again, housing markets undid some of the intended benefits of the policy. Not only did the in-migration of higher-achieving students bump some existing enrollees – those on the cusp of being in the top decile of their class – out of the program, but increased housing prices almost certainly displaced families who could no longer afford to live in these areas.[20]

Tim DeRoche reminded me of another recent example of housing markets undoing heartfelt efforts to improve educational opportunity for disadvantaged kids. It started with a series of tragedies. In the early 1990s, many American cities faced an unprecedented crime wave fueled by crack cocaine and the gangs that sold it. Philadelphia was one of these cities, and several University of Pennsylvania community members got caught in the crossfire. In 1994, teenagers murdered a doctoral student, and two years later, another researcher was killed while walking home on Halloween with his fiancée.

The murders shook the community and prompted the university's then-president to unveil the West Philadelphia Initiatives, a targeted investment program to improve the rough area near the campus. As part of this effort, the university partnered with the Philadelphia school district to open the Penn Alexander School, an elementary campus near the university named after Sadie T.M. Alexander, Penn's first Black graduate and the first African-American to receive a PhD in economics in the country.

The efforts worked, and the school became an academic standout in a low-performing school district. In a 2010 profile, the *Philadelphia Inquirer* wrote that Penn Alexander "has helped make the community one of the most sought-after in the city, bringing rapid change in a neighborhood that was seen as gasping for air 15 years ago" (Seplow, 2010). The school's success raised the stakes surrounding attendance boundaries: "Debates about the boundaries for the catchment area were bitter, dealing as they did with two basic concerns: education and property values," the newspaper reported. While some asked that the school to operate on an open-enrollment model – accepting any student

---

[20] It is possible that the net effect may have made housing in slightly better school zones relatively more affordable, but these students still had to pay the high academic costs associated with school and residential mobility.

living in the University City area – the university insisted on attendance boundaries.

As word about the school's positive reputation spread, housing costs in its catchment area went through the roof. Between 1998 and 2011, home prices in the attendance zone tripled, greatly outpacing the appreciation in the broader university area. "People who have the means to send their children to one of the city's best schools pay a premium to buy there," the *Philadelphia Inquirer* reported (Graham and Russ, 2023). Predictably, gentrification and displacement followed. "And very soon you had a school that was mainly serving white, wealthy families, even though it was located in a formerly African American part of town," DeRoche told me, "because people came swooping in and bought up all that real estate."

When the school first opened in 2002, its students were 57 percent African-American. By 2023, Black enrollment had declined to just 13 percent. The daughter of the school's namesake, Rae Minter-Alexander, told the local newspaper she was disturbed by the changes in demographic composition of the school. "My mother was a civil rights advocate, sat on the first civil rights committee that President Truman put together, and fought for the lives and the ability of people who were marginalized to have access to the larger frills of society," Minter-Alexander remembered. What happened at the school is "enough to break my heart. It isn't what my mother what would want. It isn't what the family wants" (Graham and Russ, 2023).

CAN HOMEOWNERS DO WELL BY DOING GOOD?

As this chapter has shown, it is impossible to separate the educational opportunities available to American children from their addresses. Rational concerns about property values encourage homeowners to use their considerable political influence to pressure school districts to adopt exclusionary policies. Purchasing a home in a good neighborhood is the ticket to obtaining a spot in a desirable school. As a result, families who most desperately need high-quality schools to compensate for the many academic disadvantages their children face outside of the classroom are often the ones deprived of access to such schools.

What can be done to address the resulting inequities? Radical reformers like Tim DeRoche advocate for an abolition of school attendance boundaries – in effect, making every public school an open-enrollment school. I am skeptical, both because I doubt this approach is politically viable and because there are reasons to worry about how such a system might play out.

San Francisco provides a cautionary tale. In the early 2000s, the city scrapped its racial quota system used for school assignment – designed to increase integration – due to legal concerns and moved toward a lottery model in which parents would submit applications to their schools of choice. The district then used a lottery to allocate spots in oversubscribed buildings – giving preference to siblings of current students and families residing in neighborhoods with the lowest test scores. The system effectively broke the link between where students lived and the school they attended.

In many ways, this is exactly the kind of system reformers would love. The problem is that parents did not like it. Many resented the lack of predictability and the fact that their children had extended bus commutes every day, cutting into time for extracurricular and homework. Others were frustrated when the lottery didn't place their kid into any of their top-ranked choices, relegating them to schools everyone wanted to avoid. "We were shocked to find we were assigned to something that was not on our list and not in our neighborhood," one parent told a reporter in 2018 (Schwartz, 2018).

Such frustrations led to predictable results: Many families with school-aged children simply left the city and the school district. "San Francisco Asks: Where Have All the Children Gone?" read one memorable *New York Times* headline (Fuller, 2017). At 13 percent of the city population, San Francisco had the lowest share of children of any major American city – just half the levels of Chicago and New York. In fact, San Francisco residents had more dogs than children. "In many areas of the city, pet grooming shops seem more common than schools," the article noted. And many of the families that remained opted out of the public school system, giving ultraprogressive San Francisco one of the highest private school penetration rates in the country. Eventually, the district relented and brought back geographic zones, to provide parents the predictability they demanded.

If radical changes like the one tried in San Francisco are off the table and housing markets are here to stay, serious reforms should take incentives seriously. Although current market dynamics create an educational system plagued by unfairness and inequality, this can be changed because incentives can be reworked.

Fischel's *Homevoter Hypothesis* provides a useful starting point. In the early pages of the book, he anticipates the inevitable pushback against the claim that self-interested obsession with property values can foster democratic engagement and encourage investment in public goods. "I don't mean to say that people who are concerned about these good things act solely because of how it affects their property values," Fischel writes. "Nor do I mean that if good schools and other public amenities did not map into higher home values that they would not be good things (though I guess I would take a second look at them in that case). What I am arguing as a normative matter is that the world will get more of these good things if the motive to do good is lined up with the motive to do well" (p. 18).

In Chapter 9, I turn to this question, describing a basket of reforms that can help align the motives to do good and do well. As it turns out, the policy levers that can overcome the perverse incentives that contribute to educational NIMBYism are the same ones that have the potential to improve educational governance more broadly.

9

A Framework for Education Reform

> Kids don't vote.
> —"The Wire," Season 4, Episode 13

As is true for a lot research on local politics, many of the insights in this book have been articulated before – in the hit HBO series "The Wire." The show was created by a former *Baltimore Sun* reporter and a Baltimore homicide-detective-turned-middle-school-teacher, and it offers a lightly fictionalized account of that city's struggles circa 2005. Season 4 focuses on the Baltimore school system and conveys the political logic I tried to lay out in this volume more powerfully and clearly than I could ever hope to do.

The season begins with an election of a fresh-faced, charismatic new mayor who truly cares about Baltimore and its residents. He has passion, energy, and great ideas for improving its government. Once in office, however, he confronts an unexpected crisis: The city school system is running an unreported budget deficit in the tens of millions of dollars. There is a lot of ineptitude to go around, but it seems like the money was spent on educational programming and not defrauded or embezzled.

The mayor has to find a way to plug this fiscal gap, which threatens to derail his entire agenda. He, a white Democrat representing an overwhelming Black and Democratic city, decides to reach out to the Maryland governor, a Republican, for a bailout. The governor offers him the money – but on the condition that the state take over the bankrupt district and unilaterally change the teachers' union contract to allow for the firing of tenured teachers for cause. The mayor has to decide whether to take the deal. Over the course of several episodes, we see the mayor wrestling with the difficult decision and speaking to many political and policy advisors.

"The choice comes down to this: We take the state money, and instead of being fucked up and broke, our schools go back to being merely fucked up," one advisor tells the mayor. No program cuts or layoffs will be necessary. "We don't take the money, it looks like we're shorting our own kids. We take the money, we're giving up local control of education, which is going to lose us a lot of middle class Black folks."

"Not to mention the problem you might have two years from now, running [for governor] in the D.C. suburbs explaining how you needed their money to bail out your schools," the city council president pipes in.

"Take the money, we need it," the budget director advises. The mayor looks around the room, some are nodding in agreement, others are shaking their head in opposition. He turns to the city council president. "Oh, don't look at me," she tells him. "If you take it, you're selling out the teachers, and that's my base. If you don't take it, you're selling out the kids. Either way, I will probably rip you and half of the [city] council will, too. Just glad I'm not the mayor."

In the final episode of the season, it's decision time. The mayor is in his office with his two closest advisors. "So I take the money, and two years from now, when I shake the hand of any voter in the D.C. suburbs, they say, 'Oh yeah, you're the guy who needed my tax dollars to bail out your school system,'" the mayor says. You take the money, the advisor reminds him, and you lose three major counties in the next gubernatorial election. And if you're not the governor, you can't help the city – or its school system – from the state capitol, where the real resources are.

"He's the mayor *now*!" the second advisor responds. "I agree we can't fix the city schools, but we can't let them get any worse, either. Go back to Annapolis. Eat his shit. If we lose local control the schools, [the city council president] and the teachers will rip you. But the rest of the city will see you did it for them kids."

The mayor looks over to the other advisor. "Kids don't vote," he responds. The mayor ... doesn't take the money.

It is a perfect, albeit fictional, illustration of how democratic pressures affect educational policymaking. The theory behind democracy is that it incentivizes elected officials with career ambitions to be responsive to their constituents. "Out of step, out of office," as one famous study concluded (Canes-Wrone, Brady and Cogan, 2002). But this logic doesn't work in public education. Kids can't vote, and as I showed in Chapter 2, most of people who can (and do) aren't particularly concerned about their learning. Instead, elected officials face pressure to respond to adults, and "The Wire" makes perfectly clear the types of considerations – partisanship, racial and identity politics, and employment concerns – that adults seem to care most about.

That is not to suggest that every elected official makes calculated, deliberate decisions they know will end up screwing kids. Many school board members may be oblivious to the incentives I describe. They are the ones who get voted out of office, just like James Ragland, the Columbus school board member I profiled in Chapter 1. Others may be unwilling to do what is required to remain electorally viable and step down instead of running for reelection, as nearly half of incumbents do (see Chapter 2). In the long run, the result is the same: School board members who choose to remain in office and succeed in keeping their seats are the ones who are willing to play by the rules of adult politics. In democracy, the logic of elections creates clear Darwinian selection pressures, and only the most politically fit survive.

John Chubb and Terry Moe made this point three decades ago in *States, Markets, and America's Schools*. "Almost everyone's first impulse is to think that the purpose of schools is to provide children with academic training, with essential information about society and the world, with an understanding of citizenship in a democracy, or something of the sort," they wrote. "On reflection, however, it should be apparent that schools have no immutable or transcendent purpose. What they are supposed to be doing depends on who control them and what those controllers want them to do" (p. 30).

As we have seen, those who control the schools seem to prioritize many other considerations well ahead of student learning, even if they come at the expense of academic achievement. This was true when Chubb and Moe wrote their book, and perhaps even more true today. Growth in partisan polarization, increasing nationalization, and the economic decline of local news sources have all worked to turn the school governance dial toward adult interests and away from academic considerations.

Chapters 1–8 of this book were all about the problems, so it is now time to turn to possible solutions. Readers will be disappointed to find that this is the shortest chapter, in part because there are no obvious silver bullets in sight. The perverse incentives that encourage school board members to be responsive to adult interests are hardwired into our democratic institutions, and no one has found a compelling alternative. As

British Prime Minister Winston Churchill was famously quoted as saying, democracy may indeed be the worst form of government except for all those other forms that have been tried from time to time. He wasn't talking about local democracy or school boards, but his insights likely apply here as well.

The graveyard of education reform is filled with overhyped initiatives that ended up failing or even making things worse. Most of these interventions focused on classroom practices, not governance processes, but even here our track record is disappointing. For example, promising ideas for improving how schools are governed – from mayoral control to state takeovers to "portfolio" management – have largely failed to deliver, especially when tried at scale and for extended periods of time (New York State Education Department, 2024; Schueler and Bleiberg, 2022).

In DC, mayoral control fueled a wave of reform under Michelle Rhee – until her political patron, Mayor Adrian Fenty, was booted out of office in large part due to (adult) disapproval of his education agenda and mobilization by the city's teachers' union.[1] In Denver, portfolio management seemed to be working well in improving student academic outcomes, until the teachers' union and its allies won local elections, took over the school board, and dismantled almost all of the reforms. Even in New Orleans, the state-run, all-charter model proved difficult to sustain. Facing mounting political pressure, control of the district was handed back to local voters in 2018. Chicago, once discussed as a case study of successful urban school turnaround, recently elected a mayor who is a former teachers' union organizer, and he vowed to put other union leaders in charge of education policy.

None of the reforms proved to be durable or sustainable because they did not address or remove the perverse political incentives that constrain the decisions of elected officials or the preferences and behaviors of adult voters. Simply trying to change the elected political principals in charge, or hoping that local school board members will credibly commit to resist political temptations in the future, as portfolio management tries to do, doesn't work because it doesn't change the underlying politics. These reforms are a bit like rearranging the deck chairs on the Titanic. Short-term improvements are possible but over the long run, the political ship will go down.

---

[1] Fenty's successor installed a less divisive and firebrand district leader than Rhee, who kept most of her policies in place. But forward progress stalled.

That is not to say that things can't be made better on the margin, and I describe some concrete proposals worth considering. I should, however, be transparent about the small magnitude of the benefits these reforms are likely to produce, the considerable uncertainty that remains about their effectiveness, and the political impediments that stand in the way of their adoption.

To preview, my reforms focus on (1) encouraging voters to care more about student outcomes and (2) shifting political power to adults with the most skin in the game in order to (3) try to align the electoral and political incentives of office holders with the interests of students. These reforms are synergistic. Individually, each might move the needle modestly, but they are likely to work best when implemented as a package.

In laying out the case for each, I will begin by summarizing the logic – what in medical research might be called the "mechanism of action" – before turning to the available evidence on "real-world efficacy." In the concluding sections, I will widen the aperture beyond specific proposals and describe a more general framework that we should apply to other proposals moving forward.

REFORM 1: HOLD SCHOOL BOARD ELECTIONS IN NOVEMBER OF EVEN YEARS

Scheduling school board elections to be held in November of even years, at the same time as presidential and midterm elections, is a good place to start. The idea is not controversial and makes obvious sense to almost everyone. As political scientist Michael Hartney has shown, holding school board elections off-cycle – the norm today – is the most potent mechanism of voter suppression ever invented. Off-cycle elections reduce turnout in local elections by orders of magnitude more than voter identification requirements or prohibitions on mail voting (Hartney, 2021).

Democrats love on-cycle elections because they disproportionately increase turnout among Democratic voters (Hajnal, Kogan and Markarian, 2022; Kogan, Lavertu and Peskowitz, 2018). Republicans love on-cycle elections because they are thought to reduce the political power of school employees and their unions (Anzia, 2011, 2012, 2013). Indeed, both deep blue California and deep red Texas have passed legislation in recent years to sync the timing of school board elections with higher-level offices.

There are multiple mechanistic arguments about why on-cycle elections might produce better academic outcomes, but for me, the most compelling one is related to the findings in Chapter 2. If the problem is that voters have too little skin in the game, we need to think about ways to increase it. On-cycle elections fit the bill because they significantly increase the share of voters who are also parents (Kogan, Lavertu and Peskowitz, 2018) – the types of adults who should care about student academic outcomes the most. As a bonus, on-cycle elections also reduce the overrepresentation of homeowners, perhaps softening the political power of education NIMBYs.

As I mentioned in Chapter 2, this mechanism is borne out in the data. As Julia Payson's research shows, voters appear to hold school board incumbents more accountable for improvements in academic achievement (or lack thereof) when school board elections are held on-cycle (Payson, 2017). And her work is not the only one finding such a result. In his dissertation project, researcher Ethan Sherer (2014) also examined California school board elections, but during an earlier era, as the state first rolled out its school accountability system. The new ratings represented an unexpected and generally negative information shock, and Sherer looked to see if they had any impacts on local school board elections. He found that incumbents were held accountable for performance – but only during elections held in November of even years. "We can conclude that, during these high turnout years, information matters," he wrote.

Of course, California is just one state. To be fully confident in these results, we would love to see them replicated elsewhere. And, although on-cycle elections may increase accountability pressures on school boards, there is less evidence that this pressure ultimately translates into better student outcomes. The only study on this subject I am aware of, which also focuses on California and leverages districts that change the timing of their school board elections, finds no meaningful improvement in achievements when school board elections are moved to November of even years (Berry and Gersen, 2011).

There are two other important caveats to keep in mind. First, although we often talk about "off-cycle" and "on-cycle" elections, the evidence really suggests that we should be thinking about presidential elections and everything else. Even Payson finds accountability only in elections held in November of even years when the president is on the ballot but not during the midterms. The data on voter composition also suggests that the boost in parent voting is limited to presidential elections. As long as school districts continue to stagger their board terms, only half of the board is likely to be elected concurrently with the president's race.

Second, election timing effects voter composition on many different margins, and we might imagine other, countervailing effects. For example, there is evidence that the marginal voters who turnout only for high-profile presidential races but stay home otherwise are particularly uninformed and lean heavily on third-party cues and endorsements to decide how to cast their ballots (de Benedictis-Kessner, 2018). If the endorsements they turn to come from adult interest groups – such as teachers' unions (Kogan and Hartney, 2024) or political parties – we can imagine the reform backfiring. That is why pairing changes in election timing with informational interventions is critical.

REFORM 2: MAKE *GOOD* PERFORMANCE INFORMATION MORE SALIENT

Throughout this book, I have emphasized two points. First, most voters don't seem to care about student learning. And second, when they do care, adults tend to prioritize the wrong performance metrics – ratings that mostly reflect the demographic composition of the students schools serve, not the amount of learning that takes place within them. Thus, just encouraging voters to pay more attention to achievement without also pushing them to use better measures would almost certainly make things worse, not better. It would encourage the kinds of perverse gaming behaviors I warned about in Chapter 1 and the intentional efforts to exclude disadvantaged students I documented in Chapter 8.

The good news is that the information both voters and parents use to anchor their perceptions of school quality is highly malleable. There are of course many factors that go into their evaluations, but the evidence is overwhelming that the official accountability ratings states put out directly impact perceptions. Parents, for example, change their views about their children's school when state accountability ratings change – even for arbitrary reasons (Chingos, Henderson and West, 2012; Wang and Kim, 2024).

My favorite example of this phenomenon comes from a natural experiment that New York City carried out about a decade ago. At the time, all New York schools received a letter grade, ranging from an "A" for the best to an "F" for the worst. One day, the city's school chancellor, Joel Klein, decided that the grades were too high. Although 97 percent of New York City schools were receiving an "A" or a "B" grade, Klein did not think that 97 percent of the schools were actually good. In 2009, he decided to raise the bar, making it harder for schools to attain the highest marks, and the performance ratings predictably tanked.

The key was that many (but not all) schools suddenly received lower grades because the formula changed, not because student performance declined. In fact, in some affected buildings, test scores actually *increased*. But parents seemed to respond to the grades, not to test scores on which the ratings were based. School satisfaction, as measured by surveys that parents completed every year, went down in the schools that were downgraded (Jacobsen, Saultz and Snyder, 2013). Something similar happened in Florida, when the state changed its school ratings formula. Schools that experienced declining grades as a result saw their PTA donations plummet (Figlio and Kenny, 2009). And parent satisfaction is not the only thing that seems to respond to changes in official school performance ratings – housing prices do as well (Figlio and Lucas, 2003).

These findings point to an obvious policy prescription: In rating schools, states should put much more weight on "value added" – growth in achievement over time – and much less weight on average test scores, which unfairly penalize schools serving disadvantaged students. And they should make these new, better ratings much more salient. For example, they might time the school accountability data to be released in close proximity with school board elections, recognizing that voters seem to put much more weight on recent performance (Healy and Lenz, 2014). They might go further and even print the performance ratings right on the ballot, next to the school board candidate names.

Instead, some states seem to be going in the opposite direction. A few years ago, Tennessee voted to add partisan labels to the ballot for what were previously nonpartisan school board elections. North Carolina did something similar about a decade ago and several other states are now mulling such a policy. Party labels might make sense if our goal is to help adults pick candidates that shared their ideological agendas. But they don't make sense if what we want is electoral incentives that encourage improvements in student performance. Indeed, evidence from judicial elections suggest that party labels crowd out objective performance information (Lim and Snyder, 2015) – the exact opposite of what we want.

There are also worrying developments on the political left. A decade ago, the California State Board of Education replaced the state's school accountability system – which assigned each district a numerical Academic Performance Index score – with a new "dashboard" containing a smorgasbord of data. The ostensible reason was to provide parents more information, but the effect – intended or not – was to bury the important academic performance measures and make them less visible. In a number of cities, school boards have pursued the same changes after teachers' union-backed slates won majorities. This is the educational equivalent of the "flood the zone with shit" strategy pioneered by President Trump's advisor Steve Bannon – overwhelming the public with misleading or irrelevant information to prevent them from making informed choices.

Improving elections are not the only reason to make it easier for the broader public to access information about student growth. Even parents, who have the most skin in the game and who are obviously invested in their kids' education, often struggle to separate good schools from bad ones. Just like homeowners, parents seem to prefer schools that enroll high-achieving students but don't seek out schools that actually produce high achievement. Many parents, in other words, use average peer achievement as a proxy for school quality, even though we know it is not a very good one (Abdulkadiroğlu et al., 2020; Glazerman and Dotter, 2017).

"It's something that we see over and over again. The schools that are in demand among parents are those that are high-performing, but they're not necessarily high-performing because of 'value added'," MIT economist Parag Pathak, who has published some of the foundational studies in this field, told me. "What do we make of this? Something I'm worried about is, if schools are in demand because they have selected the best students, as a school leader, I should devote a lot of attention to selecting the best students and that might crowd out other things that would make that schools perform better."

The question of why parents seem willing to leave so much value added on the table when choosing schools is a hotly contested one. Some scholars argue that parents are savvy and realize that school quality is multidimensional (Beuermann et al., 2023). When they forgo schools that do the best job increasing test scores, or voluntarily enroll their children in programs that seem to make them worse off academically (e.g., Abdulkadiroğlu, Pathak and Walters, 2018), it is because parents are prioritizing other considerations that are more important for their students' long-term success (Beuermann et al., 2023). They know test scores aren't everything.

But it is clear this is not the whole story. When value-added information is accessible to parents – either because school ratings make it salient or because schools are similar on other relevant dimensions – they do choose schools that are more effective at improving test scores (Campos and Kearns, 2024; Haderlein, 2022; Harris and Larsen, 2023b). And one way to make value-added information more salient is to provide parents school ratings highlighting these measures. Economists Justine Hastings and Jeffrey Weinstein (Hastings and Weinstein, 2008) leveraged just such an intervention in a randomized experiment in Charlotte a number of years ago. They provided parents with a short information sheet describing school options ahead of the district's annual school choice lottery and found that the intervention nudged parents into choosing higher-performing schools for their children. Economist Jason Campos found the same thing in a similar informational experiment in Los Angeles recently (Campos, 2023). The bottom line is that better information can help parents make better decisions for their children.[2]

Improving official school quality ratings and increasing their visibility is an obvious win–win proposal. It improves democratic accountability, orients housing markets around real school quality instead of racist and classist stereotypes, and aids parents in choosing the best schools for their kids. And it is light-touch intervention – everyone is free to ignore this information if they want to. Rarely can we find reforms with so much promise and so little downside risk.

The challenge is that elected officials don't have much incentive to adopt this reform and many reasons to oppose it. Unable to continue claiming credit for the unearned performance of their students, incumbents in high-achieving but low-growth districts would suffer, especially if property values in their communities declined as a result. There is no easy solution to this problem – my hope is that another political crisis could help catalyze the necessary policy change, just as the 1984 *Nation at Risk* report and President Obama's Race to the Top program did previously. When the next policy window opens, changes to school performance ratings should be at the top of the reform agenda.

REFORM 3: PROMOTE SMART SCHOOL CHOICE OPTIONS

In *Politics, Markets, and America's Schools*, Chubb and Moe went beyond diagnosing the problem – poorly performing schools are the

---

[2] As I noted in Chapter 8, parents might prefer more advantaged, higher-achieving peers for other rational reasons that have little to do with learning and school quality (e.g., school safety), which contributes to school segregation and social stratification. Informational interventions will almost certainly never eliminate such preferences but could help reduce their impact on school choice decisions.

result of democratic processes and bureaucratic calcification that such processes produce. They also offered a solution, summarized apply by the title of an accompanying paper: "Choice Is A Panacea" (Chubb and Moe, 1990a). The alternative to controlling schools through the political process is to use market mechanisms instead – removing decision-making power from voters, politicians, and special interests and handing it to parents instead. And they sketched out what such a system would look like: "Schools compete for the support of parents and students, and parents and students are free to choose among schools. The system is built on decentralization, competition, and choice" (p. 6).

The last thirty years have provided a wealth of policy experiments that tried to put this idea into practice. We saw the growth of charter schools (publicly funded but typically operated by independent nonprofits), the introduction of private school vouchers, and, most recently, a wave of legislation to create "education savings accounts." These experiments have also yielded a deep base of empirical findings, too voluminous to summarize faithfully here. There are three key lessons: When done well, school choice can improve education – for everyone, not just the students who take advantage of these options. But doing school choice well is hard to pull off in the real world, in part because of the same vested adult interests described in this book. It also requires overcoming strong incentives school operators face to "cream skim," by selectively attracting the highest performing students or pushing out the most disadvantaged, and building in sufficient quality controls. Although promising, choice as done in the real world and subject to political constraints has proven to be no panacea.

To be sure, one reason why choice has not lived up to its promise is that most of the programs we have tried have lacked important features Chubb and Moe argued were essential. They envisioned a carefully designed, highly regulated system – involving liaisons who meet with parents to help them compare options, weighted funding carefully calibrated to incentivize schools to enroll disadvantaged or difficult students, and a system that makes performance information easily accessible to parents. Some choice programs have had elements of these features, but few have had them all. Worryingly, the latest iterations – such as the education savings accounts – have none.

Unlike my previous two proposals, the topic of school choice is controversial and has become even more polarized along partisan lines over the past fifteen years. Much of the popular debate is filled with appeals to emotion rather than reason. Some opponents of private school vouchers, for example, note that they were used in the South by racist white families to avoid integrated public schools. (True!) Supporters argue that early prohibitions on publicly funded vouchers, known as the Blaine amendments, were clearly motivated by anti-Catholic prejudice. (Also true!) Evidence is often cherry-picked to support whatever talking point an advocate wants to make.

In my reading of the extensive body of research, the following facts appear to be true (although one can always find exceptions):

- When provided options, parents don't always prioritize academic considerations. Driving distance and travel time are major constraints, and parents sometimes focus on their own convenience – for example, choosing low-performing schools with free after-school care over better schools without latchkey programs. In New Orleans, parents put a lot of weight on high school football teams and marching bands, and these often trump student achievement concerns.
- Perhaps because academics aren't always at the top of the list, the quality of choice options is highly varied. On average, charter schools perform about as well as the traditional public schools their students would have attended instead. But charter schools have gotten better over time – primarily because of increased accountability requirements imposed by states. In places like Ohio and Texas, once known as the wild west of chartering, the states really had to crack down and actively drive bad providers out of the market. Charter schools in urban areas tend to outperform the public schools, mostly because of the quality of the alternatives available to families is so poor.
- Private school voucher programs have had some success when tried in disadvantaged urban districts. But especially when implemented at scale statewide, they appear to have null to negative effects on achievement. This could be because private schools don't teach to the test or follow different curricula – most are religious, and so perhaps parents choose them for nonacademic reasons. It could be because only the lowest-quality providers choose to accept vouchers. Or it could be because the kinds of students who choose to attend private schools are higher-achieving to begin with, making it difficult for other families considering them to differentiate programs that attract smart students from programs that make their students smart through high growth. Evidence on longer-term

outcomes aside from test scores is limited although it appears to be more positive than for achievement. Private schools also sometimes respond to new voucher programs by raising their tuition, capturing the new revenues without increasing access.[3] When vouchers are universally available, a large number of families who use them would have attended private schools anyway had the vouchers not existed, significantly increasing program costs for taxpayers with little apparent educational benefit.

- In contrast to the effects of choice programs on the students who use them ("participant effects"), which are highly variable, the effects on students who stay behind in the public schools ("competition effects") are generally positive in the short run, but modest in size. When facing competition, school leaders may respond by improving their programming – sometimes in ways that boosts academic achievement and sometimes by enhancing other amenities that parents find appealing. In terms of thinking through the aggregate impacts of choice, the competitive effects are probably more important than the participant effects because most students will continue to attend public schools.
- In most places, only the state share of funding follows the students who leave the public schools, while local property taxes stay in the district. As a result, revenue per student in the public schools often increases as more students exercise choice options. But many operating costs are fixed and districts struggle to trim them in proportion to the enrollment decline, so spending per student often goes up without any improvements in service quality. Over the longer run, enrollment losses due to increased choice can lead to serious budget problems, and how the districts respond is critical. If they close the lowest-quality buildings, student achievement can improve. If they paper over budget deficits in other ways, achievement can decline. Because of the pathologies of politics, school districts have a hard time using their extra money productively and struggle to cut back in ways in responsible ways (see Chapter 7).
- Even when choice programs improve achievement, there may be concerning effects on other outcomes. For example, racial segregation between schools can increase somewhat. This may be due to

---

[3] It is possible, perhaps even likely, that many of these issues will work out over the long term as general equilibrium effects kick in and supply adjusts in response to the new incentives.

parents preferring to send their children to schools where their racial or ethnic group represents the numerical majority and because choice programs often offer specialized programming that may be particularly attractive to certain populations of families.
- School choice programs can decouple property values from "perceived" school quality by weakening the connection between home address and school assignment. Depending the precise programs, this can occur by increasing home prices in neighborhoods previously zoned for low-achieving schools or slowing the growth of prices for properties previously zoned for desirable buildings. In the case of the latter, residential segregation by race, income, and education all decrease as a result, and some of the perverse incentives I discuss in Chapter 8 are muted.

How one combines all of these findings into policy recommendations is ultimately a judgement call requiring the consideration of difficult trade-offs. My view is that school choice is generally a good thing but must be implemented carefully to minimize the unintended consequences by including many of the safeguards Chubb and Moe laid out (see also Moe, 2008). Charter schools are better than private school vouchers, both because it is easier for parents to find apples-to-apples performance information and make more informed choices and because charter schools cannot discriminate in their admissions.[4] Allowing disadvantaged students to take advantage of choice programs requires publicly funded transportation. A unified application for all schools is better and imposes fewer administrative burdens than separate admission processes.

And highly targeted programs, designed for students who lack good options, are strongly preferable to universal programs. This last point is essential but also controversial. To the extent that we think choice improves public education by injecting market competition, *who* the public schools are forced to compete to retain is important. The kinds of things school leaders do to be attractive to poor and disadvantaged families are almost certainly different than the things they do to compete for wealthy students. At a minimum, universal programs water down the kinds of competitive pressures we want choice to create, and they could actually make things worse for students trapped in the worst public schools.

---

[4] Racial discrimination is illegal, but religious institutions may set admission policies that keep out other disadvantaged groups, such as LGBT students.

More generally, my ideal choice program would work as a "gun behind the door" – a credible threat that changes the internal operations and politics of a school district for the better while rarely having to go off (see, e.g., Gerber, 1996).

Unfortunately, the politics of choice seems to be moving in the opposite direction. Democrats, once champions of charter schools, have dropped their support due to pressure from their teachers' union allies. During the 2000 election, the Democratic Party's official platform vowed to "triple the number of charter schools in the nation" and proclaimed that "we must allow experimentation in our public schools to find out what works." Two decades later, the platform called for a ban on for-profit charter schools, "more stringent guardrails" on charter operations, "measures to increase accountability for charter schools," and giving local districts veto power over whether new charters open within their boundaries. Never fans of vouchers, party elites now view even limited programs as toxic – although the same is not true of rank-and-file Democratic voters, especially Democrats of color.

Republicans have shifted their position as well, embracing vouchers and pushing to expand them to wealthier families with minimal guardrails around discrimination in admissions or quality. At the state level, Republican leaders have also promoted new education savings accounts, allowing families to take the dollars that would have gone to their local schools – regardless of whether families had ever seriously considered attending them – and spend it on all sorts of education-adjacent services. Both programs have proven to be more expensive than expected, and very poorly targeted – going mostly to families whose public schools were decent to begin with.

10% LESS DEMOCRACY?

Election timing, informational interventions, and increased choice might be the most promising policy levers we have available today to improve academic achievement in this country. But smart reformers could come up with new ideas in the future, so I want to propose a simple framework we can use to evaluate them.

The first part is obvious – student outcomes should be our North Star. Reforms should be judged by how they impact what students know and can do, not by how adults feel about them.

The second part may seem more radical: We should be willing to sacrifice some amount of democratic control if doing so produces better schools. "Local control" should not be treated as a political trump card to block reform the way it is often used today. We should not take more versus less democracy as prima facie evidence that a proposal to reform education governance is normatively good or bad. Upon closer reflection, this is not such a radical idea after all.

Since I noted the parallels between housing and education NIMBYs in Chapter 8, housing offers a great example of a policy domain where the idea that more democracy might lead to worse outcomes is accepted by scholars and practitioners alike. It is now widely understood that taking straw polls of attendees at planning commission meetings is a terrible way to make land-use decisions, because the people who show up are not at all representative (Einstein, Palmer and Glick, 2019; Sahn, 2025). Many have also recognized that electoral incentives can make housing too expensive, because city council members stand to gain few votes from approving the construction of affordable units that won't be finished for years. By the time low-income beneficiaries move in and establish residency for voting purposes, the incumbents worry they will have been voted out of office by angry homeowners who can vote *now* and are upset about the impact on their property values. Democracy encourages elected officials to respond to their current constituents, not some hypothetical future voters who would benefit from the development. If expensive housing keeps poor people out today (preventing them from voting in your local elections) and makes your current constituents unhappy, all of the incentives push against affordability (see Chicago Area Fair Housing Alliance, 2018).

Some of the most fascinating recent work in this area examines electoral institutions. We have long known that electing city councils in geographic districts (or wards) as opposed to citywide can dramatically increase the number of minorities who win elections. Indeed, under certain circumstances, Section 2 of the Voting Rights Act requires local governments to use district elections. Yet recent studies suggest that this also makes housing more expensive (Hankinson and Magazinnik, 2023; Mast, 2024). Housing development imposes geographically concentrated costs on neighbors through increased traffic and reduced parking but produces geographically diffuse benefits – increased housing supply and lower housing prices. Under a ward system, elected officials internalize all of the costs but only some of the benefits, because the benefits accrue to everyone in the community, including voters living in other city council districts. This encourages elected officials to oppose residential development their municipalities desperately need to make housing affordable because their political calculus puts more weight on the cost side of the equation. Ward elections may be more democratic, but they can also produce worse policy.

That an electoral arrangement increasing minority political representation might also lead to undesirable housing policies is unfortunate but not particularly controversial. Serious scholars of election law or housing policy do not write book-length screeds accusing affordable housing advocates of being neoliberal shills seeking to put African-Americans back in chains. But such pieces regularly appear in leading education journals – I cited several examples in Chapter 6 in the context of the debate surrounding the New Orleans school reforms. It is time for education scholars, advocates, and practitioners to take seriously the idea that a little bit less democracy may sometimes be a good thing.

Housing is not the only area where giving up some direct voter control may be necessary to achieve important goals our society broadly agrees on. We have given independent central banks control over monetary policy because elected officials face too much temptation to open up the spending taps before elections, creating excessive inflation. In earlier eras, Congress delegated responsibility for identifying and closing unneeded military bases to an independent commission because its members understood how parochial politics would prevent them from doing the job themselves. We accept that federal judges need the protection of lifetime tenure to shield them from populist passions in the administration of justice. "Life is often about trade-offs, choosing one imperfect bundle of options rather than another," economist Garett Jones wrote in his book *10% Less Democracy* (2020), which argues for exactly what the title says. My argument is not that we should give up completely on local democratic control of schools, only that we should seriously consider sacrificing a little bit of it if a reform proposal that we expect to benefit students comes along.

FROM SATAN TO OTHER DELUDERS

Future conversations about education reform should begin by acknowledging that local democratic control of schools, although the default, is not the only option. The US Constitution doesn't require it – indeed, the constitution doesn't mention education (or local government) at all. Our system is a historically contingent accident that emerged directly out of adult political interests and agendas – in the case of the system's founders, an adult moral panic.

We can trace the origins of local democratic control to the Massachusetts Bay Colony. In 1647, the colonial assembly passed a piece of legislation that began: "It being one chief project of that old deluder, Satan, to keep men from the knowledge of the Scriptures, as in former times by keeping them in an unknown tongue, so in these latter times by persuading from the use of tongues." The legislation, known as the Old Deluder Satan Law, required every township with at least fifty families to hire an educator to teach children to read and write, so they could access the Scriptures to protect their souls from the devil. Larger townships, with at least 100 families, were mandated to set up a "grammar school." Failure to comply resulted in a fine.

If a time machine brought Puritans to the modern era, they would no doubt see the parallels between the governance system they developed and school boards as they exist and operate today. Yet in many ways, our education system has evolved significantly from the 1600s. In the 1800s, for example, most public schools charged tuition (Fischel, 2009). Until the early 1900s, almost all were one-room school houses that ended in eighth grade. In large cities controlled by party machines, teaching jobs were a form of political patronage handed out to favored ethnic groups to win votes (Cremin, 1961; Erie, 1990).

Governance has changed too. The creation of high schools required much larger attendance boundaries, which resulted in consolidation of tiny local districts into bigger political units with shared elected boards. Progressive reformers pressed for the appointment of professionally trained "superintendents" to take over the day-to-day oversight of school operations from elected officials (Tyack, 1974). Starting in the 1960s, both the state and federal governments stepped in to supplement local property taxes in order to equalize resources and provide targeted financial support to schools serving economically disadvantaged students. In the 1990s, states adopted curriculum standards, began annual testing, and rolled out accountability systems. In 2001, the federal government got into the accountability game as well (Henig, 2013).

Not all of these reforms made education better. Indeed, Chubb and Moe trace the roots of the bureaucratization they blame for many of our problems to the reforms of the Progressive era. But the main lesson I take away from this history is that changes in education governance is possible because we have done it in the past – usually in response to perceived crises, technological revolutions, or big social transformations.

If the past is any guide, a political window of opportunity for meaningful reform will eventually open again. It is important that this opportunity not be squandered and that our efforts focus on the central problem in education system – the institutions through which schools are governed and the political processes that privilege the interests of adults over the learning of America's students.

References

Abdulkadiroğlu, Atila, Joshua D. Angrist, Susan M. Dynarski, Thomas J. Kane and Parag A. Pathak. 2011. "Accountability and Flexibility in Public Schools: Evidence from Boston's Charters and Pilots." *Quarterly Journal of Economics* 126(2):699–748.

Abdulkadiroğlu, Atila, Parag A. Pathak and Christopher R. Walters. 2018. "Free to Choose: Can School Choice Reduce Student Achievement?" *American Economic Journal: Applied Economics* 110(1):175–206.

Abdulkadiroğlu, Atila, Parag A. Pathak, Jonathan Schellenberg and Christopher R. Walters. 2020. "Do Parents Value School Effectiveness?" *American Economic Review* 110(5):1502–1539.

Abott, Carolyn, Vladimir Kogan, Stéphane Lavertu and Zachary Peskowitz. 2020. "School District Operational Spending and Student Outcomes: Evidence from Tax Elections in Seven States." *Journal of Public Economics* 183:104142.

Abt, Thomas. 2019. *Bleeding Out: The Devastating Consequences of Urban Violence – and a Bold New Plan for Peace in the Streets*. New York: Basic Books.

Achen, Christopher H. and Larry M. Bartels. 2017. *Democracy for Realists: Why Elections Do Not Produce Responsive Government*. Princeton, NJ: Princeton University Press.

Adkins, Deborah, G. Gage Kingsbury, Michael Dahlin and John Cronin. 2007. "The Proficiency Illusion." https://fordhaminstitute.org/national/research/proficiency-illusion

Adnot, Melinda, Thomas Dee, Veronica Katz and James Wyckoff. 2017. "Teacher Turnover, Teacher Quality, and Student Achievement in DCPS." *Educational Evaluation and Policy Analysis* 39(1):54–76.

Adukia, Anjali, Benjamin Feigenberg and Fatemeh Momeni. 2023. "From Retributive to Restorative: An Alternative Approach to Justice." EdWorkingPaper: 23-854. https://doi.org/10.26300/k310-w337

Afrouzi, Hassan, Carolina Arteaga and Emily K. Weisburst. 2023. "Is It the Message or the Messenger? Examining Movement in Immigration Beliefs." National Bureau of Economic Research Working Paper No. 31385.

American Bar Association Commission on Homelessness and Poverty. 2018. *Educating Students Experiencing Homelessness: A Primer on Legal Requirements and Implementation Strategies for Educators, Advocates and Policymakers, Fifth Edition*. American Bar Association.

Angrist, Joshua D. and Jörn-Steffen Pischke. 2009. *Mostly Harmless Econometrics: An Empiricist's Companion*. Princeton, NJ: Princeton University Press.

Anstreicher, Garrett, Jason Fletcher and Owen Thompson. 2022. The Long Run Impacts of Court-Ordered Desegregation. Working Paper 29926 National Bureau of Economic Research. www.nber.org/papers/w29926

Anzia, Sarah F. 2011. "Election Timing and the Electoral Influence of Interest Groups." *Journal of Politics* 73(2):412–427.

Anzia, Sarah F. 2012. "The Election Timing Effect: Evidence from a Policy Intervention in Texas." *Quarterly Journal of Political Science* 7(3):209–248.

Anzia, Sarah F. 2013. *Timing and Turnout: How Off-Cycle Elections Favor Organized Groups*. Chicago: University of Chicago Press.

Anzia, Sarah F. and Terry M. Moe. 2015. "Public Sector Unions and the Costs of Government." *Journal of Politics* 77(1):114–127.

Arold, Benjamin W. 2024. "Evolution vs. Creationism in the Classroom: The Lasting Effects of Science Education." *Quarterly Journal of Economics* 139(4):2331–2375.

Ashmore, Harry S. 1954. *The Negro and the Schools*. Chapel Hill, NC: University of North Carolina Press.

Associated Press. 1994. "Plan to Teach U.S. History Is Said to Slight White Males." *New York Times*. www.nytimes.com/1994/10/26/us/plan-to-teach-us-history-is-said-to-slight-white-males.html

Auditor of the State of California. 2019. "K-12 Local Control Funding." www.auditor.ca.gov/pdfs/reports/2019-101.pdf

Barabak, Mark Z. 1998. "Fierce Governor's Race Draws Voters to the Polls." *Los Angeles Times* p. VYA1.

Barber, Michael and Jeremy C. Pope. 2019. "Does Party Trump Ideology? Disentangling Party and Ideology in America." *American Political Science Review* 113(1):38–54.

Barnum, Matt. 2016. "Study: The Real Reason Some People Don't Like ObamaCore, Er, Common Core." *The 74*. www.the74million.org/article/study-the-real-reason-some-people-dont-like-obamacore-er-common-core/

Barnum, Matt. 2023. "The Public is Souring on American Education, but Parents Still Give Own Child's School High Marks." *Chalkbeat*. www.chalkbeat.org/2023/9/5/23859890/parents-polling-surveys-schools-american-education-pandemic/

Barrow, Lisa and Diane Whitmore Schanzenbach. 2012. "Education and the Poor." In *Oxford Handbook of the Economics of Poverty*, ed. Philip N. Jefferson. Oxford: Oxford University Press pp. 316–343.

Bell, Jr., Derrick A. 1980. "*Brown v. Board of Education* and the Interest-Convergence Dilemma." *Harvard Law Review* 93(3):518–533.

Berkman, Michael B. and Eric Plutzer. 2005. *Ten Thousand Democracies: Politics and Public Opinion in America's School Districts*. Washington, DC: Georgetown University Press.

Berkman, Michael B. and Eric Plutzer. 2010. *Evolution, Creationism, and the Battle to Control America's Classrooms*. New York: Cambridge University Press.

Berry, Christopher R. 2009. *Imperfect Union: Representation and Taxation in Multilevel Government*. New York: Cambridge University Press.

Berry, Christopher R. and Jacob E. Gersen. 2011. "Election Timing and Public Policy." *Quarterly Journal of Political Science* 6(2):103–135.

Berry, Christopher R. and William G. Howell. 2007. "Accountability and Local Elections: Rethinking Retrospective Voting." *Journal of Politics* 69(3):844–858.

Bertrand, Ariell Rose, Melissa Arnold Lyon and Rebecca Jacobsen. 2024. "Narrative Spillover: A Narrative Policy Framework Analysis of Critical Race Theory Discourse at Multiple Levels." *Policy Studies Journal* 52(2):391–423.

Bertrand, Marianne, Esther Duflo and Sendhil Mullainathan. 2004. "How Much Should We Trust Differences-in-Differences Estimates." *Quarterly Journal of Economics* 119(1):249–275.

Beuermann, Diether W., C. Kirabo Jackson, Laia Navarro-Sola and Francisco Pardo. 2023. "What is a Good School, and Can Parents Tell? Evidence on the Multidimensionality of School Output." *Review of Economic Studies* 90(1):65–101.

Biasi, Barbara, Julien M. Lafortune and David Schönholzer. 2025. "What Works and For Whom? Effectiveness and Efficiency of School Capital Investments across the U.S." Quarterly Journal of Economics, https://doi.org/10.1093/qje/qjaf013

Bifulco, Robert and David J. Schwegman. 2020. "Who Benefits from Accountability-Driven School Closure? Evidence from New York City." *Journal of Policy Analysis and Management* 39(1):96–130.

Black, Sandra E. 1999. "Do Better Schools Matter? Parental Valuation of Elementary Education." *Quarterly Journal of Economics* 114(2):577–599.

Bowler, Shaun, Stephen P. Nicholson and Gary M. Segura. 2006. "Earthquakes and Aftershocks: Race, Direct Democracy, and Partisan Change." *American Political Science Review* 50(1):146–159.

Boyarsky, Bill. 1981. *Ronald Reagan: His Life and Rise to the Presidency*. New York: Random House.

Bross, Whitney, Douglas N. Harris and Lihan Liu. 2023. "The Effects of Performance-Based School Closure and Restart on Student Performance." *Economics of Education Review* 94:102368.

Brummet, Quentin. 2014. "The Effect of School Closings on Student Achievement." *Journal of Public Economics* 119:108–124.

Buck, Stuart. 2011. *Acting White: The Ironic Legacy of Desegregation*. New Haven, CT: Yale University Press.

Bullock, John G., Alan S. Gerber, Seth J. Hill and Gregory A. Huber. 2015. "Partisan Bias in Factual Beliefs about Politics." *Quarterly Journal of Political Science* 10(4):519–578.

Bullock, John G. and Gabriel Lenz. 2019. "Partisan Bias in Surveys." *Annual Review of Political Science* 22:325–442.

Buras, Kristen L. 2015. *Charter Schools, Race, and Urban Space: Where the Market Meets Grassroots Resistance*. New York: Routledge.

Burnett, Craig M. and Vladimir Kogan. 2017. "The Politics of Potholes: Service Quality and Retrospective Voting in Local Elections." *Journal of Politics* 79(1):302–314.

Burtis, Eloise and Sofoklis Goulas. 2023. "Declining School Enrollment since the Pandemic." www.brookings.edu/articles/declining-school-enrollment-since-the-pandemic

Campbell, Robert F. and Frank Richardson. 1968. "How Are the Negro Teachers Faring?" *Southern Education Report* 4.

Campbell, Travis. 2024. "Black Lives Matter's Effect on Police Lethal Use-of-Force." *Journal of Urban Economics* 141:103587.

Campos, Christopher. 2023. "Social Interactions, Information, and Preferences for Schools: Experimental Evidence from Los Angeles." http://dx.doi.org/10.2139/ssrn.4352040

Campos, Christopher and Caitlin Kearns. 2024. "The Impact of Public School Choice: Evidence from Los Angeles's Zones of Choice." *Quarterly Journal of Economics* 139(2):1051–1093.

Canes-Wrone, Brandice, David W. Brady and John F. Cogan. 2002. "Out of Step, Out of Office: Electoral Accountability and House Members' Voting." *American Political Science Review* 91(1):127–140.

Cannon, Lou. 1978. "Poll Shows Californians Support Controversial Initiatives." *Washington Post*.

Carlson, Deven and Stéphane Lavertu. 2016. "Charter School Closure and Student Achievement: Evidence from Ohio." *Journal of Urban Economics* 95:31–48.

Carlson, Deven and Stéphane Lavertu. 2018. "School Improvement Grants in Ohio: Effects on Student Achievement and School Administration." *Educational Evaluation and Policy Analysis* 40(3):287–315.

Carmines, Edward G. and James A. Stimson. 1980. "The Two Faces of Issue Voting." *American Political Science Review* 74(1):78–91.

Carr, Sarah. 2013. *Hope against Hope: Three Schools, One City, and the Struggle to Educate America's Children*. New York: Bloomsbury Press.

Cascio, Elizabeth U. and Ebonya Washington. 2014. "Valuing the Vote: The Redistribution of Voting Rights and State Funds Following the Voting Rights Act of 1965." *Quarterly Journal of Economics* 129(1):379–433.

Chait, Jonathan. 2021. "Unlearning an Answer." *New York*. https://nymag.com/intelligencer/2021/01/unlearning-democrats-answer-on-charter-schools.html

Chait, Jonathan. 2023. "Indoctrination Nation." *New York* pp. 18–23.

Charles, Guy-Uriel E. and Luis Fuentes-Rohwer. 2016. "*Reynolds* Revisited." In *Election Law Stories*, ed. Joshua D. Douglas and Eugene D. Mazo. St. Paul, MN: Foundation Press pp. 21–61.

Chen, Jowei and Jonathan Rodden. 2013. "Unintentional Gerrymandering: Political Geography and Electoral Bias in Legislatures." *Quarterly Journal of Political Science* 8(3):239–269.

Chetty, Raj, John N. Friedman and Jonah E. Rockoff. 2014. "Measuring the Impacts of Teachers II: Teacher Value-Added and Student Outcomes in Adulthood." *American Economic Review* 104(9):2633–2679.

Chetty, Raj, John N. Friedman, Nathaniel Hilger, Emmanuel Saez, Diane Whitmore Schanzenbach and Danny Yagan. 2011. "How Does Your Kindergarten Classroom Affect Your Earnings? Evidence from Project STAR." *Quarterly Journal of Economics* 126(4):1593–1660.

Chicago Area Fair Housing Alliance. 2018. "A City Fragmented: How Race, Power, and Aldermanic Prerogative Shape Chicago's Neighborhoods." www.povertylaw.org/wp-content/uploads/2019/09/CityFragmentedLowRes-1.pdf

Chin, Mark, Thomas J. Kane, Whitney Kozakowski, Beth E. Schueler and Douglas O. Staiger. 2019. "School District Reform in Newark: Within- and Between-School Changes in Achievement Growth." *ILR Review* 72(2):323–354.

Chingos, Matthew M. 2013. "Class Size and Student Outcomes: Research and Policy Implications." *Journal of Policy Analysis and Management* 32(2):411–438.

Chingos, Matthew M., Grover J. Whitehurst and Michael R. Gallaher. 2015. "School Districts and Student Achievement." *Education Finance and Policy* 10(3):378–398.

Chingos, Matthew M., Michael Henderson and Martin R. West. 2012. "Citizen Participation of Government Service Quality: Evidence from Public Schools." *Quarterly Journal of Political Science* 7(4):411–445.

Chotiner, Isaac. 2021. "How San Francisco Renamed Its Schools." *New Yorker*. www.newyorker.com/news/q-and-a/how-san-francisco-renamed-its-schools

Chubb, John E. and Terry M. Moe. 1990a. "America's Public Schools: Choice Is a Panacea." *Brookings Review* 8(3):4–12.

Chubb, John E. and Terry M. Moe. 1990b. *Politics, Markets, and America's Schools*. Washington, DC: Brookings Institution Press.

Collins, Courtney A. and Erin K. Kaplan. 2022. "Demand for School Quality and Local District Administration." *Economics of Education Review* 88:102252.

Collins, Jonathan E. 2021. "Does the Meeting Style Matter? The Effects of Exposure to Participatory and Deliberative School Board Meetings." *American Political Science Review* 115(3):790–804.

Collins, Sharon M. 1997. *Black Corporate Executives: The Making and Breaking of a Black Middle Class*. Philadelphia: Temple University Press.

Columbus Dispatch. 2007. "Reprehensible – Rejection of School-Board Candidate Is a Shameful Moment for Democrats, Union." p. 10A. www.dispatch.com/story/opinion/columns/2007/10/18/editorial-reprehensible-rejection-school-board/23748058007/

Cook, Jason, Stéphane Lavertu and Corbin Miller. 2021. "Rent-Seeking through Collective Bargaining: Teachers Unions and Education Production." *Economics of Education Review* 85:102193.

Cortes, Kalena E. and Andrew I. Friedson. 2014. "Ranking Up by Moving Out: The Effect of the Texas Top 10% Plan on Property Values." *National Tax Journal* 67(1):51–76.

Cox, Oliver C. 1953. "Negro Teachers: Martyrs to Integration?" *Nation* 176:347–348.

Crawford, James. 1989. *Bilingual Education: History, Politics, Theory, and Practice*. Trenton: Crane Publishing Company.

Cremin, Lawrence A. 1961. *The Transformation of the School: Progressivism in Education, 1876-1957*. New York: Alfred A. Knopf.

Cullen, Julie Berry, Mark C. Long and Randall Reback. 2013. "Jockeying for Position: Strategic High School Choice under Texas' Top Ten Percent Plan." *Journal of Public Economics* 97:32–48.

Dahl, Robert A. 1971. *Polyarchy: Participation and Opposition*. New Haven, CT: Yale University Press.

de Benedictis-Kessner, Justin. 2018. "Off-Cycle and Out of Office: Election Timing and the Incumbency Advantage." *Journal of Politics* 80(1):119–132.

de Chaisemartin, Clément and Xavier D'Haultfœuille. 2020. "Two-Way Fixed Effects Estimators with Heterogeneous Treatment Effects." *American Economic Review* 110(9):2964–2996.

DeBonis, Mike. 2010. "Fenty Says Education Reform Cost Him Re-election." *Washington Post*. https://web.archive.org/web/20101022034547/; http://voices.washingtonpost.com/debonis/2010/10/fenty_presses_education-reform.html

Dee, Thomas S. 2012. "School Turnarounds: Evidence from the 2009 Stimulus." National Bureau of Economic Research Working Paper No. 17990.

Dee, Thomas S. and James Wyckoff. 2015. "Incentives, Selection, and Teacher Performance: Evidence from IMPACT." *Educational Evaluation and Policy Analysis* 34(2):267–297.

Dee, Thomas S., Jessalynn James and Jim Wyckoff. 2021. "Is Effective Teacher Evaluation Sustainable? Evidence from District of Columbia Public Schools." *Education Finance and Policy* 16(2):267–297.

Deming, David J., Sarah Cohodes, Jennifer Jennings and Christopher Jencks. 2016. "School Accountability, Postsecondary Attainment, and Earnings." *Review of Economics and Statistics* 98(5):848–862.

DeRoche, Tim. 2020. *A Fine Line: How Most American Kids Are Kept Out of the Best Public Schools*. Los Angeles: Redtail Press.

DeRoche, Tim. 2023. "Educational Redlining, Rezoning and the Bitter Politics of School Closures." *The 74*. www.the74million.org/article/educational-redlining-rezoning-and-the-bitter-politics-of-school-closures/

DeRoche, Tim, Hailly T. N. Korman and Harold Hinds. 2023. *When Good Parents Go to Jail: The Criminalization of Address Sharing in Public Education*. Available to All. https://availabletoall.org/report-when-good-parents-go-to-jail/

Devi, Tanaya and Roland G. Fryer, Jr. 2020. "Policing the Police: The Impact of 'Pattern-or-Practice' Investigations on Crime." National Bureau of Economic Research Working Paper No. 27324.

DiPierro, Amy and Corey Mitchell. 2023. "Homeless Students Needed Help: Schools Showed Them the Door." *Chalkbeat*. www.chalkbeat.org/philadelphia/2023/8/29/23844399/pennsylvania-homeless-students-schools-disenrolled/

Domina, Thurston, Andrew McEachin, Andrew Penner and Emily Penner. 2015. "Aiming High and Falling Short: California's Eighth-Grade Algebra-for-All Effort." *Educational Evaluation and Policy Analysis* 37(3):275–295.

Dotter, Dallas, Duncan Chaplin and Maria Bartlett. 2021. "Impacts of School Reforms in Washington, DC on Student Achievement." www.mathematica.org/publications/impacts-of-school-reforms-in-washington-dc-on-student-achievement

Druckman, James N., Samara Klar, Yanna Krupnikov, Matthew Levendusky and John Barry Ryan. 2021. "Affective Polarization, Local Contexts and Public Opinion in America." *Nature Human Behavior* 5:28–38.

Duncan, Arne. 2018. *How Schools Work: An Inside Account of Failure and Success from One of the Nation's Longest-Serving Secretaries of Education*. New York: Simon & Schuster Paperbacks.

Dunn, Joshua. 2012. *Complex Justice: The Case of* Missouri v. Jenkins. Chapel Hill, NC: University of North Carolina Press.

Egalite, Anna J. 2024. "What We Know about Teacher Race and Student Outcomes." *Education Next* 24(1).

Einstein, Katherine L., David M. Glick and Maxwell Palmer. 2020. *Neighborhood Defenders*. New York: Cambridge University Press.

Einstein, Katherine L., Maxwell Palmer and David M. Glick. 2019. "Who Participates in Local Government? Evidence from Meeting Minutes." *Perspectives on Politics* 17(1):28–46.

Engberg, John, Brian Gill, Gema Zamarro and Ron Zimmer. 2012. "Closing Schools in a Shrinking District: Do Student Outcomes Depend on Which Schools Are Closed?" *Journal of Urban Economics* 71:189–203.

Erie, Steven P. 1990. *Rainbow's End: Irish-Americans and the Dilemmas of Urban Machine Politics, 1840–1985*. Berkeley: University of California Press.

Erikson, Robert S., Gerald C. Wright and John P. McIver. 1993. *Statehouse Democracy: Public Opinion and Policy in the American States*. New York: Cambridge University Press.

Ethridge, Samuel B. 1979. "Impact of the 1954 *Brown vs. Topeka Board of Education* Decision on Black Educators." *Negro Educational Review* 30(4):217–332.

Ewing, Eve L. 2018. *Ghosts in the Schoolyard: Racism and School Closings on Chicago's South Side*. Chicago: University of Chicago Press.

Fahle, Erin M., Belen Chavez, Demetra Kalogrides, Benjamin R. Shear, Sean F. Reardon and Andrew D. Ho. 2021. "Stanford Education Data Archive (Version 4.1)." http://purl.stanford.edu/db586ns4974.

Fallows, Deborah. 2014. "A Creative Way to Educate Low-Income Students." *Atlantic*. www.theatlantic.com/education/archive/2014/10/a-creative-way-to-educate-low-income-students/381461/

Fenwick, Leslie T. 2022. *Jim Crow's Pink Slip: The Untold Story of Black Principal and Teacher Leadership*. Cambridge, MA: Harvard Education Press.

Festerwald, John. 2023. "Newsom Vows again to Send Social Studies Textbooks to Temecula Valley Unified with Hefty Fine." *EdSource*. https://edsource.org/2023/newsom-again-vows-to-order-social-studies-textbooks-for-temecula-valley-with-a-hefty-fine/694455

Figlio, David N. 2006. "Testing, Crime and Punishment." *Journal of Public Economics* 98(4–5):837–851.

Figlio, David N. and Lawrence W. Kenny. 2009. "Public Sector Performance Measurement and Stakeholder Support." *Journal of Public Economics* 93(9-10):1069–1077.

Figlio, David N. and Maurice E. Lucas. 2003. "What's in a Grade? School Report Cards and the Housing Market." *American Economic Review* 94(3):591–604.

Fischel, William A. 1989. "Did "Serrano" Cause Proposition 13?'." *National Tax Journal* 42(4):465–473.

Fischel, William A. 2001a. *The Homevoter Hypothesis: How Home Values Influence Local Government Taxation, School Finance, and Land-Use Policies.* Cambridge, MA: Harvard University Press.

Fischel, William A. 2001b. "Why Are There NIMBYs?" *Land Economics* 77(1):144–152.

Fischel, William A. 2009. *Making the Grade: The Economic Evolution of American School Districts.* Chicago: Chicago University Press.

Fishback, Price V., Jessica LaVoice, Allison Shertzer and Randall Walsh. 2020. "Race, Risk, and the Emergence of Federal Redlining." National Bureau of Economic Research Working Paper No. 28146.

Fiske, Edward B. 1985. "One Language or Two?" *New York Times* p. ES1.

Fowler, Anthony. 2020. "Partisan Intoxication or Policy Voting?" *Quarterly Journal of Political Science* 15(2):141–179.

Friday, Cameron and Tucker Smith. 2023. "Turning around Schools (and Neighborhoods?): School Improvement Grants and Gentrification." *Economics of Education Review* 94:102382.

Frisvold, David E. 2015. "Nutrition and Cognitive Achievement: An Evaluation of the School Breakfast Program." *Journal of Public Economics* 124:91–104.

Fryer, Jr., Roland G. and Paul Torelli. 2010. "An empirical analysis of 'Acting White'." *Journal of Public Economics* 94(5–6):380–396.

Fryer, Jr., Roland G. 2014. "Injecting Charter School Best Practices into Traditional Public Schools: Evidence from Field Experiments." *Quarterly Journal of Economics* 129(3):1355–1407.

Fuller, Kathleen, Jeffry Netter and Mike Stegemoller. 2002. "What Do Returns to Acquiring Firms Tell Us? Evidence from Firms That Make Many Acquisitions." *Journal of Finance* 57(4):1763–1793.

Fuller, Thomas. 2017. "San Francisco Asks: Where Have All the Children Gone?" *New York Times*. www.nytimes.com/2017/01/21/us/san-francisco-children.html

Fuller, Thomas. 2022. "In Landslide, San Francisco Forces Out 3 Board of Education Members." *New York Times*. www.nytimes.com/2022/02/16/us/san-francisco-school-board-recall.html

Gailmard, Sean and John W. Patty. 2007. "Slackers and Zealots: Civil Service, Policy Discretion, and Bureaucratic Expertise." *American Journal of Political Science* 51(4):873–889.

Garvin, Glenn. 1998. "Loco, Completamente Loco." *Reason* pp. 18–29.

Gelman, Andrew and Gary King. 1993. "Why Are American Presidential Election Campaign Polls so Variable When Votes Are So Predictable?" *British Journal of Political Science* 23(1):409–451.

Gerber, Elisabeth R. 1996. "Legislative Response to the Threat of Popular Initiatives." *American Journal of Political Science* 40(1):99–128.

Gillani, Nabeel, Doug Beeferman, Christine Vega-Pourheydarian, Cassandra Overney, Pascal Van Hentenryck and Deb Roy. 2023. "Redrawing Attendance Boundaries to Promote Racial and Ethnic Diversity in Elementary Schools." *Educational Researcher* 52(6):348–364.

Gilmour, John B. 2001. "The Powell Amendment Voting Cycle: An Obituary." *Legislative Studies Quarterly* 26(2):249–262.

Gilraine, Michael and Nolan G. Pope. 2021. "Making Teaching Last: Long-Run Value-Added." National Bureau of Economic Research Working Paper No. 29555.

Glazerman, Steven and Dallas Dotter. 2017. "Market Signals: Evidence on the Determinants and Consequences of School Choice from a Citywide Lottery." *Educational Evaluation and Policy Analysis* 39(4):593–619.

Goldstein, Dana. 2021. "Schools Are Open, but Many Families Remain Hesitant to Return." *New York Times*. www.nytimes.com/2021/05/09/us/covid-school-reopening-virtual-learning.html

Good, Ryan M. 2017. "Histories That Root Us: Neighborhood, Place, and the Protest of School Closures in Philadelphia." *Urban Geography* 38(6):861–883.

Good, Ryan M. 2019. "Invoking Landscapes of Spatialized Inequality: Race, Class, and Place in Philadelphia's School Closure Debate." *Journal of Urban Affairs* 39(3):358–380.

Gordon, Molly F., Marisa de la Torre, Jennifer R. Cowhy, Paul T. Moore, Lauren Sartain and David Knight. 2018. "School Closings in Chicago: Staff and Student Experiences and Academic Outcomes." https://consortium.uchicago.edu/publications/school-closings-chicago-staff-and-student-experiences-and-academic-outcomes

Graham, Kristen A. and Valerie Russ. 2023. "Sadie Alexander's Daughter Is 'Heartbroken' at the State of the Philly School Named for Her Mother." *Philadelphia Inquirer*. www.inquirer.com/education/penn-alexander-sadie-minter-alexander-gentrification-20230815.html

Green, Jon, Matthew A. Baum, James Druckman, David Lazer, Katya Ognyanova, Matthew Simonson, Roy Perlisand and Mauricio Santillana. 2020. "Identifying and Measuring Conditional Policy Preferences: The Case of Opening Schools during a Pandemic." https://osf.io/zsh8u/

Greene-Bell, Danielle Marie and Francis A. Perlman II. 2024. "Racialized Closures and the Shuttering of Black Schools: Evidence from National Data." *Harvard Education Review* 94(2):187–210.

Grossmann, Matt, Sarah Reckhow, Katharine O. Strunk and Meg Turner. 2021. "All States Close but Red Districts Reopen: The Politics of In-Person Schooling during the COVID-19 Pandemic." *Educational Researcher* 50(9):637–648.

Guryan, Jonathan. 2004. "Desegregation and Black Dropout Rates." *American Economic Review* 94(4):919–943.

Haderlein, Shira Alicia Korn. 2022. "How Do Parents Evaluate and Select Schools? Evidence from a Survey Experiment." *American Educational Research Journal* 59(2):381–414.

Hajnal, Zoltan L., Vladimir Kogan and G. Agustin Markarian. 2022. "Who Votes: City Election Timing and Voter Composition." *American Political Science Review* 116(1):374–383.

Hall, Andrew B. and Jesse Yoder. 2022. "Does Homeownership Influence Political Behavior? Evidence from Administrative Data." *Journal of Politics* 84(1):351–366.

Han, Chunping, Margaret E. Raymond, James L. Woodworth, Yohannes Negassi, W. Payton Richardson and Will Snow. 2017. "Lights Off: Practice and Impact of Closing Low-Performing Schools." https://credo.stanford.edu/wp-content/uploads/2021/08/closure_final_volume_i.pdf

Handel, Danielle Victoria and Eric A. Hanushek. 2023. "U.S. School Finance: Resources and Outcomes." In *Handbook of the Economics of Education, Volume 7*, ed. Eric A. Hanushek, Stephen Machin and Ludger Woessmann. Amsterdam: North Holland pp. 143–226.

Hanford, Emily. 2019. "There Is a Right Way to Teach Reading, and Mississippi Knows It." *New York Times* (5). www.nytimes.com/2019/12/05/opinion/mississippi-schools-naep.html

Hankinson, Michael and Asya Magazinnik. 2023. "The Supply-Equity Trade-Off: The Effect of Spatial Representation on the Local Housing Supply." *Journal of Politics* 85(3):1033–1047.

Hannah-Jones, Nikole. 2019. "It Was Never about Busing." *New York Times*. www.nytimes.com/2019/07/12/opinion/sunday/it-was-never-about-busing.html

Hanushek, Eric A., Paul E. Peterson, Laura M. Talpey and Ludger Woessmann. 2019. "The Achievement Gap Fails to Close." *Education Next* 19(3). www.educationnext.org/achievement-gap-fails-close-half-century-testing-shows-persistent-divide/

Harris, Douglas N. 2020a. *Charter School City: What the End of Traditional Public Schools in New Orleans Means for American Education*. Chicago: Chicago University Press.

Harris, Douglas N. and Matthew F. Larsen. 2023a. "Taken by Storm: The Effects of Hurricane Katrina on Medium-Term Student Outcomes in New Orleans." *Journal of Human Resources* 58(5):1608–1643.

Harris, Douglas N. and Matthew F. Larsen. 2023b. "What Schools Do Families Want (and Why)? Evidence on Revealed Preferences from New Orleans." *Educational Evaluation and Policy Analysis* 45(3):496–519.

Harris, Douglas N. and Valentina Martinez-Pabon. 2023. "Extreme Measures: A National Descriptive Analysis of Closure and Restructuring of Traditional Public, Charter, and Private Schools." *Education Finance and Policy* 19(1):32–60.

Harris, Leslie M. 2020b. "I Helped Fact-Check the 1619 Project. The Times Ignored Me." *Politico Magazine*. www.politico.com/news/magazine/2020/03/06/1619-project-new-york-times-mistake-122248

Hartney, Michael T. 2021. "Revitalizing Local Democracy: The Case for On-Cycle Local Elections." Manhattan Institute. https://media4.manhattan-institute.org/sites/default/files/MI-issue-brief-hartney-election-timing.pdf

Hartney, Michael T. 2022a. *How Policies Make Interests: Group Lobbying in American Education*. Chicago: University of Chicago Press.

Hartney, Michael T. 2022b. "Teachers' Unions and School Board Elections: A Reassessment." *Interest Groups and Advocacy* 11(2):237–262.

Hartney, Michael T. and Leslie K. Finger. 2022. "Politics, Markets, and Pandemics: Public Education's Response to COVID-19." *Perspectives on Politics* 20(2):457–473.

Harvey, Anna and Taylor Mattia. 2024. "Reducing Racial Disparities in Crime Victimization: Evidence from Employment Discrimination Litigation." *Journal of Urban Economics* 141:103459.

Hastings, Justine S. and Jeffrey M. Weinstein. 2008. "Information, School Choice, and Academic Achievement: Evidence from Two Experiments." *Quarterly Journal of Economics*, 123(4):1373–1414.

Healy, Andrew and Gabriel S. Lenz. 2014. "Substituting the End for the Whole: Why Voters Respond Primarily to the Election-Year Economy." *American Journal of Political Science* 58(1):31–47.

Henig, Jeffrey R. 2013. *The End of Exceptionalism in American Education: The Changing Politics of School Reform.* Cambridge, MA: Harvard Education Press.

Henig, Jeffrey R., Rebecca Jacobsen and Sarah Reckhow. 2019. *Outside Money in School Board Elections: The Nationalization of Education Politics.* Cambridge, MA: Harvard Education Press.

Henig, Jeffrey R., Richard C. Hula, Marion Orr and Desiree S. Pedescleaux. 2001. *The Color of School Reform: Race, Politics, and the Challenge of Urban Education.* Princeton, NJ: Princeton University Press.

Hess, Frederick M. and Michael Q. McShane, eds. 2018. *Bush-Obama School Reform Lessons Learned.* Cambridge, MA: Harvard Education Press.

Hill, Carolyn J., Howard S. Bloom, Alison Rebeck Black and Mark W. Lipsey. 2008. "Empirical Benchmarks for Interpreting Effect Sizes in Research." *Child Development Perspectives* 2(3):172–177.

Hill, Paul T., Christine Campbell and Betheny Gross. 2013. *Strife and Progress: Portfolio Strategies for Managing Urban Schools.* Washington, DC: Brookings Institution Press.

Holbein, John. 2016. "Left Behind? Citizen Responsiveness to Government Performance Information." *American Political Science Review* 110(2):353–368.

Homans, Charles. 2023. "How a Sexual Assault in a School Bathroom Became a Political Weapon." *New York Times Magazine.* www.nytimes.com/2023/08/05/magazine/loudoun-county-bathroom-sexual-assault.html

Hooker, Robert W. 1970. *Displacement of Black Teachers in the Eleven Southern States.* Nashville, TN: Race Relations Information Center.

Hopkins, Daniel J. 2018. *The Increasingly United States: How and Why American Political Behavior Nationalized.* Chicago: University of Chicago Press.

Houston, David. 2024. "Polarization, Partisan Sorting, and the Politics of Education." *American Educational Research Journal* 61(3):508–540.

Huntington, Samuel P. 1991. *The Third Wave: Democratization in the Late Twentieth Century.* Norman, OK: University of Oklahoma Press.

Imai, Kosuke and Kabir Khanna. 2016. "Improving Ecological Inference by Predicting Individual Ethnicity from Voter Registration Records." *Political Analysis* 24(2):263–272.

Imberman, Scott A. and Michael F. Lovenheim. 2016. "Does the Market Value Value-Added? Evidence from Housing Prices after a Public Release of School and Teacher Value-Added." *Journal of Urban Economics* 91:104–121.

Indianapolis News. 1915. "Gabriel L. Jones, Widely Known Colored Man, Dead." p. 11.

Ingram, Carl. 1998. "Wilson Backs Ballot Measure to Ban Bilingual Education." *Los Angeles Times* p. A1A.

Irvine, Janice M. 2004. *Talk about Sex: The Battles over Sex Education in the United States.* Berkeley: University of California Press.

Jackson, C. Kirabo. 2018. "What Do Test Scores Miss? The Importance of Teacher Effects on Non-Test Score Outcomes." *Journal of Political Economy* 126(5):2072–2107.

Jackson, C. Kirabo and Claire L. Mackevicius. 2024. "What Impacts Can We Expect from School Spending Policy? Evidence from Evaluations in the United States." *American Economic Journal: Applied Economics* 16(1):412–446.

Jackson, C. Kirabo, Rucker C. Johnson and Claudia Persico. 2016. "The Effects of School Spending on Educational and Economic Outcomes: Evidence from School Finance Reforms." *Quarterly Journal of Economics* 131(1):157–218.

Jackson, C. Kirabo, Shanette C. Porter, John Q. Easton and Sebastián Kiguel. 2022. "Who Benefits from Attending Effective High Schools." National Bureau of Economic Research Working Paper No. 28194.

Jacobs, Joanne. 2022. "School Board Shakeup in San Francisco: Arrogance, Incompetence, and Woke Rhetoric Trigger Successful Recall Effort." *Education Next* 22(3):26–43.

Jacobsen, Rebecca, Andrew Saultz and Jeffrey W. Snyder. 2013. "When Accountability Strategies Collide: Do Policy Changes That Raise Accountability Standards Also Erode Public Satisfaction?" *Educational Policy* 27(2):360–389.

Jacobson, Gary C. 2006. *A Divider, Not a Uniter: George W. Bush and the American People.* New York: Longman.

Jacobson, Louis. 2014. "State School Superintendents and the Messy Business of Politics." *Governing.* www.governing.com/archive/gov-state-school-superintendents-messy-business-politics.html

Jaffe, Harry S. and Tom Sherwood. 1994. *Dream City: Race, Power, and the Decline of Washington, D.C.* New York: Simon and Schuster.

Jeffers, Elizabeth K. 2024. "Beyond the Parameters of 'Choice': An Obliterated Vision for Traditional Public Schooling and the Contamination of the New Orleans Charter Restart Model." *Educational Policy* 38(3):566–603.

Jeffers, Elizabeth K. and Adrienne D. Dixson. 2024. "The Plantation 'All Charter' Model and the Long Durée of Resistance for Black Public High Schools in New Orleans." *Educational Evaluation and Policy Analysis* 46(4):673–708.

Jensen, Amalie, William Marble, Kenneth Scheve and Matthew J. Slaughter. 2021. "City Limits to Partisan Polarization in the American Public." *Political Science Research and Methods* 9(2):223–241.

Jochim, Ashley and Patrick McGuinn. 2016. "The Politics of the Common Core Assessments: Why States Are Quitting the PARCC and Smarter Balanced Testing Consortia." *Education Next* (16):44–52.

Johnson, Rucker C. 2011. Long-Run Impacts of School Desegregation and School Quality on Adult Attainments. Working Paper 16664 National Bureau of Economic Research. www.nber.org/papers/w16664

Johnson, Rucker C. 2023. "School Funding Effectiveness: Evidence From California's Local Control Funding Formula." Learning Policy Institute. https://files.eric.ed.gov/fulltext/ED642549.pdf

Jones, Garett. 2020. *10% Less Democracy: Why You Should Trust Elites a Little More and the Masses a Little Less*. Stanford, CA: Stanford University Press.
Jongco, Angelica K. 2016. "Keeping the Promise of LCFF: Key Findings and Recommendations after Two Years of LCFF Implementation." Public Advocates. https://publicadvocates.org/wp-content/uploads/report_public_advocates_keeping_the_promise_of_lcff.pdf
Jost, Kenneth. 1995. "Teaching History." *CQ Press*.
Kane, Thomas J., Stephanie K. Riegg and Douglas O. Staiger. 2006. "School Quality, Neighborhoods, and Housing Prices." *American Law and Economics Review* 8(2):183–212.
Kemple, James J. 2016. "School Closures in New York City." *Journal of Policy Analysis and Management* 16(4):66–75.
Kennedy, David M. 2011. *Don't Shoot: One Man, A Street Fellowship, and the End of Violence in Inner-City America*. New York: Bloomsbury.
Kenworthy, E.W. 1964. "Dirksen Shaped Victory for Civil Rights Forces in Fight to Bring Measure to Vote." *New York Times* p. 11. www.nytimes.com/1964/06/20/archives/dirksen-shaped-victory-for-civil-rights-forces-in-fight-to-bring.html
Kernell, Samuel. 1997. *Going Public: New Strategies of Presidential Leadership*. Washington, DC: CQ Press.
Kim, James S. 2004. "Research and the Reading Wars." In *When Research Matters: How Scholarship Influences Education Policy*, ed. Frederick M. Hess. Cambridge, MA: Harvard University Press, pp. 89–111.
King, Kenneth James. 1971. *Pan-Africanism and Education: A Study of Race, Philanthropy, and Education in the Southern States of America and East Africa*. Oxford, UK: Clarendon Press.
Kirchick, James. 2022. *Secret City: The Hidden History of Gay Washington*. New York: Henry Holt and Company.
Kliebard, Herbert M. 1995. *The Struggle for the American Curriculum, 1893–1958, Second Edition*. New York: Routledge.
Kogan, Vladimir. 2017. "Administrative Centralization and Bureaucratic Responsiveness: Evidence from the Food Stamp Program." *Journal of Public Administration Research and Theory* 27(4):629–646.
Kogan, Vladimir. 2021a. "What's behind Racial Differences in Attitudes toward School Reopening (and What to Do about Them)." www.aei.org/research-products/report/whats-behind-racial-differences-in-attitudes-toward-school-reopening-and-what-to-do-about-them/
Kogan, Vladimir. 2021b. "What's behind the Racial Divide on School Reopening?." https://crpe.org/whats-behind-the-racial-divide-on-school-reopening/
Kogan, Vladimir. 2022. "Locally Elected School Boards Are Failing: Pandemic Stress-Tested School Governance, Revealing Many Flaws." *Education Next* 22(3):9–13.
Kogan, Vladimir. 2023. "New NAEP Scores Reveal the Failure of Pandemic Academic Recovery Efforts." *The 74*. www.the74million.org/article/new-naep-scores-reveal-the-failure-of-pandemic-academic-recovery-efforts/
Kogan, Vladimir and Michael T. Hartney. 2024. "The Politics of Teachers' Union Endorsements." *American Journal of Political Science*.

Kogan, Vladimir, Stéphane Lavertu and Zachary Peskowitz. 2025. "High Turnover with Low Accountability: Local School Board Elections in 16 States."
Kogan, Vladimir, Stéphane Lavertu and Zachary Peskowitz. 2016. "Do School Report Cards Produce Accountability through the Ballot Box?" *Journal of Policy Analysis and Management* 35(3):639–661.
Kogan, Vladimir, Stéphane Lavertu and Zachary Peskowitz. 2018. "Election Timing, Electorate Composition, and Policy Outcomes: Evidence from School Districts." *American Journal of Political Science* 62(3):637–651.
Kogan, Vladimir, Stéphane Lavertu and Zachary Peskowitz. 2021. "The Democratic Deficit in U.S. Education Governance." *American Political Science Review* 115(3):1082–1089.
Kogan, Vladmir. 2020. "Columbus Audit Offers Sobering Lessons for Ohio Teacher Evaluations." *Ohio Gadfly Daily.* https://fordhaminstitute.org/ohio/commentary/columbus-audit-offers-sobering-lessons-ohio-teacher-evaluations
Koski, William S. and Jesse Hahnel. 2015. "The Past, Present, and Possible Futures of Educational Finance Reform Litigation." In *Handbook of Research in Education Finance and Policy, 2nd Edition*, ed. Helen F. Ladd and Margaret E. Goertz. New York: Routledge pp. 41–49.
Kozol, Jonathan. 1991. *Savage Inequalities: Children in America's Schools.* New York: Crown Publishers, Inc.
Kraft, Matthew A. 2019. "Teacher Effects on Complex Cognitive Skills and Social-Emotional Competencies." *Journal of Human Resources* 54(1):1–36.
Kraus, Neil and Todd Swanstrom. 2001. "Minority Mayors and the Hollow-Prize Problem." *PS: Political Science and Politics* 34(1):99–105.
Kuziemko, Ilyana and Ebonya Washington. 2018. "Why Did the Democrats Lose the South? Bringing New Data to an Old Debate." *American Economic Review* 108(10):2830–2867.
Labaree, David. 1997. "Public Goods, Private Goods: The American Struggle over Educational Goals." *American Educational Research Journal* 34(1):39–81.
Ladd, Helen F. 2012. "Education and Poverty: Confronting the Evidence." *Journal of Policy Analysis and Management* 31(2):203–227.
Lafortune, Julien, Jesse Rothstein and Diane Whitmore Schanzenbach. 2018. "School Finance Reform and the Distribution of Student Achievement." *American Economic Journal: Applied Economics* 10(2):1–26.
Laird, Jennifer. 2017. "Public Sector Employment Inequality in the United States and the Great Recession." *Demography* 54:391–411.
Lam, Kit. 2022. "San Francisco School Board Recall Organizer: Gross Mismanagement, Not Racism, Motivated Me." *USA Today.* www.usatoday.com/story/opinion/voices/2022/03/08/san-francisco-school-board-recall/6974316001/
Larsen, Matthew F. 2020. "Does Closing Schools Close Doors? The Effect of High School Closings on Achievement and Attainment." *Economics of Education Review* 76:101980.
Larson, Edward J. 2003. *Trial and Error: The American Controversy over Creation and Evolution, Third Edition.* New York: Oxford University Press.
Lastra-Anadón, Carlos X. and Paul E. Peterson. 2023. "The Efficiency-Equity Trade-Off in a Federal System: Local Financing of Schools and Student Achievement." *Publius: The Journal of Federalism* 53(2):174–200.

Lax, Jeffrey R. and Justin H. Phillips. 2012. "The Democratic Deficit in the States." *American Journal of Political Science* 56(1):148–166.
Lay, Celeste J. 2022. *Public Schools, Private Governance*. Philadelphia: Temple University Press.
Lebo, Lauri. 2008. *The Devil in Dover: An Insider's Story of Dogma v. Darwin in Small-Town America*. New York: New Press.
Lee, David S. 2008. "Randomized Experiments from Non-Random Selection in U.S. House Elections." *Journal of Econometrics* 142:675–697.
Lee, Hojung, Kenneth Shores and Elinor Williams. 2022. "The Distribution of School Resources in the United States: A Comparative Analysis across Levels of Governance, Student Subgroups, and Educational Resources." *Peabody Journal of Education* 97(4):395–411.
Lee, JoonHo, Bruce Fuller and Sophia Rabe-Hesketh. 2021. "How Finance Reform May Alter Teacher and School Quality: California's $23 Billion Initiative." *American Educational Research Journal* 58(6):1225–1269.
Lemann, Nicholas. 1997. "The Reading Wars." *Atlantic Monthly* 280(5):128–134.
Lenz, Gabriel S. 2013. *Follow the Leader? How Voters Respond to Politicians' Policies and Performance*. Chicago: University of Chicago Press.
Levine, Larence W. 1965. *Defender of the Faith: William Jennings Bryan: The Last Decade, 1915-1925*. New York: Oxford University Press.
Lewis, David E. 2008. *The Politics of Presidential Appointments: Political Control and Bureaucratic Performance*. Princeton, NJ: Princeton University Press.
LiCalsi, Christina, Martyna Citkowicz, Lawrence B. Friedman and Megan Brown. 2015. "Evaluation of Massachusetts Office of District and School Turnaround Assistance to Commissioner's Districts and Schools: Impact of School Redesign Grants." https://files.eric.ed.gov/fulltext/ED583091.pdf
Lijphart, Arend. 1999. *Patterns of Democracy: Government Forms and Performance in Thirty-Six Countries*. New Haven, CT: Yale University Press.
Lim, Claire S. H. and James M. Snyder, Jr. 2015. "Is More Information Always Better? Party Cues and Candidate Quality in U.S. Judicial Elections." *Journal of Public Economics* 128:107–123.
Lincove, Jane Arnold, Nathan Barrett and Katharine O. Strunk. 2017. "Did the Teachers Dismissed after Hurricane Katrina Return to Public Education?." https://educationresearchalliancenola.org/files/publications/ERA-1705-Policy-Brief-Labor-Market_170804_161710.pdf
Little Hoover Commission. 1993. "A Chance to Succeed: Providing English Learners with Supportive Education." https://lhc.ca.gov/report/chance-succeed-providing-english-learners-supportive-education
Liu, Jing, Michael S. Hayes and Seth Gershenson. 2022. "From Referrals to Suspensions: New Evidence on Racial Disparities in Exclusionary Discipline." *Journal of Urban Economics* 141:103453.
Liu, Jing, Susanna Loeb and Ying Shi. 2022. "More than Shortages: The Unequal Distribution of Substitute Teaching." *Education Finance and Policy* 17(2):285–308.
Loveless, Tom. 2021. *Between the State and the Schoolhouse: Understanding the Failure of Common Core*. Cambridge, MA: Harvard Education Press.

Loveless, Tom. 2022. "San Francisco's Detracking Experiment." *Education Next*. www.educationnext.org/san-franciscos-detracking-experiment/

Lovenheim, Michael F. and Alexander Willén. 2019. "The Long-Run Effects of Teacher Collective Bargaining." *American Economic Journal: Economic Policy* 11(3):292–324.

Lyda, John W. 1953. *The Negro in the History of Indiana*. Terre Haute, IN: No Publisher.

Manna, Paul. 2011. *Collision Course: Federal Education Policy Meets State and Local Realities*. Washington, DC: CQ Press.

Mansouri, Kavahn and Kate Grumke. 2023. "St. Louis-Area School District Aggressively Audits Student Housing, Citing 'Educational Larceny'." *St. Louis Public Radio*. www.stlpr.org/education/2023-11-02/st-louis-area-school-district-aggressively-audits-student-housing-citing-educational-larceny

Marschall, Melissa J., Anirudh V. S. Ruhil and Paru R. Shah. 2010. "The New Racial Calculus: Electoral Institutions and Black Representation in Local Legislatures." *American Journal of Political Science* 54(1):107–124.

Martin, Isaac W. 2008. *The Permanent Tax Revolt: How the Property Tax Transformed American Politics*. Stanford: Stanford University Press.

Martin, Isaac W. 2015. *The Gay Revolution: The Story of the Struggle*. New York: Simon and Schuster.

Martin, Jonathan. 2014. "As G.O.P. Wedge, the Common Core Cuts Both Ways." *New York Times* p. 1.

Mast, Evan. 2024. "Warding off Development: Local Control, Housing Supply, and NIMBYs." *Review of Economics and Statistics* 106(3):671–680.

Mathews, Mitford M. 1966. *Teaching to Read: Historically Considered*. Chicago: University of Chicago Press.

Matsusaka, John G. 2001. "Problems with a Methodology Used to Evaluate the Voter Initiative." *Journal of Politics* 63(4):1250–1256.

Matsusaka, John G. 2010. "Popular Control of Public Policy: A Quantitative Approach." *Quarterly Journal of Political Science* 5(2):133–167.

May, Henry, Aly Blakeney, Pragya Shrestha, Mia Mazal and Nicole Kennedy. 2023. "Long-Term Impacts of Reading Recovery through 3rd and 4th Grade: A Regression Discontinuity Study." *Journal of Research on Educational Effectiveness* 17(3):433–458.

Mayhew, David R. 1974. *Congress: The Electoral Connection*. New Haven, CT: Yale University Press.

McCluskey, Neal. 2019. "Correlates of Values and Identity-Based Conflicts in Public School Districts and States." Working Paper.

McCrummen, Stephanie. 2010. "D.C. Principal's Hands-on Tack Transforms Sousa Middle but Also Ruffles Feathers." *Washington Post*. www.washingtonpost.com/wp-dyn/content/article/2010/07/05/AR2010070502915.html

McGahan, Jason. 2023. "Violence Erupts over Embrace of Pride by Glendale Schools." *Los Angeles Magazine*. https://lamag.com/news/violence-erupts-over-embrace-of-pride-by-glendale-schools

McKenna, Michael C., Steven A. Stahl and David Reinking. 1995. "A Critical Commentary on Research, Politics, and Whole Language." *Journal of Reading Behavior* 26(2):211–233.

McMillan, Penelope. 1978. "Briggs Points to Gay Teachers in North as Example." *Los Angeles Times* p. B3.
Melnick, R. Shep. 2020. "Desegregation, Then and Now." *National Review* 42: 100–118.
Mezvinsky, Norton. 1961. "Scientific Temperance Instruction in the Schools." *History of Education Quarterly* 1(1):48–56.
Miller, Mathew. 1999. "Man on a Mission." *New Republic* 221(3–4):24–29.
Milner, H. Richard IV. 2020. "Disrupting Racism and Whiteness in Researching a Science of Reading." *Reading Research Quarterly* 55(S1):S249–S253.
Mintrom, Michael. 1997. "Policy Entrepreneurs and the Diffusion of Innovation." *American Journal of Political Science* 41(3):738–770.
Mixner, David. 1996. *Stranger among Friends*. New York: Bantam Books.
Moe, Terry M. 2019. *The Politics of Institutional Reform: Katrina, Education, and the Second Face of Power*. New York: Cambridge University Press.
Moe, Terry M. 2006. "Political Control and the Power of the Agent." *Journal of Law, Economics, and Organization* 22(1):1–29.
Moe, Terry M. 2008. "Beyond the Free Market: The Structure of School Choice." *Bringham Young University Law Review* 2008(2):557–592.
Moe, Terry M. 2009. "Collective Bargaining and the Performance of the Public Schools." *American Journal of Political Science* 53(1):156–174.
Moe, Terry M. 2011. *Special Interest: Teachers Unions and America's Public Schools*. Washington, DC: Brookings Institution Press.
Moe, Terry M. 2015. "Vested Interests and Political Institutions." *Political Science Quarterly* 130(2):277–318.
Monarrez, Tomás and Carina Chien. 2021. "Dividing Lines: Racially Unequal School Boundaries in US Public School Systems." Center on Education Data and Policy, Urban Institute.
Moran, Jeffrey P. 2003. "Reading Race into the Scopes Trial: African American Elites, Science, and Fundamentalism." *The Journal of American History* 90(3):891–911.
Morel, Domingo. 2018. *Takeover: Race, Education, and American Democracy*. New York: Oxford University Press.
Morel, Domingo and Sally A. Nuamah. 2020. "Who Governs? How Shifts in Political Power Shape Perceptions of Local Government Services." *Urban Affairs Review* 56(5):1503–1528.
Mosher, Clayton J., Terance D. Miethe and Dretha M. Philips. 2002. *The Mismeasure of Crime*. Thousand Oaks, CA: Sage Publications.
Muller, Brittany. 2023. "Hillsborough County Schools Superintendent to Present Re-zoning Recommendation to School Board." *WFLA*. www.wfla.com/news/hillsborough-county/hillsborough-county-schools-superintendent-to-present-re-zoning-recommendation-to-school-board/
Mumma, Kirsten Slungaard. 2024. "Politics and Children's Books: Evidence from School Library Collections." *American Educational Research Journal* 61(5):883–914.
Mummolo, Jonathan, Erik Peterson and Sean Westwood. 2019. "The Limits of Partisan Loyalty." *Political Behavior* 43:949–972.

Murphy, Tim. 2014. "State School Superintendents and the Messy Business of Politics." *Mother Jones*. www.motherjones.com/politics/2014/09/common-core-education-reform-backlash-obamacare/

Napolitano, Jo. 2024. "San Francisco Voters Overwhelmingly Support Algebra's Return to 8th Grade." *The 74*. www.the74million.org/article/san-fran-voters-overwhelmingly-support-algebras-return-to-8th-grade/

Nash, Gary B., Charlotte Crabtree and Ross E. Dunn. 1997. *History on Trial: Culture Wars and the Teaching of the Past*. New York: Alfred A. Knopf.

Natanson, Hannah. 2023a. "Covid Changed Parents' View of Schools – and Ignited the Education Culture Wars." *Washington Post*. www.washingtonpost.com/education/2023/03/18/pandemic-schools-parental-involvement/

Natanson, Hannah. 2023b. "She Challenges One School Book a Week: She Says She'll Never Stop." *Washington Post*. www.washingtonpost.com/education/2023/09/28/virginia-frequent-school-book-challenger-spotsylvania/

Neal, Derek and Diane Whitmore Schanzenbach. 2010. "Left behind by Design: Proficiency Counts and Test-Based Accountability." *Review of Economics and Statistics* 92(2):263–283.

New York State Education Department. 2024. "Mayoral Control of New York City Schools." www.nysed.gov/sites/default/files/mayoral-control-of-new-york-city-schools-final-pdf

Noel, Hans. 2012. "The Coalition Merchants: The Ideological Roots of the Civil Rights Realignment." *Journal of Politics* 74(1):156–173.

Nuamah, Sally A. 2023. *Closed for Democracy: How Mass School Closure Undermines the Citizenship of Black Americans*. New York: Cambridge University Press.

Nye, John V. C., Ilia Rainer and Thomas Stratmann. 2015. "Do Black Mayors Improve Black Relative to White Employment Outcomes? Evidence from Large US Cities." *Journal of Law, Economics, and Organization* 31(2):383–430.

Office of the Inspector General. 2006. "The Reading First Program's Grant Application Process: Final Inspection Review." U.S. Department of Education, ED-OIG/I13-F0017.

Orfield, Gary. 1969. *The Reconstruction of Southern Education: The Schools and the 1964 Civil Rights Act*. New York: Wiley-Interscience.

Ornstein, Joseph T. 2018. "Election Timing and the Politics of Urban Growth." Washington University Working Paper.

Owens, Emily G. 2014. "The American Temperance Movement and Market-Based Violence." *American Law and Economics Review* 16(2):433472.

Pane, John F., Daniel F. McCaffrey, Nidhi Kalra and Annie J. Zhou. 2008. "Effects of Student Displacement in Louisiana during the First Academic Year after the Hurricanes of 2005." www.rand.org/content/dam/rand/pubs/reprints/2008/RAND_RP1379.pdf

Paterson, Frances R. A. 2000. "The Politics of Phonics." *Journal of Curriculum and Supervision* 15(3):179–211.

Payson, Julia A. 2017. "When Are Local Incumbents Held Accountable for Government Performance? Evidence from US School Districts." *Legislative Studies Quarterly* 42(3):421–448.

Pearson, P. David. 1989. "Reading the Whole-Language Movement." *Elementary School Journal* 90(2):230–241.
Pearson, P. David. 2004. "The Reading Wars." *Educational Policy* 18(1):216–252.
Peterson, Paul E., Michael B. Henderson, Martin R. West and Samuel Barrows. 2017. "Common Core Brand Taints Opinion on Standards." *Education Next* (17):8–17.
Pitkin, Hanna F. 1967. *The Concept of Representation*. Los Angeles, CA: University of California Press.
Polikoff, Morgan. 2021. *Beyond Standards: The Fragmentation of Education Governance and the Promise of Curriculum Reform*. Cambridge, MA: Harvard Education Press.
Pondiscio, Robert. 2022. "Exit Interview: NCTQ's Kate Walsh." American Enterprise Institute. www.aei.org/op-eds/exit-interview-nctqs-kate-walsh/
Powell, Michael. 2014. "A School Board That Overlooks Its Obligation to Students." *New York Times*. www.nytimes.com/2014/04/08/nyregion/a-school-board-that-overlooks-its-obligation-to-students.html
Przeworski, Adam, Michael E. Alvarez, José Antonio Cheibub and Fernando Limongi. 2000. *Democracy and Development: Political Institutions and Well-Being in the World, 1950–1990*. Cambridge, MA: Cambridge University Press.
Pyle, Amy. 1996. "80 Students Stay Out of School in Latino Boycott." *Los Angeles Times* p. 1.
Ravitch, Diane. 1983. *The Troubled Crusade: American Education, 1945–1980*. New York: Basic Books.
Reardon, Sean F., John P. Papay, Tara Kilbride, Katherine O. Strunk, Joshua Cowen, Lily An and Kate Donohue. 2019. "Can Repeated Aggregate Cross-Sectional Data Be Used to Measure Average Student Learning Rates? A Validation Study of Learning Rate Measures in the Stanford Education Data Archive." Stanford Center for Education Policy Analysis Working Paper No. 19-08.
Reinhold, Robert. 1991. "California Rewrites History." *San Francisco Chronicle* p. Z1.
Rhodes, Jesse Hessler. 2011. "Progressive Policy Making in a Conservative Age? Civil Rights and the Politics of Federal Education Standards, Testing, and Accountability." *Perspectives on Politics* 9(3):519–544.
Rich, Wilber C. 1996. *Black Mayors and School Politics: The Failure of Reform in Detroit Gary, and Newark*. New York: Garland Publishing.
Riker, William H. 1986. *The Art of Political Manipulation*. New Haven, CT: Yale University Press.
Rivera, Roman G. and Bocar A. Ba. 2023. "The Effect of Police Oversight on Crime and Allegations of Misconduct: Evidence from Chicago." *Review of Economics and Statistics*.
Rogers, Steven. 2023. *Accountability in State Legislatures*. Chicago: University of Chicago Press.
Rohter, Larry. 1985. "The Politics of Bilingualism." *New York Times* p. ES46.

Romero, Gloria. 2014. "From Topeka, to Adelanto, and Montgomery County: Brown v. School Board of Education Continues." *Whittier Journal of Child and Family Advocacy* 13(1):20–35.

Rothstein, Richard. 2018. *The Color of Law: A Forgotten History of How Our Government Segregated America*. New York: W.W. Norton and Company.

Sacerdote, Bruce. 2011. "Peer Effects in Education: How Might They Work, How Big Are They and How Much Do We Know Thus Far?" In *Handbook of the Economics of Education, Volume 3*, ed. Eric A. Hanushek, Stephen Machin and Ludger Woessmann. Amsterdam: North Holland pp. 249–277.

Sahn, Alexander. 2025. "Public Comment and Public Policy." *American Journal of Political Science* 69(2):685–700. DOI: 10.1111/ajps.12900

Sass, Tim R. and Stephen L. Mehay. 1995. "The Voting Rights Act, District Elections, and the Success of Black Candidates in Municipal Elections." *Journal of Law and Economics* 38(2):367–392.

Saunders-Hastings, Emma. 2022. *Private Virtues, Public Vices: Philanthropy and Democratic Equality*. Chicago: University of Chicago Press.

Scanlon, Donna M. and Kimberly L. Anderson. 2020. "Using Context as an Assist in Word Solving: The Contributions of 25 Years of Research on the Interactive Strategies Approach." *Reading Research Quarterly* 55(S1):S19–S34.

Schalin, Jay. 2019. "The Politicization of University Schools of Education." James G. Martin Center for Academic Renewal.

Schecker, Justin. 2023. "South Tampa Parents Rally against Proposed School Boundary Changes." *WFLA*. www.wfla.com/news/education/south-tampa-parents-rally-against-proposed-school-boundary-changes/

Scheer, Robert. 1978. "A *Times* Interview with Sen. John Briggs." *Los Angeles Times* p. A4.

Scherer, Ethan. 2014. "Three Essays on Education Reform in the United States." Pardee RAND Graduate School. www.rand.org/content/dam/rand/pubs/rgs_dissertations/RGSD300/RGSD335/RAND_RGSD335.pdf

Schneider, Jack. 2017. *Beyond Test Scores: A Better Way to Measure School Quality*. Cambridge, MA: Harvard University Press.

Schoenberg, Tom. 1995. "On Campaign Trail, Senator Dole Denounces History Standards." *Chronicle of Higher Education*. www.chronicle.com/article/on-campaign-trail-senator-dole-denounces-history-standards/?sra=true&cid=gen_sign_in

Schueler, Beth E. and Joshua F. Bleiberg. 2022. "Evaluating Education Governance: Does State Takeover of School Districts Affect Student Achievement?" *Journal of Policy Analysis and Management* 41(1):162–192.

Schuit, Sophie and Jon C. Rogowski. 2017. "Race, Representation, and the Voting Rights Act." *American Journal of Political Science* 61(3):513–526.

Schultz, Jr., Michael John. 1970. *The National Education Association and the Black Teacher*. Coral Gables, FL: University of Miami Press.

Schwartz, Amy Ellen and Michah W. Rothbart. 2020. "Let Them Eat Lunch: The Impact of Universal Free Meals on Student Performance." *Journal of Policy Analysis and Management* 39(2):376–410.

Schwartz, Katrina. 2018. "How the San Francisco School Lottery Works, and How It Doesn't." *KQED*. www.kqed.org/news/11641238/how-the-san-francisco-school-lottery-works-and-how-it-doesnt-2

Seplow, Stephen. 2010. "Penn Neighborhood Blooms around a Top School." *Philadelphia Inquirer*. www.inquirer.com/philly/education/20100405_Penn_neighborhood_blooms_around_a_top_school.html

Shanahan, Timothy. 2020. "What Constitutes a Science of Reading Instruction?" *Reading Research Quarterly* 55(S1):S235–S247.

Shapiro, Eliza. 2020. "How Trump's Push to Reopen Schools Backfired." *New York Times*. www.nytimes.com/2020/08/13/us/trump-schools-reopen.html

Sharkey, Patrick and Michael Friedson. 2019. "The Impact of the Homicide Decline on Life Expectancy of African American Males." *Demography* 56(2):645–663.

Shi, Lan. 2009. "The Limit of Oversight in Policing: Evidence from the 2001 Cincinnati Riot." *Journal of Public Economics* 93(1-2):99–113.

Simon, Cecilia Capuzzi. 2016. "Making America Great Again." *New York Times*.

Sirinides, Philip, Abigail Gray and Henry May. 2018. "The Impacts of Reading Recovery at Scale: Results from the 4-Year i3 External Evaluation." *Educational Evaluation and Policy Analysis* 40(3):179–211.

Skelton, George. 1997. "In Any Language, Escalante's Stand Is Clear." *Los Angeles Times* p. A3.

Slothuus, Rune and Martin Bisgaard. 2021. "How Political Parties Shape Public Opinion in the Real World." *American Journal of Political Science* 65(4):896–911.

Smith, Adam and Bruce Yandle. 2014. *Bootleggers and Baptists: How Economic Forces and Moral Persuasion Interact to Shape Regulatory Politics*. Washington, DC: Cato Institute.

Smith, Daniel A. 1998. *Tax Crusaders and the Politics of Direct Democracy*. New York: Routledge.

Smith-Silverman, Sara. 2020. "Partisan Bias in Surveys." *Journal of the History of Sexuality* 29(1):79–107.

Sonenshein, Raphael J. 1993. *Politics in Black and White: Race and Power in Los Angeles*. Princeton, NJ: Princeton University Press.

Stanovich, Keith E. 2000. *Progress in Understanding Reading: Scientific Foundations and New Frontiers*. New York: Guilford Press.

Steinberg, Matthew P. and John M. MacDonald. 2019. "The Effects of Closing Urban Schools on Students' Academic and Behavioral Outcomes: Evidence from Philadelphia." *Economics of Education Review* 69:25–60.

Steiner, David and Susan D. Rozen. 2004. Preparing Tomorrow's Teachers: An Analysis of Syllabi from a Sample of America's Schools of Education. In *A Qualified Teacher in Every Classroom? Appraising Old Answers and New Ideas*, ed. Frederick M. Hess, Andrew J. Rotherham and Katie Walsh. Cambridge, MA: Harvard University Press, pp. 119–148.

Stemper, Sam. 2022. "School Segregation, Student Achievement, and Parental Preferences." University of Auckland Working Paper. https://samstemper.com/files/school_boundaries.pdf

Stern, Sol. 2008. "Too Good to Last: The True Story of Reading First." Thomas B. Fordham Institute. https://fordhaminstitute.org/national/research/too-good-last-true-story-reading-first

Strauss, Steven L. 2005. *The Linguistics, Neurology, and Politics of Phonics: The Silent "E" Speaks Out*. Mahwah, NJ: Lawrence Erlbaum Associates.

Sun, Min, Emily K. Penner, and Susanna Loeb. 2017. "Resource- and Approach-Driven Multidimensional Change: Three-Year Effects of School Improvement Grants." *American Educational Research Journal* 54(4):607–643.

Taub, James. 1993. "The Hearts and Minds of City College." *New Yorker*.

Taubes, Gary. 2016. *The Case against Sugar*. New York: Anchor Books.

Tausanovitch, Chris and Christopher Warshaw. 2014. "Representation in Municipal Government." *American Political Science Review* 108(3):605–641.

Thomas, Paul. 2019. "Mississippi Miracle or Mirage?." https://plthomasedd.medium.com/mississippi-miracle-or-mirage-f116490f8257

Thompson, Charles Henry. 1951. "Editorial Comment: Negro Teachers and the Elimination of Segregated Schools." *Journal of Negro Education* 20(2):135–139.

Thompson, Owen. 2022. "School Desegregation and Black Teacher Employment." *Review of Economics and Statistics* 104(5):962–980.

Thompson, Paul N. 2016. "School District and Housing Price Responses to Fiscal Stress Labels: Evidence from Ohio." *Journal of Urban Economics* 94:54–72.

Thompson, Paul N. 2019. "Are School Officials Held Accountable for Fiscal Stress? Evidence from School District Financial Intervention Systems." *Economics of Education Review* 72:44–54.

Thornbrough, Emma Lou. 1957. *The Negro in Indiana before 1900: A Study of a Minority*. Indianapolis, IN: Indiana Historical Bureau.

Trounstine, Jessica. 2018. *Segregation by Design: Local Politics and Inequality in American Cities*. New York: Cambridge University Press.

Tucker, Jill. 2021a. "S.F. Schools See Learning Gaps Widen during Pandemic." *San Francisco Chronicle*. www.sfchronicle.com/bayarea/article/S-F-schools-see-learning-gaps-widen-during-15912588.php

Tucker, Jill. 2021b. "S.F. Schools Superintendent Vincent Matthews Agrees to Stay if Board Behaves." *San Francisco Chronicle*. www.sfchronicle.com/local/article/SF-schools-superintendent-agreed-to-stay-if-the-16108691.php

Tucker, Jill. 2021c. "S.F. Seniors Might Go Back to School for Only One Day before Term Ends. Parents Are Furious." *San Francisco Chronicle*. www.sfchronicle.com/education/article/S-F-seniors-might-go-back-to-school-for-only-one-php

Tucker, Jill and Annie Vainshtein. 2022. "S.F. School Board Recall: Alison Collins, Gabriela López and Faauuga Moliga Ousted." *San Francisco Chronicle*. www.sfchronicle.com/sf/article/S-F-school-board-recall-Alison-Collins-16922351.php

Tucker, Jill and Bob Egelko. 2021. "SF School Board Member Alison Collins Sues District, Colleagues over Response to Her Tweets." *San Francisco Chronicle*. www.sfchronicle.com/education/article/SF-school-board-member-Alison-Collins-sues-16068075.php

Turnbull, Geoffrey K. and Minrong Zheng. 2021. "A Meta-Analysis of School Quality Capitalization in U.S. House Prices." *Real Estate Economics* 49(4):1120–1171.

Tyack, David B. 2001. "School Reform Is Dead (Long Live School Reform)." *American Prospect*. https://prospect.org/features/school-reform-dead-long-live-school-reform/

Tyack, David B. 1974. *The One Best System: A History of American Urban Education*. Cambridge, MA: Harvard University Press.

Tyack, David B. and Thomas James. 1985. "Moral Majorities and the School Curriculum: Historical Perspectives on the Legalization of Virtue." *Teachers College Record* 86(4):513–537.

Tyack, David B. and Elisabeth Hansot. 1981. "Conflict and Consensus in American Public Education." *Daedalus* 110(3):1–25.

United States Civil Rights Commission. 1968. Political Participation. Technical report. www.crmvet.org/docs/ccr_voting_south_6805.pdf

Upchurch, Daniel F. 2016. *Pyrrhic Victory: The Cost of Integration*. Charlotte, NC: Information Age Publishing.

Urban, Wayne J. 2000. *Gender, Race, and the National Education Association: Professionalism and Its Limitations*. New York: RoutledgeFalmer.

Verba, Sidney, Kay Lehman Schlozman and Henry E. Brady. 1995. *Voice and Equality: Civic Voluntarism and American Politics*. Cambridge, MA: Harvard University Press.

Vlachos, Jonas, Edvin Hertegård and Helena B. Svaleryd. 2021. "The Effects of School Closures on SARS-CoV-2 among Parents and Teachers." *Proceedings of the National Academy of Sciences* 118(9):e2020834118.

Wallace-Wells, Benjamin. 2021. "How a Conservative Activist Invented the Conflict over Critical Race Theory." *New Yorker*. www.newyorker.com/news/annals-of-inquiry/how-a-conservative-activist-invented-the-conflict-over-critical-race-theory

Walsh, Bryan. 2021. "The Racial Divide in Returning to the Classroom." *Axios*. www.axios.com/2021/02/06/racial-divide-reopening-schools-coronavirus

Wang, Weijie and Taek Kyu Kim. 2024. "Do Government Performance Signals Affect Citizen Satisfaction?" *Journal of Policy Analysis and Management* 43(3):846–870.

Weisburst, Emily K. 2019. "Patrolling Public Schools: The Impact of Funding for School Police on Student Discipline and Long-Term Education Outcomes." *Journal of Policy Analysis and Management* 38(2):338–365.

White, Rachel S., Sarah Stitzlein, Kathleen Knight Abowitz, Derek Gottlieb and Jack Schneider. 2023. "Are Locally Elected School Boards Really Failing?" *Education Next* 23(1):68–71.

Whitmire, Richard. 2011. *The Bee Eater: Michelle Rhee Takes on the Nation's Worst School District*. San Francisco: Jossey-Bass.

Wildermuth, John. 1986. "How Miami Adjusted to Its Bilingual Ban." *San Francisco Chronicle* p. 7.

Wilson, George. 1997. "Pathways to Power: Racial Differences in the Determinants of Job Authority." *Social Problems* 44(1):38–547.

Wilson, James Q. 1989. *Bureaucracy: What Government Agencies Do and Why They Do It*. New York: Basic Books.
Wilson, William Julius. 1978. *The Declining Significance of Race*. Chicago: Chicago University Press.
Yoder, Jesse. 2020. "Does Property Ownership Lead to Participation in Local Politics? Evidence from Property Records and Meeting Minutes." *American Political Science Review* 114(4):1213–1229.
Zaller, John R. 2012. *The Nature and Origins of Mass Opinion*. Cambridge, MA: Cambridge University Press.
Zimmerman, Jonathan. 2022. *Whose America? Culture Wars in the Public Schools, Second Edition*. Chicago: University of Chicago Press.
Zweig, David. 2025. *An Abundance of Caution*: American Schools, the Virus, and a Story of Bad Decisions. Cambridge, MA: MIT Education Press.

Index

10% Less Democracy (Jones), 273, 275
1619 Project, 98–103, 106, 125
1776 Commission, 102

abstention rates, 121
abstinence-only education, 98
Abt, Thomas, 27
academic achievement, 1, 9–11, 17, 18, 21, 22, 25, 32, 51, 53–55, 57, 62, 85, 113, 120, 135, 137, 138, 140, 158, 176, 177, 181, 182, 185, 188, 194, 202, 205, 211–213, 215, 216, 218, 220, 226, 227, 236, 245, 246, 248, 252, 253, 261, 264, 270, 271, 273
academic growth, 22, 56, 57, 142, 215–218, 225, 226, 233, 244–246, 248, 265, 267
accreditation (of schools and districts), 198, 236
achievement gaps, 14, 15, 51, 52, 62, 69, 95, 129, 140, 179
Adams, Darryl, 131, 132
admissions lotteries, 16
adult employment, 17, 156, 157, 159, 176, 189. *See also* Black teachers; teachers' unions
adult interests, 4, 7, 8, 13, 16, 18, 25, 29, 35, 57, 134, 186, 233, 261, 265, 269, 277
adult opinions, 66
affective polarization, 77
Affeldt, John, 63, 64
affirmative action, 82, 89, 160, 253

African-Americans, 12, 13, 98, 106, 159–161, 164, 165, 171, 175, 184, 275
Afrocentric education, 105
Aid to Families with Dependent Children (AFDC), 230
Al Jazeera, 132
Alameda County Democratic Party, 198
algebra-for-all policies, 40
Alpert, Dede, 87, 88, 91–93
American Civil Liberties Union (ACLU), 5
American Conservative, 82
American Federation of Teachers (AFT), 168
American Psychiatric Association, 78
Ansari, Zakiyah, 205, 206, 210
AP U.S. History (APUSH), 104
Arab Americans, 131
Arab-American Anti-Discrimination Committee (ADC), 131, 132, 137
Arkansas, 58, 78, 79, 102, 172
Arkansas Gazette, 164
Ashmore, Harry, 163, 164, 166
Asian Americans, 37, 45
Atlantic Monthly, 98
attendance zones, 178, 182, 191, 231, 232, 238, 239, 244, 250–253, 255, 256, 276. *See also* NIMBYism
Axios, 69

Baker v. Carr, 12
Baltimore, 156, 162, 259
Baltimore Sun, 259

Bankman-Fried, Sam, 83
Bannon, Steve, 267
Baptists (and Bootleggers), 190, 195, 210, 211, 228
Barrow, Lisa, 14, 20
Barry, Marion, 161, 162
bathroom policies, 37, 148
Bee Eater (Whitmire), 27, 158
Belkin, Lisa, 234
Bell, Derrick, 172, 184
Bell Curve (Murray and Herrnstein), 82
Bennett, William, 85
Berkman, Michael, 38, 40–42, 129
Berry, Chris, 55–57
Biden, Joe, 40, 102
bilingual education, 66, 81, 84–91, 93
Black, Sandra, 244, 250
Black mayors, 160
Black Power movement, 190
Black teachers, 13, 154–156, 164–167, 170, 172–175, 184, 185
Black voters, 12, 174, 175
Blaine amendments, 270
Blanco, Kathleen, 177
Bloomberg, Michael, 205
Boaler, Jo, 40
Bootleggers (and Baptists), 190, 211
Boston, 15, 16, 185, 240
Boudin, Chesa, 46
Bradley, Tom, 160
Breed, London, 36, 44
Briggs, John, 77–81
Brookings Institution, 18, 62, 113, 195
Brooks, Jeff, 149, 150
Brown, Kathleen, 83
Brown, Michael, 148
Brown v. Board of Education, 12, 62, 73, 84, 158, 163–170, 172, 173, 237
Bryan, William Jennings, 5, 6
Bryant, Anita, 78
Buckingham, Bill, 133
bully pulpit, 125
Bush, George H. W., 86
Bush, George W., 73, 98, 115, 116
Bush, Jeb, 73, 244
Bush, Neil, 115
Buzzfeed, 132
Byrnes, James F., 164

California (state), 1, 36, 40, 50, 56, 58, 62, 63, 66, 68, 72, 77–81, 83, 84, 86–93, 98, 102, 109, 111–114, 120, 128, 131, 137, 151, 158, 229–231, 239, 240, 249, 263, 264
California State Board of Education, 266
California Supreme Court, 249
Callaghan, Alice, 88
Campos, Jason, 268
cancellation, 29
Carr, Sarah, 177, 184
Carter, Jimmy, 85
Casserly, Michael, 126, 180, 181, 185
Castro Valley Elementary, 229, 230
Catalist, xiv, 49–51, 240, 241, 246
Cato Institute, 135, 136, 142, 149
CCPA (Coliseum College Prep Academy), 197
Center for Educational Freedom, 136
Center for Public Integrity, 235
Chait, Jonathan, 94, 95, 152
charter schools, 15, 16, 29–31, 34, 95, 117, 144, 178, 181, 182, 188, 195, 198, 199, 202, 203, 214, 223, 226, 231, 246, 262, 269, 270, 272, 273
Cheney, Dick, 104
Cheney, Lynne, 103
Chetty, Raj, 20
Chicago, 22, 68, 104, 106, 109, 185, 193, 201, 203, 205, 206, 210, 212, 214, 220, 257, 262
Chicago Tribune, 109
"Choice Is A Panacea" (Chubb and Moe), 269
Christie, Chris, 73
Chubb, John, 16–18, 261, 268, 269, 272, 276
Churchill, Winston, 262
citizenship, 11, 207, 261
Civil Rights Act of 1964, 160, 169, 175
civil service reforms, 159
Civil War, 103
Clay, Marie, 117
Clinton, Bill, 90, 103
Closed for Democracy (Nuamah), 210
Coachella Valley Unified School District, 131, 132, 134, 135, 137, 146
Cohen, Rachel, 69
collective bargaining, 15, 16, 60, 187, 228. *See also* teachers' unions
college- and career-readiness, 73
College Board, 104
Collins, Alison, 37, 45

Color of School Reform, The (Henig, Hula, Orr, and Pedescleaux), 162
Columbus Dispatch, 30, 32
Columbus Education Association (CEA), 30–32
Columbus school board, 1, 25, 30, 31, 67, 186, 187, 261
Common Core of Data (CCD), 214
Common Core standards, 65, 73–75, 77, 96, 122, 125, 126, 130
community institutions (schools as), 23–26, 203, 208
community perceptions, 203
community schools, 25
composition effects, 42, 43, 45–47, 53, 56, 69, 138, 145, 172, 180, 198, 213–216, 218, 220, 223, 225, 227, 233, 244, 245, 247, 249, 253, 256, 264, 265
Confederate flags, 137
congruence (responsiveness measure), 40
consolidation. *See* school closures
contestation, 43
Cotton, Tom, 102
Council of Great City Schools, 126, 180
Covid-19 pandemic, 1–3, 35, 36, 44, 48, 52, 65–69, 75–77, 82, 118–120, 141, 195
Covington, John, 200
Cowen Institute, 182
Cox, Oliver, 165, 166, 174, 184
Crabill, AJ, xiv, 34, 180, 181, 198–200, 204, 209
Cremin, Lawrence, 8, 276
Cristo Rey, 29, 30
Critical Race Theory (CRT), 2, 98, 99, 102, 111, 120–123, 127–129, 149, 152, 172, 173, 209
culture wars, 85, 135, 137, 151, 153
curriculum standards, 5, 7, 8, 20, 21, 30, 34, 52, 73, 74, 94, 97–99, 101–106, 111, 113–117, 120, 122–125, 128–133, 136, 144, 145, 150–152, 191, 192, 196, 254, 276

Darwin, Charles, 6
data scrubbing, 191
declining enrollment, 34, 37, 61, 124, 144, 166, 173, 190–196, 198, 199, 201–206, 208, 211, 214, 216, 218–220, 222, 223, 225–227, 231, 236, 238, 253–256, 271

democratic control (of schools), 3, 4, 17, 18, 59, 95, 159, 161, 175, 176, 189, 273, 275, 276
democratic deficit (in school governance), 51, 61, 62
democratic processes, 42, 43, 269
democratic representation, 12, 37–41, 50, 105, 175, 233, 264, 275
Denver, 262
DeRoche, Tim, 236, 238–240, 250, 251, 255, 256
desegregation, 26, 158, 163, 173, 188, 199, 203, 234
Desmond, Matthew, 101
Detroit, 162, 203
Deukmejian, George, 86, 88
DeVos, Betsy, 31, 73
Dewey, John, 106
DeWine, Mike, 65, 67
Diagnostic and Statistical Manual, 78
Diamond, Linda, 109, 111, 113, 128
DiAngelo, Robin, 127
difference-in-differences models, 135, 138, 141
Dirksen, Everett McKinley, 169
displacement (of low-income families), 101, 172, 180, 181, 184, 252, 253, 256
diversity, equity, and inclusion (DEI), 102, 127
Dole, Bob, 104
Dover Area School District, 133
dropout factories, 192
Du Bois, W. E. B., 10
Duncan, Arne, 73, 126, 190, 193, 194, 205, 219
dyslexia, 118

East Ramapo School District, 60, 61
education committees (legislative), 122, 123
Education Next, 3, 23, 74
education savings accounts, 269, 273
Education Week, 119, 121
educational attainment, 22
effect sizes, 56, 57, 115
Einstein, Katie, 233, 240, 241, 274
electoral participation, 42
electorate composition, 18, 29, 35, 40, 42, 43, 47, 49, 52, 81, 246, 247, 262

Elementary and Secondary Education Act (ESEA), 169
elite opinion leadership, 92
English immersion, 85, 88
equity, 40, 68, 110, 136, 137, 233, 243, 249, 253
Escalante, Jaime, 90
Ethridge, Samuel, 169
eugenics, 6
evolution (teaching of), 5, 6
Ewing, Eve, 206, 207

Fauci, Anthony, 72
Fenty, Adrian, 157, 158, 200, 201, 262
Ferguson effect, 148
Festerwald, John, 151
Figlio, David, 21, 244, 266
final passage votes, 121
A Fine Line (DeRoche), 239
First Reader (Schlafly), 109
Fischel, William, 242, 243, 246, 248, 249, 257, 258, 276
Flesch, Rudolph, 106, 107
Floyd, George, 35, 68, 102, 227
Ford Foundation, 164, 166
Franklin County Democratic Party, 29, 32
Frederick Douglass Academy High School, 201
Freire, Paulo, 109
Fremont Unified School District, 198
Friday, Cameron, 253

gaming (of accountability systems), 21, 265
Gates, Bill, 202
Gates Foundation, 73
Gay Pride Month, 2
gay rights movement, 78
Gelman, Andrew, 94
Gender Queer (book), 152
gender-affirming care, 4
Germantown High School, 208
gerrymandering, 13, 28, 43, 59, 174, 191, 250, 251
Glendale Unified School District, 2
Glick, David, 233, 240, 241, 274
Goals 2020, 103
Going Public (Kernell), 125
Goldwater, Barry, 109
Gonzales, Shanthi, 196–198, 200, 225
Good, Ryan, 204
good intentions (of adults), 4

governance (of schools), xiii, 4, 9, 12, 13, 16, 18, 34, 35, 38, 42, 43, 51, 60–62, 134, 148, 159, 176, 178–183, 200, 211, 232, 258, 261, 262, 274, 276
government jobs, 159–161
Gray, Vincent, 201
Great Recession, 63, 73
Groce, Stephanie, 31, 32
growth (academic). *See* academic growth
gubernatorial races, 92

Hall, Andy, 241
Hanford, Emily, 99, 116, 119, 120, 125, 209
Hannah-Jones, Nikole, 100, 101, 163
Hansot, Elisabeth, 95
Harris, Doug, xiv, 4, 177, 179–182, 211, 215
Harris, Gene, 191
Harris, Leslie, 101
Hartney, Michael, xiv, 15, 57, 68, 263, 265
Harvard University, 3, 74, 186
Hastings, Justine, 34, 268
Hazelwood School District, 235
Heineman (publisher), 115, 120
Hess, Rick, 72, 94
High School and Beyond Survey, 17
history wars, 103, 104
Hoffenblum, Allan, 89
hollow-prize problem, 187
home equity, 232
home prices, 18, 225, 232, 234, 243–245, 249, 251, 252, 254, 256, 272
homelessness, 88, 236
homeowners (interests of), 23, 232–234, 240–243, 246–248, 256, 264, 267, 274
homeschooling, 195, 223
Homevoter Hypothesis (Fischel), 242, 257
homevoters, 243, 246–251
Honig, Bill, 112, 113, 128
housing markets, 231, 238, 239, 246, 248, 249, 251–253, 255, 257, 268
Houston, David, xiv, 95
Howard University, 166
Howell, Will, 55–57
Hurricane Katrina, 117, 158, 176–185, 188

Imberman, Scott, 245
immigration, 84, 86, 89, 91, 137

Index

impossible trinity, 189
incentives (electoral and political), 4, 14, 18, 20, 21, 54, 55, 57, 59, 60, 62, 68, 73, 77, 152, 161, 185, 188, 209, 233, 248, 249, 257, 258, 260–263, 266, 269, 271, 272, 274
incumbents (on school boards), 43, 44, 49, 52, 55, 56, 59, 133, 135, 162, 198, 200, 261, 264, 268, 274
Indiana, 125, 154–156, 165
Indianapolis, 154–156, 165, 187
Indianapolis Freeman, 156
Institute for Education Sciences (IES), 116, 117
integration, 12, 155, 156, 163, 165–175, 191, 198, 199, 239, 251, 257
intelligent design, 133, 152
interest alignment, 43
IQ scores, 82, 83

Jackson, Kirabo, 21, 22
Jacobs, Joanne, 86
Jarvis, Howard, 80
Jeffries, Leonard, 105, 106
Jim Crow, 13, 163, 183
Johnson, Kevin, 157
Johnson, Lyndon, 26, 169
Jones, Gabriel, 154–156, 187
Jones, Garett, 275
Joseph, Marion, 113
Journal of Negro Education, 166, 167
Journey for Justice Alliance, 202, 215

Kansas City, 180, 198–200, 203, 204, 208, 228
Kauffman, Christina, 133
Kayden, Xandra, 89
Kendi, Ibram X., 127
Kennedy, John F., 168
Kernell, Sam, 125
Kerner Commission, 26
Kim, James, 107, 109
King, Gary, 94
King, Martin Luther, Jr., 103
Kirst, Michael, 62, 63
Klein, Joel, 205, 265
Knowledge Is Power Program (KIPP), 178
Knox, George, 156
Kozol, Jonathan, 14

Labaree, David, 10
Ladd, Helen, 20
Larson, Edward, 5
Latino Caucus, 87, 91
Lau v. Nichols, 84
Lautenberg Amendment, 229
Lavertu, Stéphane, xiv, 15, 48, 51–54, 56, 58, 62, 209, 212, 213, 252, 263, 264
Lax, Jeff, 40
Lemann, Nicholas, 98, 99, 112, 113
Lensmire, Timothy, 129
Lenz, Gabe, 75–77, 95, 266
Lerum, Eric, 200, 201, 204–207
LGBT people, 2, 5, 39, 150–152, 272
libertarians, 87, 195
Lincoln University, 165
Linden-McKinley High School, 190–192, 196, 199, 206, 208
Little Hoover Commission, 87
local democracy, 14, 29, 33–35, 38, 39, 41, 60, 62, 63, 66, 188, 262
local property taxes, 13, 113, 199, 203, 237, 239, 248, 271, 276
"Locally Elected School Boards Are Failing" (Kogan), 3
lockdowns, 67
Los Angeles Times, 79, 81, 88, 113, 244
lotteries, 16, 257, 268
Loudoun County effect, 148
Louisiana, 177
Louisville Municipal College for Negroes, 166
Loveless, Tom, xiv, 40, 73, 113, 129, 130
Lovenheim, Michael, 15, 245
Lowell High School, 37
Lungren, Dan, 91
Lyon, G. Reid, xiv, 114, 115, 209

magnet programs, 199, 254
malapportionment, 12
Mann, Horace, 106
Mariel boatlift, 85
market mechanisms, 269
Marshall-Brennan Constitutional Literacy Project, 200
Martinez-Pabon, Valentina, 211, 214, 215
mascots, 4, 34, 131, 132, 134, 135, 137
Massachusetts, 3, 106, 216, 240, 244
Massachusetts Bay Colony, 276
Massive Resistance, 163
Mathematica, 157

Matsusaka, John, 39, 41
Matthews, Vince, 38
Mayhew, David, 18
mayoral control, 34, 262
McCarthy, Joe, 111
McCluskey, Neal, 136, 138
McLaury, Bruce, 18
McWhorter, John, 99
measurement, 9, 21, 22, 38–40, 42, 52, 53, 165, 206, 212, 214, 227, 246, 265
merit pay, 118
Mexican American Legal Defense and Educational Fund, 87
Milk, Harvey, 151
Minter-Alexander, Rae, 256
Mississippi (state), 58, 113, 120, 124
Mississippi Miracle, 120
Missouri, 50, 58, 124, 164, 165
Mixner, David, 79–81
Mock, Corey, 97, 98, 122, 124, 125
Moe, Terry, xiii, 15–18, 134, 159, 177–179, 188, 261, 268, 269, 272, 276
Monarrez, Tomás E., 250, 251
Morel, Domingo, 34, 182, 183, 185, 186
multiculturalism, 85, 105, 112, 127
Murray, Charles, 82
Musk, Elon, 83
"Myth of American Meritocracy" (Unz), 82

NAACP Legal Defense Fund, 173
Nashville, 253
Nation at Risk report, 19, 268
National Advisory Commission on Civil Disorders, 26
National Assessment of Educational Progress (NAEP), 1, 2, 113, 120
National Association for the Advancement of Colored People (NAACP), 119, 173, 187
National Commission on Excellence in Education, 19
National Council of Teaching Quality (NCTQ), 118
National Education Association (NEA), 168–170
National Institute of Child Health and Human Nutrition, 114
National Reading Panel, 109, 114–116, 124

nationalization (of education politics), 32, 34, 97, 122, 124, 125, 261
"Negro Teachers: Martyrs to Integration?" (Cox), 166
neoliberalism, 161, 183, 197, 231, 275
Nevada, 58, 124
New Orleans, 158, 175–185, 188, 214, 262, 270, 275
New Republic, 81
New York City, 67, 265
New York Times, 44, 45, 48, 70, 85, 98–100, 104, 257
Newark, 162, 185
Newsom, Gavin, 38, 47, 151
NIMBYism, 229, 233, 234, 236, 238, 239, 243, 248, 249, 258, 264, 274
No Child Left Behind Act (NCLB), 21, 53, 73, 115, 126, 209
No More Lines Coalition, 232
"non-cognitive" outcomes, 21
Normandy School District, 236
North Carolina, 201, 266
North Dakota, 97–99, 122, 125
Nuamah, Sally, 182, 183, 185, 193, 210

Oakland Unified School District, 196
Obama, Barack, 27, 65, 72–74, 94, 96, 116, 117, 122, 126, 132, 193, 209, 252, 268
Of Pandas and People (textbook), 133
off-cycle elections, 52, 76, 233, 241, 263, 264
Ohio (state), 50, 54–56, 65, 136, 186, 190, 270
Ohio State University, 67, 190
Oklahoma, 50, 58, 73, 78, 123
Old Deluder Satan Law, 276
on-cycle elections, 263, 264
O'Neill, Tip, 193
Orfield, Gary, 165, 168, 169

Palmer, Max, 233, 240, 241, 274
parent voting, 264
parental satisfaction, 19
parents, 4, 5, 7, 9, 10, 17, 19, 30, 44, 47, 50, 51, 53, 56, 61, 67, 69–71, 74, 87, 88, 99, 118, 119, 137, 148, 152, 158, 173, 183, 186, 187, 192, 195, 205–207, 213, 218, 227, 229, 230, 236, 245, 254, 257, 264–272
Parker, Francis Wayland, xiv, 106

participation, 22, 42, 55, 60, 143, 188, 207, 240–242
Paterson, Frances, 114, 122
Pathak, Parag, 267
patronage, 159, 186, 188, 276
Paul, Rand, 72
Payson, Julia, 56, 57, 264
Pearson, P. David, 97, 111
Pedagogy of the Oppressed (Freire), 109
Penn Alexander School, 255
Penncrest School District, 149–151
Pennsylvania, 50, 133, 149
Perenchio, Jerrold, 90, 91, 93
Peskowitz, Zachary, xiv, 48, 51–54, 56, 58, 62, 263, 264
Phi Delta Kappa, 30, 126
Philadelphia, 204, 208, 210, 235, 255, 256
Philadelphia Inquirer, 255, 256
Phillips, Justin, 40
phonics instruction, 98, 99, 106–120, 122, 124–126, 128, 129
Picard, Cecil, 177
pilot schools, 15, 16
Pittman, Ajay, 123, 124
plantation complex, 183
Plutzer, Eric, 38, 40–42, 129
polarization, 11, 28, 39, 42, 47, 52, 66, 68, 71–77, 85, 86, 91–97, 99, 103, 108, 110, 114–116, 121, 122, 125–127, 152, 159, 196, 232, 251, 261, 266, 269
policing, 27, 148
Polikoff, Morgan, 129, 130
political elites, 66, 75, 76
political identity, 75
Politico, 101
Politics, Markets, and America's Schools (Chubb and Moe), xiii, 16, 268
portfolio models, 262
poverty, 7, 14, 21, 25–28, 30, 169, 177, 180, 188, 197, 218
Powell, Adam Clayton, 167–169
primary elections, 92
private schools, 29, 34, 47, 123, 191, 195, 201, 202, 214, 223, 226, 232, 241, 257, 269, 270, 272
privatization, 161, 197, 202
prohibition (of alcohol), 5, 7
property taxes, 61, 78, 225, 239, 243, 249

property values, 23, 51, 225, 234, 239, 242, 243, 247, 248, 254–256, 258, 268, 272, 274
Proposition 5, 80
Proposition 6, 92
Proposition 13, 78, 80, 113, 239, 249
Proposition 187, 83, 84, 89, 90, 93
Proposition 209, 89
Proposition 227, 81, 83, 84, 88–94, 96
puberty blockers, 4
Public Advocates, 63
public education (purpose of), 9, 11
public goods, 95
public opinion, 38–40, 66, 68, 69, 71, 75–77, 80, 96, 97, 126, 134, 158, 183
Purdue, Sonny, 74
Pyrrhic Victory (Upchurch), 173

Race to the Top program, 73, 268
racial disparities, 26, 37, 68–70, 126, 149, 159, 216, 227
racism, 4, 25–28, 35, 37, 45, 68, 70, 100, 103, 105, 111, 129, 131, 132, 159–161, 163, 165, 166, 177, 194, 195, 202–205, 209, 219, 234, 248, 268, 270
Ragland, James, 29–33, 261
Ravitch, Diane, 8, 86
Reading First program, 115–117, 126
Reading Recovery program, 117, 119
reading wars, 98, 107, 109–111, 118, 123, 126, 129
Reagan, Ronald, 66, 79–81, 85, 96, 104
real estate markets, 18
Reason magazine, 87
Recovery School District (RSD), 178, 182
redlining, 250
Reed, Vince, 161
referenda, 66, 77, 78, 92
regression discontinuity designs, 116
Reidy, Rick, 89
reopening debates, 35, 37, 38, 44, 65–72, 74–76, 96, 178, 191, 214
Report of Task Force Survey of Teacher Displacement in Seventeen States (NEA), 170
Republican National Committee, 104
Republican Party, 84, 89, 109, 114
residency investigators, 235
responsiveness, 38–42, 66, 134

restructuring (of schools), 209, 211, 212, 215
retention (of third-graders), 120, 124
retrospective voting, 49, 55
revealed preferences, 35
Reynolds v. Sims, 13
Rhee, Michelle, 27, 157, 158, 187, 200, 201, 262
Rich, Wilbur, 162
Riker, William, 168
Roberts, John, 28
Rogers, Steve, 58
Romero, Gloria, 231
root causes, 25–27, 61, 177, 232
Rufo, Christopher, 99, 102, 103, 127, 209
Rugg, Harold, 105

San Diego Unified School, 28
San Francisco, 9, 35, 36, 38, 40, 43–50, 52, 56, 57, 84, 112, 151, 196, 257
San Jose Mercury News, 86
Sanchez, José Bernardo, 36
Savage Inequalities (Kozol), 14
Schanzenbach, Diane Whitmore, 14, 20, 21
Schlafly, Phyllis, 109
Schneider, Jack, 3
school accountability systems, 231, 244, 264, 266
school board elections, xiv, 5, 15, 18, 32, 35, 38, 42, 43, 48–59, 135, 144, 193, 198, 240, 241, 246, 247, 263, 264, 266
school choice, 26, 94, 226, 268, 269, 271, 272
School Choice Ohio, 30, 32
school closures, 16, 23, 65, 67, 68, 156, 193, 194, 196, 197, 200, 202, 204–228
school funding, 13–15
School Improvement Grants (SIGs), 209, 252, 253
school quality (measures of), 15, 17, 18, 20–23, 52, 53, 55, 96, 174, 197, 203, 206, 213, 216, 218, 226, 232, 233, 243–245, 248–253, 265, 267, 268, 272
school safety, 268
Schreiber-Beck, Cynthia, 122
science of reading, 99, 109, 118, 120–125, 129, 209
scientific racism, 6

Scopes, John T., 5, 6, 98, 133
segregation, 12, 13, 26, 40, 154, 155, 163–170, 172–174, 198, 204, 250, 251, 268, 271, 272
selective-admission processes, 37, 187
Serrano v. Priest, 249
Service Employees International Union, 196
sex education, 8, 98
sexual assault, 148
Shakespeare Elementary, 193
Shanahan, Tim, 109, 116, 120, 125
Sharkey, Patrick, 26, 27
Sherer, Ethan, 264
Sir Francis Howell School District, 237
skin in the game, 43, 48, 51, 52, 57, 61, 77, 233, 263, 264, 267
slavery, 11, 36, 98, 100, 101, 103, 126, 183, 184
Smith, Abigail, 201
Smith, Dan, 78
Smith, Tucker, 253
social Darwinism, 6
social emotional skills, 22
social justice, 148, 196, 197, 200, 202
Sousa Middle School, 158
South Carolina, 55, 56, 73, 164
Southern California Democratic Club, 111
Southern Poverty Law Center, 81
Soviet Union, 105, 106, 153, 199, 229
special interests, 269
Spencer Foundation, xiv, 48
Springsteen, Bruce, 133
St. Louis, 235, 236
Stalin, Joseph, 105
standardized test scores, 3, 9, 10, 17, 20, 24, 26, 52, 56, 74, 96, 129, 134, 135, 144, 159, 173, 179, 181, 185, 186, 213, 216, 226, 247, 252, 263, 264, 273
Stanford Education Data Archive, 49, 53, 135, 137, 138, 141–144, 214, 216, 217, 220, 223
Stanovich, Keith, 110, 128
State of Missouri ex rel. Gaines v. Canada et al, 164
state takeovers, 34, 183, 185, 186, 259, 262
States, Markets, and America's Schools (Chubb and Moe), 261
STEM curricula, 191, 192

Stevenson, Adlai, 168
structural racism, 216
student behavior, 10, 226
student learning, xiii, 3, 4, 16, 17, 21, 23, 25, 26, 28, 29, 35, 43, 49, 53, 57, 60, 64, 85, 130, 134, 135, 144, 145, 148, 152, 156, 181, 188, 196, 212, 214, 226–228, 233, 238, 246, 247, 261, 262, 264, 265
Students for Fair Admissions v. Harvard, 82
students' interests, 23, 35, 43, 156, 186, 188, 263
Supplemental Nutrition Assistance Program (SNAP), 41
Swan, Jocelyn, 237
Sweatt v. Painter, 165
Sweden, 67

Tampa school board, 238
Taubes, Gary, 4
tax effort, 249
Tea Party activism, 74
Teach for America, 178, 201
teacher attendance, 30
teacher evaluations, 22, 117
teacher quality, 16, 21, 22, 25, 53, 228
teachers' unions, 13, 15–17, 24, 30–33, 36, 38, 57, 60, 68, 70, 95, 109, 124, 177, 178, 195, 197, 198, 202, 209–211, 223, 228, 231, 259, 262, 263, 265, 267, 273
Temecula (California), 151
Ten Thousand Democracies (Berkman and Plutzer), 38
Tennessee, 3, 5, 133, 154, 172, 216, 253, 266
Texas, 58, 115, 151, 165, 172, 180, 240, 253, 254, 263, 270
textbooks, 104, 105, 112, 151
This American Life, 61
Thomas B. Fordham Institute, 118
Thompson, Charles Henry, xiv, 54, 55, 104, 105, 165–167, 174
Thompson, Owen, 170
Thompson, Paul, 54, 55
three-cueing methods, 109, 124, 151
top-down opinion change, 76, 95, 96
top-down opinion formation, 76
Toppo, Greg, 170
tracking, 2, 9, 39, 40, 91, 170, 173

tradeoffs, 163, 186
transgender youth, 4, 148, 149
Trump, Donald, 31, 32, 45, 67, 72, 73, 96, 102, 103, 118, 125, 267
Tulane University, 179, 183
turnout (electoral), 35, 45–47, 49, 52, 55, 60, 76, 134, 150, 175, 241, 242, 263–265
two-way fixed effects regression analyses, 146
Tyack, David, 7, 8, 84, 95, 276

UC Berkeley Statewide Database, 92
underfunding, 195, 204
University of Pennsylvania, 255
Unz, Ron, 81–84, 87–93
Unz Review, 81, 82
Upchurch, Daniel, 173
USA Today, 44, 170

value added (growth measure), 213, 216, 226, 227, 244, 248, 266–268
vested interests, 17, 18, 159, 178, 205
Vinson, Fred, 165
Voice of San Diego, 28
voter preferences, 51, 96
voters (interests of), 13
Voting Rights Act of 1965, 175, 274
vouchers, 31, 34, 195, 270, 271

Waldron, John, 123
Walsh, Kate, 69, 118
Warren, Earl, 12, 13
Washington, DC, 27, 68, 156, 157, 161, 185, 187, 200, 201, 203, 207
Watson, Nana, 187
Wayne, John, 80
WCTU (Women's Christian Temperance Union), 7, 8
Weaver, Kareem, 119
Weinstein, Jeffrey, 268
What Works Clearinghouse, 117
White, Rachel, 3
white flight, 173, 187, 190, 198, 203
white supremacy, 35, 44, 45, 177
Whitehurst, Russ, 25, 116, 117, 127
Whitmire, Richard, 27, 157, 158
whole language reading approaches, 86, 107, 109–118, 120, 126, 128, 129
Why Johnny Can't Read (Flesch), 106
Wilson, James Q., 127

Wilson, Pete, 66, 83, 84, 91, 96
Wilson, William Julius, 160
Wilson, Woodrow, 5
Women's Christian Temperance Union (WCTU), 7
Woodson, Robert, 101
World War I, 84, 104

Yandle, Bruce, 194, 195
Yoder, Jesse, 240–242
York Dispatch, 133

Zaller, John, 75, 76
ZIP codes, 231
Zuckerberg, Mark, 83

For EU product safety concerns, contact us at Calle de José Abascal, 56–1°, 28003 Madrid, Spain or eugpsr@cambridge.org.

www.ingramcontent.com/pod-product-compliance
Lightning Source LLC
LaVergne TN
LVHW020341260326
834688LV00045B/1468